D0903955

RA
564.8
.P748
1999

Park, Denise C.

 Processing of medical
information in aging
patients

Processing
of Medical Information
in Aging Patients

୫ଞ୍ଜ

Cognitive and Human Factors
Perspectives

RA
564.8
.P748
1999

Processing
of Medical Information
in Aging Patients

಼ೞ

Cognitive and Human Factors
Perspectives

Edited by

Denise C. Park
University of Michigan

Roger W. Morrell
University of Georgia

Kim Shifren
University of Michigan

LEA LAWRENCE ERLBAUM ASSOCIATES, PUBLISHERS
1999   Mahwah, New Jersey   London

Copyright © 1999 by Lawrence Erlbaum Associates, Inc.
All rights reserved. No part of this book may be reproduced in any form, by photostat, microfilm, retrieval system, or any other means, without prior written permission
of the publisher.

Lawrence Erlbaum Associates, Inc., Publishers
10 Industrial Avenue
Mahwah, NJ 07430

Cover design by Kathryn Houghtaling Lacey

Library of Congress Cataloging-in-Publication Data

Processing of medical information in aging patients : cognitive and human factors perspectives / edited by Denise C.
Park, Roger W. Morrell, Kim Shifren.
        p. cm
    Includes bibliographical references and index.
    ISBN 0-8058-2889-3
    1. Aged–Medical care. 2. Patient compliance. 3. Cognition in
old age. 4. Health education. 5. Medical personnel and patient.
6. Clinical health psychology.   I. Park, Denise C.   II. Morrell,
Roger.   III. Shifren, Kim.
RA564.8.P748 1999
362.1'9897–dc21   98-30256
                                                      CIP

Books published by Lawrence Erlbaum Associates are printed
on acid-free paper, and their bindings are chosen for strength
and durability.

Printed in the United States of America
10   9   8   7   6   5   4   3   2   1

Contents

Preface   vii

PART I: INTRODUCTION

1   Aging and the Controlled and Automatic Processing of Medical   3
Information and Medical Intentions
Denise C. Park

2   The Challenge of Communicating Health Information to Elderly   23
Patients: A View From Geriatric Medicine
Jeffrey B. Halter

PART II: MEDICAL DECISION MAKING

3   Decision Making and Aging   31
J. Frank Yates and Andrea L. Patalano

4   Cognitive Processes and Medical Decisions   55
Melissa D. Zwahr

5   Medical and Psychosocial Predictors of Breast Cancer Treatment   69
Decisions
Gail M. Williamson, Deborah J. Jones, and Lori A. Ingram

6   Frequency Reports of Physical Symptoms and Health Behaviors: 93
How the Questionnaire Determines the Results
Norbert Schwarz

7   Neurocognitive Changes Associated With Loss of Capacity   109
    to Consent to Medical Treatment in Patients With
    Alzheimer's Disease
    Daniel Marson and Lindy Harrell

8   Medical Expertise and Cognitive Aging   127
    Vimla L. Patel and José F. Arocha

PART III: MEDICATION ADHERENCE

9   Psychosocial Factors in Medication Adherence: A Model   145
    of the Modeler
    Elaine A. Leventhal, Howard Leventhal, Chantal Robitaille,
    and Susan Brownlee

10 Cognition and Affect in Medication Adherence   167
    Odette N. Gould

11 Issues in the Measurement of Medication Adherence   185
    Roger W. Morrell and Kim Shifren

12 Problem Solving on Health-Related Tasks of Daily Living   199
    Sherry L. Willis, Melissa M. Dolan, and Rosanna M. Bertrand

PART IV: HUMAN FACTORS

13 How Do I Work This Thing? Cognitive Issues in Home   223
    Medical Equipment Use and Maintenance
    Marilyn Sue Bogner

14 What Does It Say? Text Design, Medical Information,   233
    and Older Readers
    James Hartley

15 Designing Medication Instructions for Older Adults   249
    Daniel Morrow and Von O. Leirer

16 Maximizing the Effectiveness of the Warning Process: 267
    Understanding the Variables That Interact With Age
    Wendy A. Rogers, Gabriel K. Rousseau, and Nina Lamson

17 Research on Pharmaceutical Labeling: An Information   291
    Processing Approach
    Michael S. Wogalter and Russell J. Sojourner

    Author Index   311

    Subject Index   325

Preface

As people age, the cognitive resources they have available to process information become more limited. There is convincing evidence in the basic processes literature on cognitive aging that demonstrates that the speed at which information can be processed declines with age and that online cognitive capacity (often referred to as working memory) shows similar declines. Although there are hundreds of studies documenting these findings in the laboratory, relatively little is known about the implications of this decline in processing capacity for functioning in everyday life. One domain in which age-associated decline in cognitive processing resources may be of particular importance is the medical domain. Older adults frequently must decide about conditions and issues for which they have limited information, and the consequences of a decision often have implications for their physical well-being and even for their survival. Given the more limited cognitive resources available to older adults, it seems likely that they comprehend and remember less than younger adults of the information presented to them by their physicians and other health providers. Also, the factors that are important to them in making a medical decision or representing their health conditions, may be somewhat different than those of younger adults. Moreover, because older adults typically have more experience with illness and medical settings due to their longer life history and increasing consumption of medical care with age, on average, they bring more general medical experience and expertise to treatment settings than younger adults do. Does this increased expertise compensate for processing declines? Does limited processing capacity combined with expertise qualitatively change the manner in which older adults process information in the medical setting? When older adults are at a disadvantage due to cognitive declines, how can medical information and the medical environment be restructured to be compatible with the cognitive system of the older adult?

The present volume addresses these issues, focusing on understanding the impact of age-related decline in cognitive abilities on medical decisions and the implementation of medical instructions. In addition to exploring the meaning of cognitive decline for functioning within the medical environment, we also examine how medical information and the medical environment can be restructured to accommodate the decreased cognitive function associated with aging. The issues addressed in this volume are of critical importance in providing effective health care. Yet they have been largely neglected in the national debate over provision of health services for our increasingly aging population. It is essential that we begin to understand how to present information so that informed choices are made and so that patients have sufficient comprehension to follow correctly the treatment regimens prescribed for them and understand why they are important. Medications that are not taken and diets and exercise programs that are not followed due to limited comprehension of one's medical condition and the proposed interventions are not effective treatments. A failure of an older adult to represent accurately a health condition requiring intervention may be the initial link in an unsuccessful treatment of a condition. Over time, this poor comprehension will lead to ineffective treatment, resulting in declining health with ever more expensive and invasive treatments.

The volume is divided into four sections. In the Introduction, Park (chap. 1) presents a general overview of the major findings in the cognitive aging literature and their implications for medical information processing. She distinguishes between processes that rely primarily on controlled, effortful processing and those that are automatic and unconscious, and she argues for the importance of contextual and environmental cues in the medical environment that may have substantive effects on decision-making and adherence behaviors. In chapter 2, Halter, from the perspective of a geriatric physician, discusses the importance of accurately communicating health information to older adults.

The second part of the volume addresses the issues of aging and medical decision making. Yates and Patalano (chap. 3) review the decision-making literature and discuss important areas where older adults may differ from younger adults. Following this benchmark chapter, Zwahr (chap. 4) integrates aspects of age-related declines in basic cognitive mechanisms with differences in the medical decisions and information-seeking behaviors of older adults. Following this, Williamson, Jones, and Ingram (chap. 5) discuss the medical and psychosocial context in which breast cancer treatment decisions are made by women of different ages. Schwarz (chap. 6) then presents a series of intriguing findings that demonstrate that the particular structure, order, and format of questions about health create substantial biases in the self-report of symptoms. He suggests these effects may be compounded with age, due to limitations in working memory function. Marson and Harrell (chap. 7) then address the troubling issue of determining when frail older adults are no longer competent to make medical decisions, despite the fact that they may meet legal standards of competence. They provide an innovative, empirically tested framework that relates cognitive ability to the quality and complexity of decisions with which older adults may be faced. This section closes with a chapter by Patel and Arocha (chap. 8), which examines the implications of cognitive aging for the decisions made by providers, that is, the role of expertise and aging in treatment decisions of physicians.

In the third part of the volume, the issue of aging and medication adherence is discussed. E. A. Leventhal, Robitaille, H. Leventhal, and Brownlee (chap. 9) discuss the role of emotional and other psychosocial factors in medication adherence and how these factors change with age. In chapter 10, Gould presents work that integrates the relationship between affect and cognitive aging in medication adherence behaviors. Then, Morrell and Shifren (chap. 11) present a framework that addresses methodological and statistical issues associated with the study and measurement of adherence behaviors in the field. This section closes with chapter 12, authored by Willis, Dolan, and Bertrand, which provides a broad overview of the issue of medication adherence within a framework of problem-solving capabilities of older adults.

In the final part of the book, the focus is on human factors design and remediation of some age-related information-processing problems. Bogner (chap. 13) presents a compelling chapter describing the problems older adults with limited cognitive abilities presently have in managing the home health care and health maintenance that is increasingly required of older adults as hospital stays become more and more limited. Hartley (chap. 14) discusses issues of text design that would improve the readability and comprehensibility of medical text and information for older adults. Following this, Morrow and Leirer (chap. 15) present specifications for designing medical instructions that are optimal for older adults. Rogers, Rousseau, and Lamson (Chap. 16) follow with a detailed discussion on aging and warning labels, and Wogalter and Sojourner (chap. 17) close with detailed specifications for the design of medication labels.

This book is the result of a conference sponsored by the Center for Applied Cognitive Research on Aging (sponsored by the National Institute on Aging) and by a conference grant to the authors from the National Institute on Aging. The editors of this volume are deeply grateful to Denise L. Taylor-Moon for organizing the conference and providing staff support for the production of this volume. Finally, the consistent support of the National Institute on Aging is gratefully acknowledged. We particularly appreciate the efforts of Jared Jobe of the Behavioral and Social Research Program of the National Institute on Aging in providing support and advice for the integration of basic cognitive aging research with issues of practical relevance in the everyday lives of older adults.

Denise Park
Roger Morrell
Kim Shifren

I

Introduction

1

Aging and the Controlled and Automatic Processing of Medical Information and Medical Intentions

Denise C. Park
The University of Michigan

Medical patients of all ages are frequently faced with complex information and decisions about medical conditions and treatment alternatives. The decisions that medical patients make have substantial implications for their future well-being and even their survival. As we age, we are increasingly involved in medical interactions and decisions. In fact, older adults consume a disproportionate amount of medical care and services relative to their presence in the population (Institute of Medicine, 1994, 1997). Although we know that cognitive function in later adulthood declines on a number of dimensions, the role played by differences in cognitive function between younger and older adults in comprehending and acting on medical information is poorly understood. In the present chapter, and indeed in this entire volume, we consider this important issue. This issue has far-reaching implications not only for individuals with health conditions but also for our entire society, as the consumption of health services becomes an increasingly significant factor in determining economic well-being in developed countries. Before we begin a detailed discussion of the role of age-related decline and cognitive function in medical interactions and decisions, let us consider the following two scenarios.

3

Scenario 1

Dorothy Wood, age 67, is a widowed homemaker who suffers from hypertension and osteoarthritis, and she is also experiencing some age-related decline in her hearing that is not too serious and remains uncorrected. She takes a beta blocker and potassium supplement twice daily for her hypertension and also takes a nonsteroidal anti-inflammatory drug on a regular basis for her osteoarthritis. She has had surgery in the past for gall bladder disease and for fibroid tumors. She was recently diagnosed with a Stage 2 breast cancer after a routine mammogram screening followed by a surgical biopsy. She is now faced with a decision about how to treat her breast cancer. She meets briefly with her physician and at her daughter's insistence, has her daughter along for the visit. She is offered several options that include mastectomy followed by chemotherapy, lumpectomy with radiation and chemotherapy, and a radical mastectomy without radiation or chemotherapy. Breast reconstruction is also offered either during or after either of the mastectomy procedures. She does not want to seek a second opinion and does not seek out additional reading materials. Her physician thinks it is best that she have a mastectomy followed by chemotherapy, but tells her that she would not be at increased risk if she took up to a month to make her decision about what to do. A few days after meeting with the physician, she schedules the surgery. She has the surgery and follows up with three months of chemotherapy. She decides not to have reconstruction surgery. After surgery, she is prescribed four new medications that she takes in addition to her other two medications. She is very careful to organize her life around her medication schedule and rarely forgets to take her medication accurately. Three months later, after she is finished with treatment, she finds her life is getting back to normal. Although she was distressed by the news about the cancer, she believes that she has made a full recovery and does not think about what happened very much after she finishes chemotherapy.

Scenario 2

Candace Leggett, age 39, is a high-powered investment banker who is single, has no concomitant health conditions, and had surgery once as a child for appendicitis. She was recently diagnosed with a Stage 2 breast cancer after routine mammographic screening, which was followed by surgical biopsy. She is now faced with a decision about how to treat her breast cancer. She meets with the surgeon who performed her biopsy. The surgeon favors a mastectomy followed by chemotherapy, but she also presents Candace with other options, which include a lumpectomy with radiation and chemotherapy and a radical mastectomy without radiation or chemotherapy. Should Candace choose a mastectomy, she may also elect to have a breast reconstruction as part of the initial surgery or delay it until later, after she finishes chemotherapy. The surgeon advises her that she is not at increased risk if she takes up to a month to make this decision. After meeting with her physician, she schedules an appointment with an oncologist and another surgeon to get additional opinions. She reads several books written for women faced with this decision and also secures additional information from the World-Wide Web. Based on information she found on the Web, she becomes part of an Internet support and information exchange group. After a month of appointments and consultations, Candace opts for a mastectomy followed by chemotherapy. She decides to wait and see how she feels about reconstructive surgery after she finishes the chemotherapy. After surgery, she is prescribed four new medications that she is to take in addition to her daily vitamin. She goes back to work in a month and continues with her chemotherapy for two more months. She has trouble remembering to take her medications after she goes back to work, as she is very busy and has quite a lot of work to catch up. Three months after the surgery, she is finished with the chemotherapy and finds that her life is getting back to normal. Nevertheless, she continues to feel deeply distressed by her diagnosis and experiences considerable worry about a recurrence of the cancer and her uncertain future.

In the preceding scenarios, the two women are faced with similar decisions and prognoses. Although both women arrive at the same decision, their approaches to the decision process differ considerably. Dorothy Wood, age 67, takes relatively little time to make a decision, relying on the expertise of her physician and the opinion of her daughter. She reports considerably less distress than 39-year-old Candace Leggett and is also able to take her medication reliably. In contrast to Dorothy, Candace seeks out a great deal of information but, after considerable deliberation and consultation, makes the same decision as Dorothy. She rates her distress at her situation higher than Dorothy and, despite her superior cognitive abilities, has difficulty taking her medication reliably.

Although there are little data on the topic of medical decision making, extant data do suggest that age-related differences in cognitive processes, as well as differences in expertise in dealing with the medical establishment, may account for the contrasting processes used by Dorothy and Candace to arrive at the same decision. In the present chapter, it is hypothesized that there are fundamental differences in the cognitive function of younger and older adults that substantially influence medical decisions, treatments, and compliance behaviors. It is also hypothesized that unconscious, automatic processes play an important role in understanding medical behaviors and that older adults may be more susceptible to automatic influences due to more familiarity and experience with medical interactions and interventions as well as due to decreased amounts of controlled processing. A brief overview of cognitive function in young and old adults is presented, followed by a discussion of how these differences affect the comprehension of medical information, the process of making medical decisions, and adherence to treatment instructions. The importance of both controlled, effortful cognitive processes as well as unconscious, automatic processes in understanding medical information and the completion of medical intentions is discussed.

COGNITION AND AGING

The classic pattern of findings with respect to aging and cognition is one of age invariance on tasks that rely primarily on automatic processes with growth across the life span in acquired knowledge, such as vocabulary and world knowledge. With age, however, there is pronounced decline on cognitive tasks that require effortful or controlled processing (Craik & Byrd, 1982; Craik & Jennings, 1992; Park et al., 1996).

Effortful or controlled processing occurs in the individual in situations that require the conscious search for information from memory, active manipulation of retrieved information, or a conscious attempt to solve a problem. There is evidence that, compared to young adults, older adults have less cognitive resource for such effortful processing. The best index of processing resource is of some debate in the cognitive aging literature. Salthouse (1996) demonstrated that older adults are slower at processing information in nearly any situation and argued that this slowed rate of processing of information is an index of cognitive resource and the fundamental cause of age differences in cognitive performance. Others suggested limits in working memory capacity as an index of processing resource (Craik & Jennings, 1992; Smith, 1996; Wingfield, Stine, Lahar, & Aberdeen, 1988). Working memory is the capacity one has to process, store, and retrieve information online. Working memory declines with age (Park et al., 1996) and is measured by tasks that assess the ability of subjects to both answer questions about material presented while simultaneously remembering aspects of the stimulus presented (Salthouse & Babcock, 1991). Finally, Hasher and Zacks (1988) and Zacks and Hasher (1997) suggested that older adults are deficient in their ability both to direct and to inhibit their attention to irrelevant information. They argue that poor inhibitory function accounts for the decreased cognitive ability of older adults.

Regardless of the mechanism driving the cognitive deficits evidenced by the elderly, it is clearly the case that they are slower at processing information, that they have less capacity with which to process new information, and that they appear to have some difficulty focusing attention on the most relevant and important information in their environment. As a result of these basic declines in cognitive resources, older adults show deficits in types of memory that are effortful, such as free and cued recall (Park et al., 1996), although they do perform better on less demanding memory tasks such as picture recognition (Park, Puglisi, & Smith, 1986), spatial memory (Park et al., 1996; Park, Cherry, Smith, & Lafronza, 1990; Park, Puglisi, & Sovacool, 1983), and prospective memory (Einstein & McDaniel, 1990; Kidder, Park, Hertzog, & Morrell, 1997; Park, Hertzog, Kidder, Morrell, & Mayhorn, 1997). Similarly, older adults show deficits in reasoning tasks relative to younger adults (Salthouse, 1992) and on tasks that require inferences based on the information presented to them (Cohen, 1988).

In contrast to effortful processes, automatic processes are not age-impaired or are impaired only slightly with age. Automatic processes are viewed by cognitive psychologists to be low or no resource tasks that require little mental capacity to perform and may develop as a result of repeated experience, such as driving a car or other highly practiced tasks. Fisk and Rogers (1991) demonstrated age equivalence in automatic processes at the attentional level, and in a thorough review/meta-analysis of the implicit memory/priming literature, LaVoie and Light (1994) concluded that priming differences between young and old are substantially smaller than differences in explicit memory. Park and Shaw (1992), in a careful study with high power, found no differences in implicit memory between young and old but large differences in explicit (controlled) memory. Finally, Jacoby, Jennings, and Hay (1996) developed a new technique that permits estimates of the familiarity (automatic) and explicit (controlled) aspects of a memory from a single recall protocol. They found that the automatic/familiarity component of memory was age invariant but that young adults showed substantial superiority to old adults on the controlled component of memory.

Social psychologists have a broader conceptualization of automatic processes than the highly specified cognitive resource view described here. It is a view that is of considerable importance for understanding the behavior of older adults in medical settings. Bargh (1994, 1996) described an automatic process as an unconscious mental state, that, when combined with a particular set of conditions or specific environmental trigger, results in a behavior predicted by the unconscious mental state. Examples of subtle, automatically driven real-world behaviors as defined by Bargh might include overestimating the probability that your son would get rejected at Harvard after receiving negative feedback about your work from your boss, or a self-evaluation that you are too tired to go running when you get home from work after watching a frail, older woman get on the bus. Jacoby et al. (1996) postulated that the familiarity component of memory, which he observed in the laboratory, is the basis for these automatic, everyday behaviors described by Bargh, and it is this definition—the notion that unconscious processes automatically guide everyday behaviors—that may be of particular importance in understanding medical behaviors.

A second domain of cognitive function evidencing age invariance is that of knowledge structures. There is abundant evidence that knowledge structures remain intact with age and that semantic memory deteriorates only when brain pathology is present. Both Howard (1983) and Light (1992) presented evidence that priming effects that depend on semantic knowledge are similar for young and old adults, suggesting that semantic memories are structured similarly for old and young people. Additionally, association norms to pictures and words do not differ as a function of age (Howard, 1980; Puglisi & Park, 1987), reinforcing this view. Finally, vocabulary scores and other measures of crystallized intelligence are largely age invariant until about 80 years of age (Park et al., 1996).

For the purposes of the present topic, it is important to note that there is also some evidence that older adults, despite declines in other cognitive domains, are adept at producing and comprehending speech (Tun & Wingfield, 1993), a skill that may be of considerable importance in medical interactions. The amount of redundancy in language, the possibility that speech is a highly protected mechanism at the neurobiological level, and the vast experience older adults have with processing speech are possible explanations for the protected status of speech. Data suggest that older adults will be as adept as younger at comprehending speech presented at a normal or even somewhat rapid rate. There is also evidence that older adults have little difficulty comprehending written materials, except in cases where inferences are required or the grammatical structure places a high working memory load on the individual by requiring that they remember antecedent information to interpret later information (Kemper, 1998; Light, 1992). Nevertheless, data also indicate that, when older and younger adults are asked what they remember from a conversation or written text, older adults show less memory for the material (Kemper, 1992).

AGING AND MEDICAL INFORMATION PROCESSING

Thus, data on basic cognitive function suggest it is likely that older adults bring more experiences, familiarity, and information to medical situations, which they can draw upon, than younger adults, given that older adults have had more medical encounters, on average, than their younger counterparts. The greater familiarity and experiences of older adults with medical situations may play an important role in determining the choices they make due to the operation of environmental cues and automatic processes in controlling their behavior (Park, 1997). Data also suggest that although older adults may initially understand the information presented to them by a health professional, they may have trouble remembering the information presented to them, particularly novel information that does not build on existing knowledge. They will be slow to process information that often is presented quite rapidly in verbal interactions with nurses and physicians, and they may not have the cognitive resources required to make inferences about information presented to them, particularly when they have to hold it in working memory because it was presented verbally.

Thus, an older adult like Dorothy Wood would not fare very well if a physician presented her with a complex diagnosis of a staged breast cancer with particular cell characteristics and then proceeded to discuss causes, disease trajectory, and treatment with her. This verbal interaction requires Dorothy to integrate a large amount of unfamiliar information rapidly. In contrast, Candace would fare better at understanding and integrating the information presented online at the time of initial diagnosis. She would have the ability to make rapid inferences about her condition and might have more questions for her physician than Dorothy. This is a speculative suggestion, as it is not known at this time if older adults ask fewer questions than younger adults. One might expect that due to limited processing resources, older adults would make fewer inferences about their conditions based on information presented to them and, as a result, might have fewer questions for their physicians at the time of diagnosis. Additionally, due to rapid forgetting of information, they might have fewer questions later as well. Finally, they may be more likely to maintain their behavior through environmental cues and highly practiced routines that require little effortful processing and are largely automatic, explaining the better medication adherence of Dorothy Wood, despite her advanced age, when compared to Candace Leggett.

COMPREHENSION OF INFORMATION
AND INSTRUCTIONS IN A MEDICAL SETTING

It is not necessarily the case that older adults will always have more difficulties comprehending medical information than younger adults. In a situation where old adults have a great deal of information already about a preexisting medical condition, age differences would not be expected if the new information were explicitly presented to them. Indeed, if the older adult were more knowledgeable about the condition than a younger adult, one might expect that they would show superior comprehension of the information presented. For example, Dorothy Wood might show superior retention of new information about her osteoarthritis compared to Candace Leggett, due to the richer base of knowledge she has about the disorder after coping with it for 15 years. One would only expect comprehension deficits to the extent that comprehension requires an investment of cognitive resource. Thus, when presented with information that had a high working memory load (e.g., information about a tropical disease like Dengue fever that was equally unfamiliar to both Dorothy and Candace) or required considerable inference (due perhaps to incomplete information presented by the physician), one might expect age differences favoring younger adults.

One area in which there is some work examining age differences in comprehension is medication instructions, particularly instructions on prescription labels (see Morrow & Leirer, chap. 15, this volume, for a detailed discussion of this issue). Space for instructions on prescription labels is limited and, frequently, the instructions require inferences to be useful. It is due to this use of inference that we might expect age-related deficits. There is some evidence that older adults do have more difficulty than younger adults interpreting the information on prescription labels. Kendrick and Bayne (1982) reported that older adults had difficulty translating the instructions "Take every 6 hours" into a specific medication plan, and Hurd and Butkovich (1986) also found that the majority of older adults made errors when interpreting prescription labels. Morrell, Park, and Poon (1989, 1990) found that about 25% of the information in a medication plan was incorrectly comprehended by older adults, when they were presented with an array of prescription labels and asked to develop a medication schedule based on the instructions. Similarly, Park, Morrell, Frieske, Blackburn, and Birchmore (1991) found that rheumatoid arthritis patients had difficulty loading their own medications into over-the-counter medication organizers that were arranged by days of the week.

In other work, Zwahr, Park, Eaton, and Larson (1997) examined the comprehension of middle-aged and older adults regarding information presented to them about advance medical directives and power of attorney for health conditions. In 1990, Congress passed the Patient Self-Determination Act which required all health facilities receiving Medicare or Medicaid to offer patients, at the time of admission, information about advanced directives and the opportunity to prepare a living will or advanced medical directive. Zwahr et al. (1997) presented middle-aged and older adults with three versions of materials used by different hospitals to present information to patients on advanced medical directives. While controlling for prior knowledge, Zwahr et al. reported that middle-aged adults showed more learning from the materials than older adults. Moreover, the best predictors of comprehension of the materials were cognitive factors such as working memory and vocabulary as well as robust health. These data suggest that older adults are somewhat more disadvantaged than younger adults in comprehending complex medical information. The three types of documents subjects were presented with ranged from a simply worded pamphlet to a complex seven-page document. Surprisingly, type of document made no difference in the amount of information acquired and had no impact on age. Thus, a simple document containing focused information was just as effective as a complex document in assisting patients in learning the key points necessary for an adequate understanding of advanced directives. This finding is reminiscent of research conducted by Morrell, Park, Mayhorn, and Kelley (1998), who found that older adults learned computer tasks more effectively with less complete, procedural-based instructions compared to more complex, explanatory instructions.

The notion that older adults have difficulty understanding medical directives is recognized by the institutions required to provide the information to patients. Park, Eaton, Larson, and Palmer (1994) studied practices of hospitals and administrators in implementing the Patient Self-Determination Act in the state of Georgia. Hospital administrators reported that the biggest problem with implementation of the law was the inappropriateness of presenting this material at the time of admission and the difficulties patients had in comprehending the materials presented. In a follow-up study of nursing homes, Zwahr, Park, Eaton, and Larson (1997) reported that 74% of nursing home administrators reported difficulties conveying information about advanced directives to patients so that they could understand it. Nursing homes were more likely than hospitals to provide written materials for patients and to spend more time on disseminating this information to residents in recognition of the particular difficulties that the nursing home group experienced.

In summary, there is evidence that older adults have difficulty comprehending medical information, both at the level of relatively simple instructions about medications as well as for complex information that is required to make important medical decisions. Relatively more is known about how to structure specific medication instructions to support the declining cognitive capacities of older adults (Park & Jones, 1996; Morrow & Leirer, chap. 15, this volume; Wogalter & Sojourner, chap. 17, this volume), but considerable work remains to be done in determining optimal formats for the presentation of more complex instructions and information to older adults.

AGING AND MEDICAL DECISION MAKING

As a result of age-related declines in comprehension and memory, older adults have less information available to them than younger adults after being exposed to relevant information with which to make a medical decision. In addition, it appears that age-related information-processing deficits affect the components of the decision process as well. Meyer, Russo, and Talbot (1995) studied young and older women's decisions regarding treatment options for breast cancer in a laboratory setting as well as studying actual breast cancer patients. They reported that older women made decisions that were similar to those of younger women, but they based their decisions on less information, made the decision more quickly, made fewer comparative statements among perceived choices, and offered less complete rationales for their decision. Moreover, they found that effortful, controlled processes as measured by recall and comprehension ability predicted the quality of the decision process (but it is important to note, not the quality of the decision itself), thus reinforcing the important role of basic cognitive abilities in understanding age differences in medical decisions.

In a similar vein, Zwahr, Park, and Shifren (1998) examined the relationship of cognitive variables to the quality of the decision process of younger and older women about whether to elect estrogen replacement therapy as a treatment for menopause. After reading detailed information about treatment choices, they reported that older women nevertheless perceived fewer options to be available to them than younger women, they made fewer comparisons among options perceived, and the quality of their rationale for the decision was more limited than that of younger women. Moreover, path analysis indicated that the best predictors of the age-related variance in these measures were cognitive measures including speed of processing of information, reasoning ability, and reading comprehension ability.

E. A. Leventhal, H. Leventhal, Schaefer, and Easterling (1993) demonstrated as well that older adults make different decisions about seeking medical treatment compared to younger adults. They reported that older adults took markedly less time to seek treatment for possibly serious symptoms they were experiencing, whereas both age groups sought treatment quickly for symptoms that were definitely serious. They argue that older adults act quickly to conserve limited emotional/physical reserves for addressing and worrying about medical problems (see E. A. Leventhal, Robitaille, H. Leventhal, & Brownlee, chap. 9, this volume, for further discussion). Another plausible interpretation of these data is a cognitive resource interpretation, that is, due to limited cognitive resources, older adults seek the services of an expert more rapidly because they feel less able to evaluate the condition than do younger adults.

In general, then, as demonstrated in the narratives about Dorothy Wood and Candace Leggett, the extant literature indicates that, due to limited cognitive resources, older adults take less time to make a decision about treatment, seek less information about treatment alternatives, and show less evidence of complex comparison and evaluation of the information available to them (see Yates & Patalano, chap. 3, this volume; Zwahr, chap. 4, this volume, for more discussion). It is important to recognize, however, that there is no evidence at this point that older adults make medical decisions of lower quality than younger adults who process more material. It may be the case that in domains where a great deal of expertise and information processing is required, older adults are more likely to rely on knowledgeable third parties, such as their children or a physician. In fact, Cassileth, Zupkis, Sutton-Smith, and March (1980) reported that older adults were considerably more likely to defer decisions about cancer treatment to their physician (about 48% deferred) compared to younger adults (about 13% of adults ages 20 to 39 deferred). Although it is possible that some of this deference reflects cohort-specific behaviors between younger and older adults with respect to physician–patient interactions, it is also quite plausible that older patients may compensate for a decrease in controlled processing by delegating authority for decision making about treatments to an expert.

The findings discussed thus far suggest that limited cognitive resources or controlled processes contribute to differences in medical decision-making behaviors in older adults compared to younger adults. It is important to recognize, however, that the role that automatic activation of a category or stereotype by an environmental trigger may play is important in the choices and decisions we make. Because older adults show little or no decline in automatic processes, it is likely that their decisions are affected as much or even more (due to less controlled processing) by such activations than younger adults. For example, Dorothy Wood might over-report her own symptoms and feel particularly ill in a physician visit after just having a conversation with her frail older mother about her mother's myriad health problems. Or perhaps, after successfully completing a risky bicycle ride along a treacherous course on the way to the doctor's office, Candace might feel generally invulnerable and be more willing to agree to a controversial medical treatment for breast cancer. What these scenarios have in common is that a specific event primed a general feeling or construct that triggered an outcome or decision in a seemingly unrelated medical setting and that the individual was unaware of the linkage.

There are two interesting studies on automatic processes and aging that support the hypothesis that the activation of an aging stereotype in a medical setting could have powerful effects. Bargh, Chen, and Burrows (1996) reported that young adults who received subliminal presentation of words on a computer screen that were stereotypes of aging (e.g., forgetful, Florida, bingo) were demonstrably slower to walk to an elevator 40 feet away, as they left the experiment, than subjects who had received neutral primes. In a recent study, Levy (1996) demonstrated that older adults who were primed with aging stereotypes subliminally actually demonstrated poorer memory performance when compared to a baseline condition. Similarly, older adults primed with words associated with high cognitive performance (e.g., wise), were improved for the same memory test. These data suggest that the activation of an aging stereotype in older adults can profoundly affect their performance. Moreover, the demonstration of a priming effect of an aging stereotype on older adults suggests that understanding the relationship of the activation of such stereotypes to medical decisions made by older adults is of critical importance. Medical interactions frequently infantilize adults, and aging stereotypes are easily activated in medical settings by such things as the use of Elderspeak by staff (Kemper, 1998) and questioning that emphasizes age and frailty.

Although little is known about the role of automatic processes in making medical decisions and in representing health conditions, the priming literature suggests that the way information is presented in a physician's office, even the design of the environment and materials available in the waiting area, will have a substantive impact on the patient's representation of their health, their demeanor with the physicians, and their subsequent decisions. The impact on patients of interactions and environments that activate negative stereotypes about aging versus positive constructs about control, vitality, and wisdom are likely to be substantial in medical settings and appear to be a fruitful and important domain for future research.

ADHERENCE TO MEDICAL INSTRUCTIONS

The role of cognitive function in a medical interaction does not end with a visit to a physician. Typically, patients are expected to participate in the maintenance of health and management of illness by following various instructions. In fact, as health care costs increase in the United States, patients are increasingly expected to manage complex equipment and perform tasks for themselves or for family members that would have been performed in the hospital in the past (see Bogner, chap. 13, this volume, for a thorough discussion of this issue). Additionally, patients frequently must manage a complex medication schedule that requires a number of cognitive operations for accurate adherence to the medication regimen to take place. Age-related declines in controlled processes would appear to leave older adults at a disadvantage in managing these tasks correctly. However, it is also the case that automatic processes and environmental cues may play a significant role in governing adherence behavior so that older adults may be less disadvantaged than one might expect.

Park (1992) suggested that there are four controlled processing components to medication adherence. The individual taking medications must do the following:

- Comprehend the instructions as to when to take the medication and what special considerations apply to taking the medication, such as taking with food or not taking the medication with alcohol (see Rogers, Rousseau, & Lamson, chap. 16, this volume, for a discussion of medication warnings).
- Integrate the medication schedules from individual prescriptions with one another and develop a daily or weekly plan. Park (1992) conceptualizes this to be a working memory task.
- Remember the medication schedule once it is integrated (or use a memory aid to assist retention, such as a medication organizer or a written hour-by-hour schedule).
- Remember to take the medication at the appointed time, a prospective memory task.

There is evidence, some of which has already been reviewed, that older adults are disadvantaged on all of these steps. The comprehension of medical instructions typically requires some inference. For example, the individual must translate the meaning of "Take every 6 hours" into a concrete daily plan. Older adults are clearly disadvantaged on medication tasks that require inferences, as described earlier in the chapter. The integration of the medical schedule as well may prove to be a challenge, as working memory and long-term memory both decline with age, possibly posing difficulties for retention of the medication schedule. Finally, remembering to perform future actions has been demonstrated to be age-sensitive in the laboratory, both for prospective memories that are time-based (e.g., "Take medication at 5 p.m."; Einstein & McDaniel, 1990; Park et al., 1997) as well as event-based ("Take medication at breakfast"; Park et al., 1997; Kidder et al., 1997). Because of considerations like these, it is frequently suggested in the literature that older adults are at great risk of nonadherence (Bergman & Wilholm, 1981; Lamy, 1984). With the recent advent of microelectronic monitoring techniques for medication adherence, it has become possible to determine the role of age and cognitive function in medication adherence.

Park, Morrell, Frieske, and Kincaid (1992) monitored medication-adherence behaviors for 4 weeks of adults ages 60 and older who were taking three or more medications. Subjects were given bar codes for each medication they were taking and a credit-card sized scanner. They scanned the bar code for the appropriate medication at the time it was taken and returned the scanner to the experimenters after 4 weeks, providing the experimenters with a detailed record of medication-adherence behavior. The results, somewhat surprisingly, indicated that young-old adults (ages 60–77) were highly adherent and made few errors. Old-old adults (ages 78–92) however, made many more errors than young-old adults and showed improvement in adherence compared to a no-treatment control when they were provided with cognitive aids. The cognitive aids were designed to relieve the comprehension, working memory, and long-term memory component of the adherence task by providing organization of the medications and an explicit structure for what was to be done with the medication. Subjects were given both a detailed hour-by-hour schedule for their medications as well as a weekly medication organizer that had four marked slots for each day. The medications were placed in the slots, which were marked with the time as to when the medication should be taken each day. Because these aids were effective and primarily supported working memory, it appears that very old adults (in this sample, the old-old were age 77 and older) may experience sufficient amounts of cognitive decline that aids that support their working-memory function act to improve adherence. In contrast, young-old adults, although experiencing some age-related declines, appear to have sufficient cognitive function to manage medications accurately.

In later work, Morrell, Park, Kidder, and Martin (1997) monitored adults ages 30 to 80 with hypertension. Over a 2-month period, they observed that, as in Park et al. (1992), the least adherent subjects were the oldest-old and the most adherent were young-old adults. However, these data also indicated that middle-aged adults evidenced significantly more nonadherence behaviors than the young-old adults, despite the declining cognitive function of the young-old adults.

This puzzling pattern of findings led us to examine causes for nonadherence that went beyond cognition as well as traditional medical variables. We became interested in the role of noncognitive variables in adherence (Park & Mayhorn, 1996) and became familiar with the work of Leventhal and colleagues. Leventhal and Cameron (1987) suggested that individuals have an evolving conceptualization of their illnesses and that drives their illness behaviors (see also H. Leventhal, E. A. Leventhal, & Schaefer, 1992). Based on this thinking, we hypothesized that young-old adults had both sufficient cognitive abilities and also felt sufficiently vulnerable to the consequences of uncontrolled hypertension that they were both cognitively able and had an illness representation consistent with adherence. Old-old adults, in contrast, had an illness representation consistent with adherence but insufficient cognitive function to take medication correctly. Finally, middle-aged adults had adequate cognitive function for adherence but were less concerned about consequences of hypertension and did not have an illness representation compatible with adherence. This model predicts, as we found in Park et al. (1992) and Morrell et al. (1997), that young-old adults would be most adherent.

A MODEL OF MEDICATION ADHERENCE

We have developed a model of adherence behavior that explicitly integrates cognitive, psychosocial, medical, and contextual variables. Working with a multidisciplinary team and joining forces with the Leventhal team, we used structural equation modeling techniques to understand the relative contributions of each potential component to adherence behaviors (see Park, 1994; Park & Jones, 1996). We studied rheumatoid arthritis patients across the life span and administered detailed questionnaires to assess their beliefs about their illness and self-efficacy related to disease variables as well as general affect. Subjects also received a complete cognitive battery, and we also measured the role of contextual stress, by administering a self-rated busyness in everyday life scale (Park et al., 1998). We studied subjects for one month who were taking a mean of 4.18 medications. Despite the high medication load and pronounced evidence for cognitive decline relative to the younger adults in the study, 47% of the sample over age 55 did not make a single error in their medication regimen over a one month time period! Regimen complexity did not relate to nonadherence, nor did illness severity, although in the medical literature these variables have been hypothesized to be important (Bergman & Wilholm, 1981; Shimp & Ascione, 1985). As in the past, middle-aged adults were more nonadherent than the older adults. Contrary to our predictions, illness representation was not a strong predictor of nonadherence.

The single most powerful variable was self-rated busyness. That is, subjects who reported leading a very engaged, busy lifestyle that was frequently unpredictable were the most nonadherent. This, of course, is also a quality that is typical of middle-aged adults who are pressed by a peak level of professional engagement as well as by the joint needs of children and aging parents. One might consider highly engaged individuals who report being too busy as individuals engaged in a chronically high resource demanding situation so that they have insufficient cognitive resource remaining to attend to everyday needs, such as taking medications correctly or even showing up for medical appointments.

Another interpretation of this finding is that environment and lifestyle play a large role in medication adherence and that this behavior is environmentally determined and automatically driven. Subjects who reported having stable environments were more likely to take their medications. It is likely that such environments provide a plethora of cues that automatically drive adherence behavior whereas individuals who are in unpredictable, shifting environments do not have access to the day-to-day cues that are associated with taking medications. Furthermore, it would appear that the act of completing an adherence behavior in a particular environment may strengthen the probability of completing the behavior in the future in this environment. Because elderly subjects scored quite low on the busyness scale, their adherence behavior was highly accurate due to the maintenance function a stable environment provides for adherence behaviors. More study of these intriguing possibilities is needed.

Park et al. (1998) also reported in this study that performance on laboratory measures of cognition played a role in nonadherence, after age was controlled statistically. Thus, it appears that lower ability adults of all ages may be at greater risk of nonadherence than higher ability adults. Finally, we hypothesized that illness representation did not have the strong effect on adherence that we expected because we selected a group of subjects who were seriously ill with a chronic disease that provided them with frequent cues in the form of pain and fatigue. The medications for the treatment of rheumatoid arthritis are effective for both controlling pain and preventing disability. Hence, it is likely that subjects had an illness representation that was highly consonant with adherence, permitting the effects of other variables, such as the context in which one is taking medication and cognitive function, to emerge. In summary, the Park et al. (1998) data clearly demonstrated that a simple overlay of cognitive psychology to complex medical behaviors will not be effective and that more integrative approaches are necessary to understand the complex interplay among cognitive function, belief systems, environmental press, and patients' medical behaviors.

INTERVENTIONS TO IMPROVE ADHERENCE AND THE COMPLETION OF OTHER MEDICAL INTENTIONS

Rather than attempting to improve active memory (a controlled process) to enhance medication adherence and the completion of other medical intentions (e.g., adherence to an exercise program, routine breast self-examination, etc.), it may be more useful to develop interventions that build or strengthen automatic processes that will operate to increase the likelihood that an intended medical intention or behavior is completed. Gollwitzer (1996) demonstrated that it is possible to increase the probability that an intention will be carried out by strengthening automatic components of the intended behavior. Gollwitzer, Heckhausen, and Ratajczak (1990) asked subjects to describe a personal goal and how far they were from fulfilling it. All were far from their goals, which were things like moving in with a boyfriend or going on a ski vacation. Subjects were required to think of the positive consequences of achieving a goal, a variety of ways they might achieve the goal, or a single specific plan for implementation. Only subjects who considered the single specific plan made progress later toward achieving this goal. Gollwitzer (1996) hypothesized that the development of a specific intention strengthened the probability that the intention would be carried out. Gollwitzer (1993) asked students to describe a project they expected to finish over Christmas vacation and whether they had implementation expectations. After vacation, Gollwitzer found that two thirds of those with a specific plan had completed the project but only a fourth of those with a general plan did. Similarly, subjects who were required to form an implementation plan about writing a report over the vacation were much more likely to write the report (75%) compared to subjects who did not have a specific plan (33%). Brandstatter (1992) reported that subjects were much more likely to make counterarguments to a racist speech at the exact point they had planned when they had to mark where in the speech they would do this rather than merely think about where they might do it, despite the fact that all students were motivated to produce compelling counterarguments to the racist speech. When subjects had to divide a project into five specific steps, with a detailed plan for how they would complete each step, they were more likely to be successful than subjects who had to deliberate and list pros and cons of the action.

Gollwitzer (1996) hypothesized that the formation of specific intentions "alleviates the volitional problems of goal achievement. As soon as people anticipate such problems, they should form implementation intentions to protect themselves from falling prey to such problems" (p. 294). In a sense, the reinstatement of various situational cues rehearsed in planning serve as primes to energize automatically behavior in the desired direction, bypassing the role of volition. Gollwitzer (1993) suggested that the development of specific implementation intentions will be most effective for a goal about which an individual feels strongly and would very much like to achieve. It is the case that patients usually would very much like to follow their doctors' instructions to take their medications, change diet, exercise, or stop smoking. Thus, the techniques outlined by Gollwitzer (1993) could be used to enhance medication adherence behaviors or adherence to an exercise program or other medically prescribed behavior. Orbell, Hodgkins, and Sheeran (1997) reported that the use of an implementation intention training program increased the probability of breast self-examination in a college-age sample of women. As Orbell et al.'s (1997) data suggest, the potential for using these techniques to enhance medication adherence and other health behaviors would appear to be substantial.

A second mechanism for improving adherence or the completion of intentions might be to present subjects with artificial environmental cues designed to trigger the behavior. In an effort to improve medication adherence, Park, Shifren, Morrell, Watkins, and Stuedemann (1997) outfitted nonadherent hypertensive patients whose nonadherence was electronically measured with bottle caps or wristwatches that beeped at the time they were to take their medications. Subjects' adherence improved significantly over their original baseline and relative to a no-treatment control. Introducing an environmental cue to remind a subject of a medical event or behavior they need to complete not only may support the immediate prospective memory, but also may, strengthen automatically the probability that the behavior will be repeated in the same environment in the future.

Returning to the vignettes of Dorothy Wood and Candace Leggett, we see that their behavior mirrors the findings from our research program. Dorothy, age 67, although showing cognitive decline and maintaining an already high medication load, had little difficulty integrating the four new medications with the two that she was already taking. Dorothy is retired, lives alone, and is generally cognitively intact. Thus, she had the time and tended to organize her day around her illness and taking medications accurately. She developed an elaborate system for taking her medications, was home in a constant environment much of the time that provided automatic cuing of adherence, and had adequate time to prepare her medications to take with her if she were going to be out. She rarely made errors. In contrast, Candace Leggett, age 39, has a very demanding job, travels frequently, and often works 70 or more hours a week. She does not have an existing schema for taking medications, and she was only taking vitamins prior to her illness. She has multiple offices, travels often, and is frequently juggling multiple tasks. She receives little automatic support for her adherence behavior and often has trouble managing all of the daily tasks in her life, such as getting her home repaired, making appropriate medical appointments, and helping her aged mother with her health problems. As a result, she frequently forgets to take her medications and is considerably more nonadherent than Dorothy, despite higher cognitive abilities. It appears that Candace's problem is primarily prospective in nature—that is, she knows what to do with the medications, but cannot remember to do it (Park & Kidder, 1996). Based on the hypertension study completed in our lab (Park, Shifren, et al., 1997), we would likely recommend that Candace wear a programmable triathlon wristwatch that would beep every time she was to take a medication.

CONCLUSIONS

The problem of medical information processing in older adults is a complex one. On one hand, deficient controlled processes that occur with age result in decreased ability to comprehend, remember, and make inferences about medical information. However, intact automatic processes combined with considerable knowledge and expertise about illness and medical settings may compensate for declines in controlled processes. Moreover, the potential for relying on a proxy that has a high level of cognitive resources may also mitigate the impact of cognitive aging on medical behaviors. Very little is known about these issues, and it remains a challenge for future researchers to learn more about these critically important issues. The medical domain is a research area where theories about cognition, expertise, intentions, and context all have contributions to make to understanding representations of medical conditions and choices individuals make about treatment for them.

ACKNOWLEDGMENTS

This research was supported by grants to the author from the National Institute on Aging, including R13 AG14631-01, "Medical Information Processing and Aging Conference"; R01 AG09868, "Aging, Arthritis, and Medication Adherence; R01 AG06265, "Context Effects on the Aging Memory"; and P50AG11715, "The Center for Applied Cognitive Research on Aging." The author gratefully acknowledges their support. In addition, the author thanks Shari Turner for assistance in manuscript preparation.

REFERENCES

Bargh, J. A. (1994) The four horseman of automaticity: Awareness, intention, efficacy, and control in social cognition. In R. S. Wyer & T. K. Srull (Eds.), *Handbook of social cognition* (2nd ed., Vol. 1, pp. 1–40). Hillsdale, NJ: Lawrence Erlbaum Associates.

Bargh, J. A. (1996). Automaticity in social pscyhology. In E. T. Higgins & A. Kruglanski (Eds.), *Social psychology: Handbook of basic principles* (pp. 184–210). New York: Guilford.

Bargh, J. A., Chen, M., & Burrows, L. (1996). Automaticity of social behavior: Direct effects of trait construct and stereotype activation on action. *Journal of Personality and Social Psychology, 71,* 230–244.

Bergman, U., & Wilholm, B. E. (1981). Patient medicine on admission to a medical clinic. *European Journal of Pharmacology, 20,* 185–191.

Brandstatter, V. (1992). Der Einflub von Vorsetzen auf die Handlungsinitiierung. *Ein Beitrag zur willenpsychologischen Frage der Realisierung von Absichten.* Frankfurt, Germany: Peter Lang.

Cassileth, B. R., Zupkis, R. V., Sutton-Smith, K., & March, V. (1980). Information and participation preferences among cancer patients. *Annals of Internal Medicine, 92,* 832–836.

Cohen, G. (1988). Age differences in memory for text: Production deficiency or processing limitations? In L. L. Light & D. M. Burke (Eds.), *Language, memory, and aging* (pp. 171–190). New York: Cambridge University Press.

Craik, F. I. M. & Byrd, M. (1982). Aging and cognitive deficits: The role of attentional resources. In F. I. M. Craik & S. Trehub (Eds.), *Aging and cognitive processes* (pp. 191–211). New York: Plenum Press.

Craik, F. I. M. & Jennings, J. M. (1992). Human memory. In F. I. M. Craik & T. A. Salthouse (Eds.), *The handbook of aging and cognition* (pp. 51–110). Hillsdale, NJ: Lawrence Erlbaum Associates.

Einstein, G. O., & McDaniel, M. A. (1990). Normal aging and prospective memory. *Journal of Experimental Psychology: Learning, Memory, and Cognition, 16,* 717–726.

Fisk, A. D., & Rogers, W. A. (1991). Toward an understanding of age-related memory and visual search effects. *Journal of Experimental Psychology: General, 120,* 131–149.

Gollwitzer, P. M. (1993). Goal achievement: The role of intentions. In W. Stroebe & M. Hewstone (Eds.), *European review of social psychology* (Vol. 4, pp. 141–185). Chichester, England: Wiley.

Gollwitzer, P. M. (1996). The volitional benefits of planning. In P. M. Gollwitzer & J. A. Bargh (Eds.), *The psychology of action: Linking cognition and motivation to behavior* (pp. 287–312). New York: Guilford.

Gollwitzer, P. M., Heckhausen, H., & Ratajczak, H. (1990). From weighing to willing: Approaching a change decision through pre- or postdecisional mentation. *Organizational Behavior and Human Decision Processes, 45,* 41–65.

Hasher, L., & Zacks, R. T. (1988). Working memory, comprehension, and aging: A review and a new view. In G. H. Bower (Ed.), *The psychology of learning and motivation* (Vol. 22, pp. 193–225). San Diego, CA: Academic Press.

Howard, D. V. (1980). Category norms: A comparison of the Battig and Montague (1969) norms with the responses of adults between the ages of 20 and 80. *Journal of Gerontology, 35,* 225–231.

Howard, D. V. (1983). The effects of aging and degree of association on the semantic priming of lexical decisions. *Experimental Aging Research, 9,* 145–151.

Hurd, P. D., & Butkovich, S. L. (1986). Compliance problems and the older patient: Assessing functional limitations. *Drug Intelligence and Clinical Pharmacy, 20,* 228–231.

Institute of Medicine. (1994). Strengthening training in geriatrics for physicians. *Journal of the American Geriatrics Society, 42,* 559–565.

Institute of Medicine. (1997). *Pharmacokinetics and drug interactions in the elderly and special issues in elderly African-American populations.* Washington, DC: National Academy Press.

Jacoby, L. L., Jennings, J. M., & Hay, J. F. (1996). Dissociating automatic and consciously-controlled processes: Implications for diagnosis and rehabilitation of memory deficits. In D. J. Herrmann, C. L. McEvoy, C. Hertzog, P. Hertel, & M. K. Johnson (Eds.), *Basic and applied memory research: Theory in context* (Vol. 1, pp. 161–193). Hillsdale, NJ: Larwence Erlbaum Associates.

Kemper, S. (1992). Adults' sentence fragments: Who, what, when, where, and why. *Communication Research, 19*(4), 444–458.

Kemper, S. (1998). Aging and message production and comprehension. In N. Schwartz, D. Park, B. Knauper, & S. Sudman (Eds.), *Aging, cognition, and self-reports.*

Kendrick, R., & Bayne, J. R. (1982). Compliance with prescribed medication by elderly patients. *Journal of the Canadian Medical Association, 127,* 961.

Kidder, D. P., Park, D. C., Hertzog, C., & Morrell, R. (1997). Prospective memory and aging: The effects of working memory and prospective memory task load. *Aging, Neuropsychology, and Cognition, 4*(9), 3–112.

Lamy, P. (1984). Hazards of drug use in the elderly: Commonsense measures to reduce them. *Postgraduate Medicine, 76,* 50–61.

LaVoie, D., & Light, L. L. (1994). Adult age differences in repetition priming: A meta-analysis. *Psychology and Aging, 9,* 539–553.

Leventhal, E. A., Leventhal, H., Schaefer, P., & Easterling, D. (1993). Conservation of energy, uncertainty reduction and swift utilization of medical care among the elderly. *Journal of Gerontology, 48,* 78–86.

Leventhal, H., & Cameron, L. (1987). Behavioral theories and the problem of compliance. *Patient Education and Counseling, 10,* 117–138.

Leventhal, H., Leventhal, E. A., & Schaefer, P. M. (1992). Vigilant coping and health behavior. In M. G. Ory, R. P. Abeles, & P. D. Lipman (Eds.), *Aging, health, and behavior* (pp. 109–140). Newbury Park, CA: Sage.

Levy, B. (1996). Improving memory in old age through implicit self-stereotyping. *Journal of Personality and Social Psychology, 71,* 1092–1107.

Light, L. L. (1992). The organization of memory in old age. In F. I. M. Craik & T. A. Salthouse (Eds.), *The hankbook of aging and cognition* (pp. 111–166). Hillsdale, NJ: Lawrence Erlbaum Associates.

Meyer, B. J. F., Russo, C., & Talbot, A. (1995). Discourse comprehension and problem solving: Decisions about the treatment of breast cancer by women across the life span. *Psychology and Aging, 10,* 84–103.

Morrell, R. W., Park, D. C., Kidder, D. P., & Martin, M. (1997). Adherence to anti-hypertensive medications over the lifespan. *The Gerontologist, 37,* 609–619.

Morrell, R. W., Park, D. C., Mayhorn, C. B., & Kelley, C. L. (1998). *The effects of age and instructional format on teaching older adults how to use ELDERCOMM: An electronic bulletin system.* Manuscript submitted for publication.

Morrell, R. W., Park, D. C., & Poon, L. W. (1989). Quality of instructions on prescription drug labels: Effects on memory and comprehension in young and old adults. *Gerontologist, 29,* 345–354.

Morrell, R. W., Park, D. C., & Poon, L. W. (1990). Effects of labeling techniques on memory and comprehension of prescription information in young and old adults. *Journals of Gerontology, 45,* 166–172.

Orbell, S., Hodgkins, S., Sheeran, P. (1997). Implementation intentions and the theory of planned behavior. *Personality and Social Psychology Bulletin, 23*(9), 945–954.

Park, D. C. (1992). Applied cognitive aging research. In F. I. M. Craik & T. A. Salthouse (Eds.), *Handbook of cognition and aging* (pp. 449–493). Hillsdale, NJ: Lawrence Erlbaum Associates.

Park, D. C. (1994). Self-regulation and control of rheumatic disorders. In S. Maes, H. Leventhal, & M. Johnson (Eds.), *International handbook of health psychology* (pp. 189–217). New York: Wiley.

Park, D. C. (1997). Psychological issues related to competence: Cognitive aging and instrumental activities of daily living. In W. Schaie & S. Willis (Eds.), *Social structures and aging* (pp. 66–82). Mahwah, NJ: Lawrence Erlbaum Associates.

Park, D. C., Cherry, K. E., Smith, A. D., & Lafronza, V. N. (1990). Effects of distinctive context on memory for objects and their locations in young and elderly adults. *Psychology and Aging, 5,* 250–255.

Park, D. C., Eaton, T. A., Larson, E. J., & Palmer, H. T. (1994). Implementation and impact of the patient self-determination act. *Southern Medical Journal, 87* (10), 971–977.

Park, D. C., Hertzog, C., Kidder, D., Morrell, R., & Mayhorn, C. (1997). Effects of age on event-based and time-based prospective memory. *Psychology and Aging, 12,* 314–327.

Park, D. C., Hertzog, C., Leventhal, H., Morrell, R. W., Leventhal, E., Birchmore, D., Martin, M., & Bennett, J. (In press). *Medication adherence in rheumatoid arthritis patients: Older is wiser.*

Park, D. C. & Jones, T. R. (1996). Medication adherence and aging. In A. D. Fiske & W. A. Rogers (Eds.), *Handbook of human factors and the older adult* (pp. 257–288). San Diego, CA: Academic Press.

Park, D. C., & Kidder, D. (1996). Prospective memory and medication adherence. In M. Brandimonte, G. Einstein, & M. McDaniel (Eds.), *Prospective memory: Theory and applications* (pp. 369–390). Mahwah, NJ: Lawrence Erlbaum Associates.

Park, D. C. & Mayhorn, C. B. (1996). Remembering to take medications: The importance of nonmemory variables. In D. Hermann, M. Johnson, C. McEvoy, C. Hertzog, & P. Hertel (Eds.), *Research on practical aspects of memory* (Vol. 2, pp. 95–110). Mahwah, NJ: Lawrence Erlbaum Associates.

Park, D. C., Morrell, R. W., Frieske, D., Blackburn, A. B., & Birchmore, D. (1991). Cognitive factors and the use of over-the-counter medication organizers by arthritis patients. *Human Factors, 31*(3), 57–67.

Park, D. C., Morrell, R. W., Frieske, D., & Kincaid, D. (1992). Medication adherence behaviors in older adults: Effects of external cognitive supports. *Psychology and Aging, 7*(2), 252–256.

Park, D. C., Puglisi, J. T., & Smith, A. D. (1986). Memory for pictures: Does an age-related decline exist? *Psychology and Aging, 1,* 11–17.

Park, D. C., Puglisi, J. T., & Sovacool, M. (1983). Memory for pictures, words, and spatial location in older adults: Evidence for pictorial superiority. *Journal of Gerontology, 38,* 582–588.

Park, D. C. & Shaw, R. J. (1992). Effect of environmental support on implicit and explicit memory in younger and older adults. *Psychology and Aging, 7,* 632–642.

Park, D. C., Shifren, K., Morrell, R. W., Watkins, K., & Stuedemann, T. (1997, November). Improving medication adherence in African Americans with hypertension: A cognitive intervention strategy. In

K. Pillemer (Chair), *Promoting productive aging: New ideas from the Roybal Centers on Applied Gerontology*. Symposium conducted at the 50th Annual Scientific Meeting of the Gerontological Society of America, Cincinnatti, Ohio.

Park, D. C., Smith, A. D., Lautenschlager, G., Earles, J., Frieske, D., Zwahr, M., & Gaines, C. (1996). Mediators of long-term memory performance across the life span. *Psychology and Aging, 11*(4), 621–637.

Puglisi, J. T., & Park, D. C. (1987). Perceptual elaboration and memory in older adults. *Journal of Gerontology, 42*(2), 160–162.

Salthouse, T. A. (1992). Reasoning and spatial ablilities. In F. I. M. Craik & T. A. Salthouse (Eds.), *The handbook of aging and cognition* (pp. 167–212). Hillsdale, NJ: Lawrence Erlbaum Associates.

Salthouse, T. A. (1996). The processing-speed theory of adult age differences in cognition. *Psychological Review, 103,* 403–428.

Salthouse, T. A., & Babcock, R. L. (1991). Decomposing adult age differences in working memory. *Developmental Psychology, 27,* 763–776.

Shimp, L. A., & Ascione, F. J. (1985). Potential medication-related problems in noninstitutional elderly. *Drug Intelligence and Clinical Pharmacy, 19,* 766–772.

Smith, A. D. (1996). Memory. In J. E. Birren (Ed.), *The encyclopedia of gerontology* (pp. 107–119). New York: Academic Press.

Tun, A., & Wingfield, A. (1993). Is speech special? Perception and recall of spoken language in complex environments. In J. Cerella, J. Rybash, W. Hoyer, & M. L. Commons (Eds.), *Adult information processing: Limits on loss* (pp. 425–457). San Diego, CA: Academic Press.

Wingfield, A., Stine, E. L., Lahar, C. J.. & Aberdeen, J. S., (1988). Does the capacity of working memory change with age? *Experimental Aging Research, 14,* 103–107.

Zacks, R., & Hasher, L. (1997). Cognitive gerontology and attentional inhibition: A reply to Burke and McDowd. *Journal of Gerontology: Psychological Sciences, 52B*(6), P274–P283.

Zwahr, M. D., Park, D. C., Eaton, T. A., & Larson, E. J. (1997). Implementation of the patient self-determinatinon act: A comparison of nursing homes to hospitals. *Journal of Applied Gerontology, 16,* 190–207.

Zwahr, M. D., Park, D. C., & Shifren, K. (1998). *Judgments about estrogen replacement therapy: The role of age, cognitive abilities and beliefs.* Manuscript submitted for publication.

2

The Challenge of Communicating Health Information to Elderly Patients: A View From Geriatric Medicine

Jeffrey B. Halter
*The University of Michigan Geriatrics Center
and Ann Arbor Veterans Affairs Medical Center*

Communication between health care providers and patients or their caregivers is an essential component of any medical encounter. Adequacy of communication of medical information is the key first step in any therapeutic intervention, provides the basis for patient adherence to such an intervention, and is critical to the concept of informed consent. Although informed consent is not a universal doctrine for health provider-patient interactions, it has become, through both practice and legislation, a fundamental characteristic of such interactions in the United States. The issue of communication between health care providers and patients is particularly relevant when the patient is elderly. The stakes are likely to be raised with an older patient:

Both the risks and benefits of a given intervention may be higher.
The complexity of the medical situation may be greater (including a high prevalence of a coexisting disorder of cognitive function).

Elderly populations are more heterogeneous.

There are limitations resulting from a rapidly changing health system.

Health care providers may not be well equipped to communicate needed information to an older patient.

RISKS AND BENEFITS

There is a progressive increase in morbidity and mortality rates associated with a given medical condition in older people. For example, the mortality rate during hospitalization for myocardial infarction in patients older than age 80 is ten times higher than the rate for middle-aged people (Maggioni et al., 1993). Such increased risks may be due to the presence of multiple coexisting medical problems as well as a decrease in homeostatic reserve capacity of multiple key regulatory systems. For example, the age-related decline in renal function may not cause any problem for an older adult until the individual becomes acutely ill with a life-threatening illness such as acute myocardial infarction with its associated risk of kidney injury due to impaired blood flow. On the other hand, higher risks associated with illness in an older adult provide an opportunity for effective intervention. Indeed, medical or surgical interventions often show greater benefit in an older, higher risk population. For example, the number of lives saved per 1,000 people treated with thrombolytic therapy for acute myocardial infarction is greater in an older age population (Topol & Califf, 1992), and the number of strokes prevented per given number of people treated for hypertension is greater in older people (Insua et al., 1994). However, such benefits of treatment occur in a setting in which the risks of treatment are also greater, such as bleeding complications from thrombolytic therapy (Gurwitz, Avorn, Rose-Degnan, Choodnovskiy, & Ansell, 1992) or orthostatic hypotension from use of antihypertensive drugs.

One challenge to health care providers of older patients is to provide an adequate, understandable description of risks and benefits from a given intervention. This challenge is frequently further compounded by lack of specific information in an older adult population or in older adults who have the particular constellation of health problems that may be presented by a specific patient. For example, information on risks and benefits of many drugs currently in use is based on studies only in young people. Although new drugs require testing in older people, often people with multiple coexisting medical conditions are excluded from formal studies (Institute of Medicine, 1997). Thus, health care providers frequently must extrapolate from limited information in their communications with older patients.

HETEROGENEITY OF THE ELDERLY POPULATION

As a result of variation in physiologic functions as well as the presence of multiple comorbidities, the population of older adults is much more heterogeneous than a younger population. In addition, there are substantial psychosocial factors influencing people over a long life span. Differences in life experience add further to the heterogeneity of the elderly population and may influence their perception of illness, willingness to adhere to medical regimens, and ability to communicate effectively with health care providers. Substantial differences in the social history and ethnic background of different cohorts of older adults may further distance them from health care providers growing up in a different era and with different perceptions about medical illness. Thus, in dealing with elderly adults, health care providers may have to address a very broad range of physiological, medical, and psychosocial differences among individuals. This heterogeneity presents a challenge for health care providers to extrapolate from prior patient experience to address what may appear to be a similar problem in another older individual.

MEDICAL COMPLEXITY

Decisions about therapeutic interventions and the ability of elderly patients to adhere to medical regimens are also affected by the complexity of the health situation of older adults who have chronic medical conditions (Institute of Medicine, 1997). With advances in medical therapeutics, a growing array of treatment options are now available. Furthermore, the complementary nature of treatments available make multiple drug regimens for a given condition both intellectually appealing and frequently recommended by specialists. Thus, multiple drug regimens commonly are recommended for conditions such as osteoporosis, hypertension, coronary artery disease, congestive heart failure, chronic obstructive lung disease, and diabetes mellitus. Although multiple drug regimens may be attractive, they present a clear challenge to patient adherence even for the patient who has only one of these health problems. But, what about the patient who has many or even all of them? The complexity of the overall treatment program can become overwhelming.

The frequency of adverse drug reactions increases with increasing numbers of medications prescribed (Montamat, Cusak, & Vestal, 1989; Chrischilles, Segar, & Wallace, 1992). Patients with an underlying cognitive disorder appear to be at even greater risk for an adverse drug reaction (Larson, Kukull, Buchner, & Reifler, 1987). The situation may be further complicated when patients are seeing multiple specialists who are each trying to manage their component of the patient's constellation of problems. In such a situation, there are many opportunities for miscommunication, conflicting recommendations, and hopelessly complex treatment programs.

Another challenge in dealing with medically complex elderly adults is the presence of chronic disease. Medical intervention for a chronic disease, such as osteoarthritis, hypertension, or diabetes mellitus, requires different approaches and skills than management of an acute episode of illness, such as a urinary tract infection or a traumatic injury. In chronic illness, medication adherence over an extended period may require lifestyle change to accommodate the needed schedule, and other permanent lifestyle changes may be necessary, such as dietary modification. Such changes require substantial direct involvement by the patient and/or family members and consistent, ongoing effort over a long period by health care providers. Chronic care management is further complicated by social issues such as moving to a new location (either by the patient or health care provider) or a change in insurance coverage requiring the patient to change health care provider. Problems with continuity of care and involvement of multiple different health care providers can make consistent medical follow-up for the chronic illness even more difficult.

Elderly adults often have varying degrees of disability as a result of lifelong accumulation of injuries or illnesses that have resulted in permanent loss of function. Such disabilities can include loss of sensory function such as vision or hearing, loss of motor function of one or more limbs, and loss of mobility due to joint problems or damage to systems controlling balance. Such disabilities can lead to important losses of functional capability affecting communication with health care providers, obtaining medication as prescribed, and taking medication appropriately. Patients with an underlying disability are at substantially greater risk for complications arising from adverse drug effects, which might lead to only minor problems in someone without such disability.

INFLUENCE OF THE HEALTH CARE SYSTEM

The structure of the health care system may contribute to problems with treatment adherence, communication between health care providers and patients, and informed consent. Although elderly people have relatively good access to medical care by virtue of the Medicare system, there are also many limitations to Medicare. As pressure increases to control Medicare expenditures, there is a growing gap between the reimbursement that a health care provider can obtain (through Medicare and associated coinsurance) and the time and effort needed to deliver such care. Thus, health care providers may feel that they do not have the time to communicate fully to an older patient the risks, benefits, and uncertainties about a given intervention or to provide sufficient detail about a complex regimen of drugs, diet, and exercise to ensure full understanding by the patient, let alone adequate adherence to the regimen. Adherence to drug therapy in an elderly population is also limited by the lack of Medicare coverage for prescriptions and variable coverage for services of other health professionals, such as a dietitian or physical therapist, whose guidance may be essential for effective treatment.

Rapid changes in the clinical practice environment also may affect interactions between health care providers and patients. Some aspects of this evolution have a potentially positive impact on clinical care of elderly people. These include a growing emphasis on primary care and preventive health as part of managed care initiatives and a growing appreciation of the importance of a continuum of coordinated care services including provision of services in the home and integration of long-term care services into the mainstream of medicine. New Medicare-sponsored managed care initiatives include variable support for prescription drugs, which is not available in the traditional Medicare program. However, other aspects of this evolution pose threats for elderly patients. Whereas there is decreased emphasis on the hospital as a primary site for patient care services, there is increased emphasis on hospitals as the center of broader, sometimes for-profit, health care systems. Physicians are increasingly functioning as employees of such systems rather than as independent practitioners. Thus, the front line health care services can be influenced, and sometimes even dictated, by business interests. Insurers are also at times taking active roles in defining how clinical services are provided and for whom. The marketing strategies by insurers is primarily focused on groups, such as corporation employees and retirees, rather than on meeting needs of individual patients. The growing dependence on technology offers improved diagnosis and treatment capability, but higher costs associated with such technology may limit its use particularly among those with fewer resources, such as poor, frail, elderly patients.

EFFECTS OF MEDICATION ON COGNITION

All of these factors provide a background for understanding how age-related changes in cognition may affect processing of medical information, adherence to medical regimens, and adequacy of decision making by patients and their families. It is also necessary to take into account direct effects of medications on cognition. For example, minor tranquilizers such as benzodiazepines are frequently prescribed for elderly people. Such drugs cause cognitive impairment, which is greater in older people, even in those who do not have evidence of an underlying cognitive disorder (Greenblatt et al.,1991). Furthermore, the pharmacokinetics of such drugs may be altered in older people so that they remain effective for longer periods of time. The use of long-acting benzodiazipines is strongly associated with risk of hip fracture in elderly people (Ray, Griffin, Schaffner, Baugh, & Melton, 1987). The impact of such drugs on a patient's ability to understand treatment programs and adhere to them has not been adequately studied.

LIMITED MEDICAL EDUCATION IN GERIATRICS

Many health care providers have received little or no formal training to help them address these challenges to providing informed care to elderly adults (Institute of Medicine, 1994). Virtually no health professions' schools had programs or courses in geriatric medicine even in the 1970s. Even in the 1990s, many such programs are small and have limited access to trainees. Routine evaluation and documentation of a patient's cognitive function is a recent phenomenon, which is still not practiced widely. Training experiences in geriatrics are now required by some medical specialties and are being considered by others. However, the gap between the rapidly growing information base in geriatric medicine and the educational material provided to trainees and practicing health care providers remains wide.

REFERENCES

Chrischilles, E. A., Segar, E. T., & Wallace, R. B. (1992). Self-reported adverse drug reactions and related resource use. *Annals of Internal Medicine, 117,* 634–640.

Greenblatt, D. J., Harmatz, J. S., Shapiro, L., Engelhardt, N., Gouthro, T. A., & Shader, R. I. (1991). Sensitivity to triazolam in the elderly. *New England Journal of Medicine, 324,* 1691–1698.

Gurwitz, J. H., Avorn, J., Ross-Degnan, D., Choodnovskiy, I., & Ansell, J. (1992). Aging and the anticoagulant response to warfarin therapy. *Annals of Internal Medicine, 116,* 901–904.

Institute of Medicine, Committee on Strengthening the Geriatric Content of Medical Training. (1994). Strengthening training in geriatrics for physicians. *Journal of the American Geriatrics Society, 42,* 559–565.

Institute of Medicine (1997). *Pharmacokinetics and Drug Interactions in the Elderly and Special Issues in Elderly African-American Populations.* Washington, DC: National Academy Press.

Insua, J. T., Sacks, H. S., Lau, T., Lau, J., Reitman, D., Pagano, D., & Chalmers, T. C. (1994). Drug treatment of hypertension in the elderly: A meta-analysis. *Annals of Internal Medicine, 121,* 355–362.

Larson, E. B., Kukull, W. A., Buchner, D., & Reifler, B. V. (1987). Adverse drug reactions associated with global cognitive impairment in elderly persons. *Annals of Internal Medicine, 107,* 169–173.

Maggioni, A. P., Maseri, A., Fresco, C., Franzosi, M. G., Mauri, F., Santoro, E., & Tognoni, G. (1993). Age-related increase in mortality among patients with first myocardial infarctions treated with thrombolysis. *The New England Journal of Medicine, 329,* 1442–1448.

Montamat, S. C., Cusack, B. J., & Vestal, R. A. (1989). Management of drug therapy in the elderly. *New England Journal of Medicine, 321,* 303–309.

Ray, W. A., Griffin, M. R., Schaffner, W., Baugh, D. K., & Melton, L. J. (1987). Psychotropic drug use and the risk of hip fracture. *New England Journal of Medicine, 316,* 363–369.

Topol, E. J., & Califf, R. M. (1992). Thrombolytic therapy for elderly patients. *The New England Journal of Medicine, 327,* 45–47.

II

Medical Decision Making

3

Decision Making and Aging

J. Frank Yates
Andrea L. Patalano
University of Michigan

Each of us makes decisions continually. In our personal lives, we make both routine, everyday decisions—such as what to wear each day, what to eat for dinner, and what movie to see on a Friday night—as well as more difficult, novel ones—such as whether to go to college, when to have children, and what medical treatments to accept. We also make consequential decisions in our work lives. Indeed, in some of our jobs, decision making is the core of our responsibilities—what tests a patient should have, what candidate should be our company's next vice president, what plan is best for investing our client's money. Typically, our decisions have significance for more than our own well-being; they greatly affect the welfare of those around us, including our families, our employers, and our communities. The specific content of the decision situations we face undoubtedly changes over the life span. But, the need to make decisions—and to make good ones—is always present.

These observations thus motivate the primary focus of the present chapter: How and why does the character of decision making change in the later stages of normal, healthy adulthood? To anticipate, some of the changes can be construed as weaknesses and others as strengths. This therefore raises corresponding management questions as well: How might the weaknesses be offset and the strengths exploited, more than is customary today, particularly in medical contexts?

The plan of the chapter is as follows: First, we discuss the special nature of decision making. Particular attention is directed to characteristics that make it especially difficult to even discuss notions like age-related "declines," a topic of traditional importance in gerontology. We then address a concept that appears to have considerable significance for discussions of age differences in decision making—decision modes. The remaining and most extensive sections of the chapter are identified with elements of what is arguably the most central mode, "analytic" decision making. In each of those sections, we first sketch the basic decision theoretic concepts. We then discuss plausible as well as documented age differences in how and how well people approach the given activities. As space permits, we also consider the practical challenges and opportunities those differences represent.

Before continuing, we should acknowledge a surprising reality. The literature on basic and applied research on decision processes is large and diverse. And the aging literature is sizable and growing rapidly, too. But we have been struck by how remarkably small is the intersection of those literatures. This chapter therefore differs in character from most of those in this volume, attempting to provide more high-level integration than is necessary for other topics. Another consequence is that, in much of what follows, our ability to draw firm conclusions is severely limited by the dearth of hard research, empirical or otherwise. By necessity, we have been more speculative than we would like. Viewed more positively, the circumstances have permitted us to offer what we hope will prove to be a useful theoretical framework for organizing productive research on important but neglected issues.

THE SPECIAL NATURE OF DECISION MAKING

Our working definition is that a *decision* is the selection of an action with the aim of producing satisfying outcomes (cf. Yates, 1990, 1998). Thus, decision making can be seen as a special case of problem solving. The main thing that is special about decision making—its hallmark—is implicit in the expression *satisfying outcomes*: subjective value. What is satisfying to one decision maker (i.e., valued by him or her) easily can be unsatisfying to another, or even to the same decision maker at some later time. The correct solution to an algebra test problem is the correct solution for everybody—forever. But, a perfectly ideal car for one buyer could be completely repugnant to his or her best friend. (Hence, the seemingly endless variety of cars on the market.) And, even if one loves its styling today, one might be indifferent to it tomorrow. Another feature common to many decision problems, although not a defining characteristic, is uncertainty. For instance, many of the events that ultimately determine the extent to which a buyer is indeed satisfied with the car selected are uncertain at the time that choice occurs.

Suppose we wish, as we do, to address questions of decision quality, such as whether it has declined for a given individual. Value and uncertainty complicate that enterprise considerably. If what is satisfying can differ markedly from one person to the next (or from Time 1 to Time 2 for the same person), how can we, as outside observers, say for sure that the consequences of Mr. Smith's decisions are worse than they used to be? And, if the consequences of a given decision are, to some extent, uncertain propositions, how can we attribute even patently adverse outcomes to the decision maker's possibly diminished skills? Why should we not attribute them to, say, chance?

Practical concerns like these are part of the reason decision specialists have been forced to think hard about the very concept of decision quality. Those deliberations have led to implicit consensus about quality notions embodied in Yates's (1998) synthesis. In that view, a good decision is one that exhibits few serious deficiencies. Decision deficiencies, in turn, come in five varieties:

Aim Deficiencies. An aim deficiency occurs when a decision fails to meet the decision maker's explicitly formulated aim(s). Suppose a job seeker chooses a particular job with the goal of making $40,000 within 2 years. If, however, at the end of 2 years he is making only $32,000, then the original decision was deficient in the aim sense.

Need Deficiencies. People do not make decisions for no reason. Rather, decision episodes are instigated when a person senses that some need either is unmet currently or will be unmet in the future unless a decision is made. The decision maker may or may not recognize what the true need actually is, hoping to capture it in broadly conceived aims. Regardless, if the decision fails to quiet that instigating need, then a need deficiency has occurred. If our job seeker had indeed achieved his $40,000 goal, he might still have felt the emptiness he was expecting to escape by attaining that goal. His unsettling ennui made it clear that something was amiss, suggesting the need for a decision. But the decision he actually made was deficient in meeting whatever that need happened to be.

Aggregate Outcomes Deficiencies. It is not at all unusual to have decision makers report that, although a decision meets their aims (and perhaps their original needs as well), that decision is disastrous because other outcomes are negative and outweigh the aim achievement (e.g., a newly chosen job pays extremely well but is numbingly dull). Such a decision exhibits an aggregate outcomes deficiency: collectively, the entire array of outcomes from the decision leaves the decision maker worse off than some reference, for example, the status quo.

Competitor Deficiencies. Suppose that, at the time a decision is made, some other option is available (or could be created), which would leave the decision maker in a better position than the decision actually pursued. Then, even if the selected option is okay with respect to the previous criteria, it is still deficient in the competitor sense. Thus, a job that is identical to a perfectly fine job but pays $1,000 more makes the selection of that "perfectly fine job" deficient in the competitor sense.

Process Cost Deficiencies. Suppose that Decision A is the same as Decision B except that it takes twice as long to arrive at Decision A. Then, Decision A is deficient in terms of its process costs. More generally, a decision exhibits a process cost deficiency to the extent that the decision maker incurs inordinately high costs in making that decision, costs such as time, money, effort, and tolerance for aggravation of various kinds (e.g., the kind of anxiety that indecisive decision makers tend to report; Frost & Shows, 1993).

What do these observations have to do with research on decision making and aging, or actual health care practices involving older persons? Contrast the situation with that for memory and aging research. At the risk of overstatement, the appropriate criterion in the typical memory study is straightforward and uncontroversial. The research participant either does or does not freely recall a given item that was presented during the earlier learning stage of an experiment. And it is "simple" to determine whether the probability of such a recollection is higher or lower for older than for younger participants. Ideally, what would we do in order to make a similar determination about the probability of making a good decision in an ecologically representative situation? We would appraise decisions against each of the yardsticks implicit in the deficiency classes described earlier.

Although there is insufficient space here to describe all the details, it takes little to convince anyone that following the proper script for assessing decision quality is an arduous enterprise indeed. And that is why, in actual practice, decision researchers virtually never do follow it, in the context of aging or more generally. So, what does happen in practice? One strategy is to avoid the complications by ignoring them or by limiting attention to situations in which there is arguably only a single overriding consideration. The best example of this approach is provided by the vast number of studies that examine how much money (or how many reward points) participants accumulate via their decisions. Another tack is to establish by fiat some particular theoretical criterion as the yardstick against which research participants' decisions are measured. Frequently used standards include expected value, expected utility, and multiattribute utility or value (e.g., Bettman, Johnson, Luce, & Payne, 1993).

The most common and perhaps most generally defensible strategy that is used rests on assumptions or expectations about connections between ultimate decision quality (e.g., deficiencies) and specific elementary operations the decision maker might perform. Probably the best illustration of this "process approach" to decision quality assessment is implicit in the enormous literature on so-called judgmental heuristics and biases, most visibly identified with Tversky and Kahneman (e.g., Tversky & Kahneman, 1974). There, the focus has been on, for instance, how people arrive at their judgments of event chances and how good those judgments are. The latter is established by observing whether the focal events actually happen or by comparing the judgments to the prescriptions of probability or statistical theory (cf. Yates, 1982, 1990). The eminently reasonable underlying assumption is that such judgments contribute substantially to people's decisions. For instance, if a car buyer sees cars A and B as equivalent except that A is likely to have better resale value in five years, then the buyer can be expected to purchase A.

It is important to recognize that seemingly innocuous assumptions like these can be wrong. Poses, Cebul, and Wigton (1995) provided a good illustration. These investigators trained physicians to make better probability judgments for strepto-coccal pharyngitis, with the expectation that this would reduce those physicians' overprescription of antibiotics. The training did indeed markedly improve the physicians' judgments, but this had no effect at all on the treatments they selected.

The particular instantiation of the process evaluation approach we advocate (cf. Yates, 1998) differs in subtle but important ways from others that are common in the decision literature (see, for instance, Baron & Brown, 1991; Janis & Mann, 1977). It is interesting that this strategy, which we describe in the section on cardinal decision issues, just happens to be captured partly by some contemporary tech-niques for evaluating the competency of older patients for making their own treatment decisions (cf. Marson, Ingram, Cody, & Harrell, 1995). A topic for consideration by competency specialists is whether and how those techniques might be refined to correspond even more closely to current decision theoretic conceptions of decision quality. It is curious that the legal standards guiding the techniques make no acknowledgment of what we have noted makes decision making unique among cognitive functions—subjective value. Before pursuing the cardinal issues at the core of our recommended evaluation approach, we must bring attention to a class of distinctions that might well have special significance for age variations—dis-tinctions among various decision modes. As will be apparent, the recognition of such modes provides a plausible explanation for puzzles like those posed by the results of Poses et al. (1995).

DECISION MODES

Decision making can be seen as operating in three modes: analytic, rule-based, and automatic (Yates, 1998). These are qualitatively distinct patterns of procedures that people of all ages use in making decisions. A decision situation that arises routinely in driving a car—whether to try to pass a huge trailer truck ambling along in front—illustrates the distinctions:

• To a new driver who was licensed just this morning, a truck-passing decision is a terrifying one that is made by doing things like deliberatively considering and comparing the alternatives (as well as the other activities entailed in addressing the cardinal issues discussed later). New drivers make the decision via the *analytic decision mode,* effortfully reasoning through to what action makes sense given their personal representation of the circumstances.

• A driver who has been taught professionally is likely to have been given a set of rules about when one should and should not attempt a passing maneuver. An experienced untutored driver could have developed similar rules simply through that experience. Either of these drivers, however, employs the *rule-based decision mode.* In such circumstances, decision makers compare their representation of the decision problem to the preconditions, C, of a decision rule of the form C → A. If the representation-precondition correspondence is sufficiently close, the decision maker follows the rule's prescription, selecting action A.

• Drivers who have been on the road many years seem to give no thought at all to the passing decision, perhaps even continuing a normal conversation while making it. The decision appears to simply pop out quickly and effortlessly. Indeed, if asked how they arrived at their decision, they might well not recall having made a decision at all ("What truck?") and thus certainly could not describe how they did so. The decision was made in the *automatic mode,* a behavior displaying all the commonly acknowledged markers of automaticity (see the now-classic papers by Schneider & Shiffrin, 1977, and Shiffrin & Schneider, 1977). Both the rule-based and automatic decision modes rely on C → A sequences and matches between precondition C and the decision maker's representation R of the situation. In rule-based decision making, the match between C and R is a deliberative judgment. In contrast, in automatic decision making, after the representation R is constructed, if there exists a sufficiently close match between R and the precondition for some particular action sequence C → A readily available in long-term memory, then action A is evoked, essentially involuntarily.

As implicit in our illustration, we should expect decision modes to evolve, often according to the following developmental sequence:

Analytic → Rule-Based → Automatic.

That is, when untutored decision makers first encounter a particular kind of decision problem, they must deal with it analytically. After seeing similar situations repeatedly, they develop a rule for handling them, which is then invoked in the rule-based mode as pertinent cases arise. Alternatively, those rules might be provided by others, for example, mentors, as in medical training. Regardless of their original source, after those rules have been applied many times, they become automatized, and the automatic decision making mode takes the stage, that is, a habit develops (cf. Ronis, Yates, & Kirscht, 1989).

We should also anticipate a characteristic episodic sequence:

Automatic → Rule-Based → Analytic.

Thus, in a particular decision episode, given its nature, if the automatic mode can be applied, it will be applied. If it cannot, for reasons of cognitive economy (cf. Payne, 1982), because rule-based decision making is faster and less demanding than analytic, the decision maker will attempt rule-based decision making. Only as a last resort will the analytic mode be invoked.

Does reliance on different decision modes change systematically over the life span? We have seen no evidence that the issue has been addressed directly as such in the literature. This is unsurprising in view of the fact that mainstream decision researchers themselves are only presently coming to appreciate mode distinctions in general (cf. Klein, 1993). So we can only speculate about plausible age differences in mode use and suggest specific issues that future work should pursue.

It seems reasonable to expect that, as people age, they will depend less on the analytic mode and more on the rule-based and automatic modes. This expectation in part derives from the nature of the analytic mode. That mode imposes especially heavy demands on working memory, for example, in making comparisons among the strengths and weaknesses of available alternatives. Numerous studies have demonstrated convincingly the degradation of working memory functioning with advancing age (e.g., Salthouse & Babcock, 1991). Such work has also shown how declines like these interact with the slowing of cognitive operations to attenuate performance on complex tasks not unlike those required in analytic decision making (e.g., Salthouse, 1992, 1996). Now, older adults could simply continue to attempt analytic decision making as their cognitive abilities diminish, blithely accepting the resulting poor decisions. Previous decision work on cognitive economics (cf. Payne, 1982) suggests that this is unlikely, though. Instead, older adults can be expected to respond strategically to their limits, by reducing their dependence on the costly analytic mode. Indeed, some studies revealing older decision makers' abbreviated cognitive analyses have been interpreted in precisely this way, as illustrating deliberate attempts to conserve diminished resources (e.g., Meyer, Russo, & Talbot, 1995).

The anticipated changes in decision mode reliance could be simply the logical consequence of the developmental sequence we described, along with the mere fact that older adults have made more decisions than younger adults. Research on experience effects on decision behavior agrees with this expectation. Consider, for instance, the work of Myles-Worsley, Johnston, and Simons (1988). These investigators examined the abilities of radiologists to detect abnormalities in chest X-rays. They found that, as experience increased, there was a greater tendency for senior radiologists ($M = 22$ years experience) to approach the abnormality recognition task in the same way that we all recognize faces, automatically, and to accomplish it more effectively. It is interesting that greater experience appeared to diminish the radiologists' abilities to remember normal X-rays. This might be an instantiation of a more general principle whereby, with age, we lose our skills at performing unpracticed analytic decision tasks that have minimal significance to us.

Suppose the speculation about how decision mode reliance changes over the life span is true. What are its practical implications? It says that older adults (and those affected by their decisions) will profit from the usual benefits of rule-based, and especially automatic, decision making and will suffer from their drawbacks. The advantages include (ironically?) their speed (as perhaps illustrated by the unusually fast breast cancer treatment choices made by the older respondents of Meyer et al., 1995). The disadvantages include the fact that the decision maker might be more poorly prepared to accommodate novel circumstances. This then places a premium on mode control. Thus, from the perspective of a given older adult, the problem is how to ensure the appropriate application of the decision rules and action sequences acquired over the years. From the point of view of a group to which an older adult belongs (e.g., a medical practice, an executive committee, or a family), the problem is how to make certain that that member's rules and sequences are exploited to their fullest extent when applicable and are not called forth when they are inapplicable. As noted by Salthouse (1982, chapter 5), research on aging and cognitive flexibility suggests that mode control is indeed problematic for older adults when left to their own devices. For instance, at least one well-known study (Heglin, 1956) found that older adults exhibit the Einstellung effect more strongly than younger individuals. This is the phenomenon such that, when a complicated procedure for solving a class of problems has been learned, one persists in attempting that procedure on problems that are superficially similar but are actually solvable by a simpler procedure (Luchins, 1942).

AGENCY: YET ANOTHER MODE?

Curley, Eraker, and Yates (1984) presented hospital outpatients and their spouses with the following scenario:

> Suppose you find it hard to walk after going several blocks. To keep walking leads to stiffness and a dull pain in your legs. So you come to the clinic. A treatment is available, but it is risky. The treatment may work well, or it may make you worse. If the treatment works, you will be able to walk about twice as far before the stiffness begins. And the pain will be less than before the treatment.

> If the treatment does not work, you will always have stiffness in your legs when you walk. And you will begin to feel the dull pain after only a block of walking. If you do not choose to have the treatment, you will stay as you are. (p. 505)

The purpose of the study was to determine whether and to what degree patients' treatment choices in such situations are affected by the nature of the uncertainty, for example, whether the patient is told by a physician that the chances of treatment success are 5 in 10 or could range anywhere between 3 in 10 and 7 in 10 because the procedure is new. The interest here, however, is in how subjects responded to another option presented to them, to indicate: "I would rather not make the choice at all. I would prefer that the doctor decide if I would have the treatment" (p. 506).

About one third of all the subjects in the Curley et al. (1984) study deferred to the physician. But this tendency was much stronger for older than for younger respondents. For instance, whereas fewer than 20% of those in ages ranging from 16 to 39 deferred, more than 45% of those between ages 50 and 86 did so. This result provides a good illustration of a potentially important age variation in decision making—reliance on agents. It suggests that, as people advance in age, they are more likely to "commission" others to make their decisions for them. In a sense, such commissioning constitutes another decision mode beyond the analytic, rule-based, and automatic forms. Note that decision agents are not necessarily real people; they could be any of the computerized decision aids that are becoming increasingly common.

Surprisingly, we have been unable to find systematic research on the decision agency-age connection as such. Nevertheless, several issues that should be pursued by future work on the problem are apparent. First of all, there is the question of whether older adults do indeed tend to assign their decision-making chores to others more often than do younger adults. There are tantalizing suggestions that the Curley et al. (1984) results are not anomalous. For instance, other research also reveals an inclination for older adults to forego risky decision-making opportunities when they can (e.g., Calhoun & Hutchison, 1981). Or consider Deber, Kraetschmer, and Irvine's (1996) finding that older patients tend to ask for less information from their doctors. If the treatment decision is to be turned over to the physician, it makes sense to ask few questions about it. Studies also indicate that older adults tend to have higher "powerful others" scores than younger adults on locus of control scales. This might be especially significant in that other research reveals a negative association between "powerful others" scores and inclinations to request medical information (see Rogers, 1997).

Suppose that older adults are in fact strongly inclined to call upon decision agents. Why is this so? Several possible answers to this question should be pursued:

• One potential explanation is that the age-agency association is a cohort artifact. Participative health care decision making is somewhat popular now. But when today's older adults first came in contact with the health care system, paternalistic health care was the norm. Thus, those individuals' strong inclination to defer to physicians might reflect mere ingrained custom rather than a deliberate metadecision to assign decision-making functions to others.

• A second possibility is that older adults—rightly or wrongly—suspect that their personal decision skills are diminishing. They hence quite sensibly seek to compensate for this loss by deferring to those with better skills.

• A third reason might focus on effort. Even if an older adult believes he or she is fully capable of performing some decision task, he or she might not have or wish to expend the energy required to do so (an implicit recognition of the process cost form decision deficiencies can assume).

• Yet another alternative is also economic in the broad sense. In direct and opportunity costs, it is less expensive to have a mechanic repair one's car than to try to do it oneself. Similarly, especially in terms of opportunity costs, it is far more cost effective to have a clerk who makes $15,000 a year sort $70,000-a-year professors' mail than to have the professors do it for themselves. The typical older adult has had many opportunities to gain an appreciation for such principles. Moreover, many older adults have risen on the economic ladder such that they are quite accustomed to delegating various functions. Therefore, for them, commissioning the services of a decision agent is anything but an admission of diminished abilities, but is instead merely an exercise in intelligent executive action.

• A final possibility is mindful of variations observed in cross-cultural psychology. In the culture of the United States, the ability to decide is regarded as a fundamental right that should be protected at all costs. Witness, for instance, how debates about abortion and managed care are often couched, that is, in terms of a woman's right to choose what happens to her body and a patient's ability to select his or her own doctor, respectively. The preoccupation in the United States with making one's own choices is often interpreted as simply one element of a more general Western value for an independent construal of the self. (Parents exhort their children to be self-reliant, to "stand on your own two feet.") It is significant that this value is not universally shared, with numerous non-Western cultures regarding interdependence with others more positively (cf. Markus & Kitayama, 1991). In the same way, it may be that the significance of personal involvement in making decisions diminishes in later adulthood. Indeed, the sharply reduced vigor with which older adults invest themselves in decision tasks (e.g., Meyer et al., 1995) is consistent with such a value change. Perhaps they reason, "I just no longer think it's all that important."

The practical questions raised by older adults' greater use of decision agents mainly center on the management problems that occupy the attention of agency theory (cf. Eisenhardt, 1989). One of those problems is selection: How do older adults choose their decision agents, and how effectively do they do that? Are they, for instance, so eager to defer that they are insufficiently vigilant in screening the potential agents who just happen to come along? The other big problem is the central concern of formal agency theory: How can older adults assure that an agent, once chosen, attempts to make decisions that are truly in their interests? Put another way, how can such a principal compensate the agent such that it is in the agent's interests to make decisions that are good from the principal's perspective? There are plenty of stories in the news describing how unscrupulous entrepreneurs victimize older adults by exploiting their vulnerabilities. Why should we not expect similar attempts in the arena of decision agency?

CARDINAL DECISION ISSUES

A careful examination of real-life, practical decision episodes reveals a limited set of fundamental issues that tend to recur (cf. Yates, 1998). Careful analysis also suggests that the quality of the eventual decision that is made depends on how well those issues are resolved. Their frequency and significance thus justify calling these issues "cardinal." At minimum, cardinal decision issues provide a framework for examining systematically the potential differences in how two populations, such as older and younger adults, decide. But they also provide a defensible means of getting at quality issues. To the extent that particular issues are handled well, we can be reasonably confident that the resulting decisions will exhibit few serious deficiencies. Here we review several of the cardinal issues distinguished in Yates's (1998) analysis, focusing on those for which age differences in how they are addressed are most plausible.

Options

In the voice of the decision maker, the options issue is this: "What are the actions I could take in this situation?" This issue speaks most directly to the competitors form of decision deficiency. That is, in mishandling the options issue, the decision maker fails to even consider an available alternative whose aggregate outcomes are superior to those of the option ultimately selected. Conversely, decision makers handle the options issue well if they do, in fact, bring to mind (or create) a set of alternatives that includes those that actually are most suitable. Of course, effective handling of the options issue also requires that the collection of options presented for careful deliberation does not also include an overwhelming variety of unsuitable options.

How should we expect older and younger adults to compare in their handling of the options issue? At least superficially, the literature that is most directly relevant to this question is that concerning age differences in divergent thinking, the generation of large numbers of distinct yet acceptable solutions to a given problem. There have been repeated, careful examinations of the inevitable declines in divergent thinking in varied domains. Work by McCrae, Arenberg, and Costa (1987) is illustrative. These authors found sizable differences in the ages at which declines in scores on six different divergent thinking tests began, as well as the rates at which those declines occurred. Nevertheless, the latest point of initial decline was at about age 50.

Taken at face value, results like those of McCrae et al. (1987) suggested that skill at handling the options issue should begin deteriorating rather early in the mature adult portion of the life cycle. This is probably an inappropriate conclusion, however. That is because, as will be recalled, proper handling of the options issue prohibits the generation of large numbers of options that eventually would prove inferior. As those who study decision making in a wide variety of natural settings submit (e.g., Klein, Orasanu, Calderwood, & Zsambok, 1993), one of the last things real-world decision makers, such as fire fighters, want to do is wade through large numbers of alternatives. Instead, they want to zero in immediately on the best option, or at least one that is "good enough." There have been numerous indicators that experience, which obviously increases with age, allows people to do that. Indeed, at least one study has provided fairly direct indications that younger adults might tend to waste their energy generating excessive numbers of options that do not ultimately yield better decisions (Streufert, Pogash, Piasecki, & Post, 1990).

The usual—and quite plausible—account for such effects is "perceptual" in a particular sense. That is, over time, experienced decision makers come to recognize characteristics of problem situations that lead them to call forth solutions that are especially likely to be good ones. (Recall that this is what is expected to happen in the emergence of rule-based decision making in a given context.) Thus, brute-force chess computer programs clearly can generate and evaluate thousands of move sequences far faster than the best master. But even an old master would waste no time on most of those moves, but instead, would immediately narrow his or her attention to ones that are likely to be promising, so that the master can compete quite well against most of the best programs (cf. Charness & Bosman, 1990).

With advancing age, circumstances are likely to favor divergence, the strong suit of the young. Why? At least two reasons. First are the documented difficulties older adults have even with long-term memory retrieval (cf. Hasher & Zacks, 1988). Thus, even if older decision makers have, in fact, successfully solved an earlier decision problem similar to the current one, they might have great difficulty recalling the option pursued on that occasion—if not the decision problem itself. There is also the problem of interference. As decision makers age and accumulate more decision experiences, it becomes progressively easier for them to bring to mind at least one experience that seems somehow related to virtually any decision problem that arises. Unfortunately, the connections might be so tenuous that they mislead the decision makers, effectively leading them down blind alleys. And then, there is the fact that real life has a habit of presenting decision problems that are truly unique, in which case recognition of prior analogs is moot. In those circumstances, younger decision makers should be greatly advantaged by the "fluid intelligence" demands of the requisite analytic decision making (cf. Salthouse, 1992, 1996).

Many practical decisions are made collectively (e.g., in committees) rather than by individuals. The previous considerations suggest that such collectives would do well to seek the diversity of membership commonly recognized by group decision researchers as essential to good option generation (e.g., Valacich, Dennis, & Connolly, 1994). In particular, it is in the interests of those collectives to draw upon the option-generation efforts of both older and younger members because their contributions are likely to be quite different. Further, procedures should be developed whereby those special contributions are exploited to their fullest. For instance, in a policy decision situation, it might make sense to encourage older members to search their experiences for circumstances that are even remotely similar to the current problem. The options employed in those earlier instances might serve as useful starting points for deliberations. Given the difficulties older adults have with long-term memory retrieval, mnemonic devices—including simply the opportunity to take more time—should be provided to older group members to help them mine their experiences.

Possibilities

Again, as the decision maker might put it, the possibilities issue is the following: "What consequences could possibly result from various actions—consequences I care about?" People who make decisions they regard as disasters often report that they were "blind-sided." That is, their decisions brought about bad outcomes that never even crossed their minds when they were contemplating those decisions. In our terms, they mishandled the possibilities question.

Despite its obvious importance, the possibilities issue only rarely has been acknowledged as such in any decision literature. Thus, the best anyone can do is draw tenuous inferences from related research in speculating about age differences in how people address the possibilities problem. There are clear parallels between the options and possibilities issues. So most conclusions about the former should apply to the latter. Nevertheless, there do seem to be differences between the two issues that should imply nonidentical age effects. In particular, in a given situation, the possibilities problem seems more closely circumscribed. After all, in the possibilities stage of a decision episode, the decision maker needs to anticipate the outcomes each given option is capable of yielding, only one option at a time. This seems less daunting than trying to envision the more ill-defined (and probably generally larger) pool of options capable of producing some particular desired outcome.

There are two basic tacks a decision maker can take in addressing the possibilities issue. The first is to rely on memory. The decision maker could attempt to recall what happened in past instances when options similar to the one under consideration were pursued. In principle, older decision makers should have a marked advantage with this approach. They have directly experienced more decisions and their aftermaths. Moreover, they have had more opportunities to hear or read of cases they have not witnessed firsthand. Advantages like these should not be taken lightly. Every organization or enterprise routinely benefits from the informal institutional memory embodied almost exclusively in its older members. The psychological research community itself provides a good example. For well-known reasons, negative results are rarely published. Thus, every year new researchers routinely repeat essentially the same attempts to find plausible but nonexisting effects that earlier investigators tried and failed to find. There would be even more such futile attempts except for the advice passed along informally from older to younger colleagues.

It is unfortunate, as noted previously, that research (e.g., Hasher & Zacks, 1988) has suggested that older adults might have great difficulty exploiting the rich sources of possibilities contained in their long-term memories. Other research suggests that prospects are probably even bleaker for the alternative means of addressing the possibilities issue, that is, deductive inference. By this approach, the decision maker starts with the presumed nature of the decision circumstances and, via chains of arguments, derives the "logically feasible" potential outcomes of the options. As also noted, a variety of studies over a long period of time demonstrate how challenging comparable fluid intellectual tasks are for older adults.

Realization

In posing the realization issue, the decision maker asks: "Would the possibilities I have envisioned be realized? Would they actually occur?" The judgment tasks examined in the well-known heuristics and biases tradition we mentioned before (Tversky & Kahneman, 1974) are perhaps the most easily appreciated exemplars of how people are presumed to address the realization question. A prototypical problem in that tradition would be judging how long it would take to complete a given project. Such an assessment could have particular decision significance because it would dictate whether and when to accept other projects. There have been repeated demonstrations that people routinely underestimate project completion times and that they do so because of their mismanaged reliance on particular heuristics (e.g., Buehler, Griffin, & Ross, 1994).

We have been struck—and puzzled—by the near-total absence of research examining age variations in how people approach the realization issue. This is surprising if for no other reason than the sheer size of the judgment literature and the importance of the issue. As is well recognized, judgment accuracy imposes a strict ceiling on decision quality. Accordingly, no matter how well a contractor handles other aspects of planning decisions, if the time it will take to complete his projects is repeatedly and grossly misjudged, the contractor will go broke. At any rate, Mutter and Pliske (1994) reported the only two recent studies concerning age variations in basic judgment processes of which we are aware. It is hence of some interest to examine them with some care.

In their first study, Mutter and Pliske (1994) considered age differences in covariation judgment, that is, assessments of whether, how, and to what extent two variables are related to each other. Such judgments are clearly fundamental to good decision making. For instance, suppose a loan officer predicts applicants' repayment behavior on the basis of information that in actuality has no reliable connection to such outcomes. Then, these predictions necessarily must be worthless. Research dating from the 1960s (e.g., Chapman & Chapman, 1967) has been interpreted as indicating that people—including professionals—often perceive "illusory correlations." Thus, imagine a subject being shown a collection of cases, each describing a characteristic of a psychiatric patient (e.g., whether or not he is homosexual) and a record of that patient's interpretation of a Rorschach card (e.g., whether or not it has anal connotations, such as "a horse's rear end"). The task of the subject is to judge the (possible) association of the patients' characteristics with their Rorschach interpretations—*for the cases presented to the subject, not patients in general.* In reality, there is no statistical association at all in those cases. Nevertheless, in situations like these, subjects often report seeing associations that are consistent with intuitive associations (e.g., homosexuality and anal interpretations). Mutter and Pliske found that older subjects were even more inclined to exhibit such illusory correlations than younger subjects.

Mutter and Pliske (1994) offered plausible accounts for the observed differences in terms of memory processes, the differential ease with which older and younger adults can retrieve information consistent and inconsistent with preexisting schemas. Future work should evaluate these hypotheses more directly. In addition, however, alternative or complementary hypotheses similar to those that have appeared in other work on contingency judgment should be considered.

One alternative perspective is similar in spirit to a normative Bayesian analysis of such problems (cf. Yates, 1990, p. 182, Problem 6). Suppose that subjects failed to recognize correctly their task as judging the contingency present solely in the data presented in the experiment. Instead, suppose they thought their task was to assess the contingency based on both their prior beliefs as well as the current data. Because the older subjects would have held their prior beliefs longer, they could be expected to hold those beliefs more strongly. A Bayesian analysis would prescribe that the new data should have less impact on their assessments, as was indeed the case. (Incidentally, studies have shown that illusory correlation does in fact diminish upon exposure to large numbers of observations.)

Another alternative take on the illusory correlation-age connection entails an entirely different class of accounts for contingency judgments, one that rests on psychological association strength (cf. Price & Yates, 1995). In this view, people's reports of their judgments about event contingencies are actually translations of how strongly those events are associated psychologically. There is quite good evidence that association models often provide more parsimonious explanations for contingency judgments than the general class of models implicit in Mutter and Pliske's (1994) interpretation of their results. Those models could also comfortably account for the observed connection between age and illusory correlation. These observations further highlight the very real need for studies that examine more directly possible age variations in contingency judgment under broad conditions. Of special interest would be studies that consider contingency judgments in completely novel situations, where subjects have no prior expectations. An initial analysis suggests that the kinds of rule-based models presumed by Mutter and Pliske would predict substantial age differences because of the heavy memory demands those models entail. Association strength models would not.

Overconfidence is a topic that has attracted intense scrutiny in the decision research community. This is the phenomenon whereby people seem to believe that their judgments are more accurate than they actually are. The subject has been considered important, among other reasons, because of its presumed metacognitive implications (cf. Russo & Schoemaker, 1989). After all, if a decision maker believes that the quality of his or her judgment is better than it really is, he or she should be overly content with his or her abilities, foregoing efforts to improve those skills. Pliske and Mutter (1996) pursued the question of whether there are age differences in overconfidence, focusing on general knowledge (e.g., answers to questions of the form, "Which city is farther north: (a) London or (b) New York?"). Contrary to their expectations, Pliske and Mutter found no solid evidence that older adults were less overconfident than younger adults.

What should we make of a negative result like this? This is not entirely clear, on several grounds. Pliske and Mutter found that their older subjects successfully answered more questions than did their younger subjects. It is well known that confidence judgments exhibit a "hard-easy effect," such that people tend to exhibit overconfidence for hard items but underconfidence for easy ones (e.g., Lichtenstein & Fischhoff, 1977). This therefore raises the question of whether Pliske and Mutter would have observed a difference in overconfidence had they been able to control for item difficulty. There is also the question of exactly why such overconfidence differences may or may not occur. Pliske and Mutter anticipated that older adults would be less overconfident than younger ones on the basis of previous "adult wisdom" research suggesting that older adults should have improved recognition of their limitations. The most promising contemporary accounts for the general phenomenon of overconfidence are quite different. Contrary to common lay and scholarly beliefs (cf. Yates, Lee, & Shinotsuka, 1996), there is little evidence that overconfidence rests on people's self-assessments of their abilities. Instead, it appears to result from peculiarities of the purely cognitive mechanisms by which people arrive at their responses to individual questions, for example, their failure to bring to mind arguments contrary to their chosen answers. Only additional research can establish whether those mechanisms differ over the life span.

Value

The value issue presents this question from the decision maker's perspective: "How much would I really care about various decision consequences, were they to actually occur?" As we noted before, the values implicit in this question are at the heart of what makes decision making special. When we inquire about age differences in how the value issue is resolved, we are actually asking about two different things. The first is whether values tend to change systematically as people age. To the best of our knowledge, this question has not been addressed in the scholarly literature. But it has been considered and answered in the affirmative repeatedly in various practical contexts. Thus, marketing demographers have firmly established that age groups differ in their tastes for various goods and services. (Why such variations exist is another story, with changing physical and financial needs as well as simple cohort effects being leading explanatory candidates.)

The more interesting side of the age-value question concerns self-insight, the essence of the value issue as articulated earlier. Decision makers are said to exhibit good *self-insight* into their values to the extent that they know what those values actually are. It stands to reason that when self-insight is weak, poor decisions are inevitable. That such insight can be systematically (and sometimes surprisingly) deficient has been demonstrated in a variety of ways (e.g., Kahneman, Fredrickson, Schreiber, & Redelmeier, 1993; Kahneman & Snell, 1992). Here, we can ask whether, how, and why such self-insight would vary across the life span.

It seems intuitively compelling that people would learn more and more about their values as they grow older. A long life provides ample opportunities for "experimentally testing" one's value system to determine how it is "wired." Thus, even if you are childless, you surely have some notion of how you would respond to the various aspects of what parenthood entails (e.g., total responsibility for another life). But it is only through direct experience with your first child that you can begin to understand how nature really has equipped you to react to those elements of parenthood, to say nothing of learning what those elements actually are (cf. Yates & Stone, 1992a, pp. 63–67). You might discover that you are indifferent to (or even embrace) things you expected to find repugnant, or the other way around.

Is there any evidence that people do indeed exploit the value of learning opportunities that age provides them? As we have been forced to acknowledge so often in this review, there has been virtually no research on the question, only hints from limited related work. In the aging literature per se, studies of wisdom seem most pertinent. There have been suggestions that a significant part of wisdom is *value relativism,* as Baltes and Smith (1990) put it, an appreciation for (among other things) the widely divergent value systems that different people tend to possess. Empirical research (e.g., Baltes, Staudinger, Maercker, & Smith, 1995) shows that wisdom measures, including measures of value relativism, do not exhibit the age declines so common in other contexts. It is perhaps not too much of a stretch to infer from such findings that value self-insight itself might be relatively immune to age declines as well. So, if one recognizes that people's values in general can be surprising, one might suspect that one's own could be surprising as well and therefore scrutinize them more carefully.

Cast against such optimistic, even if tenuous, conclusions, there are pessimistic findings as well. Decision researchers have studied various forms of self-insight since the 1970s (e.g., Reilly & Doherty, 1992; Wilson et al., 1993; Zedeck & Kafry, 1977). One of the most influential self-insight studies was among the first, by Slovic, Fleissner, and Bauman (1972). That study focused on self-insight into judgment policies rather than values per se. Specifically, it examined how respondents made predictions of changes in the prices of financial securities on the basis of various characteristics of the securities, for example, price-to-earnings ratios. Subjects reported how they thought they went about the task, including the emphasis they placed on particular features. The investigators constructed models that described quite well how each respondent did indeed accomplish the task. Self-insight limitations were revealed to the extent that there were discrepancies between a given respondent's model and his or her report of how he or she made his or her judgments. For our purposes, the most significant aspect of the findings was that self-insight was inversely related to experience, with professional brokers exhibiting worse insight than master's of business administration (MBA) students.

How should we interpret findings like these, and what is their significance for the value issue? First of all, note that analogous conclusions are anticipated and found in other domains. Indeed, common conceptions of the development of expertise (e.g., Anderson, 1990) propose that we should routinely expect that, as competence emerges, our procedures for accomplishing a task become automated, and we thus lose our access to those operations. The key question is this, however: When we make repeated decisions in a certain class and then experience the consequences of those decisions, do we lose access to the polarity and intensity of our valuative experiences of those consequences? To the degree that the underlying processes are the same as those supporting more purely cognitive judgment tasks, that is indeed what we should expect. Unfortunately, we do not yet know enough about those processes to tell for sure. Nevertheless, we have seen nothing in the literature to suggest that conclusions about judgment self-insight do not generalize to value self-insight.

Conflict

The final cardinal issue we examine concerns conflict. As before, in the decision maker's voice, that issue is this: "Suppose that some considerations favor one action but others favor a competitor. How should I resolve this conflict?" In most nontrivial decision episodes, the conflict issue inevitably arises in some form or another. Imagine, for instance, a patient pondering whether to accept some new medicine prescribed by a physician. Using a commonly recommended strategy for making good decisions, the patient lists the pros and cons as follows:

Pros	*Cons*
Shorter periods of pain	High cost
Ability to work longer	Loss of appetite
	Occasional drowsiness

The patient feels that the list helps reveal the nature of the problem more clearly. But the patient is still left with the task of concluding whether the pros outweigh the cons, or vice versa. How do people work through conflicts like this, and do their resolution schemes depend on their ages?

There are actually two distinct aspects to the conflict issue, which we might call the *procedure* and *parameter* questions (Yates, 1998). Let us first consider the procedure question, which is the one most often (and most satisfactorily) addressed in the decision literature, even though it is not labeled as such. The most frequently discussed procedure distinction is that between compensatory and noncompensatory schemes. In a *compensatory* procedure, it is possible in principle for any weakness to be offset (i.e., compensated for) by one or more strengths, and vice versa. Thus, suppose our medical patient's mechanism for resolving the conflicts between the pros and cons of a newly prescribed medicine is compensatory. Then, even though the medicine is expensive, this does not rule out the possibility that the benefits of the medicine are so great that it is still acceptable. On the other hand, suppose the patient's scheme entails a budget limit and that the medicine's cost exceeds that limit. Then no matter how good the medicine might be, it cannot be used; nothing can compensate for the excessive price.

Compensatory decision schemes generally require quite thorough processing of all the information available about every option. Hence, in our example, the patient would probably contemplate all five of the pros and cons in the list if the conflict resolution approach were compensatory. In contrast, *noncompensatory* schemes often demand minimal information processing. Continuing the previous illustration, once our budget-limited patient observes that the new medicine exceeds the budget allowance, there is no need to consider anything else; it is eliminated from consideration. Careful analyses (e.g., Payne, Bettman, & Johnson, 1988) have demonstrated that noncompensatory strategies really are generally less demanding than compensatory strategies. Such analyses have also indicated that people tend to shift between the two classes of procedures adaptively in response to the constraints placed upon them, for example, calling on noncompensatory schemes when time is short.

These observations lead quite naturally to the prediction that older adults would rely more heavily on noncompensatory rather than compensatory procedures than would younger adults. This follows from the assumption that older adults are cognizant of the special difficulties they seem to have with operations that make such heavy demands on resources like working memory. And at least one study, that by Johnson (1990), reports the predicted age dependency. Besides the fact that the Johnson study is just that, one study, there are several reasons for caution in immediately accepting the conclusion that older adults' conflict resolution schemes tend toward the noncompensatory and for reasons of cognitive economy.

One especially intriguing alternative potential account for the kinds of data reported by Johnson (1990) involves a radically different perspective on conflict resolution. Pennington and Hastie's (1993) story model of juror decision making illustrated the idea nicely. These authors provide convincing evidence that one way jurors reach their decisions is by trying (typically with prompting from attorneys) to create coherent stories that account for as much of the testimony as possible, elements of which superficially appear to be inconsistent. The verdict is prescribed by whether the story that does the best job of explaining the testimony agrees with the defendant's guilt or innocence. Now, it is plausible that, as a person grows older, he acquires more and more strongly held story schemas, in a wide variety of life circumstances. Thus, we should expect greater reliance with age on story-like means of resolving the conflict issue. Effectively, such schemes will bear closer resemblance to classical noncompensatory rather than compensatory routines. But the details and the motivation are markedly different. It is hoped that research in the near future will determine whether there is anything more than plausibility to this speculation.

The parameter aspect of the conflict issue concerns precisely *how* a particular resolution procedure will be applied in a given decision episode, to dictate whether option A or option B is the one that is actually pursued. Consider yet again the plight of our medical patient. Suppose that, for whatever reason, she settles upon a compensatory conflict resolution scheme. For concreteness, imagine that that scheme can be described by an additive rule as follows. The scheme says that the medicine should be accepted if the score S is greater than 0 and rejected otherwise, and S is given by

$$S = w_R v(R) + w_W v(W) - w_C v(C) - w_A v(A) - w_D v(D) \qquad (1)$$

where R = Relief of Pain and W = Work Allowed are the pros (which contribute positively to S) and C = Cost, A = Appetite Loss, and D = Drowsiness are the cons (which affect S negatively). In Equation 1, we assume that all the considerations have been evaluated on similarly bounded value scales (the v's, ranging, say, between 0 and 100). We also assume that the coefficients applied to those evaluations (the w's) index the relative importance of those considerations (e.g., the w's range from 1 for the least important factor to 10 for the most). In this form, it is clear what remains unsettled: Exactly what are the coefficients, or "importance weights," in the given instance. It is also apparent how intimately wedded are the value and conflict issues. That is, how the conflict will be resolved (whether S is positive) depends directly on how the various factors are valued relative to one another. So, if loss of appetite is highly important (i.e., the w_A parameter is large, say, 7), then rejection of the medicine (S is 0 or smaller) is more likely than if it is less important (e.g., $w_A = 2$). It is a curious and sad fact that decision research has had little to say about how people ought to settle upon the parameters implicit in their conflict resolution schemes (e.g., "How much should I care about loss of appetite?" or, equivalently, "How big should w_A be for me?"). The field has also been silent on how people in fact arrive at their parameter conclusions; it has only considered how to determine what those conclusions are (e.g., how much a patient belives that appetite loss really matters to him or her). A corollary is that the field has had almost nothing principled to say about the basis for possible age differences in such parameters and has offered only occasional suggestions about whether particular differences might actually exist.

No discussion of age and decision making would be complete without considering risk-taking. The topic fits quite naturally into the present perspective on the conflict issue. That is because every risk taking situation can be framed as entailing a conflict between risk, on the one hand, and everything else, on the other. At its most general level, *risk* is "the possibility of loss" (Yates & Stone, 1992b). Loss being unappealing by definition, any seriously considered option that contains risk must also entail positive aspects as well; otherwise, it would be dismissed out of hand. For example, no one would entertain investing in a high-risk junk bond unless it offered an exceptionally high interest rate. Now, a commonly shared intuition is that older adults are more risk averse than younger adults. Is this true, and if so, why is it true?

The literature on the possible connection between age and risk taking is perhaps surprisingly inconsistent. Some studies find the expected increase in risk aversion with age (e.g., Wallach & Kogan, 1961) whereas others do not (e.g., Holliday, 1988), with perhaps the consensus being consistent with the expectation (e.g., MacCrimmon & Wehrung, 1986). Why do the studies accord with one another so poorly? Relatedly, how can the various effects and absences of effects be explained?

In part, the inconsistency is undoubtedly due to the generally established conclusion that risk-taking behavior is highly situation specific (e.g., Bromiley & Curley, 1992). Thus, to the extent that different researchers demand different tasks of their subjects, they have a good chance of reaching different conclusions. Nevertheless, at least a cursory comparison of various studies suggests several hypotheses that should be pursued more carefully in future research. One of the most appealing concerns data sources. It appears that most studies rely on subjects' responses to hypothetical, paper-and-pencil situations, often involving people other than themselves (e.g., the advice they would give to an engineer about whether he should change jobs). On the other hand, some studies (e.g., those of MacCrimmon & Wehrung, 1986) provide direct or indirect reports of respondents' own personal risk-taking behavior. And it is the latter which seem most believable and also indicate greater risk aversion by older adults.

Why would risk taking decrease with age? In discussions of financial risk taking, the general assumption is that the various age groups are responsive to the reality (which is also emphasized by financial planners) that, in the event they suffer major financial setbacks, younger adults have years to recover whereas older adults do not. In effect, the real risk facing young and old adults in superficially identical situations is not really the same; it is higher for older adults. Such a risk-perception basis for age differences in risk taking is also suggested by research on driving. For instance, Sivak, Soler, Trankle, and Spagnhol (1989) found that younger drivers saw significantly less risk in identical slide-projected traffic scenes than did middle-aged and older drivers.

Yet another possible "reality" basis for the age-risk aversion connection might be implicit in research on decision making and stress. There have been numerous demonstrations that time pressure tends to increase risk aversion. Ben Zur and Breznitz (1981) provided evidence about how this effect actually occurs. Specifically, time pressure induces people to pay relatively greater attention to potential losses and less to potential gains. Implicit is perhaps a strategic effect. If decision makers realize that there might be insufficient time to attend to everything, then they should pay attention to the most important things. And a wide variety of studies (e.g., Kahneman & Tversky, 1979) indicate that people are generally more sensitive to losses than to gains. Now, suppose that, in a given risky decision situation, older subjects feel compelled to decide rapidly (e.g., subjects are in a timed session) and recognize that they process information more slowly than they used to. Then, we should expect them to do what people generally do under time-pressured conditions—avoid the risks.

CONCLUDING REMARKS

Changes in basic decision processes over the life span—including declines of various sorts—are inevitable. After all, people rarely just sail along in their lives and then simply and suddenly die. We set out to create a synthesis of what has been established about the specific nature of the changes that tend to occur. As we got deeper into this enterprise, it became obvious how precious few solid facts researchers have actually determined. Thus, one of the few things that are crystal clear is how much work lies ahead. Achieving deep understanding in any given area depends heavily on having well-formed questions and a framework in which to conceptualize and pursue answers to those questions. We hope that the present effort represents at least a start in that direction.

ACKNOWLEDGMENTS

It is our pleasure to acknowledge the excellent comments and suggestions of an anonymous referee, Wendy Rogers, Denise Park, Carla Grayson, and other members of the Michigan Judgment and Decision Laboratory.

REFERENCES

Anderson, J. R. (1990). *Cognitive psychology and its implications* (3rd ed.). New York: Freeman.

Baltes, P. B., & Smith, J. (1990). Toward a psychology of wisdom and its ontogenesis. In R. J. Sternberg (Ed.), *Wisdom: Its nature, origins, and development* (pp. 87–120). New York: Cambridge University Press.

Baltes, P. B., Staudinger, U. M., Maercker, A., & Smith, J. (1995). People nominated as wise: A comparative study of wisdom-related knowledge. *Psychology and Aging, 10,* 155–166.

Baron, J., & Brown, R. V. (Eds.). (1991). *Teaching decision making to adolescents.* Hillsdale, NJ: Lawrence Erlbaum Associates.

Ben Zur, H., & Breznitz, S. J. (1981). The effect of time pressure on risky choice behavior. *Acta Psychologica, 47,* 89–104.

Bettman, J. R., Johnson, E. J., Luce, M. F., & Payne, J. W. (1993). Correlation, conflict, and choice. *Journal of Experimental Psychology: Learning, Memory, and Cognition, 19,* 931–951.

Bromiley, P., & Curley, S. P. (1992). Individual differences in risk taking. In J. F. Yates (Ed.), *Risk-taking behavior* (pp. 87–132.). Chichester, England: Wiley.

Buehler, R., Griffin, D., & Ross, M. (1994). Exploring the "planning fallacy": Why people underestimate their task completion times. *Journal of Personality and Social Psychology, 67,* 366–381.

Calhoun, R. E., & Hutchison, S. L. (1981). Decision-making in old age: Cautiousness and rigidity. *International Journal of Aging and Human Development, 13*(2), 89–98.

Chapman, L. J., & Chapman, J. P. (1967). Genesis of popular but erroneous psychodiagnostic observations. *Journal of Abnormal Psychology, 72,* 193–204.

Charness, N., & Bosman, E. A. (1990). Expertise and aging: Life in the lab. In T. M. Hess (Ed.), *Aging and cognition: Knowledge organization and utilization* (pp. 343–385). Amsterdam: Elsevier.

Curley, S. P., Eraker, S. A., & Yates, J. F. (1984). An investigation of patients' reactions to therapeutic uncertainty. *Medical Decision Making, 4,* 501–511.

Deber, R. B., Kraetschmer, N., & Irvine, J. (1996). What role do patients wish to play in treatment decision making? *Archives of Internal Medicine, 156,* 1414–1420.

Eisenhardt, K. M. (1989). Agency theory: An assessment and review. *Academy of Management Review, 14,* 57–74.

Frost, R. O., & Shows, D. L. (1993). The nature and measurement of compulsive indecisiveness. *Behavioral Research Theory, 31,* 683–692.

Hasher, L., & Zacks, R. T. (1988). Working memory, comprehension, and aging: A review and a new view. *Psychology of Learning and Motivation, 22,* 193–225.

Heglin, H. J. (1956). Problem solving set in different age groups. *Journal of Gerontology, 11,* 310–317.

Holliday, S. G. (1988). Risky-choice behavior: A life-span analysis. *International Journal of Aging and Human Development, 27,* 25–33.

Janis, I. L., & Mann, L. (1977). *Decision making.* New York: Free Press.

Johnson, M. M. S. (1990). Age differences in decision making: A process methodology for examining strategic information processing. *Journal of Gerontology: Psychological Sciences, 45,* P75–P78.

Kahneman, D., Fredrickson, B. L., Schreiber, C. A., & Redelmeier, D. A. (1993). When more pain is preferred to less: Adding a better end. *Psychological Science, 4,* 401–405.

Kahneman, D., & Snell, J. (1992). Predicting a changing taste: Do people know what they will like? *Journal of Behavioral Decision Making, 5,* 187–200.

Kahneman, D., & Tversky, A. (1979). Prospect theory: An analysis of decision under risk. *Econometrica, 47,* 263–291.

Klein, G. A. (1993). A recognition-primed decision (RPD) model of rapid decision making. In G. A. Klein, J. Orasanu, R. Calderwood, & C. E. Zsambok (Eds.), *Decision making in action: Models and methods* (pp. 138–147). Norwood, NJ: Ablex.

Klein, G. A., Orasanu, J., Calderwood, R., & Zsambok, C. E. (Eds.). (1993). *Decision making in action: Models and methods.* Norwood, NJ: Ablex.

Lichtenstein, S., & Fischhoff, B. (1977). Do those who know more also know more about how much they know? The calibration of probability judgments. *Organizational Behavior and Human Performance, 20,* 159–183.

Luchins, A. (1942). Mechanization in problem solving. *Psychological Monographs, 54,* (Whole No. 248).

MacCrimmon, K. R., & Wehrung, D. A. (1986). *Taking risks: The management of uncertainty.* New York: Free Press.

Markus, H. R., & Kitayama, S. (1991). Culture and the self: Implications for cognition, emotion, and motivation. *Psychological Review, 98,* 224–253.

Marson, D. C., Ingram, K. K., Cody, H. A., & Harrell, L. E. (1995). Assessing the competency of patients with Alzheimer's disease under different legal standards. *Archives of Neurology, 52,* 949–954.

McCrae, R. R., Arenberg, D., & Costa, P. T., Jr. (1987). Declines in divergent thinking with age: Cross-sectional, longitudinal, and cross-sequential analyses. *Psychology and Aging, 2,* 130–137.

Meyer, B. J. F., Russo, C., & Talbot, A. (1995). Discourse comprehension and problem solving: Decisions about the treatment of breast cancer by women across the life span. *Psychology and Aging, 10,* 84–103.

Mutter, S. A., & Pliske, R. M. (1994). Aging and illusory correlation in judgments of co-occurrence. *Psychology and Aging, 9,* 53–63.

Myles-Worsley, M., Johnston, W. A., & Simons, M. A. (1988). The influence of expertise on X-ray image processing. *Journal of Experimental Psychology: Learning, Memory, and Cognition, 14,* 553–557.

Payne, J. W. (1982). Contingent decision behavior. *Psychological Bulletin, 92,* 382–402.

Payne, J. W., Bettman, J. R., & Johnson, E. J. (1988). Adaptive strategy selection in decision making. *Journal of Experimental Psychology: Learning, Memory, & Cognition, 14,* 534–552.

Pennington, N., & Hastie, R. (1993). The story model of juror decision making. In R. Hastie (Ed.), *Inside the juror* (pp. 192–221). New York: Cambridge University Press.

Pliske, R. M., & Mutter, S. A. (1996). Age differences in the accuracy of confidence judgments. *Experimental Aging Research, 22,* 199–216.

Poses, R. M., Cebul, R. D., & Wigton, R. S. (1995). You can lead a horse to water—improving physicians' knowledge of probabilities may not affect their decisions. *Medical Decision Making, 15,* 65–75.

Price, P. C., & Yates, J. F. Associative and rule-based accounts of cue interaction in contingency judgment. *Journal of Experimental Psychology: Learning, Memory, and Cognition, 21,* 1639–1655.

Reilly, B. A., & Doherty, M. E. (1992). The assessment of self-insight in judgment policies. *Organizational Behavior and Human Decision Processes, 53,* 285–309.

Rogers, W. A. (1997). Individual differences, aging, and human factors: An overview. In A. D. Fisk & W. A. Rogers (Eds.), *Handbook of human factors and the older adult* (pp. 151–170). San Diego, CA: Academic Press.

Ronis, D. L., Yates, J. F., & Kirscht, J. P. (1989). Attitudes, decisions, and habits as determinants of repeated behavior. In A. R. Pratkanis, S. J., Breckler, & A. G. Greenwald (Eds.), *Attitude structure and function* (pp. 213–239). Hillsdale, NJ: Lawrence Erlbaum Associates.

Russo, J. E., & Schoemaker, P. H. (1989). *Decision traps.* New York: Doubleday.

Salthouse, T. A. (1982). *Adult cognition.* New York: Springer-Verlag.

Salthouse, T. A. (1992). Why do adult age differences increase with task complexity? *Developmental Psychology, 28,* 905–918.

Salthouse, T. A. (1996). The processing-speed theory of adult age differences in cognition. *Psychological Review, 103,* 403–428.

Salthouse, T. A., & Babcock, R. L. (1991). Decomposing adult age differences in working memory. *Developmental Psychology, 27,* 763–776.

Schneider, W., & Shiffrin, R. M. (1977). Controlled and automatic human information processing: I. Detection, search, and attention. *Psychological Review, 84,* 1–66.

Shiffrin, R. M., & Schneider, W. (1977). Controlled and automatic human information processing: II. Perceptual learning, automatic attending, and a general theory. *Psychological Review, 84,* 127–190.

Sivak, M., Soler, J., Trankle, U., & Spagnhol, J. M. (1989). Cross-cultural differences in driver risk-perception. *Accident Analysis & Prevention, 21,* 355–362.

Slovic, P., Fleissner, D., & Bauman, W. S. (1972). Analyzing the use of information in investment decision making: A methodological proposal. *Journal of Business of the University of Chicago, 45,* 283–301.

Streufert, S., Pogash, R., Piasecki, M., & Post, G. M. (1990). Age and management team performance. *Psychology and Aging, 5,* 551–559.

Tversky, A., & Kahneman, D. (1974). Judgment under uncertainty: Heuristics and biases. *Science, 185,* 1124–1131.

Valacich, J. S., Dennis, A. R., & Connolly, T. (1994). Idea generation in computer-based groups: A new ending to an old story. *Organizational Behavior and Human Decision Processing, 57,* 448–467.

Wallach, M. A., & Kogan, N. (1961). Aspects of judgment and decision making: Interrelationships and changes with age. *Behavioral Science, 6,* 23–36.

Wilson, T. D., Lisle, D., Schooler, J., Hodges, S. D., Klaaren, K. J., & LaFleur, S. J. (1993). Introspecting about reasons can reduce post-choice satisfaction. *Personality and Social Psychology Bulletin, 19,* 331–339.

Yates, J. F. (1982). External correspondence: Decompositions of the mean probability score. *Organizational Behavior and Human Performance, 30,* 132–156.

Yates, J. F. (1990). *Judgment and decision making.* Englewood Cliffs, NJ: Prentice Hall.

Yates, J. F. (1998). *Decision tools.* Manuscript submitted for publication.

Yates, J. F., Lee, J.-W., & Shinotsuka, H. (1996). Beliefs about overconfidence, including its cross-national variation. *Organizational Behavior and Human Decision Processes, 65,* 138–147.

Yates, J. F., & Stone, E. R. (1992a). Risk appraisal. In J. F. Yates (Ed.), *Risk-taking behavior* (pp. 49–85). Chichester, England: Wiley.

Yates, J. F., & Stone, E. R. (1992b). The risk construct. In J. F. Yates (Ed.), *Risk-taking behavior* (pp. 1–25). Chichester, England: Wiley.

Zedeck, S., & Kafry, D. (1977). Capturing rater policies for processing evaluation data. *Organizational Behavior and Human Performance, 18,* 269–294.

4

Cognitive Processes and Medical Decisions

Melissa D. Zwahr
Caliber Associates

This chapter highlights a shift in medical treatment selection from a paternalistic approach, in which the physician has primary responsibility for deciding which treatment is most appropriate, to a more patient-directed one, in which the patient is actively involved in the decision process. When patients are confronted with situations in which more than one treatment option is available to treat a particular medical condition, a number of factors may be involved in the evaluative process; this chapter focuses primarily on the cognitive factors involved in these types of decisions. Perception of risk associated with various treatment alternatives, the amount and type of information provided on which to base decisions, cognitive representations of the medical condition and available treatments, and the role of personal experience and/or prior knowledge of the patient in the decision process are evaluated. Additionally, the contribution of specific cognitive abilities (e.g., memory, comprehension, verbal ability, reasoning ability, and perceptual speed) to the decision process is explored. The potential implications that age-related differences in cognitive factors have on medical care decision making are discussed.

PATIENT PARTICIPATION IN MEDICAL DECISIONS

A dramatic change has occurred in the way treatment decisions are made when medically equivalent therapies are available to treat a particular medical condition

(Pierce, 1996). In contrast to traditional paternalistic approaches where the physician was primarily responsible for selecting treatments, the physician and patient now commonly share this responsibility. An individual's right to participate in decisions about proposed medical treatments is protected under the doctrine of *informed consent,* which stipulates that every adult has the right to determine what is done to his or her body, provided they are of sound mind (Altman, Parmelee, & Smyer, 1992). Under the informed consent doctrine, physicians are required by law to present information regarding ". . . the nature of the disorder and of the proposed intervention, the likely benefits, risks, and discomforts, and possible alternatives . . ." (Appelbaum & Grisso, 1988, p. 1637).

Despite the existence of the informed consent doctrine, many people may hesitate to act upon their right to be actively involved in treatment selection. In fact, some studies have shown that the desire for active participation in medical decision making is relatively low across a wide domain of medical situations and conditions. For instance, Ende, Kazis, Ash, and Moskowitz (1989) found that the number of patients making treatment decisions in a general practice setting was very low. Similar results were found in cancer patients (Bilodeau & Degner, 1996; Sutherland, Llewellyn-Thomas, Lockwood, Tritchler, & Till, 1989), in patients from a health maintenance organization, community hospital, and a Veterans administration clinic (Strull, Lo, & Charles, 1984), in college students (Krantz, Baum, & Wideman, 1980), and in low-income patients with diabetes (Pendleton & House, 1984). Other researchers have found, however, a strong desire for active involvement in treatment decisions (e.g., Cassileth, Zupkis, Sutton-Smith, & March, 1980; Haug & Lavin, 1981).

The source of the discrepancies in these studies measuring desire for patient involvement in medical decision making may lie in the fact that some people appear to be more likely to pursue an active role than others. Specifically, younger people (e.g., Beisecker, 1988; Ende et al., 1989), women (Larsson, Svardsudd, Wedel, & Saljo, 1989; Lerman et al., 1990), whites (Cassileth et al., 1980), and the better educated (Cassileth et al., 1980; Strull et al., 1984; Thompson, Pitts, & Schwankovsky, 1993) typically have stronger preferences for active involvement in decisions about treatment alternatives. Additionally, it seems that patients express more desire for involvement in some decision situations than in others. Patients express stronger desire for active participation when medical expertise is not required to evaluate treatment options (Thompson et al., 1993), when the illness was less severe (Ende et al., 1989), and when they have had experience with the effects of the medication (Strull et al., 1984).

Active involvement of the patient in the decision process may, according to some, pose an additional burden on individuals who may already be distressed (Pierce, 1996). However, according to others, active participation in treatment selection has potentially beneficial outcomes. For instance, Wallace (1986) found that active participation in medical decisions was related to faster recovery, and Morris and Royle (1987) found that breast cancer patients who were offered a choice of treatments experienced less postoperative anxiety and depression. Brody,

Miller, Lerman, Smith, and Caputo (1989) determined that active involvement was related to improved treatment effectiveness, as well as reports of greater control of and improvement in health, greater satisfaction with physicians, and less concern with illness. Moreover, Cassileth et al. (1989) reported that cancer patients who were inadequately involved in their treatment decisions become noncompliant or dissatisfied with their physicians and were more likely to reject conventional cancer treatments entirely.

Although research suggests that active participation in medical decisions may have potentially beneficial effects for patients and even identifies those who are more likely to be involved in the decision process, the factors underlying the behavior are less clear. Patients faced with making difficult decisions about medical treatment undoubtedly experience a certain amount of conflict and have difficulty in identifying the best treatment alternative. How do patients resolve decisional conflict and evaluate treatment alternatives posed by their physicians? Some research has identified several strategies that people use in decision-making situations that may aid them in their selection of a particular treatment alternative.

STRATEGIES FOR MAKING MEDICAL DECISIONS

Pierce (1996) identified several ways that people may make decisions about medical treatment. She first described people who make rapid, almost intuitive decisions with little evidence of conflict. Pierce stated that these people may have a partial commitment to a particular alternative and fail to make comparisons of this action with other actions because of this commitment. According to Pierce, this a priori commitment may stem from factors such as what patients perceive as most favored by the physician, how the physician presented the decision problem (i.e., framing effects), personal experiences of the patient, or the alternative may fall close to the patient's point of maximum reference (i.e., the choice is closest to the patient's psychological ideal).

Patients who do not have an a priori commitment to a particular treatment alternative and can not make rapid decisions follow other courses of action to make their decisions (Pierce, 1996). Pierce stated that these patients may decompose the alternatives into smaller units. This decomposition involves breaking down the alternatives into smaller units to make them more meaningful. Individual attributes are assessed and compared to the patient's set of values and goals. In assessing these attributes, patients may apply the first-difference rule (Pierce, 1996). The *first-difference rule* involves assessing attributes of the various alternatives until one feature becomes most salient or relevant. The first difference detected that makes a qualitative difference in their appraisal is what the final decision rests upon (Pierce, 1996). Alternatively, patients may use a *satisficing* strategy to make decisions (Simon, 1956). Patients using this strategy search for a course of action that meets some minimal set of standards and appears to be "good enough" (Pierce, 1996).

Although particular strategies may be used to help aid decision makers in their task of selecting treatment alternatives, the mechanisms underlying the evaluative process of treatment attributes and alternatives are relatively unknown. What factors specifically contribute to this evaluation? Some research implicates the role of cognitive factors in medical information processing and decision making. The potential contributions of various cognitive processes to these tasks are highlighted throughout the remainder of this chapter.

COGNITIVE FACTORS INVOLVED IN MEDICAL INFORMATION PROCESSING AND DECISION MAKING

Prior research underscores the importance of cognitive factors in several medical domains. For instance, cognitive functioning has long been implicated in the determination of competency, which is the capacity to make decisions about consenting to particular medical treatments. According to the President's Commission for the Study of Ethical Problems in Medicine and Biomedical and Behavioral Research (1982), capacity is a function of a patient's values and goals, ability to understand relevant information, and ability to reason about treatment choices. Venesy (1994) pointed out that clinicians often use mental status tests to assess a person's decision-making capacity. Although these tests may be informative about the capacity of the decidedly impaired to make medical decisions, Venesy (1994) cautioned that the crucial issue is whether the patient understands and appreciates the nature of the proposed treatments as well as the risks and benefits and that these issues must be addressed directly. She suggests use of a more specific instrument, such as Annas and Densberger's (1984) "knowledge and understanding" substantive test, which more clearly identifies patient understanding and appreciation of the medical situation. Thus, cognitive functioning, including knowledge, comprehension, and reasoning abilities, is important in determinations of capacity to consent to treatment.

Another medical domain in which cognitive functioning has been found to be important is in medication adherence. For instance, Morrell, Park, and Poon (1989, 1990) found that older adults' failure to comply with appropriate medication instructions was a consequence of inaccurate interpretation of dosage instructions on medicine labels. Additionally, Morrell et al. (1990) found that older adults were particularly disadvantaged when inferences were required to interpret medication instructions—a particularly demanding cognitive task. In subsequent work, Park (1992) outlined a model proposing that successful adherence to a medication regimen involved understanding medication instructions, ability to integrate medication information across a number of prescribed medications, ability to recall medication information, and remembering to take the prescribed medication. Taken together, these findings highlight the importance of cognitive functioning in appropriate medication compliance.

Various cognitive processes have been implicated in making decisions about medical treatment as well. Prior research shows that perceptions of risk associated with treatment alternatives, the amount and type of information provided about various treatment options, cognitive representations people have about their conditions and available medical therapies, and personal experiences people have with the medical conditions and treatments in question influences the medical decision-making process. Additionally, specific cognitive abilities may be important in evaluating treatment options. The contribution of specific cognitive factors to medical decision making will be discussed in the following sections of the chapter.

Perception of Risk

Patients' perceptions of the risks involved with various treatment alternatives may influence the decisions they make. Patients' perceptions of how risky treatments are have been shown to be related to treatment decisions in a number of medical situations, including whether to take estrogen replacement therapy (e.g., Hunskaar & Backe, 1992; Schmitt et al., 1991; Zwahr, 1994), treatment of breast cancer (e.g., Pierce, 1993), whether to accept a vaccine (Kaplan, Hammel, & Schimmel, 1985), decisions about elective hysterectomies (Travis, 1985), and choice of childbirth settings (McClain, 1983). In some cases, a treatment option is selected because it is perceived to be safer than rejected alternatives. For example, Pierce (1993) found that the majority of women seeking breast cancer treatments were risk-averse and preferred therapies that they perceived as safe. Similar findings were described by McClain (1983); she also found, however, that once a childbirth setting had been decided upon, women engaged in bolstering activities in which the benefits of the selected option were magnified while the risks of the rejected alternatives were exaggerated. In other cases, patients' decisions may be influenced by perceptions that certain treatments may prevent risky or undesirable outcomes. For instance, Schmitt et al., (1991) found that, when making decisions about estrogen replacement therapy (ERT), the largest group of women in their study tended to discount the risks associated with ERT (i.e., increased risk of endometrial cancer) in the presence of severe hot flashes; the here-and-now dilemma of discomforts associated with the presence of hot flashes took precedence over the long-term risk of endometrial cancer. Taken together, these findings highlight the importance of the perception of risk in the selection of treatment alternatives, regardless of whether the perception involves perceiving one treatment to be safer or less risky than others or perceiving the treatment as a way of avoiding undesirable outcomes.

Amount and Type of Medical Information Provided

The amount and type of information provided on which to base treatment decisions may influence the evaluative process of patients. Pierce (1996) reported that health care practitioners may try to minimize the amount of information they provide to patients in order to reduce cognitive overload. On the other hand, Hack, Degner,

Farber, and McWilliams (1992) and others suggested that patients are not receiving the amount or type of information they need—patients typically desire more information than they receive from their doctors (e.g., Beisecker & Beisecker, 1990; Matthews, 1983; Strull et al., 1984). Increasing the amount of information provided to patients is not without risk, however. Slovic, Fischoff, and Lichtenstein (1977) cautioned that increasing the amount of information given to people in situations in which a decision must be made may increase the variability of responses, decrease the quality of the choices, and artificially increase the confidence the decision maker has in the option selected. These cautions may be of differential importance to people of different ages; there are conflicting findings with regard to how much information younger and older people desire when making medical decisions. For instance, Beisecker and Beisecker (1990) found that older adults engaged in more information-seeking behaviors than did younger adults; Meyer, Russo, and Talbot (1995), on the other hand, found that older adults seek less information when making a treatment decision.

Although the information needs of younger and older decision makers may differ, Pierce (1996) postulated that the amount of information provided may be of less importance than its emotional impact. For example, information perceived as negative or undesirable may be especially influential in a medical decision task (Pierce, 1996). Specifically, Pierce elaborated upon findings obtained by Bocken-holt, Albert, and Aschenbrenner (1991) indicating that, in a decision context, negative information tends to be weighed more heavily than positive information. She applies this to a clinical context by stating that ". . . patients may discount one option inappropriately and begin to seek another with more attractive charac-teristics. Some individuals cannot bear to think that bad things may happen to them and, having a natural desire to escape any further unpleasantness, may avoid information" (Pierce, 1996, p. 284).

Additionally, a number of studies identify a range of types of information that are particularly important for patients to receive, including information about treatment options (Bilodeau & Degner, 1996; Hailey, Lavine, & Hogan, 1988), treatment side effects (Reynolds, Sanson-Fisher, Poole, Harker, & Byrne, 1981), likelihood of cure (Bilodeau & Degner, 1996), and stage or extent of disease (Bilodeau & Degner, 1996; Cassileth et al., 1980). In sum, these results indicate that both the amount and type of information provided may influence a patient's decision-making performance.

Cognitive Representation of Illness

Leventhal, Leventhal, and Schaefer (1992) proposed that individuals use stored knowledge about a particular illness or disease as well as information obtained from other sources (such as doctors, family, and friends) to form an internal cognitive representation, which may in turn influence decisions made about medical treat-ment. Items contained in this representation include information pertaining to a name for the disorder, beliefs about the duration of the illness, consequences of the disorder, beliefs and knowledge about controllability, and causes of the disorder. These representations are not always accurate; they are frequently flawed and based on misinformation. Regardless of potential inaccuracy, cognitive representations of illness serve as a basis for attempts people make to cope with or regulate the disease, such as by seeking treatment or more information. After a coping strategy has been adopted, individuals are involved in a continuous learning process that results in updating the representation. This modified representation drives future coping or regulatory strategies in a continuously dynamic process.

Park (1994) described how the cognitive representation of illness theory works in a person recently diagnosed with a rheumatic disease such as rheumatoid arthritis. She explained that the patient may experience considerable distress over the diagnosis as well as from the pain and symptoms of the disease, beliefs about the severity and controllability of the disease, and the information relayed from the diagnosing physician. Initial attempts at coping and regulation (e.g., through learning more about the disease, the impact of medication, etc.) will cause a change in the illness representation; this new representation will, in turn, influence future attempts at regulation and coping. Thus, it is clear that the cognitive representation held about a particular medical condition may influence initial decisions made about regulation, coping, and treatment.

Personal Experience and/or Prior Knowledge About Medical Conditions

An integral component of Leventhal et al.'s (1992) cognitive representation of illness is conceptual knowledge about the illness and potential treatments. This stored knowledge, in addition to personal experiences that people may have with regard to particular medical conditions and treatments, seems to have influenced the medical decision-making process in a number of studies. For instance, Pierce (1996) suggested that patients remember family members' or friends' experiences with particular medical situations and treatment options selected. Patients then use these memories and knowledge gleaned from these experiences as the basis for making decisions about their own treatments in similar situations. In fact, Pierce (1996) explained that patients with such personal experiences frequently make treatment decisions very rapidly; they utilize their experiences to immediately eliminate certain treatment choices and essentially make a decision before hearing about all possible alternatives.

Some researchers have examined the role of prior knowledge in medical decision making. Meyer et al. (1995) examined womens' treatment choices regarding breast cancer. Participants were given a pretest assessment of knowledge about breast cancer and its treatment prior to being given experimental materials to read. Results indicate that prior knowledge, or what women know about breast cancer and its treatment prior to reading experimental materials, is important in determining what treatment option (e.g., lumpectomy, mastectomy, radiation therapy) is selected. These authors stated that "... to some extent, beliefs a reader brings into the learning situation influence the treatment option selected, regardless of the medical information presented . . ." (Meyer et al., 1995, p. 91). In another study, Zwahr (1994) investigated the contribution of prior knowledge and other factors to decisions made about estrogen replacement therapy (ERT) to alleviate problematic postmenopausal symptoms. Using methodology similar to that of Meyer et al. (1995), Zwahr (1994) found that prior knowledge of menopause and ERT directly influenced the process of selecting a treatment alternative to alleviate postmenopausal distress. Specifically, what women knew about menopause and ERT, prior to being given information, was related to how many treatment options women perceived as available to alleviate symptoms, how frequently women made comparisons among available treatment alternatives (e.g., ERT, vitamin/herbal remedies, waiting for symptoms to pass naturally), and how well women substantiated or supported their chosen alternative. Taken together, the results of the Meyer et al. (1995) and Zwahr (1994) studies highlight the importance of prior knowledge in making medical decisions.

Cognitive Abilities

The role of specific cognitive abilities in medical decision making has not been studied as extensively as the other cognitive processes discussed thus far in the chapter. Some research does suggest, however, that certain cognitive abilities are utilized when making decisions about medical treatment. Appelbaum and Grisso (1988) postulated that, in order to make a decision about proposed medical therapies, one must (a) maintain information in memory long enough to make and communicate a choice, (b) understand and comprehend the information provided, (c) reason through the potential risks and benefits associated with the various treatment alternatives, and (d) rationally manipulate the information in order to form conclusions consistent with the information provided.

Using lines of reasoning similar to those of Appelbaum and Grisso (1988), Fitten, Lusky, and Hamann (1990) assessed decision-making ability using a series of three hypothetical clinical vignettes portraying increasingly complex treatment situations. In each vignette, information was provided about the medical condition, available treatments, potential benefits, and possible risks associated with proposed interventions as well as potential consequences of inaction. Decision-making abilities were assessed objectively (e.g., correct or incorrect responses to questions about the materials) as well as subjectively (e.g., decisions reasoned or not reasoned from the information provided). Decision-making abilities were evaluated based on subjects' ability to understand the basic facts presented in the vignettes, to understand the risks and benefits outlined, to come to a reasonable decision, and on whether the decision reached was based on the information contained in the vignettes (Fitten et al., 1990). Fitten et al, (1990) found that assessment of these factors provided a sensitive measure of decision-making ability; this method reliably discriminated among people with low, intermediate, and high decision-making ability.

The standards used by Fitten et al. (1990) to evaluate decision making are consistent with the abilities outlined by Appelbaum and Grisso (1988). Patients must first be able to remember and understand information provided. Second, patients must be able to reason through the risks and benefits associated with various treatment alternatives. Salthouse (1992) postulated that reasoning abilities are intermediate cognitive processes between simpler memory measures and more complex behaviors such as decision making and that measures of reasoning ability provide ". . . an important linkage between the level of elementary cognitive processes and real-world functioning . . ." (Salthouse, 1992, p. 167). Third, patients must logically manipulate the medical information provided and reach conclusions that are consistent with presented information in order to make medical decisions. To do this, one must utilize both memory abilities (to recall information as it was presented) and processing abilities (to manipulate information in an orderly fashion to form conclusions). This simultaneous use of memory and processing resources maps to Baddeley's (1986) conceptualization of working memory.

Thus, it seems that at least four cognitive abilities are important in the medical decision-making process: memory, comprehension, reasoning ability, and working memory. Two other cognitive abilities, verbal ability and perceptual speed, may also be important in medical decision tasks. According to Meyer et al. (1995), verbal ability, as measured by vocabulary scores, may be related to time spent reading and information gathering on various topics, including health care. Thus, women with higher verbal abilities may be better informed about health-related issues, which could impact their decision-making performance. Perceptual speed may also be important in medical decision making. Specifically, Salthouse (1993) found that measures of perceptual speed accounted for a large percentage of variance in measures of memory, working memory, and reasoning ability. Because perceptual speed has been shown to be related to cognitive abilities potentially utilized in making medical decisions, it too may be an important factor in these types of tasks. Unfortunately, very few studies have evaluated the role of specific cognitive abilities, with the possible exception of comprehension, in medical decision tasks. Some of the research that has examined these factors is summarized next.

With regard to memory and comprehension, it is generally accepted that patients need to comprehend and remember as much medical information as possible in order to make informed treatment decisions (e.g., Appelbaum & Grisso, 1988; Hodne, 1995; Venesy, 1994). A number of studies have demonstrated that these abilities are important in the decision process (e.g., Cassileth et al., 1989; Fitten et al., 1990; Meyer et al., 1995; Zwahr, 1994). As a specific example, consider work by Meyer et al. (1995) that investigated decisions made by women regarding the treatment of breast cancer. Using a free recall paradigm, Meyer and her colleagues found that substantiation of treatment decisions was related to the type of information remembered from presented experimental materials. They found large age-related deficits for prose recall, with older adults showing poorer recall of presented information that younger adults, and that the use of remembered information in supporting decisions varied accordingly as a function of age. Similar results were obtained by Zwahr (1994). Zwahr (1994) used two measures of comprehension in the examination of the decision process with regard to estrogen replacement therapy; she used an intratask measure of comprehension in which women's understanding and recall of experimental materials was assessed as well as an extratask measure of comprehension in which women read three unrelated text passages and then answered a series of questions about the readings. Both measures of memory and comprehension were important predictors of performance on the decision task.

Although there is some understanding of the importance of comprehension abilities in medical decision-making tasks, the role of other cognitive abilities has not been extensively studied, despite preliminary evidence suggesting their importance in medical decision making. Meyer et al. (1995) and Zwahr (1994) did examine the contribution of verbal ability in decision-making tasks. Both of these studies found that women with higher verbal abilities had better performance on the indices measuring the decision process. Additionally, Zwahr (1994) examined the contribution of working memory, reasoning ability, and perceptual speed in decision performance. She found that better reasoning ability and better performance on perceptual speed measures were related to better decision-making ability.

Based on the information presented here from studies conducted by Meyer et al. (1995) and Zwahr (1994), it seems that a number of cognitive abilities play an integral part in making medical decisions. Better comprehension and recall of medical information, higher verbal ability, better reasoning ability, and better performance on measures of perceptual speed are related to better performance on decision-making tasks. These findings have important implications for older adult decision makers. Specifically, it is commonly accepted that certain cognitive abilities show age-related declines—including some of those hypothesized to be involved in making decisions about medical treatment. Prior research has shown that older adults show poorer performance relative to younger adults on measures of comprehension (e.g., Cohen, 1979; Dixon, Hultsch, Simon, & von Eye, 1984), reasoning ability (e.g., Salthouse, 1993), and perceptual speed (Salthouse, 1993). Verbal ability, however, does not typically decline with age and may in fact increase (e.g., Meyer & Rice, 1989; Park et al., 1996).

IMPLICATIONS AND CONCLUSIONS

This chapter has identified a number of potential cognitive factors that may influence patients' medical decision-making processes; these factors may be particularly salient for older adult medical decision makers, given that they may more frequently face medical crisis and may be called upon more often than younger adults to make important medical decisions. The probability of suffering from disease increases markedly after age 65 (Schaie & Willis, 1996). According to Schaie and Willis (1996), people over age 65 are avid medical consumers; they account for 30% of all health care expenditures, use 25% of all drugs, fill one third of hospital beds, and account for 40% of visits to physicians' offices. Moreover, 86% of older adults have some sort of chronic condition (National Center for Health Statistics, 1994). Given certain age-related changes and differential needs of older adults, the cognitive factors involved in the medical decision-making process may be of critical importance.

For instance, cognitive factors could explain older adults' low desire for participation in medical decisions relative to younger adults. First, older adults' informational needs may not have been met. Although research findings are contradictory with regard to how much information older adults need relative to younger adults, it is clear that the two groups may require different amounts. More research needs to be conducted to clarify this issue. Second, the types of information that older and younger adult decision makers may need in order to feel comfortable participating in medical decisions may differ. Given that older adults may have experienced deficits in cognitive abilities involved in making medical decisions—comprehension abilities, for example—extra care may need to be taken to ensure that information provided is easily understood, particularly if the information is extremely complex. Using appropriate types and amounts of information as well as making allowances for declining cognitive abilities may encourage more older adults to become involved in treatment decisions.

Physicians and other health care practitioners need to recognize that older adults may have experienced age-related declines in cognitive abilities that may impact their aptitude for making informed treatment decisions. Additionally, they need to take steps to help remediate these declines. For instance, it is a well-known fact that primacy and recency effects exist for recall of presented information, including medical information. Prior research shows that medical information presented first and last is typically recalled better (Ley, 1982, 1989; Tymchuk & Ouslander, 1991). Thus, the most important or critical information on which to base treatment decisions should be presented to older adults early or later in physician/patient discussions. Additionally, comprehension and recall of medical information may be enhanced by using easier words and shorter sentences (Folstein, Folstein, & McHugh, 1975) or by using storybook formats (Tymchuk, Ouslander, & Rader, 1986). Implementing strategies such as these may make decision-making responsibilities easier for older adults and may make them more comfortable with participating in their treatment decisions.

It is important to note that, although there are strong indications that the process of making decisions about medical treatments may differ in some respects for younger and older adults (e.g., the amount and type of information needed, the differential contribution of cognitive abilities), there are some facets that are very similar. For example, younger and older adults appear to perceive risks associated with medical treatments in a similar manner and appear to use prior knowledge and/or personal experiences similarly as well (Zwahr, 1994). Moreover, there is preliminary evidence that there are no differences in the final treatment option selected by younger and older adults (Meyer et al., 1995; Zwahr, 1994). That is, Meyer et al. (1995) and Zwahr (1994) both found that, despite differences in the decision process (i.e., the extent to which treatment options were compared or how well decisions were rationalized), younger and older women made similar decisions in the end. Perhaps, then, future attention should be devoted to developing understanding of the differences in the mechanisms used by young and old decision makers in order to identify factors that may encourage older adults to take a more active role in their health care decisions.

REFERENCES

Altman, W. M., Parmelee, P. A., & Smyer, M. A. (1992). Autonomy, competence, and informed consent in long term care: Legal and psychological perspectives. *Villanova Law Review, 37,* 1671–1704.

Annas, G. J., & Densberger, J. E. (1984). Competence to refuse medical treatment: Autonomy vs. paternalism. *Toledo Law Review, 15,* 561–592.

Appelbaum, P. S. & Grisso, T. (1988). Assessing patients' capacities to consent to treatment. *The New England Journal of Medicine, 319,* 1635–1638.

Baddeley, A. D. (1986). *Working memory.* Oxford, England: Oxford University Press.

Beisecker, A. E. (1988). Aging and the desire for information and input in medical decisions: Patient consumerism in medical encounters. *Gerontologist, 28,* 330–335.

Beisecker, A. E., & Beisecker, T. D. (1990). Patient information-seeking behaviors when communicating with doctors. *Medical Care, 28,* 19–28.

Bilodeau, B. A., & Degner, L. F. (1996). Information needs, sources of information, and decisional roles in women with breast cancer. *Oncology Nursing Forum, 23,* 691–696.

Bockenholt, U., Albert, D., & Aschenbrenner, M. (1991). The effects of attractiveness, dominance, and attribute differences on information acquisition in multiattribute binary choice. *Organizational Behavior and Human Decision Processes, 49,* 258–281.

Brody, D. S., Miller, S. M., Lerman, C. E., Smith, D. G., & Caputo, G. C. (1989). Patient perception of involvement in medical care: Relationship to illness attitudes and outcomes. *Journal of General Internal Medicine, 4,* 506–511.

Cassileth, B. R., Seidmon, E. J., Soloway, M. S., Hait, H. I., Vogelzang, N. J., Kennealey, G. T., & Schellhammer, P. S. (1989). Patients' choice of treatment in Stage D prostate cancer. *Urology (Supplement), 33,* 57–62.

Cassileth, B. R., Zupkis, R. V., Sutton-Smith, K., & March, V. (1980). Information and participation preferences among cancer patients. *Annals of Internal Medicine, 92,* 832–836.

Cohen, G. (1979). Language comprehension in old age. *Cognitive Psychology, 11,* 412–429.

Dixon, R. A., Hultsch, D. F., Simon, E. W., & von Eye, A. (1984). Verbal ability and text structure effects on adult age differences in text recall. *Journal of Verbal Learning and Verbal Behavior, 23,* 569–578.

Ende, J., Kazis, L., Ash, A., & Moskowitz, M. A. (1989). Measuring patients' desire for autonomy: Decision making and information-seeking preferences among medical patients. *Journal of General Internal Medicine, 4,* 23–30.

Fitten, L. J., Lusky, R., & Hamann, C. (1990). Assessing treatment decision-making capacity in elderly nursing home residents. *Journal of the American Geriatric Society, 38,* 1097–1104.

Folstein, J., Folstein, S., & McHugh, P. (1975). Mini-mental state. *Journal of Psychiatric Research, 12,* 189–198.

Hack, T. F., Degner, L. F., Farber, J. M., & McWilliams, M. E. (1992). *Communication between cancer patients and healthcare professionals: An annotated bibliography.* Winnipeg, Canada: National Cancer Institute of Canada.

Hailey, B. J., Lavine, B., & Hogan, B. (1988). The mastectomy experience: Patients' perspectives. *Women and Health, 14,* 75–88.

Haug, M. R., & Lavin, B. (1981). Practitioner or patient—who's in charge? *Journal of Health and Social Behavior, 22,* 212–219.

Hodne, C. J. (1995). Medical decision making. In M. W. O'Hara, R. C. Reiter, S. R. Johnson, A. Milburn, & J. Engeldinger (Eds.), *Psychological aspects of women's reproductive health* (pp. 267–291). New York: Springer.

Hunskaar, S., & Backe, B. (1992). Attitudes towards and level of information on perimenopausal and postmenopausal hormone replacement therapy among Norwegian women. *Maturitas, 15,* 183–194.

Kaplan, R. M., Hammel, B., & Schimmel, L. E. (1985). Patient information processing and the decision to accept treatment. *Journal of Social Behavior and Personality, 1,* 113–120.

Krantz, D. S., Baum, A., & Wideman, M. V. (1980). Assessment of preferences for self-treatment and information in health care. *Journal of Personality and Social Psychology, 39,* 977–990.

Larsson, U. S., Svardsudd, K., Wedel, H., & Saljo, R. (1989). Patient involvement in decision-making in surgical and orthopaedic practice: The project perioperative risk. *Social Science and Medicine, 28,* 829–835.

Lerman, C. E., Brody, D. S., Caputo, G. C., Smith, D. G., Lazaro, C. G., & Wolfson, H. G. (1990). Patients' perceived involvement in care scale: Relationship to attitudes about illness and medical care. *Journal of General Internal Medicine, 5,* 29–33.

Leventhal, H., Leventhal, E., & Schaefer, P. M. (1992). Vigilant coping and health behavior. In M. G. Ory, R. P. Abeles, & P. D. Lipman (Eds.), *Aging, health, and behavior* (pp. 109–140). Newbury Park, CA: Sage.

Ley, P. (1982). Giving information to patients. In J. R. Eiser (Ed.), *Social psychology and behavioral science* (pp. 339–373). London: Wiley.

Ley, P. (1989). Improving patients' understanding, recall, satisfaction and compliance. In A. K. Broome (Ed.), *Health psychology: Processes and applications* (pp. 74–102). London: Chapman and Hall.

Matthews, J. (1983). The communication process in clinical settings. *Social Science and Medicine, 17,* 1371–1378.

McClain, C. S. (1983). Perceived risk and choice of childbirth service. *Social Science and Medicine, 17,* 1857–1665.

Meyer, B. J. F., & Rice, G. E. (1989). Prose processing in adulthood: The text, the learn, and the task. In L. W. Poon, D. C. Rubin, & B. A. Wilson (Eds.), *Everday cognition in adulthood and late life* (pp. 157–195). Cambridge, England: Cambridge University Press.

Meyer, B. J. F., Russo, C., & Talbot, A. (1995). Discourse comprehension and problem solving: Decisions about the treatment of breast cancer by women across the life span. *Psychology and Aging, 10,* 84–103.

Morrell, R. W., Park, D. C., & Poon, L. W. (1989). Quality of instructions on prescription drug labels: Effects on memory and comprehension in young and old adults. *Gerontologist, 29,* 345–354.

Morrell, R. W., Park, D. C., & Poon, L. W. (1990). Effects of labeling techniques on memory and comprehension of prescription information on young and older adults. *Journal of Gerontology, 45,* 166–172.

Morris, J., & Royle, G. T. (1987). Cancer: Pre- and postoperative levels of clinical anxiety and depression in patients and their husbands. *British Journal of Surgery, 74,* 1017–1019.

National Center for Health Statistics. (1994). Prevalence of selected chronic diseases, United States, 1990–1991. *Vital and Health Statistics, Series 2,* No. 120.

Park, D. C. (1992). Applied cognitive aging research. In F. I. M. Craik & T. A. Salthouse (Eds.), *The handbook of aging and cognition* (pp. 449–493). Hillsdale, NJ: Lawrence Erlbaum Associates.

Park, D. C. (1994). Self-regulation and control of rheumatic disorders. In S. Maes, H. Leventhal, & M. Johnson (Eds.), *International Review of Health Psychology* (Vol. 3, pp. 189–217). New York: Wiley.

Park, D. C., Smith, A. D., Lautenschlager, G., Earles, J. L., Frieske, D., Zwahr, M., & Gaines, C. L. (1996). Mediators of long-term memory performance across the life span. *Psychology and Aging, 11,* 621–637.

Pendleton, L., & House, W. C. (1984). Preferences for treatment approaches in medical care: College students versus diabetic outpatients. *Medical Care, 22,* 644–646.

Pierce, P. F. (1993). Deciding on breast cancer treatment: A description of decision behavior. *Nursing Research, 42,* 22–28.

Pierce, P. F. (1996). When the patient chooses: Describing unaided decisions in health care. *Human Factors, 38,* 278–287.

President's Commission for the Study of Ethical Problems in Medicine and Biomedical and Behavioral Research: Making Health Care Decisions. (1982). Washington, DC: U.S. Government Printing Office.

Reynolds, P. M., Sanson-Fisher, R. W., Poole, A. D., Harker, J., & Byrne, M. J. (1981). Cancer and communication: Information-giving in an oncology clinic. *British Medical Journal, 282,* 1449–1551.

Salthouse, T. A. (1992). Reasoning and spatial abilities. In F. I. M. Craik & T. A. Salthouse (Eds.), *The handbook of aging and cognition* (pp. 167–211). Hillsdale, NJ: Lawrence Erlbaum Associates.

Salthouse, T. A. (1993). Speed mediation of adult age differences in cognition. *Developmental Psychology, 27,* 763–776.

Schaie, K. W. S., & Willis, S. L. (1996). *Adult development and aging* (4th ed.). New York: HarperCollins.

Schmitt, N., Gogate, J., Rothert, M., Rovner, D., Holmes, M., Talarcyzk, G., Given, B., & Kroll, J. (1991). Capturing and clustering women's judgment policies: The case of hormonal replacement therapy for menopause. *Journal of Gerontology: Psychological Sciences, 46,* 92–101.

Simon, H. A. (1956). Rational choice and the structure of the environment. *Psychological Review, 63,* 129–138.

Slovic, P., Fischoff, B., & Lichtenstein, S. (1977). Behavioral decision theory. *Annual Review of Psychology, 28,* 1–39.

Strull, W. M., Lo, B., & Charles, G. (1984). Do patients want to participate in medical decision making? *Journal of the American Medical Association, 252,* 2990–2994.

Sutherland, H. J., Llewellyn-Thomas, H. A., Lockwood, G. A., Tritchler, D. L., & Till, J. E. (1989). Cancer patients: Their desire for information and participation in treatment decisions. *Journal of the Royal Society of Medicine, 82,* 260–263.

Thompson, S. C., Pitts, J. S., & Schwankovsky, L. (1993). Preferences for involvement in medical decision-making: Situational and demographic influences. *Patient Education and Counseling, 22,* 133–140.

Travis, C. B. (1985). Medical decision making and elective surgery: The case of hysterectomy. *Risk Analysis, 5,* 241–251.

Tymchuk, A. J., & Ouslander, J. G. (1991). Informed consent: Does position of information have an effect upon what elderly people in long-term care remember? *Educational Gerontology, 17,* 11–19.

Tymchuk, A. J., Ouslander, J. G., & Rader, N. (1986). Informing the elderly: A comparison of four methods. *Journal of the American Geriatrics Society, 34,* 818–822.

Venesy, B. A. (1994). A clinician's guide to decision making capacity and ethically sound medical decisions. *American Journal of Physical Medicine and Rehabilitation, 73,* 219–226.

Wallace, L. M. (1986). Communication variables in the design of presurgical preparatory information. *British Journal of Clinical Psychology, 25,* 111–118.

Zwahr, M. D. (1994). *A model to predict decisions made about postmenopausal estrogen replacement therapy.* Unpublished doctoral dissertation, University of Georgia, Athens.

5

Medical and Psychosocial Predictors of Breast Cancer Treatment Decisions

Gail M. Williamson
Deborah J. Jones
Lori A. Ingram
The University of Georgia

A diagnosis of breast cancer typically means that a woman must quickly make a number of decisions about a variety of treatment options at a time when she is likely to be emotionally stunned by the diagnosis itself (Morris & Ingham, 1988; Stanton & Snider, 1993). Although it is only within the last decade that women have been routinely offered a choice between mastectomy and lumpectomy (Rowland & Massie, 1996), many women now are actively involved in decisions about optimal treatment strategies (Moyer, 1997). Alternatives in the late 1990s include lumpectomy and radiation, mastectomy and reconstruction, immediate versus delayed reconstruction, adjuvant chemotherapy, and adjuvant hormone therapy. To date, we know relatively little about the factors that influence women's choices about the various types of treatment (Committee to Advise the Department of Defense [CADD], 1993).

Clearly, aspects of the tumor itself and advice of treating physicians play primary roles in the decisions of many women (e.g., Newcomb & Carbone, 1993). However, psychosocial factors also seem to influence these decisions (e.g., Blichert-Toft,

1992; Jensen, 1991; Payne, 1992; Schain, 1991). In this chapter, we briefly summarize the relevant literature on medical issues that have been investigated in this context. We also highlight psychosocial factors implicated to date in the research on breast cancer treatment decisions, and in doing so, note methodological limitations in much of this research. Finally, we describe our own research directed toward addressing some of these issues.

MEDICAL VARIABLES

Because breast cancer is "a heterogeneous disease, with varying patterns and outcomes ... it remains difficult to determine with any certainty the best therapeutic regimen for any particular woman, nor is it yet possible to advise her with certainty on her risks" (CADD, 1993, p. 10). Nevertheless, physician recommendations exert a strong influence on the treatment choices of most women with breast cancer (Ashcroft, Leinster, & Slade, 1985; Margolis, Goodman, & Rubin, 1990). Care availability likely plays a role as well (Farrow, Hunt, & Samet, 1992; Hynes, 1994; Nattinger, Gottlieb, Veum, Yahnke, & Goodwin, 1992), but may not dictate treatment choice, even when recommended treatment modalities are readily available (e.g., Squartini, Bevilacqua, Conte, & Surbone, 1993; Williamson & Schulz, 1997). However, as one would expect, medical variables do predict some breast cancer treatment decisions. For example, a larger tumor is related to increased likelihood of having a mastectomy and postoperative chemotherapy, and estrogen receptor status predicts postoperative chemotherapy, endocrine therapy, and radiation (Muss et al., 1992).

In addition, effects on quality of life both during and after treatment have been cited as major factors influencing treatment decisions (CADD, 1993) and may be as important to some women as survival advantage (e.g., McEvoy & McCorkle, 1990). Consistent with this proposition is hypothetical scenario research indicating that less toxic treatments are preferred regardless of the stage of breast cancer (Yellen & Cella, 1995) and patient age (Yellen, Cella, & Leslie, 1994). Moreover, in these scenario studies, women who have never had chemotherapy say they would be less willing to switch to alternative, more aggressive treatments than do those who have had chemotherapy, independent of survival advantage and past treatment difficulty (McQuellon et al., 1995; Yellen et al., 1994). These results have been interpreted as lending empirical support to the common clinical observation that the actual experience of chemotherapy is rarely as difficult as expected.

In sum, it is clear that medical variables (e.g., aspects of the tumor itself) are critical in decisions about breast cancer treatment. However, we suspect that medical issues may have the greatest impact on choices related to primary treatment options such as mastectomy versus lumpectomy. Like others (e.g., Blichert-Toft, 1992; Jensen, 1991; Payne, 1992), we also believe that psychosocial factors are important in the treatment decision-making process. In the following section, we review research relevant to this proposition.

PSYCHOSOCIAL VARIABLES

Age and Treatment Decisions

In predicting breast cancer treatment decisions, age at time of diagnosis is among the variables most frequently studied, although a clear picture has yet to emerge. Some research suggests that age is related to treatment decisions (McQuellon et al., 1995; Meyer, Russo, & Talbot, 1995; Muss et al., 1992; Newcomb & Carbone, 1993; Yellen et al., 1994; Wolberg, Tanner, Romsaas, Trump, & Malec, 1987), but other studies indicate that age is not a factor (Beisecker, Helmig, Graham, & Moore, 1994; Clifford, 1979). Meyer et al. (1995) found that older women take less time to make treatment decisions than do their younger counterparts, results that may be attributed to older women seeking fewer second opinions about diagnosis and treatment, consulting fewer sources of information, and viewing beginning treatment immediately as more relevant than being involved in the decision-making process. Although these results are consistent with earlier research showing that with age adults become more efficient in dealing with health-related crises (e.g., Beisecker & Beisecker, 1990; Leventhal, Leventhal, Schaefer, & Easterling, 1993), older women ultimately were neither more nor less likely to choose lumpectomy over mastectomy.

Other age-related factors also appear to play a role in treatment decisions. For example, older women may be no more compliant with physician recommendations than are younger women but rather, more likely to reject treatment because of concern about side effects (Newcomb & Carbone, 1993). In addition, when responding to hypothetical scenarios, older women say that quality of life is a more important treatment consideration than is survival advantage; younger women report that survival advantage is more important (McQuellon et al., 1995; Yellen et al., 1994).

Education and Treatment Decisions

Less educated women appear to make treatment decisions faster, and like older women, they are less likely to seek second opinions and more likely to want to begin treatment rather than be involved in the decision-making process (Meyer et al., 1995). Similarly, Hack, Degner, and Dyck (1994) found that women with less education were more likely to assume a passive role in breast cancer treatment decisions, preferring to allow their doctors to take primary responsibility. In addition, according to Muss et al. (1992), less educated women are more likely to have a mastectomy than a lumpectomy and less likely than their more educated counterparts to have postoperative chemotherapy, endocrine therapy, and radiation. These researchers discovered, however, that the association between education and postoperative treatment was no longer statistically significant after controlling for age and estrogen receptor status, results suggesting that education effects may be confounded with age because women in older cohorts are generally less educated than younger women.

Insurance and Treatment Decisions

It is often believed, and logically so, that adequate insurance coverage is related to the types of treatment patients choose to have, but evidence for such an association is inconclusive. For example, Newcomb and Carbone (1993) reported that the absence of insurance coverage did not predict treatment decisions. Although on the surface it appears that women with no insurance are more likely to have a mastectomy than a lumpectomy, Muss et al. (1992) discovered that this relation was no longer significant when tumor size and disease comorbidity were taken into account. Similarly, these researchers found that having private insurance was related to postoperative chemotherapy, endocrine therapy, and radiation treatment, but once again, this was no longer the case when age and estrogen receptor status were controlled in statistical analyses. Thus, it may well be that several other factors, rather than adequacy of insurance coverage, predict the types of treatment women receive for breast cancer.

Social Support and Treatment Decisions

Women who have higher levels of social support adjust better to a diagnosis of breast cancer (e.g., Taylor & Dakof, 1988). Less is known about the role that social support plays in women's decisions about treatment for breast cancer. Recently, however, Yellen and Cella (1995) reported that when presented with hypothetical scenarios, women with low levels of social well-being and more advanced breast cancer were less likely than those with higher social well-being to say they would accept toxic treatments even with increased survival advantage. On the other hand, women who lived with another person (and presumably, had more social support than those living alone) were more likely to say they would accept treatment for advanced breast cancer than were those who lived alone. Women living with their children were more likely to report that they would accept more toxic treatments in exchange for even minimal survival advantage. These results suggest that social support resources influence treatment decisions although the exact mechanisms underlying such an association remain unclear.

Other research indicates that spouses or similar partners are both influenced by and influential in the treatment and recovery process (e.g., Baider & Kaplan-De-Nour, 1984; Northouse, 1989; Sabo, Brown, & Smith, 1986; Wellisch, Jamison, & Pasnau, 1978). A spouse is typically the first person from whom support is sought during crises (Beach, Martin, Blum, & Roman, 1983; Blood, 1960; Burke & Weir, 1977), and other types of support may not compensate for the absence of spousal support (Brown & Harris, 1978; Coyne & DeLongis, 1986; Lieberman, 1982; O'Hara, 1986). Similarly, a woman's adjustment to breast cancer may best be predicted by her husband's coping behaviors and his ratings of the relationship (Hannum, Giese-Davis, Harding, & Hatfield, 1991; Northouse, Jeffs, Cracchiolo-Caraway, Lampman, & Dorris, 1995). It would seem, then, that marital and partner variables should influence breast cancer treatment decisions, but empirical support for this proposition is sparse.

On the other hand, it has been demonstrated that simply having choices about treatment predicts better adjustment at both the individual (e.g., Dean, 1988; Morris & Ingham, 1988; Pozo et al., 1992) and dyadic levels (Morris & Royle, 1988; Wellisch et al., 1978). For example, wives report less anxiety and depression before and after treatment when they are given choices about treatment; husbands report less anxiety and depression before treatment when their wives are given choices (Morris & Royle, 1988) and greater sexual satisfaction after treatment when they too are involved in treatment decisions (Wellisch et al., 1978). Some existing research indicates that women do consider their husbands when deciding about breast reconstruction (e.g., Rowland, Holland, Chaglassian, & Kinne, 1993). However, husbands' opinions do not seem to be a major factor in this decision. For example, most women report that their husbands or significant others were either neutral (e.g., recognized that she must make the decision herself) or opposed to reconstruction, claiming that it was not important for the relationship (Rowland et al., 1993; Rowland & Massie, 1996). It is interesting to note that it also appears that women who choose to have breast reconstruction for what they perceive to be the benefit of their relationship are more likely to feel disappointed after the surgery (Rowland et al., 1993).

Body Image/Self-Consciousness and Treatment Decisions

Research on body image and self-consciousness as factors in breast cancer treatment has primarily focused on the decision between mastectomy and lumpectomy. As would be expected, women who are concerned about body image insult, who perceive their breasts as a source of self-esteem, and who anticipate difficulty adjusting to the loss of a breast may be more likely to choose lumpectomy over mastectomy (Ashcroft et al., 1985; Margolis et al., 1990; Wolberg et al., 1987).

Some attention has also been devoted to the role of body image and self-consciousness in breast reconstruction decisions. Among the most frequently cited reasons for having reconstruction are desires to feel whole again, to regain body symmetry, and to reduce self-consciousness about appearance (Clifford, 1979; Rowland et al., 1993; Rowland & Massie, 1996). Indeed, after reconstruction, many women report feeling less preoccupied with their health (Rowland et al., 1993), and it appears that increased sexual activity, responsiveness, and satisfaction follow breast reconstruction (Gerard, 1982; Rowland et al., 1993; Teimourian & Adham, 1982).

SUMMARY

It seems obvious that women do not make treatment decisions based solely on medical factors. Rather, various psychosocial factors have been implicated in some, but not all, of the decisions women make about treatment for breast cancer (see

Table 5.1 for a summary of our review of the literature). The vast majority of this research effort has focused on the mastectomy versus lumpectomy decision, and it appears that age, education, insurance coverage, social support, and individual differences in body image and self-consciousness may exert some influence on this particular decision. Associations also have been found between having chemotherapy and age, education, and insurance coverage. The same is true for adjuvant hormone therapy and radiation. The decision to have reconstructive surgery appears to be related to components of social support as well as body image concerns and dispositional self-consciousness.

It is important to note, however, that as is often the case in the early stages of research in a new area, most studies have included only a few of the potentially influential variables and have investigated simple bivariate associations. The result is that clear pictures have not emerged from the existing literature. Notable exceptions, such as the work by Muss et al. (1992) employing multivariate analytic techniques, strongly suggest that confounding and cohort effects, for example, between age and education, account for at least some of the inconsistent findings in this literature.

FURTHER LIMITATIONS OF EXISTING RESEARCH

Caution is warranted in interpreting the results of the extant literature on breast cancer treatment decision making. From our review, it seems clear that the same factors are unlikely to predict all types of treatment decisions. Because much of the research has been limited to the mastectomy versus lumpectomy decision (e.g., Ashcroft et al., 1985; Hughes, 1993; Margolis et al, 1990; Muss et al., 1992; Wolberg et al., 1987), further work is needed to identify factors relevant to the range of treatment alternatives now available.

Another potential limitation is that the findings of several studies are based on reactions to hypothetical case scenarios (Beisecker et al., 1994; Hack et al., 1994; McQuellon et al., 1995; Meyer et al., 1995; Yellen & Cella, 1995; Yellen et al.,

TABLE 5.1
Previous Research: Psychosocial Predictors of Treatment Types

	Mastectomy vs. Lumpectomy	Chemotherapy	Radiation	Hormone therapy	Reconstructive surgery
Age	x	x	x	x	
Education	x	x	x	x	
Insurance	x	x	x	x	
Social support	x				x
Body image	x				x
Self-consciousness	x				x

1994). As such, the results may not accurately represent the actual decisions women with breast cancer make about their own treatment.

Among the most serious limitations of this body of research is that few studies take a multivariate analytic approach. As our review indicates, a number of psychosocial and medical factors have been shown to be associated with some (but not all) treatment decisions. More sophisticated analyses, however, sometimes reveal that these simple bivariate associations disappear when other factors are taken into account (e.g., Muss et al., 1992). Thus, more complex models are likely to better predict treatment decisions than are simple bivariate relations. Indeed, if we are to fully understand the ways in which women confronted with a breast cancer diagnosis go about deciding among their treatment options, it is necessary to take into account a wider range of variables and to determine the independent contribution of each to the decision-making process.

In the following section, we turn to a description of our own research directed toward beginning to address some of these issues. Based on our review of the literature, our study included a variety of demographic (e.g., age, education), medical (e.g., tumor stage, time since diagnosis), and psychosocial (e.g., self-consciousness, social support) factors thought to influence women's treatment decisions. We investigated these factors, using multivariate analyses, as predictors of six types of treatment: mastectomy, lumpectomy, reconstructive surgery, chemotherapy, radiation, and adjuvant hormone therapy. The results reported in this chapter are those that have emerged from our preliminary analyses of this data set and, as such, were primarily exploratory in nature. However, we expected to find bivariate associations consistent with those in previous research—for example, that age at diagnosis would be inversely related to having chemotherapy but positively correlated with hormone therapy. We also expected that women higher in self-consciousness and concern about appearance would be more likely to opt for reconstructive surgery following mastectomy.

Our primary goal, however, was to investigate—in an exploratory fashion—the independent contributions of our variables to each type of treatment when the effects of multiple predictors were considered simultaneously. We felt this was an important first step in beginning the process of disentangling inconsistencies in the existing literature, many of which, we believe, may be resolved by including more variables and using a multivariate rather than bivariate analytic approach.

METHOD

Participants

In this study, women (*N* = 95) diagnosed with Stage I (*N* = *36), Stage II (N* = 49), or Stage III (*N* = 10) breast cancer completed mail surveys (most often anonymously). These women were either identified and referred by their surgeons or recruited from breast cancer support groups. Of the women who agreed to participate in the study after being recruited in this manner ($N = 103$), 92.2% completed and returned their surveys. The vast majority (96.8%) of these women were white, a sampling bias that precluded analyses of the effects of ethnic origin.

Because they have been implicated in previous research, demographic variables used in the present analyses included current marital status, household income, percentage of medical expenses covered by insurance, education, and age at time of diagnosis. Most of the women in our sample were married or living as married (71.6%); the remainder were single and never married ($N = 9$), divorced ($N = 12$), or widowed ($N = 6$). For purposes of analyses, they were classified dichotomously ($1 = not\ married$, $2 = married$). Median household income was greater than $50,000 per year, and most of these women were college graduates (70.6%), with over half (53.7%) having graduate or professional training. As would be expected given the education and income levels in this sample, the vast majority (91.6%) had insurance coverage that paid 75% or more of their medical bills. Mean age at time of breast cancer diagnosis was 46.8 years ($SD = 9.7$, range 26–74), with almost one third (30.5%) having been 50 years of age or older when diagnosed with breast cancer (11.6% were age 60 or older). Age was not correlated with education in this sample ($r = -.06$, ns).

Measures

Medical Treatment Variables.   Outcome measures were simply the presence or absence ($0 = no$, $1 = yes$) of six different medical treatments for breast cancer at the time a woman completed the survey: (a) mastectomy, (b) lumpectomy, (c) reconstructive surgery, (d) chemotherapy, (e) radiation, and (f) hormone (Tamoxifen) therapy. Because some treatment modalities are highly related to each other, they were included as predictor/control variables in some multivariate analyses as well. Most, but certainly not all, participants (67.4%) had a course of chemotherapy, 42.1% had radiation, and 52.6% had Tamoxifen therapy. With respect to surgical variables in this sample, about three fourths (73.7%) had mastectomies, 40% had lumpectomies (11 women had both types of surgery and 8 women had neither), and 38.9% had reconstructive surgery. For analyses predicting mastectomy, lumpectomy, and reconstruction, women who had experienced both mastectomy and lumpectomy (mastectomy most often followed earlier lumpectomy in this group) were classified according to the type of surgery they had first.

Medical Predictor Variables.   In addition to the medical treatment variables, several other medical factors were considered in these analyses because of their potential influence on types of treatment. These were time (in months) since diagnosis when the survey data were collected, stage of breast cancer when diagnosed, and history of breast cancer in the family ($0 = no$, $1 = yes$). The average woman in our study was more than 2 years postdiagnosis ($M = 27.1$ months), but there was considerable variability ($SD = 25.8$ months, range, 1 to 128 months). As noted previously, most had either Stage I or Stage II malignancies when diagnosed. Less than one third (28.4%) reported a family history of breast cancer.

Psychological Predictor Variables. Of the psychological variables included in our survey, three are considered in these analyses, primarily because these variables have been implicated in previous research on breast cancer treatment decisions. Body image investment was assessed with the Concern About Appearance subscale of the Measure of Body Apperception (MBA; Carver et al., 1997) designed to measure trait-like concerns related to how much a woman values a good physical appearance. The Concern About Appearance subscale contains four items (e.g., "It's important to me to look my best all the time," If a woman doesn't look good to others, she can't possibly feel good about herself"). Participants responded to these items on a scale of 1 (*I disagree a lot*) to 4 (*I agree a lot*). Carver et al. (1997) reported test-retest reliabilities in a sample of college students of .75 or better over a 4-week period. In a sample of patients interviewed before and after original surgery for breast cancer, test-retest reliability over a 1-year period was .67. In the Carver et al. (1997) study, internal reliability was .78, and in our sample, Cronbach's alpha was .76.

We also measured public self-consciousness with the 7-item subscale of the revised version of the Self-Consciousness Scale (Scheier & Carver, 1985). Public self-consciousness refers to the inclination to attend to aspects of the self that are easily accessible to public scrutiny and from which others can readily form impressions and evaluations. Items include such statements as: "I care a lot about how I present myself to others," and "I usually worry about making a good impression." Participants indicated the degree to which each item was like them (1 = *not at all*, 4 = *a lot*). This instrument was devised for use in the general population and has been shown to be psychometrically sound and stable across time (e.g., 4-week test-retest = .74; Scheier & Carver, 1985). In the present sample, internal reliability was .79.

Finally, we included a measure of perceived social support, the 6-item version of the Interpersonal Support Evaluation List (ISEL; Cohen, Mermelstein, Kamarck, & Hoberman, 1985) employed successfully in our previous research with medically compromised populations (e.g., Williamson & Schulz, 1992). Participants rated such statements as "When I need suggestions on how to deal with a personal problem, I know someone I can turn to," and "There is at least one person I know whose advice I really trust" (0 = *definitely true,* 3 = *definitely false*). In this study, Cronbach's alpha was .82.

RESULTS

Bivariate Associations

Total Sample. Correlations between predictor variables and five types of treatment for the total sample are shown in Table 5.2. Because no women in our sample who first chose lumpectomy had reconstruction in conjunction with lum-

TABLE 5.2

Correlations Between Treatment and Predictor Variables for the Full Sample ($n = 95$)

	Types of Treatment for Breast Cancer				
	Mastectomy	Lumpectomy	Chemotherapy	Radiation	Tamoxifen[b]
Demographic variables					
Age at diagnosis	-.07	-.12	-.26**	-.26**	.19*
Marital status[a]	.13	.02	.11	.02	-.13
Income	.12	.09	.11	-.03	-.01
Education	.14	-.05	.09	-.05	-.05
Insurance coverage	.02	.00	-.06	-.04	.03
Psychological variables					
MBA-appearance	.13	-.24**	.08	-.25**	-.08
Self-consciousness	.17*	-.17*	.10	-.12	-.18*
Social support	-.08	.02	-.01	-.04	.15
Medical variables					
Time since diagnosis	.16	-.08	.04	.14	.19*
Stage of tumor	.37***	-.27**	.40***	.20*	.15
Family history[b]	.10	.02	.19*	-.21*	-.10
Mastectomy[b]	—	-.79***	.22*	-.25**	.11
Lumpectomy[b]		—	-.13	.41***	-.02
Reconstruction[b]			.10	-.38***	-.06
Chemotherapy[b]			—	.18*	.01
Radiation[b]				—	.13

[a] 1, *not married*, 2, *married*

[b] 0, *no*, 1, *yes*

* $p < .05$; ** $p < .01$; *** $p < .001$

pectomy (although four women in this group later had mastectomy followed by reconstruction), analyses for correlates of reconstruction (the sixth type of treatment) were conducted using only women whose first surgery was mastectomy, and results are reported later.

We turn first to the primary surgical variables. No demographic variables were related to either mastectomy or lumpectomy. As would be expected, stage of tumor was associated with both mastectomy and lumpectomy, such that more advanced tumor stage predicted greater likelihood of mastectomy and less likelihood of lumpectomy. Also, as would be expected, mastectomy and lumpectomy were strongly inversely correlated. It is interesting and somewhat counterintuitive that lumpectomy was inversely related to concerns about appearance and public self-consciousness; women who were more self-conscious and concerned about their appearance were less likely to opt for lumpectomy. Similarly, women who were more self-conscious were more likely to choose mastectomy.

With regard to the adjuvant therapies, of the demographic variables, only age at time of diagnosis was a significant predictor with older women being less likely to have chemotherapy and radiation and more likely to take Tamoxifen. Of the medical variables assessed in this study, only longer time since diagnosis was related to a greater likelihood of Tamoxifen therapy. However, medical variables were more consistently associated with chemotherapy and radiation. Specifically, women with more advanced stage cancer, a family history of breast cancer, and who had undergone mastectomy were more likely to have chemotherapy. In addition, several medical variables predicted greater likelihood of radiation: more advanced stage cancer, no family history of breast cancer, having a lumpectomy rather than a mastectomy, not having reconstructive surgery, and having chemotherapy. Moreover, as with the finding for concerns about appearance and lumpectomy, women who were less concerned about appearance were more likely to have radiation. Finally, women high in public self-consciousness were less likely to have Tamoxifen therapy.

Mastectomy Group (N = 52).   Correlations between treatment and predictor variables for women whose first (or only) surgery was mastectomy are shown in Table 5.3. As can be seen, no demographic variables and no relevant medical variables were correlated with the likelihood of having reconstructive surgery. The same was true for concerns about appearance and perceptions of social support. The only significant correlate of reconstruction following mastectomy was public self-consciousness.

As in the total sample, a larger stage of tumor at diagnosis was positively related to likelihood of having chemotherapy. However, remaining bivariate associations took on a somewhat different pattern among mastectomy patients than in the total sample. Specifically, in this group, chemotherapy was not related to age at diagnosis, most likely because the vast majority (76.9%) of women in this group had chemotherapy. In addition, although the magnitude of the correlation between chemotherapy and family history of breast cancer was the same as in the total

TABLE 5.3

Correlations Between Treatment and Predictor Variables for Mastectomy ($n = 52$) and Lumpectomy ($n = 37$) Patients

	Reconstruction	Chemotherapy		Radiation		Tamoxifen[b]	
	(Mast. Only)	Mast.	Lump.	Mast.	Lump.	Mast.	Lump.
Demographic variables							
Age at diagnosis	-.22	-.14	-.29*	-.20	-.23	.03	.41**
Marital status[a]	.11	.03	-.01	.07	-.16	-.19	-.11
Income	-.03	-.18	.18	-.28*	.07	.04	-.18
Education	-.02	.02	.15	-.18	.04	.05	-.19
Insurance coverage	-.09	-.25*	.09	-.22	.19	-.01	.04
Psychological variables							
MBA-appearance	.13	-.03	.08	-.13	-.07	-.07	.00
Self-consciousness	.40***	.03	-.04	-.15	.07	-.14	-.24
Social support	.11	-.03	.01	-.12	.05	.12	.24
Medical variables							
Time since diagnosis	.10	.02	.00	.10	.39**	.12	.38**
Stage of tumor	-.20	.50***	.17	.62***	-.19	.10	.22
Family history[b]	.01	.19	.18	-.29*	-.31*	-.15	-.08
Reconstruction[b]	—	.20	—	-.19	—	-.12	—
Chemotherapy[b]	—	—	—	.27*	.13	-.01	-.03
Radiation[b]	—	—	—	—	—	.15	.13

[a]1, *not married*, 2, *married*

[b]0, *no*, 1, *yes*

* $p < .05$; ** $p < .01$; *** $p < .001$

sample, it was not significant in this subsample analysis. Finally, unlike the total sample, an association between better insurance coverage and less likelihood of having chemotherapy emerged in this group.

Among mastectomy patients, correlates of radiation were somewhat more consistent with those observed in the total sample. That is, likelihood of having radiation was positively related to tumor stage and chemotherapy and negatively associated with family history. Associations observed in total sample analyses were not significant for age at diagnosis or reconstruction. However, an inverse correlation between radiation and income emerged in this subgroup that was not present in analyses of the total sample.

Finally, among mastectomy patients, none of our variables were related to Tamoxifen therapy. Thus, the associations observed in the total sample between adjuvant hormone therapy and age at diagnosis, self-consciousness, and time since diagnosis were not apparent in the subsample of mastectomy patients.

Lumpectomy Group (N = 37).   The results of bivariate analyses for women whose first (or only) surgery was lumpectomy are also shown in Table 5.3. As in the total sample, age at diagnosis was inversely related to likelihood of having chemotherapy among lumpectomy patients, a result that, when combined with the lack of a similar association in the mastectomy group, suggests the correlation observed in the total sample was due primarily to older women who have lumpectomies being less likely to have chemotherapy.

With respect to correlates of radiation, only two significant predictors emerged. As in the total sample and also the mastectomy group, having a family history of breast cancer was related to less likelihood of having radiation. Unlike results for the total sample and the mastectomy group, more time elapsed since diagnosis was related to having had radiation. No other variables predicted radiation among lumpectomy patients including effects observed in the total sample for age at diagnosis, concerns about appearance, stage of tumor, and chemotherapy.

Finally, among lumpectomy patients, two associations observed in the total sample were also found in analyses of predictors of adjuvant hormone therapy. That is, unlike results for the mastectomy group, age at diagnosis and time since diagnosis were related to Tamoxifen therapy in the subsample of lumpectomy patients. The small inverse correlation between self-consciousness and Tamoxifen found in the total sample approached significance in lumpectomy patients ($p < .07$). As in the total sample and the subsample of mastectomy patients, no other variables were related to taking Tamoxifen. This pattern of results suggests that the significant predictors of adjuvant hormone therapy identified in total sample analyses are due, in large part, to analogous associations in the lumpectomy patient group.

Multivariate Analyses

A primary goal of this study was to go beyond simple bivariate associations to determine the independent contribution of each predictor variable to treatment choice, controlling for the variance accounted for by other predictor variables. Consequently, a series of simultaneous logistic regression analyses was conducted, one for each type of treatment. To minimize the number of variables included in these analyses (and because the goals of this study did not include investigating either suppressor or interaction effects), demographic, psychological, and medical variables that were significant bivariate correlates of each type of treatment were entered as predictor variables in the regression equations. Results of these analyses are shown in Table 5.4.

Mastectomy Versus Lumpectomy.   For the 87 women whose first (or only) surgery was either mastectomy or lumpectomy, variables (i.e., significant bivariate correlates—see Table 5.2) entered into the logistic regression equation predicting the mastectomy versus lumpectomy decision were stage of tumor, concern about appearance, and public self-consciousness. After controlling for the variance attributable to stage of tumor, neither concerns about appearance nor self-consciousness were significant. However, stage of tumor alone correctly classified a significant portion of these patients (overall, 64%), with better predictability for mastectomy (72%) than lumpectomy (54%).

Reconstruction.   Among the 52 women who had undergone mastectomy, only one variable—public self-consciousness—was a significant bivariate correlate of reconstruction (see Table 5.3). In logistic regression, this variable alone correctly classified 74% of the women who had reconstruction and 56% of those who had not (overall, 65%). Women were more likely to choose reconstructive surgery if they were highly self-conscious.

Chemotherapy.   In multivariate analysis of the total sample, the significant predictors of chemotherapy were younger age, more advanced stage malignancy, and family history of breast cancer. After controlling for these variables, bivariate relations with mastectomy (found in the total sample) and insurance coverage (found only in the mastectomy group) were no longer significant. Age at diagnosis, tumor stage, and family history correctly classified 88% of the women who had chemotherapy and 61% of those who had not (overall, 79%). Consistent with previous research, older age at time of diagnosis predicted less likelihood of chemotherapy (e.g., Muss et al., 1992; Newcomb & Carbone, 1993), and this was the case after controlling for all other significant bivariate correlates.

Radiation.   The eight bivariate correlates of radiotherapy in the total sample (see Table 5.2) plus income (which was correlated with radiation only among mastectomy patients) and time since diagnosis (which was correlated with radiation only among lumpectomy patients) were entered in the simultaneous logistic regression analysis predicting likelihood of having radiation. Concerns about appearance, mastectomy, lumpectomy, and chemotherapy were no longer significant predictors.

TABLE 5.4
Beta Coefficients, Simultaneous Logistic Regression Analyses: Predictors of Types of Treatment for Breast Cancer

	Types of Treatment for Breast Cancer				
	Mastectomy vs. Lumpectomy (n = 87)	Reconstruction (n = 52)	Chemotherapy (n = 95)	Radiation[a] (n = 95)	Tamoxifen[a] (n = 95)
Demographic variables					
Age at diagnosis	—	—	-.07**	-.08*	.06*
Income	—	—	—	-.28	—
Insurance coverage	—	—	-.03	—	—
Psychological variables					
MBA-appearance	-.10	—	—	-.08	—
Self-consciousness	-.08	.21**	—	—	-.07
Medical variables					
Time since diagnosis	—	—	—	.16	.20*
Stage of tumor	-1.20***	—	1.82***	1.56**	—
Family history[a]	—	—	1.33*	-1.95***	—
Mastectomy[a]	—	—	.29	-.67	—
Lumpectomy[a]	—	—	—	2.14	—
Reconstruction[a]	—	—	—	-1.83*	—
Chemotherapy[a]	—	—	—	1.24	—
Model chi-square	14.81**	9.18*	29.83***	55.77***	12.07**

Note. Only significant bivariate predictors (see Table 5.2) were included in regression models for each type of treatment.

[a] 0, *no*, 1, *yes*.

* $p < .05$; ** $p < .01$; *** $p < .001$

The same was true for income and time since diagnosis. However, as with chemotherapy, older women were less likely than younger women to have radiation as were those with a family history of breast cancer and those who had not opted for reconstructive surgery. In addition, women with more advanced stage tumors were more likely to have radiation, a finding that, when considered in conjunction with similar associations between tumor stage and chemotherapy, indicates that radiation is common not only following lumpectomy but also as a component of an aggressive course of treatment for more advanced cancer that includes both chemotherapy and radiation. The total equation correctly classified 79% of the total sample (75% of those who had radiation and 82% of those who had not).

Hormone (Tamoxifen) Therapy.   Three variables were related to Tamoxifen therapy in bivariate analyses: age at diagnosis (in the total sample and the lumpectomy group), self-consciousness (in the total sample), and time since diagnosis (in the total sample and lumpectomy group). Public self-consciousness was no longer a significant predictor of Tamoxifen therapy after controlling for the variance attributable to age at diagnosis and time elapsed since diagnosis. Thus, of the variables included in these analyses, likelihood of taking Tamoxifen was predicted only by older age and more time postdiagnosis. The regression equation correctly classified 72% of the women who took Tamoxifen and 64% of those who did not (overall, 68%).

DISCUSSION

Breast cancer is the most common type of cancer and the second leading cause of death due to cancer among women (CADD, 1993; Marshall, 1993). Yet, remarkably little is known about the factors that influence the choices a woman diagnosed with breast cancer must make about the range of treatments likely to be available to her. In this chapter, we reviewed existing literature on medical and psychosocial contributors to these decisions, pointing out inconsistencies in results across studies and offering some suggestions about ways in which these inconsistencies might be resolved. In particular, we advocate more complex models encompassing a wide range of predictor variables and multivariate analytic strategies to determine independent contributions of each variable to treatment choice. Finally, we presented results of preliminary analyses of our own data.

Before turning to our interpretations of the findings of this study, we emphasize that the sample of women who completed our survey were far from representative of the population of breast cancer patients. These women were affluent, highly educated, almost exclusively white, and from a cursory look at the qualitative data they provided, well-informed about breast cancer and treatment alternatives. Caution is therefore warranted in attempting to generalize these results to other groups of breast cancer patients (e.g., minorities and women who are less affluent, educated, and informed about the disease). Still, even with these caveats, our data support the utility of multivariate models that include demographic, psychological, and medical variables for purposes of determining the best predictors of a particular type of treatment.

Demographic Variables

Overall, demographic factors were poor predictors of treatment types. Whether a woman was married or not was unrelated to any of the treatment modalities assessed in this study. This null result is not unlike previous research suggesting that, although spousal support is an important factor in adjustment (e.g., Hannum et al., 1991; Northouse et al., 1995), it may not predict actual decisions about treatment (e.g., Rowland & Massie, 1996). It remains to be seen whether qualitative aspects of the marital relationship are related to any of the treatment modalities we assessed.

Insurance coverage also was largely unrelated to treatment choice, and others have reported a similar lack of association (e.g., Muss et al., 1992; Newcomb & Carbone, 1993). It is heartening to find that poorer insurance coverage does not appear to prevent women from receiving the treatment they need and/or prefer. On the other hand, before we dismiss insurance coverage as inconsequential, it should be noted that the lack of results in our study could simply reflect a ceiling effect, because over 90% of these women had good insurance coverage. Much the same can be said for household income. In this relatively affluent sample, although higher income was associated with decreased likelihood of radiation among mastectomy patients in bivariate analysis, income was not a significant factor in multivariate analysis. Education also was not related to any of our treatment variables, nor was it associated with age at time of diagnosis, null results that may be attributed to the fact that the women in our study were highly educated.

Finally, of the demographic variables, a woman's age at the time she was diagnosed with breast cancer was a strong and consistent predictor of adjuvant therapies, even after controlling for medical variables. Like other researchers (e.g., Muss et al., 1992; Newcomb & Carbone, 1993), we found that older women were less likely to have chemotherapy. Our data also revealed that they were less likely to have radiation and more likely to take Tamoxifen. Age did not, however, predict any of the surgical variables (mastectomy, lumpectomy, and reconstruction). These results did not corroborate those of previous research suggesting that older women are more likely to opt for mastectomy (e.g., Muss et al., 1992; Wolberg et al., 1987), but they are consistent with other research that has similarly produced no evidence for an age effect in the decision about whether to have a mastectomy or a lumpectomy (e.g., Meyer et al., 1995). Still, it should be noted that there is evidence that, although older and younger women may ultimately make similar decisions, the process through which they arrive at these decisions differs substantially (e.g., Beisecker & Beisecker, 1990; Leventhal et al., 1993; Meyer et al., 1995).

Medical Variables

As we suspected and as others (e.g., Muss et al., 1992) have found, medical variables were important contributors to the types of treatment women in our study had experienced. In multivariate analyses, except for the effect for age noted in the previous section, elapsed time since diagnosis was the only predictor of Tamoxifen therapy. This most likely reflects the fact that many women begin taking Tamoxifen following a course of chemotherapy. Stage of tumor at diagnosis predicted mastectomy versus lumpectomy, chemotherapy, and radiation; women whose cancer was more advanced were more likely to have had mastectomy, chemotherapy, and radiation. The treatment modalities themselves were interrelated in predictable ways. For example, mastectomy was negatively related to lumpectomy and radiation. There is a reassuring aspect to these results. That is, it appears that this sample of educated, informed women were prone to choose the types of treatment currently recommended as the most efficacious for their particular situation.

One factor included in our list of medical variables bears further investigation. Specifically, having breast cancer in one's family was related to greater likelihood of chemotherapy and less likelihood of radiation. Because mastectomy followed by a course of chemotherapy is often viewed as the safer approach to breast cancer, it may be that women with a history of breast cancer in their families wanted to take the more aggressive path in order to offset their biological disadvantage as much as possible. Another possibility is that, having witnessed breast cancer treatment first hand, they realized that mastectomy and chemotherapy may not be as difficult to handle as is commonly believed.

Psychological Variables

In selecting the variables to be included in these analyses, one goal was to minimize the bias inherent in retrospective research. That is, we chose variables that seemed unlikely to be biased by memory or to change substantially over time. It appears that we were at least moderately successful with respect to our demographic and medical variables but somewhat less so in our selection of psychological variables. In particular, we now realize that the lack of results for perceived social support may indicate measurement problems rather than that this variable has no bearing on treatment decisions. Indeed, there are reasons to suspect that social support does, in fact, play a role. That is, research indicates that aspects of social support are related to treatment preferences among breast cancer patients (e.g., Yellen & Cella, 1995). Our measure of social support, however, assessed perceptions of support available at the time surveys were completed, rather than when women were actually faced with making decisions about treatment. In choosing our measure of social support, we assumed a certain amount of stability over time. We now doubt this is the case, and we have some evidence to support these doubts. Specifically, in an open-ended format, we asked the women in our study whether "anything positive or good happened to you as a result of your diagnosis" and if so, what.

Over 70% of these women responded that their existing relationships had improved, they had made new friends (e.g., through support groups), and/or they were surprised and overwhelmed by the amount of support and caring they received from members of their social networks during diagnosis and treatment. Thus, we suspect that a diagnosis of breast cancer may have substantial—many times, positive—influence on a woman's perceptions of social support. In this case, there would be little reason to expect perceived social support to predict treatment decisions retrospectively.

On the other hand, a variable shown in previous research to be stable over time—public self-consciousness (Scheier & Carver, 1985)—did emerge as a (and, indeed, the only) predictor of one type of treatment. Specifically, women who were higher in public self-consciousness were more likely to have chosen reconstructive surgery following mastectomy, a finding that is both intuitive and consistent with earlier research (e.g., Clifford, 1979; Rowland et al., 1993). An interesting question for future investigation is whether reconstruction interacts with public self-consciousness in predicting adjustment following a diagnosis of breast cancer. That is, do women high in public self-consciousness adapt better (e.g., in terms of interpersonal relationships, depression) than their counterparts who do not have reconstruction?

Concluding Comments

The overall picture emerging from our research is that, at least among women who are relatively affluent, well-educated, and well-informed about breast cancer treatment options, choices may be made based on the best information available. These women also appeared to take the road most likely to be aggressive in terms of preventing or forestalling recurrence and/or metastasis. That is, the women in our sample chose mastectomy and chemotherapy when the tumor was more advanced at diagnosis and there was a history of breast cancer in the family. Our interpretation is consistent with recent evidence indicating that family history of breast cancer and higher levels of concern about breast cancer foster self-protective behavior (McCaul, Branstetter, Schroeder, & Glasgow, 1996; McCaul, Schroeder, & Reid, 1996).

The women in our study most likely brought their considerable resources to bear when deciding about treatment for breast cancer. We suspect these women knew how to access the information they needed, were adept at processing complex information, and had the financial and social resources to support their decisions. It appears that, generally speaking, their goal was to maximize their outcomes in terms of both survival advantage and cosmetic results. Women who were high in public self-consciousness were more likely to choose reconstruction following mastectomy. In conjunction with earlier evidence that mastectomy followed by reconstruction can produce cosmetic outcomes superior to lumpectomy (Cady & Stone, 1990; Taylor et al., 1985), this finding suggests that concerns about the cosmetic results of lumpectomy being less than satisfactory contributed to the decision to have mastectomy plus reconstruction. In fact, many of the women in our study reported choosing mastectomy because they were advised that the size and/or location of their cancer would preclude a favorable cosmetic outcome with lumpectomy. Other women reported being told the radiation that typically accompanies lumpectomy would cause scarring that might interfere with later reconstructive surgery.

Finally, as we have emphasized, the research reported in this chapter is limited in several ways, including its retrospective nature and probable lack of generalizability to breast cancer patients who are less advantaged than the women who participated in our study. It should also be noted that the mean age of the women in our sample was relatively young (i.e., approximately 47 years old when diagnosed with breast cancer). However, there was considerable variability in age at diagnosis, and nearly one third of the participants were 50 years of age or older when diagnosed, with about 12% having been 60 years of age or older. Nevertheless, no woman in our study was more than 75 years old. Thus, we cannot say with certainty that our results would generalize to include women in the older cohorts.

An additional limitation is that these data say little about the actual cognitive processes involved in making treatment decisions. This study was designed to gather preliminary information on a broad range of factors thought to influence choices about a variety of treatments, and the analyses reported here represent only the beginning phases of our investigation into the quantitative and qualitative data provided by these women. Still, we believe that our results have yielded numerous interesting directions for future research. One such direction is the issue of whether women actually are given choices about each type of treatment and why this may or may not be the case. Questions such as these may be particularly important in understanding the apparent effects of age on treatment decisions. For example, it well may be that older women have fewer decisions to make because they are offered fewer options (e.g., Newcomb & Carbone, 1993). This could be the case for a variety of reasons including age-related differences in the tumor itself and coexisting health conditions that may preclude the more aggressive forms of treatment.

ACKNOWLEDGMENTS

The research reported in this chapter was supported by a grant from The Center for Applied Cognitive Research on Aging (G.M. Williamson, principal investigator). Manuscript preparation was facilitated by funds from the Institute for Behavioral Research at The University of Georgia.

REFERENCES

Ashcroft, J. J., Leinster, S. J., & Slade, P. A. (1985). Breast cancer-patient choice of treatment: Preliminary communication. *Journal of the Royal Society of Medicine, 78,* 43–46.
Baider, L., & Kaplan-DeNour, A. (1984). Couple's reactions and adjustment to mastectomy: A preliminary report. *International Journal of Psychiatry Medicine, 14,* 265–276.
Beach, S. R. H., Martin, J. K., Blum, T. C., & Roman, P. M. (1993). Effects of marital and co-worker relationship on negative affect: Testing the central role of marriage. *American Journal of Family Therapy, 21,* 313-323.

Beisecker, A. E., & Beisecker, T. D. (1990). Patient information seeking behaviors when communicating with doctors. *Medical Care, 28,* 19–28.

Beisecker, A. E., Helmig, L., Graham, D., & Moore, W. P. (1994). Attitudes of oncologists, oncology nurses, and patients from a women's clinic regarding medical decision making for older and younger breast cancer patients. *The Gerontologist, 34,* 505–512.

Blichert-Toft, M. (1992). Breast-conserving therapy for mammary carcinoma: Psychosocial aspects, indications, and limitations. *Annals of Medicine, 24,* 445–451.

Blood, R. O. (1960). *Husbands and wives.* New York: The Free Press.

Brown, G. W., & Harris, T. O. (1978). *Social origins of depression: A study of psychiatric disorder in women.* New York: The Free Press.

Burke, R. J., & Weir, T. (1977). Marital helping relationships: The moderators between stress and well-being. *Journal of Psychology, 95,* 121-130.

Cady, B., & Stone, M. D. (1990). Selection of breast-preservation therapy for primary invasive breast carcinoma. *Surgical Clinics of North America, 70,* 1047–1059.

Carver, C. S., Pozo-Kaderman, C., Price, A. A., Noriega, V., Harris, S. D., Derhagopian, R. P., Robinson, D. S., & Moffatt, F. L. (1997). *Concern about aspects of body image: Predicting adjustment to early stage breast cancer.* Unpublished manuscript, University of Miami.

Clifford, E. (1979). The reconstruction experience: The search for restitution. In N. G. Georgiade (Ed.), *Breast reconstruction following mastectomy* (pp. 22–34). St. Louis, MO: Mosby.

Cohen, S., Mermelstein, R., Kamarck, T., & Hoberman, H. M. (1985). Measuring the functional components of social support. In I. G. Sarason & B. R. Sarason (Eds.), *Social support: Theory, research, and application* (pp. 73–94). Dordrecht, The Netherlands: Martinus Nijhoff.

Committee to Advise the Department of Defense. (1993). *Strategies for managing the breast cancer research program: A report to the U. S. Army Medical Research and Development Command.* Washington, DC: National Academy Press.

Coyne, J. C., & DeLongis, A. (1986). Going beyond social support: The role of social relationships in adaptation. *Journal of Consulting and Clinical Psychology, 54,* 454-460.

Dean, C. (1988). The emotional impact of mastectomy. *British Journal of Hospital Medicine, 39,* 30–39.

Farrow, D. C., Hunt, W. C., & Samet, J. M. (1992). Geographic variation in the treatment of localized breast cancer. *New England Journal of Medicine, 326,* 1097–1101.

Gerard, D. (1982). Sexual functioning after mastectomy: Life vs. lab. *Journal of Sex and Marital Therapy, 8,* 305–315.

Hack, T. F., Degner, L. F., & Dyck, D. G (1994). Relationship between preferences for decisional control and illness information among women with breast cancer: A quantitative and qualitative analysis. *Social Science and Medicine, 39,* 279-289.

Hannum, J. W., Giese-Davis, J., Harding, K., & Hatfield, A. K. (1991). Effects of individual and marital variables on coping with cancer. *Journal of Psychosocial Oncology, 9,* 1-19.

Hughes, K. K. (1993). Psychosocial and functional status of breast cancer patients: The influence of diagnosis and treatment choice. *Cancer Nursing, 16,* 222-229.

Hynes, D. M. (1994). The quality of breast cancer care in local communities: Implications for health care reform. *Medical Care, 32,* 328–340.

Jensen, A. B. (1991). Psychosocial factors in breast cancer and their possible impact upon prognosis. *Cancer Treatment Reviews, 18,* 191–210.

Leventhal, E. A., Leventhal, H., Schaefer, P., & Easterling, D. (1993). Conservation of energy, uncertainty reduction, and swift utilization of medical care among the elderly. *Journals of Gerontology, 48,* 78–86.

Lieberman, M. A. (1982). The effects of social support on response to stress. In L. Goldberger & S. Breznitz (Eds.), *Handbook of stress: Theoretical and clinical aspects* (pp. 764-784). New York: Academic Press.

Margolis, G., Goodman, R. L., & Rubin, A. (1990). Psychological effects of breast conserving cancer treatment and mastectomy. *Psychosomatics, 31,* 33–39.

Marshall, E. (1993). Search for a killer: Focus shifts from fat to hormones in special report on breast cancer. *Science, 259,* 618–621.

McCaul, K. D., Branstetter, A. D., Schroeder, D. M., & Glasgow, R. E. (1996). What is the relationship between breast cancer risk and mammography screening? A meta-analytic review. *Health Psychology, 15,* 423–429.

McCaul, K. D., Schroeder, D. M., & Reid, P. A. (1996). Breast cancer worry and screening: Some prospective data. *Health Psychology, 15,* 430–433.

McEvoy, M. D., & McCorkle, R. (1990). Quality of life issues in patients with disseminated breast cancer. *Cancer, 66,* 1416–1421.

McQuellon, R. P., Muss, H. B., Hoffman, S. L., Russell, F., Craven, B., & Yellen, S. B. (1995). Patient preferences for treatment of metastatic breast cancer: A study of women with early stage breast cancer. *Journal of Clinical Oncology, 13,* 858-868.

Meyer, B. J. F., Russo, C., & Talbot, A. (1995). Discourse comprehension and problem solving: Decisions about the treatment of breast cancer by women across the life-span. *Psychology and Aging, 10,* 84–103.

Morris, J., & Ingham, R. (1988). Choice of surgery for early breast cancer: Psychosocial considerations. *Social Science and Medicine, 27,* 1257–1262.

Morris, J., & Royle, G. T. (1988). Offering patients a choice of surgery for early breast cancer: A reduction in anxiety and depression in patients and their husbands. *Social Science and Medicine, 26,* 583–585.

Moyer, A. (1997). Psychosocial outcomes of breast-conserving surgery versus mastectomy: A meta-analytic review. *Health Psychology, 16,* 284–298.

Muss, H. B., Hunter, C. P., Wesley, M., Correa, P., Chen, V. W., Greenberg, R. S., Eley, J. W., Austin, D. F., Kurman, R., & Edwards, B. K. (1992). Treatment plans for Black and White women with stage II node-positive breast cancer. *Cancer, 70,* 2460-2467.

Nattinger, A. B., Gottlieb, M. S., Veum, J., Yahnke, D., & Goodwin, J. S. (1992). Geographic variation in the use of breast-conserving treatment for breast cancer. *New England Journal of Medicine, 326,* 1102–1107.

Newcomb, P. A., & Carbone, P. P. (1993). Cancer treatment and age: Patient perspectives. *Journal of the National Cancer Institute, 85,* 1580–1584.

Northouse, L. L. (1989). The impact of breast cancer on patients and husbands. *Cancer Nursing, 12,* 276–284.

Northouse, L. L., Jeffs, M., Cracchiolo-Caraway, A., Lampman, L., & Dorris, G. (1995). Emotional distress reported by women and husbands prior to breast biopsy. *Nursing Research, 44,* 196-201.

O'Hara, M. (1986). Social support, life events, and depression during pregnancy and the puerperium. *Archives of General Psychiatry, 43,* 569-573.

Payne, S. A. (1992). A study of quality of life in cancer patients receiving palliative chemotherapy. *Social Science Medicine, 35,* 1505–1509.

Pozo, C., Carver, C. S., Noriega, V., Harris, S. D., Robinson, D. S., Ketcham, A. S., Legaspi, A., Moffat, F. L., & Clark, K. C. (1992). Effects of mastectomy versus lumpectomy on emotional adjustment to breast cancer: A prospective study of the first year postsurgery. *Journal of Clinical Oncology, 10,* 1292–1298.

Rowland, J. H., Holland, J. C., Chaglassian, T., & Kinne, D. (1993). Psychological response to breast reconstruction: Expectations for and impact on postmastectomy functioning. *Psychosomatics, 34,* 241–250.

Rowland, J. H., & Massie, M. J. (1996). Psychologic reactions to breast cancer diagnosis, treatment, and survival. In J. R. Harris, M. E. Lippman, M. Morrow, & S. Hellman (Eds.), *Diseases of the breast* (pp. 919–938). Philadelphia: Lippencott-Raven.

Sabo, D., Brown, H., & Smith, C. (1986). The male role and mastectomy: Support groups and men's adjustment. *Journal of Psychosocial Oncology, 4,* 19–31.

Schain, W. (1991). Psychosocial factors in mastectomy and reconstruction. In R. B. Noone (Ed.), *Plastic and reconstructive surgery of the breast* (pp. 327–343). Philadelphia: Decker.

Scheier, M. F., & Carver, C. S. (1985). The self-consciousness scale: A revised version for use with general populations. *Journal of Applied Social Psychology, 15,* 687–699.

Squartini, F., Bevilacqua, G., Conte, P. F., & Surbone, A. (Eds.). (1993). *Breast cancer: From biology to therapy.* New York: The New York Academy of Sciences.

Stanton, A. L., & Snider, P. R. (1993). Coping with a breast cancer diagnosis: A prospective study. *Health Psychology, 12,* 16–23.

Taylor, S. E., & Dakof, G. A. (1988). Social support and the cancer patient. In S. Spacapan & S. Oskamp (Eds.), *The social psychology of health* (pp. 95–116). Newbury Park, CA: Sage.

Taylor, S. E., Lichtman, R. R., Wood, J. V., Bluming, A. Z., Dosik, G. M., & Lebowitz, R. L. (1985). Illness-related and treatment-related factors in psychological adjustment to breast cancer. *Cancer, 55,* 2506–2513.

Teimourian, B., & Adham, M. (1982). Survey of patients' response to breast reconstruction. *Annals of Plastic Surgery, 9,* 321–325.

Wellisch, D. K., Jamison, K. R., & Pasnau, R. O. (1978). Psychosocial aspects of mastectomy. II. The man's perspective. *American Journal of Psychiatry, 135,* 543–546.

Williamson, G. M., & Schulz, R. (1992). Physical illness and symptoms of depression among elderly outpatients. *Psychology and Aging, 7,* 343–351.

Williamson, G. M., & Schulz, R. (1997). Unpublished data [Home care needs of women with recurrent breast cancer]. University of Georgia.

Wolberg, W. H., Tanner, M. A., Romsaas, E. P., Trump, D. L., & Malec, J. F. (1987). Factors influencing options in primary breast cancer treatment. *Journal of Clinical Oncology, 5,* 68–74.

Yellen, S. B., & Cella, D. F. (1995). Someone to live for: Social well-being, parenthood status, and decision-making in oncology. *Journal of Clinical Oncology, 13,* 1255–1264.

Yellen, S. B., Cella, D. F., & Leslie, W. T. (1994). Age and clinical decision making in oncology patients. *Journal of the National Cancer Institute, 86,* 1766-1770.

6

Frequency Reports of Physical Symptoms and Health Behaviors: How the Questionnaire Determines the Results

Norbert Schwarz
University of Michigan

The frequency with which a patient experiences physical symptoms is of considerable interest in medical research and practice. Moreover, many studies include questions about the frequency of health relevant behaviors, ranging from the number of cigarettes smoked to the weekly hours of exercise or the number of sexual partners. Although these questions may seem straightforward at first glance, answering them poses considerable cognitive demands. In this chapter, I review the cognitive tasks involved in answering behavioral frequency questions and highlight how apparently formal features of the questionnaire may determine respondents' reports. In clinical practice, health care providers are likely to draw on additional information about the patient, thus limiting the practical relevance of questionnaire-induced context effects. In contrast, self-reports in response to standardized questions are the primary source of information in many epidemiological studies, including studies that compare the health status of younger and older adults. To the extent that features of the questionnaire have a differential impact on older and younger respondents, they may lead to inappropriate conclusions about age-related differences in the behaviors studied.

RESPONDENTS' TASKS

As an introduction to the issues raised in the present chapter, you may want to answer the following questions:

1. During the 2-week (reference) period, on the days when you drank liquor, about how many drinks did you have? (Health Interview Survey Supplement; National Center for Health Statistics)
2. Now, I'd like to read you a short list of different kinds of pain. Please say for each one, on roughly how many days—if any—in the last 12 months you have had that type of pain. How many days in the last year have you had (headaches; backaches; stomach pains; joint pains; muscle pains; dental pains)? (Health Interview Survey Supplement; National Center for Health Statistics)
3. How often do you have headaches?
   ( ) twice a month or less
   ( ) once a week
   ( ) twice a week
   ( ) daily
   ( ) several times a day
   ( ) less than once a year

Answering quantitative autobiographical questions of this type involves several tasks. First, respondents need to understand what the question refers to and which behavior they are supposed to report. Second, they have to recall or reconstruct relevant instances of this behavior from memory. Third, if the question specifies a reference period, they must determine if these instances occurred during the reference period. Similarly, if the question refers to their usual behavior, respondents have to determine if the recalled or reconstructed instances are reasonably representative or if they reflect a deviation from their usual behavior. Fourth, as an alternative to recalling or reconstructing instances of the behavior, respondents may rely on their general knowledge, or other salient information that may bear on their task, to infer an answer. Finally, respondents have to provide their report to the researcher. They may need to map their report onto a response scale provided to them, and they may want to edit it for reasons of social desirability (see Strack & Martin, 1987; Sudman, Bradburn, & Schwarz, 1996, chap. 3, for a more detailed discussion).

Next, I address each of these tasks in more detail, paying particular attention to the impact of quantitative response alternatives of the type shown in example 3.

QUESTION COMPREHENSION

The key issue at the question comprehension stage is whether the behavior that the respondent identifies as the referent of the question does or does not match what the researcher had in mind. As a general rule, question comprehension is considerably poorer than most researchers would like to believe, even for apparently simple questions (Belson, 1981). What, for example, are "the last 2 weeks?" If interviewed on a Wednesday, does this refer to the last two calendar weeks or to the 2-week period including today? And what exactly is "a drink" or qualifies as a "headache?" Does the latter, for example, only refer to intense headaches, or does it include the discomfort experienced after long hours of working at a computer? Not surprisingly, respondents' personal history (e.g., a medical history of migraine) as well as the context of the questionnaire may profoundly affect their interpretation of the headache question.

To understand the influence of questionnaire context at the comprehension stage, it is important to realize that it is not enough to understand the literal meaning of the question, that is, the words. Instead, respondents have to determine the pragmatic or intended meaning of the question, that is, what the researcher is interested in. When asked, "What have you done today?" all respondents are likely to understand the words—yet, what are they to report? Should they include that they took a shower or not? Consistent with the tacit assumptions that govern the conduct of conversation in daily life (Grice, 1975), respondents are unlikely to report behaviors that they consider uninteresting or that the researcher may take for granted anyway, unless the questionnaire indicates otherwise. Hence, few respondents would spontaneously report that they took a shower, but many would check this behavior if it were included in a list of daily activities presented to them. Accordingly, questions using an open-response format yield lower reports of mundane behaviors than questions presenting a list that includes these behaviors (see Schwarz & Hippler, 1991, for a review). On the other hand, any behavior omitted from the list is likely not to be reported at all, even when the list offers an "other" alternative with the option to fill in omitted behaviors. Both of these influences reflect that the questionnaire informs respondents about the researcher's interests and that respondents attempt to be cooperative communicators, who provide the information that is of interest to the recipient (Schwarz, 1996).

Although the preceding example may seem rather obvious, the extent to which quantitative response alternatives may serve a similar function is often overlooked. Consider the question: "How often do you feel really irritated?" To answer this question, respondents have to decide what the researcher means by "really irritated." Does this refer to major irritations, such as fights with one's spouse, or does it refer to minor irritations, such as having to wait for service in a restaurant? If respondents have no opportunity to ask for clarification, or if a well-trained interviewer responds, "Whatever you feel is really irritating," they may pick up some pertinent information from the questionnaire. One such piece of information is the frequency range provided by the scale. For example, respondents who are asked to report how often they are irritated on a scale ranging from *several times daily* to *less than once a week* may relate the frequency range of the response alternatives to their general knowledge about the frequency of minor and major annoyances. Assuming that major annoyances are unlikely to occur *several times a day,* they may consider instances of less severe irritation to be the target of the question than may respondents who are presented a scale ranging from *several times a year* to *less than once every 3 months.* Experimental data support this assumption (Schwarz, Strack, Müller, & Chassein, 1988). Respondents who reported their experiences on the former scale subsequently reported less extreme examples of annoying experiences than respondents who were given the latter scale. Accordingly, the same question combined with different frequency scales is likely to assess different experiences.

Reiterating this point, Gaskell, O'Muircheartaigh, and Wright (1995) observed that the range of frequency response alternatives changed the interpretation of the question, "How often are your teeth cleaned?" When this question was presented with a scale ranging from *less often than once a year* to *more than once a month,* respondents assumed that it referred to getting one's teeth cleaned by a dental hygienist. But when presented with a scale ranging from *less often than once a week* to *more than once a day,* they assumed that the question pertained to their own brushing or flossing.

Theoretically, the impact of the response alternatives on respondents' interpretation of the question is the more pronounced the less clearly the target behavior is defined. For this reason, questions about subjective experiences may be particularly sensitive to the impact of response alternatives because researchers usually refrain from providing a detailed definition of the target experience so as not to interfere with its subjective nature. It is ironic that assessing the frequency of a behavior with precoded response alternatives may result in doing just what is avoided in the wording of the question.

At present, data bearing on age-related differences in the impact of response alternatives on question comprehension are not available. In general, however, age-related differences in language comprehension are limited to tasks that present a high working memory load (see Kemper, 1992, for a review). The relatively simple pragmatic inferences addressed here are unlikely to fall into this category. If so, the above effects should be observed in much the same way for older and younger respondents, although this hypothesis deserves empirical testing.

RECALL AND ESTIMATION STRATEGIES

After respondents determined which behavior the researcher is interested in, they need to retrieve relevant information about the behavior under study from memory. Ideally, most researchers would like the respondent to identify the boundaries of the reference period; to retrieve all instances that match the target behavior; to determine if they fall within the reference period; and if so, to count them to determine the overall frequency of the behavior during this period. This, however, is the route that respondents are least likely to take (see the contributions to Schwarz & Sudman, 1994). Moreover, older respondents may find it particularly difficult to complete this sequence of tasks due to general constraints on working memory capacity (cf. Smith, 1996).

In fact, except for rare and very important behaviors, respondents of any age are unlikely to have detailed representations of numerous individual instances of a behavior stored in memory. Instead, the details of numerous instances blend into one global representation of the behavior under study (e.g., Linton, 1982; Neisser, 1986). This renders individual episodes indistinguishable or irretrievable due to interference from other similar instances (Wagenaar, 1986; Baddeley & Hitch, 1977), fostering the generation of knowledge-like representations that "lack specific time or location indicators" (Strube, 1987, p. 89). Accordingly, a "recall-and-count" model does not provide an appropriate description of how people answer quantitative questions about frequent behaviors or experiences. Rather, their answers are likely to be based on some fragmented recall and the application of various inference rules to compute a frequency estimate. Bradburn, Rips, and Shevell (1987), Sudman et al. (1996, chaps. 7–9) and Schwarz (1990) extensively review these strategies, which are beyond the scope of this chapter. Here I focus on a specific strategy that is particularly important for the format in which reports of physical symptoms and health behaviors are typically assessed in health research, namely respondents' reliance on the frequency scale presented to them.

FREQUENCY SCALES AS A FRAME OF REFERENCE: THEIR IMPACT ON BEHAVIORAL REPORTS

Reports of the frequency of physical symptoms are typically assessed by asking respondents to check the appropriate category on a set of numeric response alternatives provided to them. For example, the most widely used German symptoms checklist (Fahrenberg, 1975) offers five response alternatives, ranging from *never* to *nearly daily*. Although the selected alternative is assumed to inform the researcher about the respondent's behavior, it is frequently overlooked that a given set of response alternatives may be far more than a simple measurement device—it may also constitute an important source of information for the respondent. Bringing the assumptions that govern the conduct of conversation in daily life to the research setting (Schwarz, 1996), respondents assume that every contribution to the ongoing conversation is relevant to its aims. A researcher's contributions, however, include the apparently formal features of the questionnaire he or she designed. In the case of frequency scales, this implies that the researcher presumably constructed a meaningful scale, based on his or her knowledge about the distribution of the symptoms or behaviors under study—after all, the researcher is probably an expert on the topic. Hence, respondents assume that the typical or average frequency of the behavior is reflected in the middle range of the scale, whereas the extremes of the scale correspond to the extremes of the distribution.

Given these assumptions, respondents can simplify their task by using the scale as a frame of reference in estimating their own behavioral frequencies. This estimation strategy results in higher frequency reports along scales that present high rather than low frequency alternatives. This influence of frequency scales has been observed in numerous studies pertaining to a diverse range of behaviors, including watching television (Schwarz, Hippler, Deutsch, & Strack, 1985), buying consumer products (Menon, Rhagubir, & Schwarz, 1995), masturbating (Schwarz & Scheuring, 1988), or having sex (Tourangeau & Smith, 1996). Next, I review some health-relevant examples in more detail and subsequently address age-related differences in the impact of response alternatives on frequency estimates.

Physical Symptoms

In a study that addressed the impact of response alternatives on frequency reports of physical symptoms, Schwarz and Scheuring (1992) asked 60 patients of a German psychosomatic clinic to report the frequency of 17 symptoms along one of the scales shown in figure 6.1. Reports along these scales can be compared by assessing the percentage of respondents who report having a given symptom more than twice a month.

The frequency range of the scales had a pronounced influence on patients' reports, which replicated the findings obtained in other domains. Across 17 symptoms, 62% of the respondents reported average frequencies of more than twice a month when presented with the high frequency scale, whereas only 39% did so when presented with the low frequency scale, resulting in a mean difference of 23 percentage points.

This impact of response alternatives was most pronounced for the ill-defined symptom of "responsiveness to changes in the weather," where 75% of the patients reported a frequency of more than twice a month along the high frequency scale, whereas only 21% did so along the low frequency scale. Conversely, the influence of response alternatives was least pronounced for the better defined symptom, "excessive perspiration," with 50% versus 42% along the high and low frequency scales, respectively. As these findings illustrate, a researcher's conclusions about the frequency with which this patient population experiences a wide variety of symptoms would be strongly affected by the nature of the research instrument used.

Low Frequency Scale

( )   *never*
( )   *about once a year*
( )   *about twice a year*
( )   *twice a month*
( )   *more than twice a month*

High Frequency Scale

( )   *twice a month or less*
( )   *once a week*
( )   *twice a week*
( )   *daily*
( )   *several times a day*

FIG. 6.1. Frequency response alternatives for reporting physical symptoms.

Differential Effects on
Older and Younger Respondents

These methodological complications are further compounded by the possibility that response alternatives may have a differential impact on older and younger respondents. Specifically, respondents rely on the response alternatives as a frame of reference when they cannot recall individual episodes. Hence, the impact of response alternatives is attenuated when the behavior is well represented in memory (Menon et al., 1995). If so, we may assume that older respondents are generally more likely to be affected by response alternatives because they find detailed recall tasks more taxing (see Smith, 1996, for a review). On the other hand, older respondents may be more likely than many younger respondents to monitor their health and to pay close attention to physical symptoms (see Deeg, Kardaum, & Fozard, 1996). If so, physical symptoms may be well represented in older respondents' memory, thus attenuating their need to rely on estimation strategies.

The limited data available support these conjectures and suggest that older respondents are more likely to be affected by response alternatives than younger respondents when the question pertains to mundane behaviors, but are less likely to be affected by response alternatives when the question refers to physical symptoms. Specifically, Schwarz, Park, and Knäuper (1998) asked 143 younger respondents (ages 29–40) and 154 older respondents (ages 60–90) to report the frequency of mundane behaviors and health symptoms along low or high frequency scales. The questions pertained to buying birthday presents (*once a year* to *6 times a year or more* vs. *5 times a year or less* to *10 times a year or more*), eating red meat (*once a month or less* to *10 times a month or more* vs. *8 times a month* to *30 times a month or more*), and suffering from headaches or from heartburn (*about once a year* to *about twice a month or more* vs. *once a month or less* to *daily*). Table 6.1 shows the results.

All respondents reported that they eat red meat or buy birthday presents more often when presented with a high rather than low frequency scale. The impact of scale range was significant for both age groups but was more than twice as large for older than for younger respondents. Conversely, younger respondents also reported that they suffer from headaches and heartburn more frequently when presented a high rather than low frequency scale. The reports provided by older respondents, however, were not significantly affected by scale range. These findings are consistent with the general observation that the impact of response alternatives increases as a recall-based strategy becomes more difficult (e.g., Menon et al., 1995; Schwarz & Bienias, 1990). Accordingly, we may expect that older respondents are generally more likely to resort to estimation strategies than younger respondents. It is important to note, however, that they may pay more attention to their physical health, thus reversing the otherwise obtained pattern in this particular domain. This conjecture deserves additional testing.

Finally, the data shown in Table 6.1 have important methodological implications for researchers interested in age differences in the behaviors under study. For

TABLE 6.1

The Impact of Response Alternatives on Behavioral Reports
as a Function of Content and Respondents' Age

| | Frequency Scale | | |
	Low	High	Difference
Mundane behaviors			
Eating red meat			
Young	24%	43%	19%
Old	19%	63%	44%
Buying birthday presents			
Young	42%	49%	7%
Old	46%	61%	15%
Physical symptoms			
Headaches			
Young	37%	56%	19%
Old	11%	10%	1%
Heartburn			
Young	14%	33%	19%
Old	24%	31%	7%

Note. Younger respondents are ages 29–40, older respondents, 60–90. Shown is the percentage of respondents reporting eating red meat more than 10 times a month or more often; buying

example, we would conclude that there are only minor, if any, cohort differences in red meat consumption or the frequency of buying birthday presents when low frequency scales are used. In contrast, we would conclude that the cohort differences in these behaviors are pronounced when high frequency scales are used. In fact, use of the latter scales results in apparent cohort differences of about four times the size obtained on the former scales. Accordingly, the differential impact of response alternatives on the frequency estimates provided by older and younger respondents may result in misleading substantive conclusions.

Recommendations

To avoid systematic influences of response alternatives on behavioral reports, it is advisable to ask frequency questions in an open-response format, such as, "How many times a month do you eat red meat? ___ times a month." Note that such an open format needs to specify the relevant units of measurement, for example, "times a month" to avoid answers like "occasionally."

As another alternative, researchers are often tempted to use vague quantifiers, such as sometimes, frequently, and so on. Given that respondents can rarely provide an exact numeric answer, not much may seem lost by using these terms. Nevertheless, this is the worst possible choice as a large number of studies has demonstrated (see Pepper, 1981, for a review). Most important, the same expression denotes different frequencies in different content domains. Thus, "frequently" suffering from headaches reflects higher absolute frequencies than "frequently" suffering from heart attacks. Moreover, different respondents use the same term to denote different objective frequencies of the same behavior. For example, suffering from headaches "occasionally" denotes a higher frequency for respondents with a medical history of migraine than for respondents without a migraine history. In general, the use of vague quantifiers reflects the objective frequency relative to respondents' subjective standard, rather than the objective frequency per se. To the extent that different age groups hold different subjective standards, this completely undermines the comparability of their reports. Accordingly, vague quantifiers cannot be recommended for the assessment of objective frequencies despite the popularity of their use.

SUBSEQUENT JUDGMENTS

In addition to affecting respondents' frequency reports, the range of the response alternatives has been found to influence subsequent judgments pertaining to these behaviors. The specific form of these influences depends on the nature of the judgment, as a few examples may illustrate.

Comparative Judgments

Many judgments of interest to health researchers are comparative in nature. When asked how satisfied we are with our health, for example, we need to determine relative to what standard we are to make this evaluation, for example, relative to our own health when we were younger or relative to other people our age? In many cases, different standards are potentially applicable and numerous studies have shown that we are likely to use the one that is cognitively most accessible at the time of judgment (see Schwarz & Strack, 1991). One standard that is highly accessible after respondents have provided a frequency report is entailed by the frequency range of the scale. Recall that respondents assume that the scale reflects the researcher's knowledge about the distribution of the behavior. Given this assumption, checking a response alternative that describes one's own behavior on one of the scales is the same as locating one's position in the distribution. For example, a respondent who checks a headache frequency of "twice a month" along one of the scales shown in figure 6.1 may infer that this frequency is above average when presented with the low frequency scale but below average when presented with the high frequency scale. Hence, respondents may extract comparison information from their own location on the frequency scale and may use this information in making subsequent judgments.

Accordingly, the frequency scales used to assess patients' physical symptoms influenced reports of health satisfaction in Schwarz and Scheuring's (1992) study.

As expected, the patients reported higher health satisfaction when they had given their symptom reports along the high frequency scale ($M = 8.3$ on an 11-point scale, with $11 = very\ satisfied$) rather than along the low frequency scale ($M = 7.2$). This reflects that the former scale suggested that their symptom frequency is below average, whereas the latter suggested it is above average. Note that these reports of higher (lower) health satisfaction were obtained despite the fact that the same respondents had just reported higher (lower) absolute symptom frequencies along the respective scales. This reflects that judgments of health satisfaction are comparative in nature and that respondents extracted comparison information about others' symptoms from the scale.

NONCOMPARATIVE JUDGMENTS

Note, however, that not all evaluative questions require a comparison with others. For example, respondents may be asked how much their symptoms affect them in daily life. In this case, they may be likely to turn to the perceived absolute frequency of their symptoms. If so, they should report that their symptoms affect them more when the high frequency scale led them to estimate a high frequency, than when the low frequency scale led them to estimate a low frequency. To address this possibility, 34 other patients were asked to report their symptom frequencies along the same scales used by Schwarz and Scheuring (1992; see fig. 6.1), but had to evaluate how much their symptoms affected them in daily life ($1 = not\ at\ all$; $11 = very\ much$; Schwarz, 1992). As expected, respondents who had reported their symptoms along the high frequency scale now reported that their symptoms affect them more ($M = 9.3$) than respondents who had reported their symptoms on the low scale ($M = 6.7$).

In combination, these findings illustrate that the response alternatives influence subsequent absolute and comparative judgments in opposite directions. When asked how satisfied they are with their health, respondents drew on their relative placement on the scale and reported higher health satisfaction when the high frequency scale suggested that their symptoms are below average in frequency. But, when asked how much their symptoms affect them in daily life, respondents drew on the absolute frequency of their symptoms and reported higher distress when the same scale evoked a higher estimate of symptom frequency. Hence, the same behavioral frequency scale may elicit subsequent reports of higher distress as well as of higher health satisfaction, in contrast to what common sense would suggest. Needless to say, a researcher may again draw rather different conclusions about these patients, depending on the frequency scale used and the type of subsequent judgment assessed.

Physicians' Judgments

Finally, the frame of reference provided by frequency scales may also influence the users of respondents' reports. To explore this possibility, Schwarz, Bless, Bohner, Harlacher, and Kellenbenz (1991, Experiment 2) asked first-year students of medicine and practicing physicians (with an average professional experience of 8.5 years) to participate in a study allegedly designed to "test if a standard health survey could be shortened without a decrease in usefulness and reliability." As part of this study, subjects were presented with vignettes that described a patient who had allegedly reported his or her symptoms along one of the scales shown in figure 6.2.

For example, in one vignette, "Mr. Z., 25 years old" checked that he suffered twice a week from "aching loins or back," and in another vignette, "Mrs. K., 41 years old" checked that she suffered from a "lack of energy," also twice a week. Note that "twice a week" constitutes a high response on the low frequency scale, but a low response on the high frequency scale. Subjects were asked to rate the severity of the reported symptom (0 = *not at all severe* to 10 = *very severe*) and the necessity to consult a doctor (0 = *not at all necessary to consult a doctor* to 10 = *absolutely necessary to consult a doctor*). Table 6.2 shows the results.

Low Frequency Scale

( )	( )	( )	( )	(X)	( )
less than once a month	about once a month	about once in 2 weeks	about once a week	about twice a week	more often

High Frequency Scale

( )	(X)	( )	( )	( )	( )
less than twice a week	about twice a week	about four times a week	about six times a week	about once every 24 hours	more often

FIG. 6.2. Response alternatives used in medical judgment study.

TABLE 6.2
Mean Severity and Consultation Necessity Ratings
as a Function of Scale Range and Expertise

	Expertise			
	Doctors		Students	
	Frequency Range of Scale			
	high	low	high	low
Severity of symptoms				
Aching loins or back	3.09	4.72	4.94	5.95
Lack of energy	2.30	4.13	2.92	5.35
Necessity to Consult Doctor				
Aching loins or back	4.48	6.25	6.00	7.07
Lack of energy	3.42	4.62	3.06	5.15

Note. Range of values is 0 to 10; higher values indicate higher severity and higher necessity to consult a doctor.

As expected, suffering from a given symptom "twice a week" was rated as more severe and as more likely to require consultation when "twice a week" represented a high rather than a low frequency response on the respective scale. Moreover, the impact of scale range was independent of subjects' expertise and was obtained for experienced practitioners as well as first-year medical students. In fact, the only expertise effect that emerged reflected that first-year medical students were more likely to consider all symptoms as severe and to recommend consultation under most conditions.

REPORTING THE ANSWER

After having determined an estimate of the frequency of the target behavior, respondents have to report their estimate to the researcher. The communicated estimate may deviate from their private estimate due to considerations of social desirability and self-presentation (see DeMaio, 1984, for a review). Survey researchers have developed a number of techniques to reduce this editing of the communicated response. Most of these techniques emphasize the respondent's anonymity and the confidentiality of the collected data (see Sudman & Bradburn, 1983, for a review and good practical advice).

In the context of the preceding discussion of frequency scales, one may wonder if these scales contribute to response editing: Do respondents hesitate to endorse a frequency that seems "deviant" in the context of the scale? This possibility has been suggested by Bradburn and Danis (1984) in a discussion of higher reports of alcohol consumption in an open-response than in a closed response format. In contrast to this self-presentation hypothesis, I suggested that such differences reflect that respondents rely on the frequency range of the scale to arrive at an estimate. The empirical evidence supports the latter hypothesis.

One way to differentiate between these two proposed mechanisms is to compare the impact of response alternatives on reports of one's own behavior (self-reports) and on reports about the behavior of other persons (proxy reports). In general, the two process assumptions lead to opposite predictions for both types of reports. If the impact of response alternatives is mediated by self-presentation concerns, scale effects should be stronger when respondents report their own behavior than when they report the behavior of friends or distant acquaintances. This follows from the assumption that they presumably are concerned more about their own self-presentation than about the image they present of others. If respondents use the values presented in the scale to compute an estimate, on the other hand, the impact of scale range should be more pronounced the less other information is available to compute an answer. Therefore, the effect of scale range should be smaller when respondents report their own behavior than when they report the behavior of friends or distant acquaintances, because they can draw upon a broader base of information that allows the reconstruction of relevant episodes for self-reports.

To address these issues, Schwarz and Bienias (1990, Experiment 1), asked undergraduates in the United States to report either their own weekly television consumption, the weekly television consumption of a close friend, or the weekly television consumption of a "typical undergraduate" of their university on a scale ranging from *up to 2½ hours per week* to *more than 10 hours,* or on a scale ranging from *up to 10 hours* to *more than 25 hours.* As predicted by the frame of reference hypothesis, the impact of scale range was most pronounced when respondents estimated the television consumption of a "typical undergraduate." Specifically, 71% provided estimates of more than 10 hours per week on the high frequency response scale, but only 13% did so on the low frequency scale, resulting in a difference of 58 percentage points. The impact of scale range was least pronounced, on the other hand, when respondents reported their own TV consumption, with a difference of 32 percentage points. This pattern of results is opposite to the one predicted by the self-presentation hypothesis, which holds that self-reports should be most strongly affected. Reports about the behavior of close friends fell in between these extremes, as both hypotheses would predict, with a difference of 37 percentage points.

These findings suggest that respondents use the range of the response alternatives as a frame of reference in estimating behavioral frequencies and that they are the more likely to rely on this frame the less other information they have. Nevertheless, it is conceivable that self-presentation concerns elicited by highly threatening questions may be compounded if the respondent discovers that his or her report requires the endorsement of a response alternative that seems extreme in the context of the scale. If so, response alternatives may also affect behavioral reports at the editing stage of the response sequence, although strong empirical evidence for this possibility has yet to be provided.

CONCLUSIONS

The reviewed findings illustrate how apparently irrelevant variations in question format may strongly affect the obtained results, introducing systematic bias. In contrast to researchers' expectations, frequency reports of mundane behaviors or physical symptoms are rarely based on recollections of specific episodes but are generated on the basis of estimation strategies. Given that frequent episodes of the same behavior blend into a generic representation that lacks time and space markers (see Bradburn et al., 1987; Schwarz, 1990; Sudman, Bradburn, & Schwarz, 1996, for reviews), respondents are unable to recall relevant episodes and count their number, in contrast to what the researcher would want them to do. Hence, they try to come up with a reasonable estimate, and they rely on information that seems highly relevant to their task, namely the response scale provided by the researcher. Assuming that the researcher is an expert on the issue under investigation, respondents believe that the scale reflects expert knowledge about the distribution of the behavior. When this assumption is called into question, the impact of scale range is attenuated (Schwarz, 1996). Unless informed otherwise, however, respondents have little reason to assume that the researcher constructed a haphazard scale and are therefore extracting relevant information that serves as input into frequency estimates and comparative judgments. These observations have important methodological implications for the assessment of self-reports (see Schwarz, 1990; Schwarz & Hippler, 1987, for more detailed discussions).

First, the numeric response alternatives presented as part of a frequency question may influence respondents' interpretation of what the question refers to. Hence, the same question stem in combination with different frequency alternatives may result in the assessment of somewhat different behaviors. This is more likely the less well defined the behavior is.

Second, respondents' use of the frequency scale as a frame of reference influences the obtained behavioral reports. Aside from calling the interpretation of the absolute values into question, this also implies that reports of the same behavior along different scales are not comparable, often rendering comparisons between different studies difficult.

Third, the impact of response alternatives is more pronounced the less respondents can recall relevant episodes from memory. This implies that reports of behaviors that are poorly represented in memory are more affected than reports of behaviors that are well represented. When behaviors of differential memorability are assessed, this may either exaggerate or reduce any actual differences in the frequency of the behaviors.

Fourth, for the same reason, respondents with poorer memory are more likely to be influenced by response alternatives than respondents with better memory. Accordingly, the impact of response alternatives is likely to be more pronounced for older than for younger respondents, as seen earlier. However, the observed age-related differences depended on the specific behavior under study, presumably reflecting differences in how well the specific behavior was represented in memory. Note that any differential impact of response alternatives on the reports provided by different groups of respondents can result in misleading conclusions about actual differences in the behavior under study.

Fifth, respondents may use their own behavioral frequency estimate as input into subsequent judgments. Hence, they may arrive at different conclusions when the scale elicited a high rather than low frequency estimate.

Finally, the range of response alternatives may further influence subsequent judgments by providing a salient standard of comparison, relative to which respondents assess their own situation. Such comparison effects have even been observed under conditions where respondents' own behavior was sufficiently well represented in memory to render the behavioral report immune to response scale effects (e.g., Menon et al., 1995). Accordingly, respondents' may arrive at evaluative judgments that are highly context dependent and may not reflect the assessments they would be likely to make in daily life.

To avoid these biases, researchers are well advised to ask behavioral frequency questions in an open-response format. In doing so, however, it is important to structure the question in a way that elicits numeric responses rather than vague verbal answers, as discussed earlier. Yet, the most important lesson that emerges from this research is more general in nature (Schwarz, 1995, 1996): As researchers, we tend to view our questionnaires as "measurement devices" that elicit information from respondents. What we frequently overlook is that our questionnaires are also a source of information that respondents draw on in order to determine their task and to arrive at a useful and informative answer. Far from reflecting artifacts or shallow responding, findings of the type reviewed here indicate that respondents do their best to be cooperative communicators. Consistent with the assumptions that underlie the conduct of conversation in daily life, they assume that all contributions of the researcher are relevant to the goals of the ongoing exchange, and they take these contributions into account in arriving at an answer. These contributions include formal features of questionnaire designs and we need to be sensitive to what respondents learn from our questionnaires if we want to avoid surprises of the type reviewed in this chapter.

REFERENCES

Baddeley, A. D., & Hitch, G. J. (1977). Recency reexamined. In S. Dornic (Ed.), *Attention and performance* (Vol. 6, pp. 647–667). Hillsdale, NJ: Lawrence Erlbaum Associates.

Belson, W. A. (1981). *The design and understanding of survey questions.* Aldershot: Gower.

Bradburn, N., & Danis, C. (1984). Potential contributions of cognitive research to survey questionnaire design. In T. B. Jabine, M. L. Straf, J. M. Tanur & R. Tourangeau (Eds.), *Cognitive aspects of survey methodology: Building a bridge between disciplines* (pp. 101–129). Washington, DC: National Academy Press.

Bradburn, N. M., Rips, L. J., & Shevell, S. K. (1987). Answering autobiographical questions: The impact of memory and inference on surveys. *Science, 236,* 157–161.

Deeg, D. J. H., Kardaum, J. W. P. F., & Fozard, J. L. (1996). Health, behavior, and aging. In J. E. Birren & K. W. Schaie (Eds.), *The handbook of the psychology of aging* (pp. 129–149). San Diego, CA: Academic Press.

DeMaio, T. J. (1984). Social desirability and survey measurement: A review. In C. F. Turner & E. Martin (Eds.), *Surveying subjective phenomena* (Vol. 2, pp. 257–281). New York: Russell Sage.

Fahrenberg, J. (1975). Die Freiburger Beschwerdenliste FBL. *Zeitschrift für Klinische Psychologie, 4,* 79–100.

Gaskell, G. D., O'Muircheartaigh, C. A., & Wright, D. B. (1995). *How response alternatives affect different kinds of behavioural frequency questions.* Unpublished manuscript, London School of Economics.

Grice, H. P. (1975). Logic and conversation. In P. Cole & J. L. Morgan (Eds.), *Syntax and semantics: Vol. 3. Speech acts* (pp. 41–58). New York: Academic Press.

Kemper, S. (1992). Language and aging. In F. I. M. Craik & T. A. Salthouse (Eds.), *The handbook of aging and cognition* (pp. 213–270). Hillsdale, NJ: Lawrence Erlbaum Associates.

Linton, M. (1982). Transformations of memory in everyday life. In U. Neisser (Ed.), *Memory observed: Remembering in natural contexts* (pp. 77–91). San Francisco: Freeman.

Menon, G., Raghubir, P., & Schwarz, N. (1995). Behavioral frequency judgments: An accessibility-diagnosticity framework. *Journal of Consumer Research, 22,* 212–228.

Neisser, U. (1986). Nested structure in autobiographical memory. In D. C. Rubin (Ed.) *Autobiographical memory* (pp. 71–88). Cambridge, England: Cambridge University Press.

Pepper, S. C. (1981). Problems in the quantification of frequency expressions. In D. W. Fiske (Ed.), *Problems with language imprecision* (New directions for methodology of social and behavioral science, Vol. 9, pp. 25–41). San Francisco: Jossey-Bass.

Schwarz, N. (1990). Assessing frequency reports of mundane behaviors: Contributions of cognitive psychology to questionnaire construction. In C. Hendrick & M. S. Clark (Eds.), *Review of Personality and Social Psychology: Vol. 11. Research methods in personality and social psychology* (pp. 98–119). Beverly Hills, CA: Sage.

Schwarz, N. (1992). [Frequency scales and noncomparative judgments.] Unpublished raw data.

Schwarz, N. (1995). What respondents learn from questionnaires: The survey interview and the logic of conversation. *International Statistical Review, 63,* 153–177.

Schwarz, N. (1996). *Cognition and communication: Judgmental biases, research methods, and the logic of conversation.* Mahwah, NJ: Lawrence Erlbaum Associates.

Schwarz, N., & Bienias, J. (1990). What mediates the impact of response alternatives on frequency reports of mundane behaviors? *Applied Cognitive Psychology, 4,* 61–72.

Schwarz, N., Bless, H., Bohner, G., Harlacher, U., & Kellenbenz, M. (1991). Response scales as frames of reference: The impact of frequency range on diagnostic judgment. *Applied Cognitive Psychology, 5,* 37–50.

Schwarz, N., & Hippler, H. J. (1987). What response scales may tell your respondents: Informative functions of response alternatives. In H. J. Hippler, N. Schwarz, & S. Sudman (Eds.), *Social information processing and survey methodology* (pp. 163–178). New York: Springer-Verlag.

Schwarz, N., & Hippler, H. J. (1991). Response alternatives: The impact of their choice and ordering. In P. Biemer, R. Groves, N. Mathiowetz, & S. Sudman (Eds.), *Measurement error in surveys* (pp. 41–56). Chichester, England: Wiley.

Schwarz, N., Hippler, H. J., Deutsch, B., & Strack, F. (1985). Response categories: Effects on behavioral reports and comparative judgments. *Public Opinion Quarterly, 49,* 388–395.

Schwarz, N., Park, D. C., & Knäuper, B. (1988). [Frequency scales and symptiom reports.] Unpublished raw data.

Schwarz, N., & Scheuring, B. (1992). Selbstberichtete Verhaltens-und Symptomhäufigkeiten: Was Befragte aus Anwortvorgaben des Fragebogens lernen [Frequency-reports of psychosomatic symptoms: What respondents learn from response alternatives]. *Zeitschrift für Klinische Psychologie, 22,* 197–208.

Schwarz, N., & Strack, F. (1991). Evaluating one's life: A judgment model of subjective well-being. In F. Strack, M. Argyle, & N. Schwarz (Eds.), *Subjective well-being* (pp. 27–47). London: Pergamon.

Schwarz, N., Strack, F., Müller, G., & Chassein, B. (1988). The range of response alternatives may determine the meaning of the question: Further evidence on informative functions of response alternatives. *Social Cognition, 6,* 107–117.

Schwarz, N., & Sudman, S. (1994). *Autobiographical memory and the validity of retrospective reports.* New York: Springer-Verlag.

Smith, A. D. (1996). Memory. In J. E. Birren & K. W. Schaie (Eds.), *The handbook of the psychology of aging* (pp. 236–250). San Diego, CA: Academic Press.

Strack, F., & Martin, L. (1987). Thinking, judging, and communicating: A process account of context effects in attitude surveys. In H. J. Hippler, N. Schwarz, & S. Sudman (Eds.), *Social information processing and survey methodology* (pp. 123–148). New York: Springer-Verlag.

Strube, G. (1987). Answering survey questions: The role of memory. In H. J. Hippler, N. Schwarz, & S. Sudman (Eds.), *Social information processing and survey methodology* (pp. 86–101). New York: Springer-Verlag.

Sudman, S., & Bradburn, N. M. (1983). *Asking questions.* San Francisco: Jossey-Bass.

Sudman, S., Bradburn, N., & Schwarz, N. (1996). *Thinking about answers: The Application of cognitive processes to survey methodology.* San Francisco: Jossey-Bass.

Tourangeau, R., & Smith, T. W. (1996). Asking sensitive questions: The impact of data collection, mode, question format, and question context. *Public Opinion Quarterly, 60,* 275–304.

Wagenaar, W. A. (1986). My memory: A study of autobiographical memory over six years. *Cognitive Psychology, 18,* 225–252.

7

Neurocognitive Changes
Associated With Loss of
Capacity to Consent to
Medical Treatment in Patients
With Alzheimer's Disease

Daniel Marson
Lindy Harrell
University of Alabama at Birmingham

The capacity to make medical treatment decisions (hereafter *consent capacity* or *competency*) is a fundamental aspect of personal autonomy. Consent capacity refers to a patient's cognitive and emotional capacity to accept a proposed treatment, to refuse treatment, or to select among treatment alternatives (Grisso, 1986; Tepper & Elwork, 1984). Consent capacity is the cornerstone of the medical-legal doctrine of informed consent, which requires that a valid consent to treatment be informed, voluntary, and *competent* (Kapp, 1992; Marson, Ingram, Cody, & Harrell, 1995; Marson, Schmitt, Ingram, & Harrell, 1994). From a functional standpoint, consent capacity may be viewed as an "advanced activity of daily life" (ADL; Wolinsky & Johnson, 1991) and an important aspect of functional health and independent living skills in older adults (see Park, 1992; Willis, 1996).

The capacity to make decisions about the care of one's body and mind is an important issue for the field of cognitive aging. First, consent capacity involves a complex set of comprehension, encoding, information-processing and decision-making abilities, which ultimately must have an explicit neurological basis (Alexander, 1988; Marson, Chatterjee, Ingram, & Harrell, 1996). Many of these abilities have been shown to undergo age-related changes and declines. Normative declines in abstract reasoning, information-processing speed, and effortful memory help explain the diminished performance of older adults on many cognitively complex tasks of daily life (Diehl, Willis, and Schaie, 1995; Schaie, 1996), including medication compliance (Park, 1992). Second, older adults are a group subject to heightened incidence and prevalence of medical illnesses and are therefore compelled to make a disproportionately high number of personal medical decisions relative to other age groups. Third, older adults are also disproportionately vulnerable to disorders of higher cortical function, which can compromise medical and other kinds of decision making (Grisso, 1986). Accordingly, study of the cognitive changes associated with declining consent capacity can yield important information about loss of functional health and independence in older adults.

Since the late 1970s, consent capacity has emerged as a distinct field of legal, clinical, and cognitive research (Kapp & Mossman, 1996; Marson & Ingram, 1996). Much work has focused on the development of standardized competency assessment instruments for specific clinical populations (Edelstein, Nygren, Northrop, Staats, & Pool, 1993; *Geropsychology Assessment Resource Guide,* 1993; Grisso & Appelbaum, 1991; Janofsky, McCarthy, & Folstein, 1992; Pruchno, Smyer, Rose, Hartman-Stein, & Henderson-Laribee, 1995; Wang, Ennis, & Copland, 1987; Willis, 1996). However, relatively little is yet known about the cognitive changes in normal and abnormal aging that may affect consent capacity. Our research group has used both psychometric assessment instruments and physician judgments to investigate cognitive changes associated with declining consent capacity in patients with Alzheimer's disease (AD; Marson, Cody, Ingram, & Harrell, 1995; Marson et al. 1996; Marson, Hawkins, McInturff, & Harrell, 1997). AD patients represent a useful patient population for studying pathological cognitive changes that mediate loss of consent capacity. AD is the most prevalent form of neurodegenerative disease among older adults, and its pattern of neurocognitive change has been staged and well-characterized (Butters, Salmon & Butters, 1994; Cummings & Benson, 1992). In addition, loss of consent capacity is an inevitable consequence of AD and can occur fairly early in the disease course (Marson, Ingram, Cody, & Harrell, 1995). Thus AD affords a relatively clear and often dramatic view of the relationship between abnormal cognition and loss of consent capacity.

In this chapter, we address the neurocognitive changes in AD that are associated with declining consent capacity. We begin by briefly outlining a cognitive neuropsychological model for understanding loss of consent capacity in AD. We then review prior cognitive studies of consent capacity in AD that have used a psychometric criterion for competency. These studies suggest that multiple cognitive functions are associated with the declining medical decision making of AD patients, including conceptualization, semantic memory, simple executive function, and verbal recall. These neurocognitive findings are discussed and related to the conceptual model. We then focus on research that has identified cognitive predictors of consent capacity of AD patients as judged by experienced physicians. The use of a physician criterion of competency has clinical relevance because physician judgments are the existing clinical standard for determining consent capacity. Based on analysis of individual physician judgments, we identify two general types of neurocognitive predictors of consent capacity in AD: (a) verbal recall and (b) executive function/judgment. These findings are also discussed and related to the conceptual model and to our prior psychometric work. Finally, limitations of this research and directions for further study are presented.

CONCEPTUAL MODEL FOR LOSS OF CONSENT CAPACITY IN AD

Our work in the area of consent capacity has led to the development of a conceptual model for loss of consent capacity in AD. This model incorporates two theoretical components: (a) a cognitive neuropsychological conceptual framework and (b) neurocognitive change in AD.

Cognitive Neuropsychological Conceptual Framework

Consent capacity may be conceptualized as consisting of three core cognitive tasks: comprehension and encoding of treatment information; information processing and making a treatment decision; and communication of the treatment decision (Alexander, 1988). These core cognitive tasks occur in a specific context: a patient's dialogue with a physician or other health care professional about a medical condition and potential treatments (Marson, Ingram, et al., 1995). The comprehension/encoding task involves oral and written comprehension and subsequent encoding of novel and often complex medical information verbally presented to the patient by the treating physician. The information-processing/decision-making task involves the patient processing (at different levels depending on the complexity of the information and treatment options) the consent and other information presented, integrating this information with established declarative and episodic knowledge (including values and risk preferences), and arriving at a treatment decision. The decision communication task involves the patient communicating his or her treatment decision to the physician in some understandable form (e.g., oral, written and/or gestural expression of consent/nonconsent).

We believe that this tripartite model is a potentially valuable theoretical basis for understanding the cognitive structure of consent capacity decisions. It can also be used as a theoretical basis for identifying potential neuropsychological predictors that may be associated with declining consent capacity in normal and demented older adults. For example, measures of memory are relevant to consent capacity because impaired learning and recall will limit the amount of encoded information available for further processing. Similarly, receptive language measures will be relevant to capacity to consent because of their sensitivity to reduced comprehension of treatment-related information. Conceptualization and executive function measures are important to consent capacity because of their relevance to organized information processing and effective reasoning. Measures of judgment and expressive language (e.g., semantic memory), in turn, may be important because of their relevance to making a decision and to communicating it effectively in the patient–physician dialogue. In this regard, it should be noted that consent capacity is a highly verbally mediated competency (the only pragmatic arguably is the signature on the form) and thus verbal measures are likely to load highly on it.

Neurocognitive Change in AD

The second component of our model concerns the dynamic of neurocognitive change in AD. AD causes a dementia syndrome associated with neurodegeneration of primarily cortical regions, beginning in hippocampus and temporal lobe structures and eventually involving anterior and posterior association cortices of both hemispheres (Butters et al., 1994). Although the progression of AD may differ across individual patients, from a neurocognitive standpoint the clinical course of AD can be usefully divided into three general stages (Cummings & Benson, 1992). In the mild stage, patients demonstrate prominent deficits in short-term and delayed memory for verbal and visual material, temporal orientation, semantic knowledge as reflected on fluency tasks, and abstract reasoning and problem solving (Butters et al. 1994; LaFleche & Albert, 1995; Monsch et al. 1992; Moss & Albert, 1988; Smith, Murdoch, & Chenery, 1989; Welsh, Butters, Hughes, Mohs, & Heyman, 1991). Mild anomic speech and difficulties with complex visuospatial construction may be present (Cummings & Benson, 1992). Attentional capacities are usually intact (Moss & Albert, 1988, 1992). Behavioral changes include apathy, depression, anxiety, and paranoia (Moss & Albert, 1992). In the moderate stage, patients demonstrate severe anterograde and increasing retrograde amnesia (Butters et al., 1994; Welsh et al., 1991), severely impaired semantic memory and executive capacities, and significant attentional loss (Moss & Albert, 1992; Berg et al., 1984). A fluent, anomic expressive aphasia and increasing receptive aphasia are present (Hodges, Salmon, & Butters, 1991). Spatial disorientation becomes common, and apraxias involving dressing and other daily activities emerge (Cummings & Benson, 1992). Behavioral disturbances such as delusions and wandering increase (Moss & Albert, 1992). In the severe stage, there is severe expressive and receptive aphasia with dysarthria, echolalia, and mutism. All intellectual functions are severely deteriorated (Cummings & Benson, 1992).

Integrating the Two Components

By integrating the cognitive neuropsychological model with neurocognitive change in AD, a conceptual framework emerges for understanding loss of different consent abilities across dementia stages in AD. First, the ability to comprehend and encode new information will be partially preserved in mild AD. However, characteristic deficits in higher order semantic knowledge and verbal learning/recall will adversely affect comprehension and particularly the encoding of complex verbal information concerning the medical problem and symptoms and treatment options with their respective risks and benefits. Mild AD patients will also retain the partial ability to process available information and will be able to arrive at a treatment decision. However, deficits in conceptualization and executive function will adversely affect the ability of mild AD patients to conceptually organize available consent information and to process it rationally in relation to existing knowledge stores (including personal values). Mild AD patients will retain the ability to communicate their treatment decision and supporting reasoning to the treating physician, as significant expressive aphasia is not characteristic of mild AD.

In moderate AD patients, in contrast, there will be more severe and global impairment of all three core consent abilities. Severe deficits in semantic knowledge, profound deficits in verbal learning and recall, and increasing receptive aphasia and attentional loss will severely compromise the ability to comprehend and encode treatment information. Severe deficits in conceptualization and executive function will preclude most rational processing of this information. A treatment decision may still be reached, but it will based on personalized or anecdotal knowledge independent of the factual treatment situation (Marson, 1996). The capacity to communicate the treatment choice itself may still be present, but increasing expressive aphasia (dysnomia, paraphasic errors, tangentiality, and circumlocution) will compromise explanation or elaboration of the treatment choice.

COGNITIVE PREDICTORS OF CONSENT CAPACITY IN AD PATIENTS USING A PSYCHOMETRIC CRITERION

In prior work, our research group used a competency assessment instrument and neuropsychological test measures to identify cognitive predictors of declining consent capacity in AD patients. Specifically, we developed an instrument consisting of two specialized clinical vignettes (vignette A-neoplasm and vignette B-cardiac) designed to test the capacity of AD patients to consent to treatment under five legal standards (Capacity to Consent to Treatment Instrument, CCTI; Marson, Ingram, 1995). Each vignette presents a hypothetical medical problem and symptoms and two treatment alternatives with associated risks and benefits. After simultaneously reading and listening to an oral presentation of a vignette, subjects answer questions designed to test consent capacity under five well-established (Appelbaum & Grisso, 1988; Roth, Meisel, & Lidz, 1977) and increasingly stringent legal thresholds or standards (LSs). These five LSs are:

LS1: the capacity simply to "evidence" a treatment choice.
LS2: the capacity to make the "reasonable" treatment choice (Vignette A only).
LS3: the capacity to "appreciate" the consequences of a treatment choice.
LS4: the capacity to provide "rational reasons" for a treatment choice.
LS5: the capacity to "understand" the treatment situation and treatment choices.

The CCTI has been used to assess consent capacity in a sample of older controls ($n = 15$) and AD patients ($n = 29$). Using Mini-Mental State Examination (MMSE) scores (Folstein, Folstein, & McHugh, 1975), AD subjects were divided into groups of mild dementia (MMSE ≥ 20; $n = 15$) and moderate dementia (MMSE ≥ 10 and < 20; $n = 14$). Performance on the five LSs was compared across groups. As shown in Table 7.1, the CCTI discriminated the performance of the normal control, mild AD, and moderate AD subgroups on three of the five LSs. Although the three groups performed equivalently on minimal standards requiring merely a treatment choice (LS1) or the reasonable treatment choice (LS2), mild AD patients had difficulty with more difficult standards requiring rational reasons (LS4) and understanding treatment information (LS5). Moderate AD patients had difficulty with appreciation of consequences (LS3), rational reasons (LS4), and understanding treatment (LS5; Marson, Ingram, et al., 1995).

Capacity status of AD patients on the LSs was classified (competent, marginally competent, incompetent) using psychometric cut off scores referenced to control group performance on each LS. Assignment of capacity status resulted in a consistent pattern of compromise (marginal competency and incompetency) among AD patients, which related both to dementia stage and stringency of LS. Mild AD patients demonstrated significant competency compromise on the two most stringent LSs (LS4, 53% and LS5, 100%). The results raised the concern that, depending on circumstances and the standard to be applied, many mild AD patients may lack consent capacity (Marson, Ingram, et al., 1995).

Instruments like the CCTI represent an important first step toward standardized evaluation of consent capacity in dementia patients. They also provide a psychometric criterion for investigating the neurocognitive basis of consent capacity in AD. We have used the CCTI and the above sample of controls and AD patients to identify cognitive predictors of declining consent capacity under four LSs (Marson, Cody, et al., 1995; Marson et al., 1996). We used stepwise multivariate regression analyses to identify key multivariate predictors of control and AD

TABLE 7.1
Performance on CCTI Legal Standards by Diagnostic Group

	N	LS1 0–4	LS2[*] 0–1	LS3 0–10	LS4 0–12	LS5 0–70
Older controls	15	4.0 (0.0)	.93	8.7[a] (1.2)	10.3[b,c] (3.8)	58.3[b] (6.6)
Mild AD	15	3.9 (0.4)	1.00	7.1 (2.0)	6.1[d] (3.4)	27.3[d] (9.6)
Moderate AD	14	3.6 (0.9)	.79	5.9 (2.7)	2.3 (2.4)	17.9 (10.6)

Note. From "Assessing the Competency of Alzheimer's Disease Patients Under Different Legal Standards," by D. Marson, K. Ingram, H. Cody, and L. Harrell, 1995, *Archives of Neurology, 52,* p. 952. Copyright 1995, American Medical Association. Adapted with permission.

[*]No group differences emerged on LS2 ($c^2 = 4.2, p = .12$)

[a]Normal mean differs significantly from moderate AD mean ($p < .001$). [b]$p < .0001$. [c]Normal mean differs significantly from mild AD mean ($p < .01$). [d]Mild AD mean differs significantly from moderate AD mean ($p < .01$).

subject performance on the LSs and parametric and nonparametric discriminant function analyses (DFA) to identify predictors classifying the competency status of the full sample under the four LSs. Table 7.2 presents stepwise multiple regression results for the AD group for these LSs.

Findings from these psychometric studies suggest that multiple cognitive functions are associated with loss of consent capacity under the CCTI LSs. Deficits in conceptualization, semantic memory, and probably verbal recall appear to be associated with the significantly impaired capacity of both mild and moderate AD patients to understand a treatment situation and choices (LS5). Deficits in executive dysfunction (word fluency) appear linked to the impaired capacity of both mild and moderate AD patients to provide rational reasons for a treatment choice (LS4) and to the impaired capacity of moderate AD patients to identify the consequences of a treatment choice (LS3). Finally, receptive aphasia and semantic memory loss (severe dysnomia) may be associated with the impaired ability of advanced AD patients to evidence a simple treatment choice (LS1). The results offer insight into the relationship between different legal thresholds of competency and the progressive cognitive changes characteristic of AD and represent an initial step toward a neurologic model of competency (Marson, Cody, et al., 1995; Marson et al., 1996).

The psychometric findings can be related to the conceptual model of consent capacity in AD presented earlier. First, it appears that consent abilities predicated on encoding and higher order processing of treatment information show the earliest decline in AD. Both mild and moderate AD patients showed severe impairment on LS5, the standard requiring factual understanding of the treatment situation and choices. Our findings suggest that cognitive deficits in conceptualization, semantic

TABLE 7.2
Stepwise Regression Predictors[*] of LS1, LS3, LS4,
and LS5 Performance for AD Group ($n = 29$)

Standard	Test[a]	R^2	p
LS1: Evidencing Choice	SAC	.44	.0001
LS3: Appreciating Consequences	CFL	.58	.0001
LS4: Rational Reasons	DRS IP	.36	.0008
LS5: Understanding Treatment	DRS CON	.70	.0001
	BNT	.11	.001

Note. From "Neuropsychological Predictors of Competency in Alzheimer's Disease Using a Rational Reasons Legal Standard" by D. Marson, H. Cody, K. Ingram, and L. Harrell, 1995, *Archives of Neurology, 52,* p. 952; copyright © 1995, American Medical Association; adapted with permission; and from "Toward a Neurologic Model of Competency: Cognitive Predictors of Capacity to Consent to Treatment in Alzheimer's Disease Using Three Legal Standards," by D. Marson, A. Chatterjee, K. Ingram, & L. Harrell, 1996, *Neurology, 46,* p. 669; copyright © 1996, American Academy of Neurology; reprinted by permission.

[*]No measures achieved univariate or multivariate significance for control group.

[a]Abbreviations: BNT, Boston Naming Test; CFL, Controlled Oral Word Fluency; DRS CON, Dementia Rating Scale Conceptualization; DRS IP, Dementia Rating Scale Initiation/Perseveration; SAC, Simple Auditory Comprehension Screen.

memory, and also verbal recall[1] may account for this global impairment of LS5 by limiting the amount of information encoded and by disrupting the organized processing of that information. Second, it appears that simple executive functions (word fluency, Trails A) may mediate organized processing of treatment information (i.e., reasoning), leading to impaired abilities of mild and moderate AD patients to provide rational reasons for a treatment choice (LS4) and to the impaired ability of moderate AD patients to identify consequences of a treatment choice (LS3). Finally, our findings suggest that simple aspects of the communication element of consent capacity are preserved in mild and moderate AD patients. Specifically, most mild and moderate AD patients retain the general ability to evidence a treatment choice (i.e., choose medication or surgery; LS1). Receptive aphasia and semantic memory loss appear to mediate this consent ability and account for the inability of some moderate AD patients to express a treatment choice.

COGNITIVE PREDICTORS OF PHYSICIAN JUDGMENTS OF CONSENT CAPACITY IN AD PATIENTS

Our psychometric studies with the CCTI led us to consider the value of pursuing cognitive studies of consent capacity using a better known and accepted criterion of competency—physician judgments. Clinician judgment embraces a broad area of observation, knowledge, and experience, which psychometric assessment does not capture. Physician judgments are the existing clinical standard for determining consent capacity (Marson, McInturff, Hawkins, Bartolucci, & Harrell, 1997). These judgments usually have the effect of legal adjudications (Grisso, 1986) and have crucial practical consequences for patients and families. Yet, surprisingly little is known about physician assessment of consent capacity (Marson & Harrell, 1996).

We conducted a study that investigated the cognitive predictors of physician judgments of capacity of AD patients to consent (Marson, Hawkins, et al., 1997). We provide some background here in order to facilitate discussion of the study's results. Subjects ($n = 45$) consisted of 16 normal older controls and 29 patients with probable AD. All AD patients in this study had mild dementia as operationalized by Mini-Mental State Examination score (MMSE $\geq$ 20). All subjects were videotaped responding to a standardized consent capacity interview (SCCI) consisting of three parts: (a) a set of standardized clinical history questions; (b) the MMSE; and (c) a brief clinical vignette with standardized questions testing capacity to consent. The clinical vignette was included as a measure of patient capacity to make a medical treatment decision. The vignette, which was written at a sixth grade level, set forth a hypothetical medical problem (atherosclerotic heart disease or "heart

---

[1]Although verbal recall was not a predictor in the stepwise analyses, factor analysis of LS5 has revealed that two of its three factors are memory based (Marson, Dymek, & Harrell, 1995). Memory measures demonstrate significant floor effects in AD and their contribution to competency changes are sometimes minimized in statistical analyses (Marson et al., 1996; Marson, Cody, et al., 1995).

blockage") in which only two treatment options, medication or surgery, were available. After hearing and reading the vignette, each subject responded to a series of questions concerning his or her treatment choice, the consequences of this choice, and the reasons supporting this choice.

All interview subjects were independently administered (off videotape) a neuropsychological test battery (see Appendix on p. 123) commonly used in dementia evaluation and comprising cognitive domains linked conceptually to competency to consent to treatment (Alexander, 1988; Marson, Cody, et al., 1995; Marson et al., 1996). These domains are Attention, Expressive Language, Receptive Language, Verbal Memory (short-term and delayed), Abstraction, Visuospatial Function, Executive Function, and Judgment.

In this study, we used the actual judgments of experienced physicians as the criterion of capacity to consent to treatment. Five physicians (2 neurologists, 1 geriatric psychiatrist, 2 geriatricians) were recruited as competency decision makers from a large tertiary care university medical center. All physicians had extensive clinical experience with both dementia and competency assessment. Each physician was board certified in his or her specialty, had an average of 7.6 years postresidency (range, 5 to 11 years), had geriatric patients comprising an average of 80% of his or her clinical practice (range, 60% to 100%), and had handled an average of 67 competency cases (range, 10 to 130). Accordingly, the study physicians constituted a group of decision makers with significant experience assessing the competency of older adults.

Each SCCI interview was videotaped such that only the interviewed subject was visible to the viewing physician. This format approximated the clinical reality of competency assessment, while controlling for the confounds and inconvenience involved in multiple physician assessments of the same subject. All 45 SCCI videotaped interviews were independently viewed by each of the study physicians. Physicians were blinded to a subject's diagnosis and neuropsychologic test performance. At the completion of a videotape, a physician judged a patient competent or incompetent to consent to treatment.

In examining the results of this study, we first address the consistency of physician judgments. Judgments of the five physicians differed markedly for AD patients but not for controls (Table 7.3). Overall, physicians showed high agreement for controls (98%) but low agreement for mild AD patients (56%). The physician group kappa for controls was 1.00 ($p < .0001$) and differed significantly ($p < .0001$) from the physician group kappa of .14 ($p = .44$) for AD patients, indicative of a real difference in the ability of study physicians to consistently judge competency across the two groups. Although preliminary and based upon a small sample of patients and physicians, our findings suggest that physician judgment is not a "gold standard" for determining the consent capacity of dementia patients. Although good reasons for the physician disagreement exist (lack of a valid gold standard for competency, lack of formal competency assessment training in medical school and residency, lack of objective competency assessment instruments), the unreliability ultimately raises concern about both the conceptual and moral bases of the compe-

TABLE 7.3
Physician Competency Judgments by Group

| Physician | Controls (N = 16) | | AD Patients (N = 29) | | Total (N = 45) | |
	Competent	Incompetent	Competent	Incompetent	Competent	Incompetent
Physician 1	15 (94%)	1 (6%)	3 (10%)	26 (90%)	18 (40%)	27 (60%)
Physician 2	16 (100%)	0 (0%)	14 (48%)	15 (52%)	30 (67%)	15 (33%)
Physician 3	16 (100%)	0 (0%)	22 (76%)	7 (24%)	38 (84%)	7 (16%)
Physician 4	16 (100%)	0 (0%)	25 (86%)	4 (14%)	41 (91%)	4 (9%)
Physician 5	16 (100%)	0 (0%)	29 (100%)	0 (0%)	45 (100%)	0 (0%)
Consensus*	16 (100%)	0 (0%)	21 (72%)	8 (28%)	37 (82%)	8 (18%)

Note. From "Consistency of Physician Judgments of Capacity to Consent in Mild Alzheimer's Disease," by D. Marson, B. McInturff, L. Hawkins, A. Bartolucci, and L. Harrell, 1997, *Journal of the American Geriatrics Society, 45,* p. 455. Copyright © 1997, by Williams and Wilkins. Reprinted by permission.

*Modal judgment of five physicians.

tency judgments being made (Marson & Harrell, 1996). Physicians (and other health care professionals) appear to differ widely in their conceptual understanding of competency, in their clinical approach to competency assessment, and in the different standards or thresholds they intuitively apply in deciding competency (Marson & Harrell, 1996). We believe that standardized assessment instruments like the CCTI and SCCI and formal training in competency assessment are needed to improve the reliability of these judgments (Marson, McInturff, Hawkins, Bartolucci, & Harrell, 1997).

In the second part of the study, we identified cognitive predictors of consent capacity in AD patients as determined by physician judgments (Marson, Hawkins, et al., 1997). Stepwise discriminant function analysis (DFA) was used to identify key cognitive predictors for the competency judgments of four physicians and of physician consensus (modal physician judgment). (No predictors were identified for Physician 5's judgments because this physician found all subjects to be competent). Parametric and nonparametric DFAs were used to determine how well these predictors classified the competency outcomes assigned by the physicians for the sample (N = 45). It is interesting that cognitive predictors differed across physicians and physician consensus (Table 7.4). Verbal recall measures (Logical Memory I and II) predicted the judgments of physicians adopting a conservative decision-making approach (Physicians 1 and 2), whereas measures of simple executive function and everyday judgment (CFL/Cognitive Competency, Trails A/WAIS-R Comprehension) predicted the judgments of more liberal physicians (Physicians 3 and 4). A simple executive function measure (CFL) also predicted physician consensus.

Each set of physician predictors accounted for a substantial portion of variance and successfully classified virtually all competency outcomes for the full sample (N = 45; Marson, Hawkins, et al., 1997).

TABLE 7.4

Cognitive Predictors of Competency Judgments By Physician ($N = 45$)

Physician[a]	Incompetency Judgment Rate[b]	Test[c]	R^2	p
1	94%	LM II	.57	.0001
		SIM	.22	.004
2	52%	LM I	.43	.0001
3	24%	CFL	.27	.0008
4	14%	Trails A	.31	.0003
		COGCOM	.11	.05
Consensus	28%	CFL	.32	.0003
		COMP	.15	.02

Note. From "Cognitive Models That Predict Physician Judgments of Capacity to Consent in Mild Alzheimer's Disease," by D. Marson, L. Hawkins, B. McInturff, and L. Harrell, 1997, *Journal of the American Geriatrics Society, 45*, p. 461. Copyright © 1997, by Williams and Wilkins. Reprinted by permission.

[a]No model available for Physician 5. [b]Incompetency judgment rate for AD patients ($n = 29$); virtually all controls were judged competent ($n = 16$). [c]Abbreviations: CFL, Controlled Oral Word Fluency; COGCOM, Cognitive Competency Test; COMP, WAIS-R Comprehension; LM I, WMS-R Logical Memory I; LM II, WMS-R Logical Memory II; SIM, WAIS Similarities.

The results suggested two very different physician approaches to determining consent capacity. Declining capacities for verbal recall predicted the judgments of physicians adopting a conservative approach to deciding competency. Physician 1 (geriatric psychiatrist) and Physician 2 (neurologist) were the strictest judges of competency, finding 90% and 52% of the mild AD patients incompetent, respectively. LM I tests auditory verbal recall of two short stories (comprising a total of 50 bits of information) immediately after the stories are presented orally, whereas LM II tests recall for the same material again after a 30-minute delay (Wechsler, 1987). Thus, rapid forgetting of verbal material (anterograde amnesia) by mild AD patients predicted judgments of incompetency by Physician 1 and Physician 2. This finding was consistent with the high rates of incompetency found by the two physicians, as impaired short-term and delayed verbal recall are defining characteristics of AD and are usually devastated even in mild AD patients (Butters et al., 1984; Welsh et al., 1991).

These findings have relevance to the conceptual model of consent capacity in AD presented earlier. The importance of verbal recall to the judgments of Physicians 1 and 2 suggests a clinical focus on a patient's capacity to comprehend and encode treatment-related information. The ability to recall general and specific facts about a medical condition and symptoms and about available treatment options and respective risks and benefits is essential to the subsequent processing of that information and the making of a treatment decision. As discussed, verbal recall is lost early in the course of AD. Mild AD patients experience substantial difficulty encoding and retaining new information and thus cannot process and incorporate it into their responses during competency interviews such as the SCCI. Clinicians like Physicians 1 and 2 may be quite sensitive to the resulting factual loss, impoverishment, and confusion in such patients' responses. For these clinicians, therefore, it may be the quantity of factual information available in the patient's responses, but not necessarily the quality of the patient's reasoning processes, that is of paramount concern in assessing competency. Accordingly, the current results indicate the importance of hippocampal and medial temporal regions to the capacity to consent to treatment. The results also suggest that assessment of verbal recall can provide valuable information in clinical evaluations of competency.

The cognitive predictors of the judgments of Physician 3 (neurologist), Physician 4 (geriatrician), and for physician consensus comprised measures of simple executive function and everyday judgment, but not verbal recall. Physician 3, Physician 4, and physician consensus were more liberal judges of competency, finding only 24%, 14%, and 28% of the mild AD patients incompetent, respectively (Marson, Hawkins, et al., 1997). For Physician 3 and physician consensus, the key predictor was phonemic word fluency (Controlled Oral Word Fluency, or CFL; Benton & Hamsher, 1978). Word fluency tasks involve the generation of words to phonemic or semantic categories within a limited time period (one minute; Lezak, 1995) and have been linked to frontal and executive function (Miceli, Caltagirone, Gainotti, Masullo, & Silveri, 1981). For Physician 4, the key predictor was visuomotor tracking/sequencing (Trails A; Reitan, 1958). Trails A is a timed measure of visuomotor tracking/sequencing that requires a subject to draw lines to connect consecutively numbered circles on a work sheet (Lezak, 1995). This task has also been linked to frontal and executive function (Eson, Yen, & Bourke, 1978; Lafleche & Albert, 1995). Finally, tasks of everyday comprehension and judgment were secondary predictors for the judgments of both Physicians 3 and 4 (Cognitive Competency, verbal reasoning subtest; and WAIS-R Comprehension).

These findings are equally relevant to the conceptual model of consent capacity in AD presented earlier. Declining capacities of mild AD patients for simple executive function and everyday judgment predicted the competency judgments of the study's two liberal physicians. The importance of these neurocognitive predictors suggests that Physician 3 and 4 (and physician consensus) clinically focused on patient capacity to process treatment information rationally in making a decision. These physicians appeared to be more sensitive to the general quality of a patient's reasoning process and less concerned as to whether factual information may be absent due to amnesia.

These results highlight the importance of frontally mediated executive functions and judgment to capacity to consent to treatment. Although such functions are impaired in mild AD (LaFleche & Albert, 1995), they are better preserved than is verbal recall (Grady et al. 1988)—consistent with the fact that Physicians 3 and 4 each found many more AD patients competent than did Physicians 1 and 2. However, as such frontally mediated executive capacities fail, the organized verbal production of responses by AD patients deteriorates significantly on competency tasks such as the SCCI vignette. In addition to the loss of specific factual material occasioned by memory impairment, patient responses increasingly are compromised by disorganized processing and strained or absent reasoning, which, in turn, compel judgments of incompetency by physicians focusing on the quality of the reasoning process. Accordingly, assessment of simple executive functions and judgment may provide important information in clinical evaluations of competency.

The present study's intrinsic models of physician judgments should be distinguished from more explicit models of physician competency decision making. Although it would be tempting to use these findings to speculate on the conscious decision-making processes of our physicians, the study design and results do not fully support such inferences (Marson, Hawkins, et al., 1997). For example, we cannot be certain that, in making their judgments, Physicians 1 and 2 explicitly focused in all cases on subject capacities for verbal recall. We can surmise, however, that these two physicians were sensitive to the effects of intrinsic memory changes on AD patients' performance and, in some cases, actually keyed on them. Future research should focus on the explicit competency decision-making processes of physicians and other clinicians (Marson & Ingram, 1996).

CAPACITY RESEARCH AND AD:
STRENGTHS AND LIMITATIONS

In our research, we have used an AD population to examine cognitive changes associated with declining consent capacity. As discussed in the Introduction, AD is, by virtue of its relentless progressive character, a useful disease with which to view the relationship between abnormal cognition and loss of capacity. At the same time, one must acknowledge that the different study results may be quite specific to the AD context and may not generalize well to other disease entities or to normal aging. Although consent capacity intuitively appears strongly related to cognitive functions of memory, conceptualization, and executive function, the identification of such predictors was probably influenced by the course and type of cognitive changes specific to AD. For this reason, it is very important to understand how normal age-related cognitive changes may affect higher order functional capacities like consent capacity (Diehl et al., 1995; Park, 1992; Willis, 1996). Little is known about whether and to what extent such normative age-related changes may affect the treatment consent capacity of nondemented older adults. Thus, studies using different age cohorts of normal adults, as well as groups with a neurodegenerative disease like AD, are necessary to understand the effects of normal and abnormal aging on consent capacity (and other functional capacities). Other directions for future research are briefly discussed below.

FUTURE DIRECTIONS

The present chapter has examined cognitive changes in mild dementia associated with competency loss as judged by psychometric instruments and experienced physicians. Future research should use such findings to develop a specific neuropsychological test battery sensitive to competency loss in dementia. Such a battery, in conjunction with direct competency assessment measures such as the SCCI or CCTI, can assist physician and other health care professionals in making more reliable and accurate judgments of competency in dementia (Marson et al., 1996). Neuropsychologic test measures can also alert clinicians to specific cognitive deficits threatening competency and thereby facilitate the use of specific cognitive interventions to support the consent capacity of patients with these deficits (Marson et al. 1996). As discussed, cognitive studies of consent capacity should also be carried out in other neurological populations and in normal older adults.

SUMMARY

The capacity to make medical decisions for oneself is a fundamental aspect of personal autonomy with important legal implications, and is a higher order functional activity of daily life. Cognitive studies of consent capacity hold considerable promise for illuminating both the normal and abnormal cognitive changes that lead to loss of functional health and independence in older adults. In the present chapter, we have presented a conceptual model for understanding loss of consent capacity in patients with AD. This model isolates three core cognitive tasks underlying consent capacity: comprehending and encoding treatment information; processing of that treatment information and arriving at a treatment decision; and communicating the treatment decision. Prior cognitive studies of consent capacity using a psychometric assessment instrument have suggested that consent abilities predicated on comprehension/encoding and processing of treatment information show the earliest and most rapid decline, due to the effects of deficits in memory, conceptualization, executive function, and semantic knowledge characteristic of mild AD. The chapter then reviewed a cognitive study of consent capacity, which used physician judgments as its competency criterion. Two very different sets of cognitive predictors of consent capacity were identified. Measures of verbal recall predicted the judgments of conservative physicians (high incompetency judgment rate) who appeared sensitive to mild AD patients' impaired capacity to comprehend and encode treatment information. Measures of executive function/everyday judgment predicted judgments of liberal physicians (low incompetency judgment rate) who appeared sensitive to mild AD patients' more intact capacities to process and reason about treatment information.

ACKNOWLEDGMENTS

This research was supported by (1) an Alzheimer's Association Investigator Initiated Research Grant (IIRG 93-051); (2) a UAB Center for Aging Pilot Grant (#200040); (3) an Alzheimer Disease Center Cores grant (NIH, NIA 1 P30 AG10163-1); and (4) an Alzheimer's Disease Program Project grant (NIH, NIA 5 P01 AG06569-05).

APPENDIX: NEUROPSYCHOLOGICAL TEST
BATTERY FOR CAPACITY TO CONSENT

Orientation: Wechsler Memory Scale-Revised (WMS-R) Information subtest examines orientation in the personal, geographical, and temporal spheres.

Attention: Dementia Rating Scale Attention subscale (DRS Attention) examines very simple aspects of both verbal and visual attention; WMS-R Digit Span (Digit Span) examines simple auditory verbal attention in simple and more complex conditions; WMS-R Mental Control examines attention in a timed format.

Expressive Language: Boston Naming Test tests confrontation naming; Controlled Oral Word Fluency (CFL) tests phonemic word fluency; Animal Naming (Animal Fluency) tests semantic word fluency; DRS Initiation/Perseveration (DRS IP; see also Executive Function below) tests semantic word fluency and other simple executive functions.

Receptive Language: Token Test (Tokens) is a short form version of test of auditory verbal propositional comprehension; auditory comprehension screen is a brief and basic test of basic auditory verbal comprehension; reading comprehension screen is a basic screen of reading comprehension comprising simple paragraphs.

Short Term Verbal Memory: WMS-R Logical Memory I (LMI) tests immediate (short term) recall for narrative verbal material; WMS-R Paired Verbal Associates I (PVAI) tests immediate (short term) associative learning for easy and hard word pairs; DRS Memory tests orientation, short term verbal recall, verbal and nonverbal recognition memory.

Delayed Verbal Memory: WMS-R Logical Memory II (LMII) tests recall for narrative verbal material after 30 minutes; WMS-R Paired Verbal Associates II (PVAII) tests associative recall for easy and hard word pairs after 30 minutes.

Abstraction: WAIS Similarities (SIM) tests verbal abstraction; DRS Conceptualization tests simple verbal and spatial conceptualization.

Judgment: WAIS-R Comprehension (COMP) tests social comprehension and judgment, proverb interpretation; Cognitive Competency Test (verbal reasoning subtest; COGCOM) tests everyday reasoning and problem solving.

Executive Function: Trails A and B are tests of visuomotor tracking/sequencing, set flexibility; DRS Initiation/Perseveration (DRS IP) tests simple executive functions; see also Expressive Language; Clock Drawing tests capacity to generate clock face and correct time.

Spatial Construction: DRS Construction is a test of simple spatial construction.

REFERENCES

Alexander, M. (1988). Clinical determination of mental competence. A theory and a retrospective study. *Archives of Neurology, 45,* 23–26.

Appelbaum, P., & Grisso, T. (1988). Assessing patients' capacities to consent to treatment. *New England Journal of Medicine, 319,* 1635–1638.

Benton, A., & Hamsher, K. (1978). *Multilingual aphasia examination.* Iowa City: The University of Iowa.

Berg, L., Danziger, W., Storandt, M., Coben, L., Gado, M., Hughes, C., Knesevich, J., & Botwinick, J. (1984). Predictive features in mild senile dementia of the Alzheimer type. *Neurology, 34,* 563–569.

Butters, M., Salmon, D., & Butters, N. (1994). Neuropsychological assessment of dementia. In M. Storandt & G. VandenBos (Eds.), *Neuropsychological assessment of dementia and depression in older adults: A clinician's guide* (pp. 33–59). Washington, DC: American Psychological Association.

Cummings, J., & Benson, D. (1992). *Dementia: A clinical approach* (2nd ed.). Stoneham, MA: Butterworth.

Diehl, M., Willis, S. L., & Schaie, K. W. (1995). Everyday problem solving in older adults: Observational assessment and cognitive correlates. *Psychology and Aging, 10,* 478–491.

Edelstein, B., Nygren, M., Northrop, L., Staats, N., & Pool, D. (1993, August). *Assessment of capacity to make medical and financial decisions.* Paper presented at the 101st Annual Convention of the American Psychological Association, Toronto, Canada.

Eson, M. E., Yen, J.K., & Bourke, R. S. (1978). Assessment of recovery from serious head injury. *Journal of Neurology, Neurosurgery, and Psychiatry, 41,* 1036–1042.

Folstein, M., Folstein, S., & McHugh, P. (1975). Mini-mental state. *Journal of Psychiatric Research, 12,* 189–198.

Geropsychology Assessment Resource Guide. (1993). Milwaukee, WI: National Center for Cost Containment, Dept. of Veterans Affairs.

Grady, C., Haxby, J., Horwitz, B., Sundarem, M., Berg, G., Schapiro, M., Friedland, R., & Rapoport, S. (1988). Longitudinal study of the early neuropsychological and cerebral metabolic changes in dementia of the Alzheimer type. *Journal of Clinical and Experimental Neuropsychology, 10,* 576–596.

Grisso, T. (1986). *Evaluating competencies: Forensic assessments and instruments.* New York: Plenum.

Grisso, T., & Appelbaum, P. (1991). Mentally ill and non-mentally ill patients' abilities to understand informed consent disclosure for medication. *Law of Human Behavior, 15,* 377–388.

Hodges, J. R., Salmon, D. P., & Butters, N. (1991). The nature of the naming deficit in Alzheimer's and Huntington's disease. *Brain, 114,* 1547–1558.

Janofsky, J., McCarthy, R., & Folstein, M. (1991). The Hopkins Competency Assessment Test: A brief method for evaluating patients' capacity to give informed consent. *Hospital and Community Psychiatry, 43,* 132–136.

Kapp, M. B. (1992). *Geriatrics and the law: Patient rights and professional responsibilities* (2nd Ed.). New York: Springer.

Kapp, M., & Mossman, D. (1996). Measuring decisional capacity: Cautions on the construction of a "Capacimeter." *Psychology, Public Policy, and Law, 2,* 73–95.

LaFleche, G., & Albert, M. S. (1995). Executive function deficits in mild Alzheimer's disease. *Neuropsychology, 9,* 313–320.

Lezak, M. (1995). *Neuropsychological assessment* (3rd ed.). New York: Oxford University Press.

Marson, D. (1996). Qualitative cognitive changes associated with declining competency to consent to treatment in Alzheimer's disease [abstract]. *The Gerontologist, 36*(1), 243.

Marson, D., Chatterjee, A., Ingram, K., & Harrell, L. (1996). Toward a neurologic model of competency: Cognitive predictors of capacity to consent in Alzheimer's disease using three different legal standards. *Neurology, 46,* 666–672.

Marson, D., Cody, H., Ingram, K., & Harrell, L. (1995). Neuropsychologic predictors of competency in Alzheimer's disease using a rational reasons legal standard. *Archives of Neurology, 52,* 955–959.

Marson, D., Dymek, M., & Harrell, L. (1995). Neuropsychological correlates of the factor structure of competency to consent in Alzheimer's disease. *Journal of the International Neuropsychological Society, 2*(1), 60.

Marson, D., & Harrell, L. (1996). Decision-making capacity: In reply. *Archives of Neurology, 53*(7), 589–590.

Marson, D., Hawkins, L., McInturff, B., & Harrell, L. (1997). Cognitive models that predict physician judgments of capacity to consent in mild Alzheimer's disease. *Journal of the American Geriatrics Society, 45,* 458–464.

Marson, D., & Ingram, K. (1996). Competency to consent to treatment: A growing field of research. *Journal of Ethics, Law and Aging, 2,* 59–63.

Marson, D., Ingram, K., Cody, H., & Harrell, L. (1995). Assessing the competency of Alzheimer's disease patients under different legal standards. *Archives of Neurology, 52,* 949–954.

Marson, D., McInturff, B., Hawkins, L., Bartolucci, A., & Harrell, L. (1997). Consistency of physician judgments of capacity to consent in mild Alzheimer's disease. *Journal of the American Geriatrics Society, 45,* 453–457.

Marson, D., Schmitt, F., Ingram, K., & Harrell, L. (1994). Determining the competency of Alzheimer's patients to consent to treatment and research. *Alzheimer's Disease and Related Disorders, 8* (Suppl. 4), 5–18.

Miceli, G., Caltagirone, C., Gainotti, G., Masullo, C., & Silveri, M. C. (1981). Neuropsychological correlates of localized cerebral lesions in nonaphasic brain-damaged patients. *Journal of Clinical Neuropsychology, 3,* 53–63.

Monsch, A., Bondi, M., Butters, N., Salmon, D., Katzman, R., & Thal, L. (1992). Comparisons of verbal fluency tasks in the detection of dementia of the Alzheimer type. *Archives of Neurology, 49,* 1253–1258.

Moss, M., & Albert, M. (1988). Alzheimer's disease and other dementing disorders. In M. S. Albert & M. B. Moss (Eds.), *Geriatric neuropsychology* (pp. 145–178). New York: Guilford Press.

Moss, M., & Albert, M. (1992). Neuropsychology of Alzheimer's disease. In R. F. White (Ed.), *Clinical syndromes in adult neuropsychology: The practitioner's handbook* (pp. 305–343). Amsterdam: Elsevier.

Park, D. (1992). Applied cognitive aging research. In F. I. M. Craik & T. Salthouse (Eds.), *The handbook of aging and cognition* (pp. 449–493). Hillsdale, NJ: Lawrence Erlbaum Associates.

Pruchno, R., Smyer, M., Rose, M., Hartman-Stein, P., & Henderson-Laribee, D. (1995). Competence of long-term care residents to participate in decisions about their medical care: A brief, objective assessment. *The Gerontologist, 35,* 622–629.

Reitan, R. (1958). Validity of the Trail Making Test as an indication of organic brain damage. *Perception and Motor Skills, 8,* 271–276.

Roth, L., Meisel, A., & Lidz, C. (1977). Tests of competency to consent to treatment. *American Journal of Psychiatry, 134,* 279–284.

Schaie, K. W. (1996). *Intellectual development in adulthood: The Seattle longitudinal study.* New York: Cambridge University Press.

Smith, S. R., Murdoch, B. E., & Chenery, H. J. (1989). Semantic abilities in dementia of the Alzheimer type: 1. Lexical semantics. *Brain and Language, 36,* 314–324.

Tepper, A., & Elwork, A. (1984). Competence to consent to treatment as a psycholegal construct. *Law and Human Behavior, 8,* 205–223.

Wang, P., Ennis, K., & Copland, S. (1987). *Cognitive competency test manual.* Toronto, Canada: Mt. Sinai Hospital.

Wechsler, D. (1987). *Wechsler Memory Scale—Revised.* New York: The Psychological Corporation.

Welsh, K., Butters, N., Hughes, J., Mohs, R., & Heyman, A. (1991). Detection and staging of dementia in Alzheimer's disease: Use of the neuropsychological measures developed for the Consortium to Establish a Registry for Alzheimer's Disease (CERAD). *Archives of Neurology, 49,* 448–452.

Willis, S. (1996). Everyday cognitive competence in elderly persons: Conceptual issues and empirical findings. *The Gerontologist, 36,* 595–601.

Wolinsky, F. D., & Johnson, R. J. (1991). The use of health services by older adults. *Journal of Gerontology: Social Sciences, 46,* S345–S357.

8

Medical Expertise and Cognitive Aging

Vimla L. Patel
José F. Arocha
McGill University

Societal trends such as an aging population, rapidly expanding medical knowledge, and the training of smaller cohorts of new physicians (for economic reasons) make it imperative that the current practitioners not only maintain but also improve upon their professional competence throughout their working lives. The result of this trend is that greater numbers of doctors are choosing to continue their work at advanced ages. So, an important and still unanswered question is, In what way does age manifest its effect on medical competence? Is it possible that experience prevails and individuals keep performing as well as they did in their younger years? Or, are certain skills maintained with age, whereas other abilities, such as the fine motor precision required of a surgeon, inevitably decline? Knowledge about how successful physicians improve upon and maintain their expert performance should result in improved training and retraining methods, which, in turn, should promote more effective use of professional resources.

As expertise in a domain increases, so does the age of the expert. With this framework in mind, we describe research in medical expertise that suggests that as expertise in a domain increases, alternative strategies are developed to deal with changes in the way knowledge is organized. What is the nature of such strategies? What is their origin? What is the relationship between expertise and aging?

To answer these questions, two models of the maintenance of expert performance with increasing age have been proposed (cf. Bäckman & Dixon, 1992). The first, which we may call the *compensatory model,* states that aging physicians develop strategies to compensate for declines in basic cognitive functions. That is, as cognitive functions decline, expert physicians begin to develop strategies that help them maintain some level of competence throughout their aging years, as a compensatory mechanism.

The second model (Ericsson, Krampe, & Tesch-Römer, 1993) proposed that early on, experts develop strategies for practice that rely not so much on basic cognitive functions, but rather on those that make heavy use of knowledge intensive processing. According to this model, aging physicians simply continue to use such *expert-like strategies,* which develop as a natural result of their deliberate practice and experience in a domain. These expert-like strategies help older physicians in maintaining their level of expertise despite possible declines in basic cognitive functioning. As long as the level of expertise is maintained by active, deliberate practice, the appropriate learning of domain-specific schemata serves as a mechanism for older physicians. In other words, it is not because they are older that they alter their strategy (Model 1), but rather because of their extensive practice and experience, a strategy that relies on resources other than those affected by cognitive aging (Model 2) happens to develop. This mechanism (Model 2) allows them to incorporate clinical information in a manner that is similar to the way that younger physicians instantiate information, while making use of processes that are less cognitively taxing. We attempt to present some evidence on the development of medical expertise in support of this position.

In this chapter, we outline an account of findings from studies of the development of expertise, in a continuum from novice to subexpert to expert. This investigation has made heavy use of detailed analysis of knowledge structures and processes underlying performance. The latter part of this continuum, after a physician has been certified to practice, involves the maintenance of expertise. As our research focuses primarily on the characterization of expert medical performance, we speculate on the complex relationship between cognitive aging and medical expertise, with particular stress on how expertise is maintained with increasing age. We also present some definitions and the frameworks underlying our research, followed by a summary of empirical studies. We describe studies that show that experts begin to use alternative strategies for interpretation of clinical case information before the aging decrements start.

MEDICAL PROBLEM SOLVING AND EXPERT PERFORMANCE

There are three classes of constraints that influence medical problem solving: epistemological (the structure of medical knowledge), cognitive (memory, knowledge, inferences, and strategies), and social/situational (group culture and norms).

These constraints interact, playing an important role in the development and maintenance of expertise. In our empirical research, we have paid special attention to the first two of these constraints: the epistemological, by investigating how the structure of medical knowledge affects clinical case comprehension, reasoning, and problem solving; and the cognitive, by investigating the mental processes involved in medical reasoning and problem solving. Each of these constraints have implications to aging research, as shall be outlined shortly.

In many fields, the concept of expertise suggests a continuum from a beginner to a specialist, which provides a basis for differentiating between subjects at various levels of expertise. Expert physicians have accrued an extensive knowledge of the general field of medicine (acquired through medical school and residency training) and an in-depth knowledge in a narrow area of specialization. Based on this, we distinguish between specific (e.g., cardiology) and generic (e.g., general medicine) expertise. An individual may possess both, or only generic expertise. Generic expertise is acquired during early medical training in medical school. After medical school, a physician enters a residency training program and specializes in a particular subdomain, thus acquiring specific expertise. However, a medical resident continues to acquire generic expertise through rotations in areas outside his or her area of specialization. We classify different levels of expertise in medicine using the following terms:

Novice: An individual who has only everyday knowledge of a domain or one who has the prerequisite knowledge assumed by the domain (e.g., first-year medical students).
Intermediate: An individual who is above the novice level but below the subexpert level (e.g., fourth year medical students).
Subexpert: An individual with generic knowledge but inadequate specialized knowledge of the domain.
Expert: An individual with a specialized knowledge of the domain.

It is important to note that, essentially, an expert is someone who consistently performs at an advanced level, with a wealth of experience and knowledge in a particular domain. This suggests the attainment of a sufficiently advanced age to have acquired this enormous amount of experience. If someone is an expert in a medical specialty, for example, cardiology, this does not imply that he or she is an expert in other medical specialties. So, being older does not automatically categorize one as expert. However, one cannot attain a level of expertise without the investment of large amounts of time and extensive practice, which goes hand in hand with being a certain minimum age.

This said, how is it that medical experts, of any age, perform so well? What makes them so good at what they do? These questions are particularly relevant given that aging research has documented general cognitive declines in normal aging humans. Do these declines affect all people? Do we expect to see these same declines (and to the same degree) in intellectually active professionals (medical experts)? Does aging affect experts in the same way as the general population? If so, how does this affect their medical performance in terms of diagnostic reasoning and conceptualization of medical information? To attempt to answer some of these questions, one first needs to comprehend how an entity as complex as a medical diagnosis is conceptualized, understood, and measured by researchers in this field. We highlight some of our main findings and venture possible extrapolations to aging research in medical expertise. Before describing the research, however, we present the general framework used in our studies.

FRAMEWORKS FOR MEDICAL DIAGNOSIS RESEARCH

Epistemological Framework

Knowledge domains can be characterized on a continuum from well-structured to ill-structured domains. In well-structured domains, such as physics (e.g., mechanics), many problems are well delineated because the constraints and the possible operations leading to the solution are well understood. At the other end of the continuum, in an ill-structured domain, such as writing composition, problems are ill structured because there are few initial constraints and no well-defined goals. Medical problems can be characterized as somewhat ill-structured, in the sense that the initial states (e.g., the presenting complaint from the patient), the definite goal state (e.g., the diagnosis), and the constraints (e.g., other information relevant to the case) are either unknown or uncertain (Simon, 1973). In a diagnostic situation, the space of potential findings (e.g., clinical signs and symptoms) and associated diagnoses is very large and becomes defined through the imposition of a set of plausible constraints that facilitate the application of specific decision strategies. Plausible constraints are produced, for example, by narrowing the range of possible diagnostic solutions, by evoking categories of disorders (e.g., cardiovascular problems), or by eliminating classes of problems.

Given the complexity of medical knowledge, there is a need for a framework differentiating between different classes of concepts. These concepts are the building blocks, in the expert's knowledge base, of an extensive network of disease models, and shape the nature and content of the diagnostic process. Following Evans and Gadd (1989), we have made use of an epistemological framework for differentiating the levels at which clinical knowledge may be organized in the medical problem-solving context (see Fig. 8.1). This epistemological framework has been used as a reference model for medical knowledge and in the coding of inferences in studies of medical reasoning (Patel, Arocha, & Kaufman, 1994) and doctor–patient interaction (Patel, Evans, & Kaufman, 1989). The framework consists of a hierarchical structure formed by observations at the lowest level, followed by findings, facets, and ultimately, diagnoses. *Observations* are units of information that are recognized as potentially relevant in the problem-solving context, but that do not constitute clinically useful facts. *Findings* are comprised of observations that

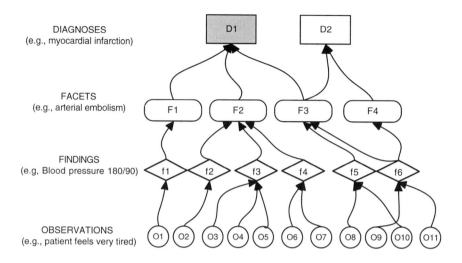

FIG. 8.1. Epistemological model of the structure of medical knowledge for problem solving. Observations are presented to the physician, who generates inferences in the form of findings. A collection of findings, or sometimes a single finding, serve to trigger a facet, which in turn lead to a diagnosis. Competing diagnoses are resolved by the amount and quality of support given by the facets.

have potential clinical significance. Establishing a finding reflects an inference made by a physician that an observation or a set of observations need to be medically accounted for. *Facets* consist of clusters of findings that indicate an underlying medical problem or class of problems. They describe a pathological process, such as aortic insufficiency or endocrine disorder, and suggest possible diagnoses. Facets also vary in terms of their levels of abstraction. We have found it useful to code for two levels of facets. A *high-level facet* may serve to partition the problem space and may be a reasonable approximation to a diagnosis. A *low-level facet* involves a more local inference that may explain one or two findings and would not advance the problem-solving process to the same extent. *Diagnosis* is the level of classification that subsumes and explains all levels beneath it. Everything above the level of observations constitute various levels of inferences, as shown in Fig. 8.1, where findings are inferred from observations, facets from findings, and diagnoses from facets.

This model constitutes an idealized description of the concepts involved in medical problems as well as the cognitive operations that a physician has to perform to arrive at a solution. The physician is presented with a set of observations about a patient. These observations are interpreted and a set of findings is generated by inferring the clinical significance of such observations. From the findings generated, the physician has to infer what pathological processes are involved and, from these, reach a single or a set of diagnoses that explains the clinical presentation. It may be interesting to investigate the circumstances for older medical experts for which this epistemological model holds true. We speculate that this model most likely applies to older physicians, but perhaps depending on the parameters of the problem space, older physicians may conceptualize a difficult case at too high a level for their knowledge. Potentially, this may occur because lower levels of abstraction demand more memory storage, whereas at higher levels of abstraction, previous experience can be drawn on to aid in the understanding of the case, rather that juggling the many case details.

Cognitive Framework

Using the previously mentioned epistemological framework, we have developed an account of diagnostic cognition that explains results in recall and memory for clinical cases, diagnostic reasoning, and problem solving, showing, not surprisingly, that accuracy of diagnostic performance increases as a function of the amount of medical practice (Patel & Groen, 1991). However, it has been extremely difficult to demonstrate superior diagnostic performance for typical cases beyond the level of performance attained during the first year of residency (Schmidt, Norman, & Boshuizen, 1990). Only with difficult cases have large differences in diagnostic accuracy been observed (Patel, Arocha, & Kaufman, 1994; Patel & Groen, 1991).

Two major findings are relevant to our discussion: The first is that, in studies of memory for routine clinical cases, there is no difference in the overall amount of information recalled or inferred (observations and findings) between experts (specialists in a medical subdomain) and subexperts (experts solving clinical cases outside their area of specialization). This finding suggests that recall of observations and findings is not related to diagnostic accuracy, although diagnostic accuracy increases with expertise. The second finding is that experts generate high-level inferences (e.g., facets, diagnoses) to account for clinical observations very early in their processing. In contrast, novices and subexperts generate lower level inferences (e.g., observations and findings). Therefore, it seems that it is the generation of high-level inferences (i.e., at the facet level) that has direct links to diagnostic accuracy.

How are experts able to do this? Following Ericsson (Ericsson & Staszewski, 1989), it has been suggested (Joseph & Patel, 1990; Patel, Arocha, & Kaufman, 1994) that expert physicians develop intermediary memory structures that allow the rapid retrieval of information in their domains of expertise, facilitate quick and easy access to compiled patient information, and make it possible to avoid extra processing of low-level clinical information. At the time of encoding, experts acquire a set of constructs that associate new clinical information with the knowledge already stored in memory. Ericsson and Kintsch (1995) termed these constructs "long-term working memory" (LT-WM), emphasizing the fact that they act as an extension of working memory. In problem-solving situations, experts use LT-WM to synthesize data (e.g., a set of clinical observations) and provide selective and rapid access to the information stored in long-term memory. Thus, instead of relying on the basic data-intensive processing needed for recalling observations or making low-level inferences, experts use alternative forms of cognitive processing, which they continue to use as they age.

In short, we suggest that with practice in a domain, the ability to rapidly interpret clinical observations (e.g., a patient's report on his or her health) increases because a list of observations is not represented in memory as a mere list, but as intermediate constructs (Arocha & Patel, 1995). This is in keeping with results (Patel, Arocha, & Kaufman, 1994) that show that experts generate more sparse clinical case descriptions and explanations than novices, suggesting that increasing medical expertise involves the generation of fewer, not more, inferences in the form of facets.

Based on these results, we would like to put forth the following line of reasoning: If there is a development of expertise with training and experience, and there exists a trend whereby experts provide their diagnoses earlier than subexperts, then one interpretation could be that older medical experts, who have been practicing for probably several decades, feel more confident in their diagnoses, and therefore provide their diagnosis earliest of all while processing the fewest pieces of data. Alternatively, one may argue that the older expert may process information slower and thus give a diagnosis much later. One can see that there is much speculation regarding the cognitive strategies of older medical experts.

EXPERTISE AND AGING RESEARCH

We shall start by stressing some points already made in our introduction. It is generally accepted that some age-related decrements in low-level cognitive functioning, such as speed of processing and working memory, are observed by the time a person reaches middle age (e.g., Salthouse, 1991). However, it is evident that high-level cognitive functioning does not necessarily show the same kind of deterioration, especially in knowledge-rich domains in which the individuals have considerable expertise. This raises the possibility that certain expert strategies associated with aging develop to compensate for deficits in lower level processes. However, an alternative hypothesis is that deliberate practice in a specific domain can maintain expert-acquired abilities in the face of age-related declines in general cognitive abilities (Ericsson, 1996). In other words, practice leads to a strategy that does not rely on cognitive resources that may be affected by the aging process.

Some research shows that age differences in short-term memory seem to be very small (e.g., Craik, 1977; Craik & Jennings, 1992; Hultsch & Dixon, 1990), except when some kind of recoding or restructuring is involved. However, larger differences have been found in long-term memory, especially in what Kausler (1985) called *intentional tasks* (i.e., when the subject is instructed to remember the material). In particular, older people are unable to perform as well as younger people on conventional free recall tasks when the material exceeds the subjects' span of immediate memory. Such effects are, however, highly influenced by factors such as instruction, context, and prior knowledge.

If there are memory declines with age, how is it that many older physicians seem to be performing as successfully and as accurately as their younger counterparts? Studies of aging in domains of expertise introduce the possibility of investigating mechanisms that may be responsible for the maintenance of expert levels of performance. In our studies, although not directed to the study of aging per se, we investigate the mechanisms by which expert performance is maintained. We believe that the discrepancy between the studies that show declines in memory with age and those that show the apparent maintenance of expert performance during old age is because the evidence for memory deficits comes mainly from studies in knowledge-lean domains, where the effects of experience with the domain are small or nonexisting.

Studying medical expertise and aging requires the use of methodologies for the analysis of connected discourse—rather than lists of words. A great deal of research has been conducted since the early 1980s that uses propositions as the basic units of information underlying discourse (van Dijk & Kintsch, 1983). Earlier studies of age differences that utilize such methodologies were performed (Cohen, 1979; Meyer, Rice, Knight, & Jessen, 1979; Spilich, 1985; Zelinski, Gilewski, & Thompson, 1980). This methodology was utilized by Patel and colleagues in their research on medical expertise, with investigations of recall and comprehension of medical texts (e.g., Patel, Groen, & Frederiksen, 1986). The work was later extended both methodologically and conceptually (Groen & Patel, 1988). From a methodological perspective, experimental paradigms and methods of analysis have been developed that are suitable for the study of expertise in medical reasoning and problem solving. On the conceptual front, Patel and colleagues investigated the comprehension and reasoning processes characteristic of experts and novices. A large part of the effort was devoted to investigating the directionality of reasoning and the time course of hypothesis generation and evaluation. The theoretical perspective consistently attempted to reconcile theories of comprehension and semantic representation (reflecting the fact that medicine is a semantically complex domain) with a problem-solving/reasoning perspective typical of most expertise research. This approach is also supported by the finding that much of expert reasoning involves the development of an initial problem representation rather than sequential problem-solving operations. Although the comprehension problem-solving approach has been used in expertise research, very little effort has been put into using it for studying the relationship between expertise and aging.

There have been, however, a few studies of age-related differences in expert performance in knowledge-rich domains. Cjifer (1966) found that physicians do not exhibit age-related decline in syllogistic reasoning. The author claimed ecological validity for this task, because it resembled a diagnostic scenario. However, Salthouse, Babcock, Skovronek, Mitchell, and Palmon (1990) demonstrated that practicing architects do show age-related decrements in facility with spatial operations. Another study by Morrow, Leirer, and Altieri (1992), which looked at the ability of young pilots, old pilots, and nonpilots to recall aviation-related and nonaviation-related narratives, showed that expertise tends to help the ability to update and recall situation models from narratives, but that aging appears to hinder these same abilities. These contradictory results indicate that it is advisable to concentrate on tasks that are identical to those encountered in the expert's everyday environment. In support of this, Denney (1990) showed that age-related differences are more pronounced when subjects are compared in artificial tasks than in ecologically valid tasks. For instance, Salthouse (1984) showed that experienced, older typists perform as accurately and rapidly as younger typists despite slower reaction time. In a replication of the Chase–Simon paradigm, Charness (1981, 1985) found that recall accuracy of chess piece positions depends on both age and skill. The more skilled a player is, the more accurately he or she recalls chess positions. However, older players recall fewer positions than their younger, skill-equivalent counterparts. This study suggests that, controlling for skill, age seems to affect recall.

These results raise a question of the extent to which similar patterns occur in more verbally rich domains of expertise. In general, Charness's results lead us to expect less literal recall but no differences in accuracy in performance with age, unless the task involves severe time constraints (Strayer & Kramer, 1994). However, there is at least one issue for which these studies do not provide a basis for prediction. This is whether there are major age-related changes in reasoning strategies. Salthouse (1991) suggested that strategies may develop to compensate for age-related deficits in elementary information processing. That such strategies do develop seems uncontroversial. However, the question is whether they develop as a compensatory mechanism for memory deficiencies or as a natural result of deliberate practice. The next section is concerned with issues of whether trade-offs in age-related processing, between knowledge-intensive (e.g., strategies, knowledge chunks) and data-intensive strategies (e.g., general memory), can be found in more knowledge-rich complex domains. We shall present some evidence in expert–novice studies that show that experts process cases in a different fashion than novices or subexperts. Their processing is based more on the exploitation of their own knowledge resources than on the processing of vast amounts of data. We shall see two examples of this: first, studies of case recall by medical experts and novices and second, studies of diagnostic reasoning.

MEDICAL EXPERTISE AND THE PROCESSING OF CLINICAL INFORMATION

Studies on Clinical Case Recall

Aging research shows that age differences in recall are affected by the knowledge of the content material that a person possesses (Hultsch and Dixon, 1990). Also, because experts are expected to possess more knowledge of the domain than novices, we should observe differences in knowledge among various levels of expertise. Where do these differences reside? In studies of memory for clinical cases, Patel, Groen, and Frederiksen (1986) found systematic differences between experts (physicians) and novices (medical students). Using clinical texts on cancer and infectious fever, they showed that novice subjects (first-year students) recalled more propositions than physicians, while inferring less than physicians. Intermediate subjects (third-year students) both recalled and inferred more propositions than physicians (see Fig. 8.2). However, when propositions were separated in terms of their relevance to the diagnosis, clear differences were found, showing a significant increase in inferences on relevant propositions by the expert physicians. This is illustrated in Fig. 8.3. These results indicate that in data-intensive tasks, such as the recall of clinical case information, novices and intermediates may show superior performance to that of the experts (Fig. 8.2), who are comparatively more advanced in age. However, when the data is separated into relevant and irrelevant propositions relative to the correct diagnosis, experts show superior recall (in terms of relevant inferences, as in Fig. 8.3). This suggests the hypothesis that, as expertise increases, there is an increasing reliance on knowledge-intensive processing and a decrease in data-intensive processing. More data-intensive processing is observed before expertise develops (in support of Model 2 on aging).

This hypothesis is further supported in research by Patel and colleagues (Coughlin & Patel, 1987; Groen & Patel, 1988), who attempted to replicate, in the medical domain, the classical studies on chess conducted by Chase and Simon (1973), who had compared recall in two experimental conditions: normal game positions and randomly generated positions. Chase and Simon showed that experts display high levels of recall only for normal chess game positions, where they have a wealth of previous experiences to draw on, but not for randomly placed positions.

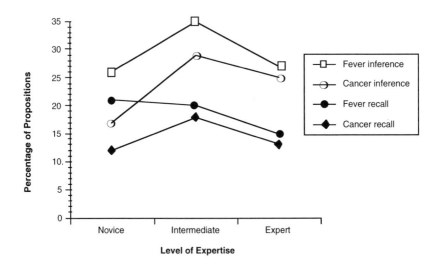

FIG. 8.2. Percentage of overall recall and inferences generated by subjects at different levels of expertise for clinical texts of cancer and fever.

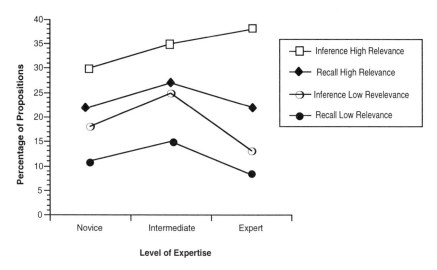

FIG. 8.3. Percentage of propositions recalled and inferred by subjects at various levels of expertise as a function of relevance for the clinical texts of cancer and fever.

Coughlin and Patel (1987) used two clinical case descriptions. Subjects were instructed to recall the case information and to provide a diagnosis. The cases were given in either structured form or scrambled form. The structured form followed the pattern of patient information given in medical case charts, widely used in clinical practice and with which physicians are highly familiar: (a) patient's personal data, (b) medical history, (c) physical examination findings, and (d) results from laboratory tests. The scrambled form presented the same information, but with the sentences randomized. Regardless of condition, the experts organized the cases according to the standard medical chart: patient description, patient complaint, history, physical examination, and laboratory tests. They used inferences in order to restructure the random texts such that they were clinically coherent in a way in which medical information is usually processed for diagnosis (e.g., patient charts) to the extent that most of the recall protocols of the randomized texts were indistinguishable from those of the structured texts. In contrast, the novices reproduced the structure of the case presentations, recalling the cases in a serial manner and keeping the sequence of information the same as was presented. These results show that as expertise in medicine increases, there is the tendency to use more inferences and less pure recall, which is consistent with the hypothesis that there is an increase in knowledge-intensive processing.

Studies on Diagnostic Reasoning

In their theory of expert performance, Chase and Simon (1973) proposed that increases in performance in a task domain are attributed to the acquisition of an increasingly larger number of and more complex patterns. According to their theory, presented information leads to recognition of patterns, which, in turn, automatically elicits the appropriate actions. This type of cognitive process, in which presented or known information evokes the desired information from memory, is called *forward reasoning* and has been found to characterize expert performance in many different domains, including medicine (Patel & Groen, 1991). Novices are unable to rely on forward reasoning because they have not acquired the necessary patterns and their associations to correct actions. Therefore, novices are forced to search actively for specific information that would allow them to reach a desired goal. They have to start with a hypothesis (e.g., a potential diagnosis) and then actively look for confirming or disconfirming evidence, a pattern of thinking that is called *backward reasoning*. Backward reasoning, from a hypothesis to a fact, involves a much greater use of working memory to keep track of the goal or the hypothesis while evaluating data. In other words, a hypothesis must be kept in working memory to be tested. This is one reason why all experts, if their knowledge base is adequate, might be expected to show a preference for the memory-efficient mode, forward reasoning.

In a number of studies, Patel and Groen (1991) showed that directionality of reasoning is associated with diagnostic accuracy and that the transition from forward to backward reasoning is strongly associated with the detection of what might be called "loose ends" in a diagnosis. In other words, when important facts in the clinical case remain unaccounted for, then a process of backward reasoning appears to be invoked. One may speculate at this point whether older experts, when confronted with a case where important facts are unaccounted for, switch into backward reasoning mode. Although our studies have found this to be so in "experts," we do not have direct data on the strategies used by "older experts." Therefore, another plausible prediction might be that the older experts, because backward reasoning might be overly taxing on their working memory, continue to utilize forward reasoning at the expense of generating errors.

To investigate these issues, a strategy has been to present clinical case descriptions in such a way that there is uncertainty about the diagnosis. This is done by giving physicians pieces of patient data in a sequential form. When physicians are given complete case descriptions, they can make use of high-level inferences to summarize the case, but when they are given incomplete cases, they should generate lower level inferences, given that they lack the context for interpreting the case in an abstract, high-level fashion. Using a case (Patel, Arocha, & Kaufman, 1994) where partial information was presented to subjects sequentially (one sentence at a time), experts and subexperts were prompted to think aloud after each piece of data was presented. Contrary to expectations, experts generated high-level inferences, as hypotheses, very early in the clinical encounter through forward reasoning and only used backward reasoning to evaluate the hypotheses generated. In contrast, subexperts generated high-level inferences later in the clinical encounter and used a combination of forward and backward reasoning. The results of the study suggest that the disease schema that eventually accounts for the case is constructed piece by piece, rather than retrieved as a whole (Patel, Arocha, & Kaufman, 1994). Facets provide access to information in long-term memory and then complete the diagnostic process on the basis of the information maintained in LT-WM. The differential use of such LT-WM is evident in the experts' repetitive use of high-level facets, which they use in a systematic way to organize and methodically evaluate the case as they process patient data. Subexperts exhibit no such systematicity in their use of retrieval structures.

How do these results with experts at the peak of their performance compare with those with experts who have many years of practice? Some data (Patel, Evans, & Kaufman, 1989) on an older physician, expert in endocrine disorders, who is considered most senior and expert in his domain, show that he exclusively focused on the signs and symptoms of a very common disorder (hyperthyroidism), while failing to recognize a rare disorder (hypokalemic periodic paralysis). Detailed analysis of the dialogue between the physician and the patient showed that the only hypothesis that this senior expert considered very early in the interview was hyperthyroidism and that he gathered data to confirm this hypothesis, ignoring relevant information that the patient provided about the condition. Even the patient's vague responses to some of the physician's questions did not alert him to the fact that there was something more to the condition than he had determined.

Could it be that older experts' performance approximates that of subexperts when encountering rare and difficult cases? We cannot say for sure, but this expert's performance underscores the risk of premature closure where the scope of reasoning is too narrow (errors of omission). An important observation suggesting another possible disorder (leg weakness) was completely ignored. Later, the expert determined without any statement from the patient to suggest this, that the patient "has been eating considerably more while losing weight," which is to be expected of patients with hyperthyroidism. It may be of interest to note that shortly after this physician had completed the case, he called back to say that he just had realized that the patient had hypokalemic periodic paralysis with hyperthyroidism! This is, of course, the correct diagnosis, which suggests that this expert simply needed more time to generate it, resembling in this case the performance of a subexpert. A similar finding has been reported by Zozula and Patel (1997). In their study, an older expert physician and a younger physician were given a clinical problem to solve. The case was in the field of expertise of both physicians (cardiology). Zozula and Patel showed that, whereas the younger physician was faster at solving the case, the older physician was more accurate in the interpretation of the case and focused on only the most relevant clinical findings, which were the only ones needed to generate the correct diagnosis, but required double the amount of time to do so.

EXPERTISE, PRACTICE, AND AGING

In this chapter, we have speculated about the maintenance of expert performance during the older years. If cognitive functions decline with age, how is it possible then that older experts maintain their level of expertise? We stated that two models of the maintenance of expertise can be used to account for the fact that older, expert, physicians perform at high levels of competence. One model proposes that experts develop compensatory strategies to overcome limitations in basic cognitive functioning (Model 1). The other hypothesis proposes that, as a natural development of expertise, experts acquire strategies for dealing with their daily tasks (Model 2). In this regard, older experts should be no different from younger experts. Although our research has not focused directly on aging as a factor, it suggests that the second hypothesis may have some merit.

We have also outlined some important aspects of expertise from novice to generic expert and from generic to specialized expertise. Recall of relevant information is positively related to diagnostic accuracy. This is true for medical students and general physicians (generic experts). Early in the medical curriculum, medical students acquire and learn the causal mechanisms of disease (*A* causes *B*), as represented in the upper part of Fig. 8.4. However, in the progression from general expert to specific expert, the learning consists of a fine-tuning of the schemata developed thus far by physicians into more abstract knowledge structures. This phase is characterized by the use of procedural knowledge, represented in the right hand side of the figure, labeled "specific expertise" (where *B* is an indicator of *A*).

Thus far, one may notice certain consistencies in the literature reviewed and our laboratory findings. These include that (a) older experts continue to perform at high levels, despite potential age-related limitations in basic cognitive functions; (b) if rushed or time constrained, older experts are more likely to make errors, particularly errors of omission; (c) if given as much time as they need, an older expert is just as accurate in his or her diagnosis and just as complete in the case conceptualization; and (d) there may be a tendency for older experts to avoid loading working memory *if* age has affected this cognitive function. At this point, one must keep in mind that

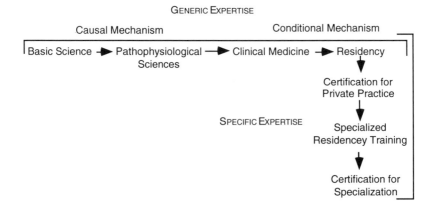

FIG. 8.4. Schematic diagram of the acquisition of diagnostic skills: Generic and specific expertise.

although the literature suggests that working memory declines with age, there is considerable individual variability. Furthermore, Shimamura, Berry, Mangels, Rusting, and Jurica (1995) provided evidence suggesting that memory is not limited by age in university professors, individuals who remain cognitively active, using general cognitive tasks (working memory and prose recall). If this can be shown in domain-lean tasks, we may argue that cognitive performance in particular domains may not decline as much as the literature on aging has previously suggested. Although in our research we have not dealt explicitly with the relationship between aging and expertise, the studies we have presented suggest that experts develop strategies for dealing with information within their domain in a manner that is different from the ones used by nonexperts. Whereas novices interpret clinical data at the lower levels and residents more at the intermediate levels, experts access higher level constructs, which are equivalent to chunks in the problem-solving literature. These chunks reflect the generation of higher order inferences seen in the pattern of recall for clinical cases in our studies.

It is through practice and learning that these intermediate constructs are activated, attended to, and stored in long term memory through a mechanism accounting for "loose ends." When physicians encounter clinical findings that are unaccountable for within the main diagnostic framework, they backtrack and search their knowledge base for alternative explanations. The detailed nature of the search will depend on the nature of the problem itself (from biomedical sciences to pathophysiology). The search stops when physicians are satisfied with their explanations, through the achievement of some criteria for coherence. Explanations, in turn, help update the knowledge structures and allow learning to take place. Although the process of backtracking is cognitively taxing, the better experts are able to successfully search for underlying information because of their highly developed disease schemata, which assist them in accessing intermediate structures. Development and maintenance of expertise, we believe, continue as long as the expert remains involved in active practice and keeps learning in their domain of expertise. This specific mechanism for maintaining expertise should not be strongly affected by aging. This depicts a more optimistic view of the aging process than that portrayed in traditional research, by stressing the changes in strategies that continuous activity in a domain fosters. Although basic level cognitive functioning may indeed decrease with age, its importance in sustaining expertise may be minor. New research specifically designed to address these issues should give us a clearer picture of the relationship between aging and expertise.

ACKNOWLEDGMENTS

The preparation of this manuscript was supported in part by a grant from the Formation de Chercheurs et l'Aide à la Recherche (FCAR) to Vimla Patel. Valuable discussions around the topics of aging, expertise, and medicine with Anders

Ericsson and Neil Charness contributed greatly to ideas in the paper. We thank Leanna Zozula for her critical suggestions and careful editing of the manuscript. We also thank the reviewers for their comments and suggestions.

REFERENCES

Arocha, J. F., & Patel, V. L. (1995). Construction-integration theory and clinical reasoning. In I. C. A. Weaver, S. Mannes, & C. R. Fletcher (Eds.), *Discourse comprehension* (pp. 359–382). Hillsdale, NJ: Lawrence Erlbaum Asociates.

Bäckman, L., & Dixon, R. A. (1992). Psychological compensation: A theoretical framework. *Psychological Bulletin, 112,* 259–283.

Charness, N. (1981). Aging and skilled problem solving. *Journal of Experimental Psychology: General, 110,* 21–28.

Charness, N. (1985). Aging and problem solving performance. In N. Charness (Ed.), *Aging and human performance* (pp. 226–260). New York: Wiley.

Chase, W. G., & Simon, H. A. (1973). Perception in chess. *Cognitive Psychology, 4,* 55–81.

Cjifer, E. (1966). An experiment on some differences in logical thinking between Dutch medical people, under and over the age of 35. *Acta Psychologica, 25,* 159–171.

Cohen, G. (1979). Language comprehension in old age. *Cognitive Psychology, 11*(4), 412–429.

Coughlin, L. D., & Patel, V. L. (1987). Processing of critical information by physicians and medical students. *Journal of Medical Education, 62,* 818–828.

Craik, F. I. M. (1977). Age differences in human memory. In J. E. Birren & K. W. Schaie (Eds.), *Handbook of the psychology of aging* (pp. 384–420). New York: Van Nostrand Reinhold.

Craik, F. I. M., & Jennings, J. M. (1992). Human memory. In F. I. M. Craik & T. A. Salthouse (Eds.), *The handbook of aging and cognition* (pp. 51–110). Hillsdale, NJ: Lawrence Erlbaum Associates.

Denney, N. W. (1990). Adult age differences in traditional and practical problem solving. In E. A. Lovelace (Ed.), *Aging and cognition: Mental process, self-awareness, and interventions* (pp. 329–349). Amsterdam: North-Holland.

Ericsson, K. A. (1996). The acquisition of expert performance: An introduction to some of the issues. In K. A. Ericsson (Ed.), *The road to excellence: The acquisition of expert performance in the arts and sciences, sports, and games* (pp. 1–50). Mahwah, NJ: Lawrence Erlbaum Associates.

Ericsson, K. A., & Kintsch, W. (1995). Long-term working memory. *Psychological Review, 102,* 211–245.

Ericsson, K. A., Krampe, R. T., & Tesch-Römer, C. (1993). The role of deliberate practice in the acquisition of expert performance. *Psychological Review, 100*(3), 363–406.

Ericsson, K. A., & Staszewski, J. J. (1989). Skilled memory and expertise: Mechanisms of exceptional performance. In D. Klahr & K. Kotovsky (Eds.), *Complex information processing: The impact of Herbert A. Simon* (pp. 235–267). Hillsdale, NJ: Lawrence Erlbaum Associates.

Evans, D. A., & Gadd, C. S. (1989). Managing coherence and context in medical problem-solving discourse. In D. A. Evans & V. L. Patel (Eds.), *Cognitive science in medicine: Biomedical modeling* (pp. 211–255). Cambridge, MA: MIT Press.

Groen, G. J., & Patel, V. L. (1988). The relationship between comprehension and reasoning in medical expertise. In M. T. H. Chi, R. Glaser, & M. J. Farr (Eds.), *The nature of expertise* (pp. 287–310). Hillsdale, NJ: Lawrence Erlbaum Associates.

Hultsch, D. F., & Dixon, R. A. (1990). Learning and memory and aging. In J. E. Birren & K. W. Schaie (Eds.), *Handbook of the psychology of aging* (3rd ed.). New York: Academic Press.

Joseph, G.M., & Patel, V. L. (1990). Domain knowledge and hypothesis generation in diagnostic reasoning. *Journal of Medical Decision Making, 10,* 31–46.

Kausler, D. H. (1985). Episodic memory: Memorizing performance. In N. Charness (Ed.), *Aging and human performance* (pp. 101–142). New York: Wiley.

Meyer, B. J. F., Rice, G. E., Knight, C. C., & Jessen, J. L. (1979). *Differences in the type of information remembered from prose by young, middle, and old adults.* (Research Report No. 5, Prose Learning Series). Tempe: Arizona State University, Department of Educational Psychology, College of Education.

Morrow, D. G., Leirer, V. O., & Altieri, P. A. (1992). Aging, expertise, and narative processing. *Psychology & Aging, 7*(3), 376–388.

Patel, V. L., Arocha, J. F., & Kaufman, D. R. (1994).Diagnostic reasoning and expertise. *The Psychology of Learning and Motivation: Advances in Research and Theory, 31,* 137–252.

Patel, V. L., Evans, D. A., & Kaufman, D. R. (1989). Cognitive framework for doctor-patient interaction. In D. A. Evans & V. L. Patel (Eds.), *Cognitive science in medicine: Biomedical modeling* (pp. 253–308). Cambridge, MA: MIT Press.

Patel, V. L., & Groen, G. J. (1991). The general and specific nature of medical expertise: A critical look. In A. Ericsson & J. Smith (Eds.), *Toward a general theory of expertise: Prospects and limits* (pp. 93–125). New York: Cambridge University Press.

Patel, V. L., Groen, G. J., & Frederiksen, C. H. (1986). Differences between students and physicians in memory for clinical cases. *Medical Education, 20,* 3–9.

Salthouse, T. A. (1984). Effects of aging and skill in typing. *Journal of Experimental Psychology: General, 113,* 345–371.

Salthouse, T. A. (1991). Expertise as the circumvention of human processing. In K. A. Ericsson & J. Smith (Eds.), *Toward a general theory of expertise: Prospects and limits* (pp. 286–300). New York: Cambridge University Press.

Salthouse, T. A., Babcock, R. L., Skovronek, E., Mitchell, D. R. D., & Palmon, R. (1990). Age and experience effects in spatial visualization. *Developmental Psychology, 26,* 128–136.

Schmidt, H. G., Norman, G. R., & Boshuizen, H. P. A. (1990). A cognitive perspective on medical expertise: Theory and implications. *Academic Medicine, 65*(10), 611–623.

Shimamura, A. P., Berry, J. M., Mangels, J. A., Rusting, C. L., & Jurica, P. J. (1995). Memory and cognitive abilities in university professors: Evidence for successful aging. *Psychological Science, 6,* 271–277.

Simon, H. A. (1973). The structure of ill-structured problems. *Artificial Intelligence, 4,* 181–201.

Spilich, G. J. (1985). Discourse comprehension across the span of life. In N. Charness (Ed.), *Aging and human performance* (pp. 101–142). New York: Wiley.

Strayer, D. L., & Kramer, A. F. (1994). Aging and skill acquisition: Learning–performance distinctions. *Psychology & Aging, 9,* 589–605.

van Dijk, T. A., & Kintsch, W. (1983). *Strategies of discourse comprehension.* New York: Academic Press.

Zelinski, E. M., Gilewski, M. J., & Thompson, L. (1980). Do laboratory memory tests relate to everyday remembering and forgetting? In L. W. Poon, J. L. Fozard, G. Cermak, D. Arenberg, & L. W. Thompson (Eds.), *New directions in memory and aging: Proceedings of the George Talland memorial conference* (pp. 519–544). Hillsdale NJ: Lawrence Erlbaum Associates.

Zozula, L., & Patel, V. L. (1997). How do they do it? Delving into the world of an aging medical expert. In M. G. Shafto & P. Langley (Eds.), *Proceedings of the Nineteenth Annual Conference of the Cognitive Science Society* (pp. 844–849). Mahwah, NJ: Lawrence Erlbaum Associates.

III

Medication Adherence

9

Psychosocial Factors in Medication Adherence: A Model of the Modeler

Elaine A. Leventhal
University of Medicine and Dentistry of New Jersey

Howard Leventhal
Chantal Robitaille
Susan Brownlee
Rutgers, The State University of New Jersey

The goal of our chapter is to elaborate a model of the cognitive and emotional factors affecting adherence. In doing so, we examine the ways in which age-related increases in morbidity and age-related changes in an individual's psychological functioning affect the self-regulation processes responsible for caring for oneself and adherence to treatment regimens. It is important to recognize that adherence is an important topic in medicine and sociology as well as psychology and that each of these disciplines approaches the issue somewhat differently (for earlier reviews of these perspectives see H. Leventhal & Cameron, 1987, and H. Leventhal, Zimmerman, & Gutmann, 1984). For example, medicine's concerns are typically of two types: (a) adherence is important for successful management of disease, and (b) adherence is critical for evaluating treatment efficacy in clinical trials because differences in adherence can reduce or even reverse the relative efficacy of two medications if adherence is less to the more effective of the two (Feinstein, 1976). Medical sociologists, on the other hand, have been concerned with the effects of institutions, social class, and roles on adherence, addressing questions such as: "Is there differential access and adherence to treatment as a function of education and/or income?" "Is adherence different in managed care and fee-for-service practice?" "Does continuity of care affect doctor-patient relationships and adherence?"

The primary focus of psychologists has been the relationship of behavioral and mental processes to adherence. For example, psychologists have examined the role of cognitive factors such as working memory and prospective memory upon adherence (Park, 1992, 1996) and the effects of beliefs about specific diseases such as the idea that symptoms are indicators of disease (Bishop, 1991; Harver & Mahler, 1997; Pennebaker, 1982), or that disease is caused by stress, has an acute or chronic time line (Heidrich, Forsthoff, & Ward, 1994), and can be controlled by medical or other means (Lau & Hartmann, 1983). Psychologists also examine the role of beliefs about personal skills, for example, self-efficacy for medication use (Lorig, Chastian, Ung, Shoor, & Holman, 1989), and the availability and risks of different procedures for the avoidance and control of disease, such as beliefs that medications are necessary but pose risks of addiction (Horne, 1997). Finally, both psychologists and sociologists examine the way in which contextual factors, such as social support, life stress, and emotional states, alter the relationship of attitudinal and skill factors to adherence within specific subsets of patients.

The differences in approach have important consequences. First, as medical practitioners are interested in outcomes, they will often express little patience for studies focusing on process. Second, the practitioner's focus on outcome data is often expressed as the need to identify factors that enhance adherence for all persons, all medications, and all diseases, in all settings. Psychologists, by contrast, do not expect to find factors that have a universal relationship to adherence. Indeed, the goal of most psychological analyses is to identify the contextual factors that alter the relationship of specific factors to adherence because data showing how contextual factors affect the relationship of specific variables to adherence will increase understanding of the process underlying adherent behavior. For example, cognitive factors such as working and prospective memory may have little or no relationship to adherence for most samples, but may be important determinants of adherence for persons over 80 years of age, particularly when these older persons have been prescribed medicatons for multiple conditions (Park, 1992). And neither memory factors nor beliefs about medications will affect adherence if the study participants are using a simple technical device to regulate use (i.e., an organizer with compartments for each day's medication; Park, Morrell, Frieske, & Kincaid, 1992) or are in a context where adherence to a regimen is regulated by a nurse or a supportive family member (Park & Jones, 1997). In short, if psychologically minded investigators are interested in examining the contribution of a particular set of variables to adherence, they must exercise great care in picking a context (disease and treatment) and population for study. They must also pay close attention to institutional and historical factors (e.g., changes in the health care system, availability of new treatments, and patient and practitioner cohort) and be prepared to persuade medical collaborators of the value of process information for clinical practice.

When trying to convince medical collaborators of the need to study the adherence process, the wise investigator will make use of case examples or what may be viewed as the "typical" problem case and not depend solely on statistical data to support a position (Nisbett & Ross, 1980). For example, what would be our expectation regarding delays in using health care and compliance with treatment for two hypothetical women, each of whom reports pain in the upper abdominal region: Alva, who is 50 years old and has no diagnosed chronic illness and Betty, who is 71 years old and has a moderate degree of osteoarthritis, scoliosis, and elevated cholesterol. Alva regards herself as being in excellent health for her age, is employed, and has full health insurance. She schedules annual checkups but rarely needs or seeks health care. Lately, she started having intermittent upper abdominal pain and burning distress that, although distinctive, is not disruptive of her daily activities. Betty, on the other hand, regards herself as being in excellent health for her age, is active in charity and volunteer work, and has full medical coverage. She schedules annual checkups and makes two to three visits per year to check on her arthritis and her cholesterol level. She has multiple symptoms (joint stiffness, pain in the lower and upper back). In addition, she recently started having intermittent upper abdominal pain and burning distress that is not disruptive of her daily activities, as the symptoms are somewhat blunted in intensity. Will Alva and Betty represent their new pain similarly? Indeed, can Betty, as clearly as can Alva, discern the "new signals" that are experienced on a complex background of somatic events and may be blunted in an older person? (E. A. Leventhal & Crouch, 1997). What procedures are they each likely to bring to bear on the experience? And if a prescribed treatment removes the intermittent symptoms more swiftly than expected, who is likely to maintain and complete the regimen "to make sure it is gone and to be sure it doesn't come back"? Considering Betty's greater ambiguity regarding the symptoms and her more frequent use of health care, will she be quicker to use care and be more adherent to prescribed treatment? Given the advancing age of the population, the reduced time spent with patients as we move to managed care, and the need for self-care for many lifelong chronic illnesses (Ory & DeFries, 1998; Stoller, 1998), it may pay to have a more complete understanding of the mental processes that drive utilization and compliance. If this understanding can enhance practice, convincing colleagues of the need for descriptive studies and intervention trials should not be an insurmountable task.

A PROCESS MODEL TO GUIDE MEDICATION ADHERENCE

A proposition at the base of our analysis of the adherence process is that individuals are problem solvers. Whether avoiding or preventing potential health threats or actively managing an ongoing health problem, these problem solvers are involved to different degrees with the tasks of defining the nature of the threat, selecting procedures for threat control, and evaluating the success of their efforts. Our model represents this problem-solving process as a pair of partially independent, parallel processing systems. Perceptual/cognitive representations of the threat and plans to perform and evaluate procedures for threat control are generated in the cognitve arm. A parallel set of emotional reactions and procedures for emotion management are generated in the affective arm, and they interact with and affect the processes under primary control of the cognitive arm (see Fig. 9.1). The self is conceived, therefore, as an active, instrumental agent attempting to construe and control environmental dangers, while simultaneously experiencing and attempting to control its emotional reactions to these dangers. As the self has and regards itself as having specific properties, the representation of the self interacts with this problem-solving process. Thus the view of a potential disease threat (e.g., an individual's perception of vulnerability to a disease such as colon cancer) and the possibility of controlling the threat will reflect both the representation of the disease and knowledge of the procedures for its prevention as well as the representation of he self (beliefs in special weaknesses of the self) and self-efficacy in executing

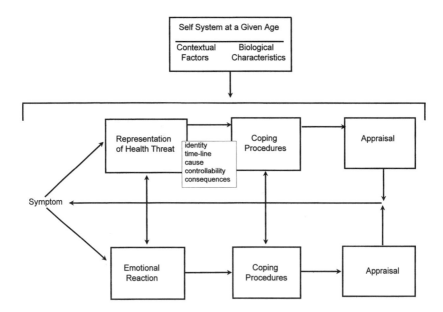

FIG. 9.1. Parallel processing model. The appearance of a symptom elicits the partially independent processing of the cognitive representation of the health threat and the emotional reaction, which, in turn, generate coping procedures and appraisals. Appraisal outcomes are continuously fed back into the system and can serve to modify any of the components in the model. The self system influences the entire model directly through both its contextual factors and biological characteristics.

preventive behaviors. In short, we regard the study of adherence to medication regimens as an empirical enterprise in which to test our skill at developing a model of a "common-sense modeler" in action (see Giere, 1988; for more recent views, see H. Leventhal, Diefenbach, & E. A. Leventhal, 1992, and H. Leventhal, E. A. Leventhal, & Contrada, in press).

How Are Illness Threats Represented?

Mental representations of threats to health, which emerge in the first step of the processing of illness information (see Fig. 9.1), have five attributes: (a) identity, its name (label) and symptoms (concrete indicators), (b) timeline, the time for the threat to develop and its duration once it develops, (c) perceived cause, the events perceived to precipitate, promote, and/or exacerbate the threat, (d) controllability, the extent to which the disease entity can be cured, controlled and/or prevented by self or expert action, and (e) consequences, the physical (death, disability, pain, etc.), lifestyle, social, emotional, and economic changes it potentiates. The illness threats or categories defined by these attributes can be organized into higher order groupings such as chronic versus acute (H. Leventhal, Easterling, Coons, Luchterhand, & Love, 1986) or life threatening versus infectious and temporary (Bishop, 1987, 1991; D'Andrade, Quinn, Nerlove, & Romney, 1972).

Each attribute exists both as an abstract concept and as a concrete perception and/or image. For example, the identity of a disease is defined by a label and a set of symptoms (Meyer, H. Leventhal, & Gutmann, 1985). Although we typically think of time in terms of numerical abstractions, such as number of minutes, hours, or days, time can also be concrete, such as perceived time or how long it "feels" for something to come to an end. Similarly, consequences can be represented in conceptual form, such as a disease being described as painful, or one can generate a vivid image of self in pain (i.e., perceptual form). Concrete perceptual experience appears to play an important role in medication adherence.

Indeed, recent studies show that perceptions can conflict with and override conceptual knowledge. For example, 80% of a sample of 50 middle-aged, hypertensive patients expressed strong agreement with the statement, "People can't tell when their blood pressure is up," a response fully in accord with the information they had been given by their physicians, but over 90% of this very same sample believed they could tell when their own blood pressure was elevated by monitoring their symptoms, and these same patients stopped taking their medications if, in their judgment, the medications did not reduce these symptoms (Meyer et al., 1985). And 58% of the patients who thought their hypertension was an acute condition, that is, as similar to illness episodes that have been typical over their life span, dropped out of treatment (Meyer et al., 1985). Indeed, even time can be experienced concretely and lead to nonadherence. Jamison (1995) reported dramatic, anecdotal examples for antidepressant medications. Conceptual time, that it takes 3 to 6 weeks for their tricyclic medications to induce positive moods, conflicts with "felt time," that is, that side effects (dry mouth, urinary retention, hypotension, etc.) appear in

1 or 2 days, persuading the patient that the medication is working but not doing its purported job, that is, enhancing mood (Jamison, 1995).

These studies make three important points: (a) a tight link exists between symptoms and disease labels; (b) symptom experience can dominate abstract knowledge in directing medication use; and (c) time frames for treatment, both abstract and concrete, can affect adherence.

Are There Procedures for Danger Control?

A vast number of procedures can be used to cope with threats to health, and a variety of categorization schemes have been offered to simplify this domain, for example, danger-based versus fear-based coping (H. Leventhal, 1970) or problem-focused versus emotion-focused coping (Lazarus & Launier, 1978). Although each classi-fication scheme is suitable for addressing a particular set of questions, it may not be useful for addressing others. For example, it would be important to determine individuals' goals in seeking social information when addressing questions respect-ing differences among age groups in the use of social information for coping with health threats. In the early stages of an illness episode, social comparisons may be aimed at identifying and evaluating the condition, for example, What is causing this pain?, whereas at a later stage, social comparisons may serve the function of evaluating treatment or enhancing the self, for example, Am I doing better than him or her? (Croyle & Jemmott, 1991; Kulik & Mahler, 1987; H. Leventhal, Hudson, & Robitaille, 1997; Wood, 1989, p. 240).

IF-THEN-ELSE Rules. Our model posits an intimate, Gestalt-like connec-tion between procedures and representations (H. Leventhal et al., 1992). This connection can be conceived as an IF-THEN rule (Anderson, 1993; H. Leventhal et al., in press), in which the IF is the suspected condition and the THEN is the procedure for further diagnosing and/or treating the condition. There is often a latent, alternative, ELSE hypothesis in this testing process, that is, if this antacid doesn't make it stop all night, maybe it's an ulcer and not just what I ate! In the initial stages of most illness episodes, the representation may be best conceived as a set of hypotheses the most available of which (often the most benign) leads to a self-care test. If this interpretation is disconfirmed, a fear response could emerge, which, depending upon the conditions, could accelerate or inhibit the adoption of an alternative procedure (e.g., care seeking) for coping with the perceived threat. The IF-THEN-ELSE formulation makes clear that representations are evolving structures and that procedures can have multiple functions, often serving as diag-nostic tools at the initial stage of symptom detection, as tools for treatment and cure or control later on, and as a means of coping with and controlling emotion throughout all stages of the illness episode.

Procedure Attributes. The attributes that define the content of repre-sentations may also be useful for defining the attributes of procedures. For example, procedures have an identity including a label (e.g., surgery), concrete experiences (e.g., pain vs. no pain), causes, or routes for causal action (e.g., if it is a tumor, then it is to be excised; else if a bacteria, then it should be killed with drugs), time lines (e.g., medication works in 24 hours vs. 2 weeks), consequences (e.g., cure and/or symptom alleviation vs. disfigurement, noxious side effects, risk of addiction, or economic costs) and can be seen as more or less controllable (e.g., a regimen may seem too complex to perform, and its consequences may be seen as uncontrollable). Commonalities on attributes should help to define IF-THEN linkages that affect the selection of a specific procedure for self-care.

Horne and colleagues' factor analytic study of commonsense views of medicines was one of the first systematic efforts to examine the attributes of a critical set of health care procedures (Horne, 1997). Their analysis produced four separate factors respecting the attributes of medication. The first two factors involved beliefs about specific medicines: (a) the perception that a medicine is necessary for controlling a disease and (b) concern or worry about taking a particular medicine. The last two factors involve beliefs about medicines in general: (c) the perception that medicines pose the danger of addiction and (d) the perception that physicians overprescribe medicines. These beliefs appear to have a major effect on treatment adherence, but little is known about the conditions limiting their impact. For example, concerns about addiction appear to be salient for both non-narcotic and narcotic pain killers, though fears about the addictive quality of narcotics can be overcome if patients are given clear instructions regarding appropriate use and reassurances that addiction is exceedingly unlikely and treatable. Addiction is indeed extremely unlikely when patients are allowed to self-administer narcotics immediately after major surgery (Bennett et al., 1982), and it is irrelevant when used by patients who are terminal. Fear of addiction is not limited to pain medications and many patients suspect that most drugs can be addictive (Horne, 1997). This belief appears to be responsible for the exceedingly low rate of willingness to use antidepressants (Hankin et al., 1982). People may develop elaborate schemes to control such fears and these can effect medication adherence.

Representations of Caregivers. A plethora of studies have identified characteristics of health providers that are related to patient satisfaction (e.g., Anderson & Zimmerman, 1993; Bertakis, Helms, Callahan, Azari, & Robbins, 1995; Hall & Roter, 1988; Kaplan, Greenfield, Gandek, Rogers, & Ware, 1996). A smaller number report associations between physician characteristics and adherence to treatment (DiMatteo, 1993; Frankel, 1995; Heszen-Klemens & Lapinska, 1984; Holt, 1991; Widmer, Cadoret, & Troughton, 1983). Similarities between physicians and patients in individual differences such as demographics, attitudes, values, and preferences have been shown to increase treatment adherence (e.g., Burgoon et al., 1987). Further, treatment adherence is positively associated with such physician interpersonal skills as levels of respect toward the patient, warmth, friendliness, and concern (Meichenbaum & Turk, 1987).

Robitaille (1998) suggested that research relating physician characteristics to treatment adherence would be invigorated and move forward more rapidly by recognizing that physicians, nurses, and other health practitioners can be represented in much the same way that investigators are conceptualizing illnesses and procedures. Thus, physicians can be represented in terms of their ability to diagnose or identify illnesses, to control symptoms and the underlying disease process (a skill factor), clarify time lines, and provide information about the causes and consequences of an illness. Physicians can also address a patient's psychological state and increase adherence to treatment by listening to patient concerns and providing information to help patients better manage their emotional reactions to both illness and treatment.

Robitaille's second point is that both the representation of the disease threat and the representation of the physician interact and influence decisions to use health care and adhere to treatment protocols. The representation of the threat, its identity, perceived causes, time line, consequences, and controllability are matched to the patient's representation of the physician on these same attributes. The matching increases the salience or importance of some physician attributes and minimizes the importance of others. Whether an individual considers seeking medical care and whether he or she is or is not compliant with that practitioner's recommendation reflect the fit between the two representations. For example, if a symptom is interpreted as a sign of a life-threatening disease such as cancer, the diagnostic and treatment skills of the physician, in particular, the physician's willingness to eliminate uncertainty and enhance disease control by immediate diagnostic and treatment efforts, become of special concern.

How Do Affective Reactions Affect Adherence?

The data from which our model originated strongly suggest that the processes underlying the use of information to construct our objectively viewed reality (i.e., the perception of danger or health threats) are largely independent of the processes involved in the construction of our emotional reactions (i.e., the active experience of fear, depression, or anger; H. Leventhal, 1970). Thus, the magnitude and time course of active, emotional reactions is quite different from that of the cognitive and skill factors involved in the motivation of behaviors to prevent, manage, and/or cure illness threats. This does not mean that the perception and/or meaning of a health threat does not affect emotion, and vice versa. It does require, however, that we identify those cognitive processes that are critical for the elicitation of emotions. For example, we proposed that the cognitions that are most likely to generate fear are those involved in direct, perceptual encounters with a threat agent, for example, scenes of accident victims and/or images of skeletonized bodies decimated by cancer, but not those verbal labels used to talk about a disease or to plan to prevent and manage it. We also hypothesized that the cognition of the health threat and the experience of fear would lead to separate procedures for their management (H. Leventhal, 1970; See also Lazarus & Launier, 1978). Later elaborations of the model proposed that emotional reactions can be elicited by minimal threat cues that automatically elicit the fear response (Furedy & Riley, 1987; H. Leventhal, 1984; H. Leventhal & Scherer, 1987; Scherer, 1984). For example, the sight of a surgical knife cutting a patient's body can elicit squirming and fear before the viewer completely represents the scene as the removal of a cancerous lung. Hence, the automatic elicitation of active, emotional reactions to minimal (impoverished) cues further supports the independence of these two processing systems.

Fear Can Facilitate and Inhibit Protective Action.   Early studies on the effects of communications about health threats identified two types of interactions between cognitive and affective reactions. One such interaction was consistent with the very obvious hypothesis that fear motivates behaviors to avoid feared objects. If fear motivates avoidance of threats such as cancer, it will motivate preventive actions (i.e., actions that move away from cancer, such as quitting smoking; e.g., H. Leventhal & Niles, 1964) and motivate avoidance of actions that bring one into contact with cancer, such as taking an X-ray to detect it (H. Leventhal & Niles, 1964; Millar & Millar, 1995). The second way in which fear affected action was by reducing confidence in one's ability to perform protective behaviors (H. Leventhal, 1970). This loss of confidence appeared when fear was "hot," that is, when it was an active state rather than something just under discussion, and it occured most often among individuals with low self-confidence. The inhibition of protective behaviors dissipated as fear "cooled," that is, inhibition lessened and protective actions resumed as time from exposure to the fear-arousing communication to the point for action increased (H. Leventhal, 1970).

The transient nature of emotional states, the need to determine the object of fear (e.g., is the individual fearful of the disease or of the treatment?), and the mode for fear management (e.g., does he or she eliminate the threat, avoid or deny the threat, or medicate the fear?) introduce considerable uncertainty in predictions as to how fear will affect adherence behaviors. These uncertainties can be reduced by the assessment of individuals' representations of the threat and the procedures for its detection, prevention, and control. For example, fear is likely to be activated and sustained if people believe that they are vulnerable to disease such as cancer, if they believe the disease is caused by prolonged exposure to stress, and if they are experiencing vague somatic symptoms (e.g., fatigue, joint pain) that they believe to be indicators of the disease (Cameron, E. A. Leventhal, & H. Leventhal, 1995; Easterling & H. Leventhal, 1989). Beliefs in vulnerability to a particular disease may also be activated by a variety of other factors such as a family history of the feared disease (Lerman et al., 1996; Brownlee, 1997), the presence of somatic changes (Meyer et al., 1985), age related morbidity in oneself and mortality in members of one's cohort. Knowledge of factors such as these may allow more precise predictions of the activation of fear, and knowledge of the individual's preferred mode of managing threat will allow one to predict the action the fear is likely to elicit. In summary, the available data suggests that active fear has short term effects on attention and over action and will have little or no effect on the depth with which people process information about health threats or the means of avoiding them.

Finally, age appears to affect emotional reactions, and older persons typically report less intense emotions, both negative and positive (Diener, Sandvik, & Larsen, 1985). Although such declines in affective intensity appear across the board, there may be specific areas in which fear is maintained, for example, fear of cancer. And, as we discuss in the following section, older persons appear to adopt generalized strategies for avoiding risk that may play a central role both in maintaining low levels of fear and high levels of protective health behaviors, including high levels of adherence to treatment recommendations.

THE SELF SYSTEM AND AGE-RELATED FACTORS AFFECTING SELF-REGULATION

Our model was developed and has been most successful in accounting for the adherence behavior of individuals in treatment for diagnosed health problems. Diagnostic illness labels and somatic changes create motivation for action by defining the presence of a threat to the self. Although the *self* was not included as a specific, conceptual entity in our earlier models (e.g., H. Leventhal, 1970; H. Leventhal, Meyer, & Nerenz, 1980), it soon became clear that we would have to give explicit recognition to the self if we were to account for adherence behavior in two important areas: (a) prevention of illness (i.e., in the absence of symptoms) or diagnosis of illness and (b) age-related changes in adherence to treatment for chronic conditions. The self is also the focus of attention when we examine issues relating to adaptation to chronic illness (H. Leventhal, 1975).

The Self in Self-Regulation

Prevention and Images of the Self.   Understanding adherence to behaviors for detecting, preventing, and managing an illness requires explicit attention to conceptions of the self and those attributes of the self that may generate feelings of vulnerability and the need to adopt preventive health behaviors. For example, conceptions of the self play a central role in the social comparisons processes that appear to account for the frequently reported increases in breast cancer concern and breast cancer screening in response to media stories of cancer in famous people (e.g., If it can happen to someone as young and well-off as she, it certainly can happen to me.). Social comparison theories do not, however, identify the specific dimensions of the self, that is, the skills, behaviors, or physical and psychological attributes that individuals will perceive as relevant for evaluating their health or susceptibility to health threats. Identifying these attributes is critical for understanding how and when social comparison will take place and whether it will create motivation to engage in or to avoid health actions (H. Leventhal, Hudson, & Robitaille, 1997).

Shared heredity is an aspect of self-identity that has emerged as a determinant of feelings of vulnerability toward specific health threats. Shared heredity, indexed by a history of cancer in one's family, is strongly related to perceptions of vulnerability to cancer (Brownlee, 1997) and to interest in testing for genetic risk (Lerman et al., 1996). Comparing symptoms among older adults is often a prelude to sharing medications. Whether people are explicitly aware, able, or willing to report on it, they are sensitive to and make use of different attributes of other persons when deciding to follow or ignore their health relevant recommendations. A study of women in the late stages of pregnancy provides a forceful illustration. Mazen and H. Leventhal (1972) had four communicators recommend rooming-in service (in which the newborn baby is kept in the room with the mother rather than in the nursery) and breast feeding to a series of pregnant women, half of whom were Black and half, White. Two of the four sources were White and two were Black. Each of the four served as communicators both when they were pregnant and after they had delivered their own babies and did so to roughly equal numbers of Black and White expectant mothers on both occasions. Thus, message recipients and communicators could be similar or different on each of two, overtly observable factors (i.e., race and pregnancy). Communicator/recipient similarity in pregnancy significantly increased favorable attitudes toward rooming-in service and actual use of the service; it had no effect on breast feeding. On the other hand, similarity in race significantly increased favorable attitudes toward breast feeding and reported use of breast feeding; it had no effect, however, on use of the rooming-in service. The data make clear that the selection of a relevant attribute for comparison is a dynamic and critical aspect of social comparison processes: attribute relevance is a function of the individual's representation of both the problem situation and the self.

The Aging Self and Self-Regulation. Chronological age has been positively correlated with treatment adherence. For example, our group found greater adherence among older than middle-aged adults to both everyday health-promoting behaviors such as the use of a low-fat diet (Prohaska, E. Leventhal, H. Leventhal, & Keller, 1985) and to treatment for hypertension and cancer chemotherapy (H. Leventhal, E. A. Leventhal, & Schaefer, 1991). Park and colleagues (1992) confirmed and extended these findings by showing that adherence to hypertension medication improves with increasing age, but declines if one extends the sample to the oldest-old adults (i.e., those over 85 years of age) who are typically managing multiple pharmacy use during a period of cognitive decline (Willis, 1996). Rather than viewing age as a direct determinant of health and health behavior, both we (H. Leventhal, E. A. Leventhal, & Schaefer, 1991) and Park (1994) view chronological age as a moderating factor in the self-regulation framework (Fig. 9.1). This approach leads us to ask whether the relationship of age to health behaviors is also mediated by differences among middle-aged, old, and oldest-old adults in cognitive competence such as prospective memory and/or by differences in how these cohorts represent illnesses, adopt procedures, and make use of general strategies to cope with potential and current health threats. If age acts through these mediating factors, and if we can identify the factors through which it operates, we will both have a more complete understanding of the effects of age on health and illness behavior, and, more important, be better able to intervene in order to optimize health-enhancing behaviors and improve the individual's quality of life.

Figure 9.1 suggests at least two additional sets of factors affecting health and illness behaviors that involve age-related changes in the self. First, age is related to differences in the somatic as well as in the social information to which people are exposed, which leads to differences in experience in managing somatic change. An important factor in the domain of social information is the age-related increase in morbidity and mortality among members of one's next older generation, followed by a similar increase in one's immediate cohort. Thus, regardless of cohort, as people age, they will find increased discussion by family and peers about managing chronic illness as well as increased mortality among these persons. These age-related changes in morbidity and mortality generate two types of statistics: the objective data collected by epidemiologists and the subjective sense of mortality that comprises the "commonsense epidemiology" of older adults (H. Leventhal, Nerenz, & Strauss, 1982). Although this subjective sense of mortality need not translate into a sense of vulnerability to any specific disease on any given day for many older persons (Brownlee, 1997), it may create a background of subjective risk, or a sense that "things can happen when you get to my age."

The second set of factors consists of age-related changes in the biological self. Age-related physiological changes alter the way specific diseases behave both in symptom manifestation and in response to treatment. Inappropriate responses to illness symptoms because of these changes may increase risk to health and result in unnecessary morbidity. Thus, our premise is that the variables that accompany chronological age, not chronological age itself, are responsible for age-related changes in both health behaviors and illness behaviors. The expression *self system at a given age* in Fig. 9.1 stands for the change in self-identity that arises from the individual's observation of mortality and morbidity in others and the experience of the physical signs of aging in the self. The facet of an individual's self-identity that may change as a function of these lifespan-related experiences is an increasing sense of nonspecific vulnerability to illness and susceptibility to harm, which, in turn, may affect older persons' decisions to act in order to prevent, diagnose, or treat physical illness.

Because changes in the strategies adopted for managing illness threats may reflect changes in procedures generated by modifications of either representations of disease threats or representations of the self and its resources, it may be difficult to isolate the determinants of age-related differences in health and illness behaviors. In the remainder of this chapter, we examine these issues drawing upon existing data whenever possible. Because the investigation of the effects of age upon illness representations and self-identity is in its infancy, we are forced at times to engage in speculation about the ways in which these age-related changes may alter health and illness behaviors.

Age Affects the Representation of Symptoms and Coping

As described in our opening scenarios of the middle-aged person (50-year-old Alva) and the older adult (71-year-old Betty), older persons typically experience more bodily symptoms than do younger persons (National Center for Health Statistics, 1995; Hale, Perkins, May, Marks, & Stewart, 1986). In addition, both the biological changes associated with normal aging and the chronic diseases common in later life develop gradually and often express themselves with less intensity. Symptoms such as fever, which depends upon a vigorous immune response (Kaesberg & Ershler, 1989), and pain associated with disease appear to present in blunted form with increasing age. Thus, the older individual has the difficult task of evaluating the significance of slowly changing, blunted symptoms against a complex background of age-related somatic changes. The increased ambiguity created by these conditions introduces a high level of uncertainty in the individual's ongoing self-appraisals and can encourage the attribution of disease-related symptoms to normal aging (Kart, 1981; Prohaska, Keller, E. A. Leventhal, & H. Leventhal, 1987). Inappropriate self-diagnoses of this type can occur because the experiencing, labeling, and seeking of treatment for blunted symptoms often lags the occurrence of these physiological changes.

Risk Avoidance and Conservation: Compensatory Strategies for Self-Regulation

How might the older Betty adjust to an increasingly ambiguous symptom environment and a growing sense that "things can happen" in order to reduce the risk of disease while maintaining quality of life? Consistent with Baltes and Baltes' (1990) proposal that older adults attempt to minimize complexity while optimizing efficiency of function, E. A. Leventhal and Crouch (1997) proposed that the elderly manage health risks in an increasingly uncertain environment by adopting an overall strategy of risk aversion and conservation of resources. This strategy may be responsible for the high levels of adherence among older cohorts.

The strongest evidence for this hypothesis has emerged from studies of the speed with which individuals seek health care in response to symptoms. In the first such study, E. A. Leventhal, H. Leventhal, Schaefer, and Easterling (1993) compared the speed of care seeking of older (more than 65 years of age) versus middle-aged (ages 40 to 55) patients. Participants were interviewed in the clinic immediately before seeing a physician (all participants were insured and thus presumably had equal access to care). The first part of the interview determined whether the current visit was patient-initiated and thus eligible for inclusion (i.e., patients with doctor-initiated follow-ups for new tests to diagnose previously reported conditions or to adjust medication for previously diagnosed conditions were excluded). The interview then defined the time line for the episode: the day that any change in health was first noticed, the day the patient decided the symptoms or change in function were medical in nature, and the day the patient called for care. Time from first notice to calling for care was defined as *total delay* and total delay was divided into two periods: *appraisal delay* (time from first notice to the decision that the changes were medical in nature) and *illness delay* (time from the decision that the changes were medical in nature to the point of calling for a provider appointment). After the temporal sequence was clearly defined, the respondent was asked about his or her thoughts at each of the three time points. These measures included what caused the symptom/health change, how serious the change was perceived to be, and why health seeking decisions may have been delayed.

The analyses showed that total delay was significantly shorter for more serious symptoms and at every level of perceived severity, total delay (in days) was less for the older than for the middle-aged patients (delay for serious symptoms: middle-aged = 2.94, older = 1.05; for possibly serious symptoms: middle-aged = 13.27, older = 1.80; for mild symptoms: middle-aged = 16.12, older = 12.01). The plot thickened with the analysis of the two components of delay: for serious and mild symptoms, appraisal delays were shorter for older than middle-aged respondents (the difference was only marginally significant for possibly serious symptoms). The findings for illness delay were more complex: for serious problems, both the older and the middle-aged adults moved swiftly (less than 1 day) from deciding they were ill to calling for care, and both groups were slow in calling for care for mild problems (3 days). However, for intermediate or possibly serious symptoms, the middle-aged were substantially slower than the older adults (middle aged = 6.98 days; older = .74 days). In fact, for middle-aged subjects, illness delay was longer for symptoms they judged as possibly serious (6.98 days) than for symptoms they judged to be mild (3.87 days).

Participants' comments on the reasons for the delay clarified the meaning of the interaction for illness delay: a significantly higher proportion of the middle-aged adult group reported avoidant behavior because they were afraid the symptom might indicate a serious problem. Other factors such as time for seeking care were equivalent in the two groups. The basic findings of less total delay and swifter appraisal among older than younger persons were confirmed in a second study (E. A. Leventhal, Easterling, H. Leventhal, & Cameron, 1995). The replication corrected for the methodological shortcoming of the prior study and nearly all other studies of care seeking by comparing the care seekers to a set of non-care-seeking controls matched on gender, age, and medical history.

Both studies support the hypothesis that the older adults are quicker to use care because they are averse to serious risk and wish to conserve resources: swift care seeking places potential threats in the hands of experts, allowing older adults to avoid distress induced by uncertainty. This strategy of avoiding risk and conserving resources by turning over threat management to expert practitioners helps to explain why older persons are more adherent to preventive (Myers et al., 1994) and treatment regimens. The strategy offers an effective way of compensating for the increase in frailty, the complexity of background symptomatology, and the ambiguity of disease-specific symptoms faced by older persons. It is also congruent with the hypothesis that older adults are motivated to optimize their ability to actively generate positive experiences by simplifying their lives and restricting their social contacts to a narrower and more select subset of persons (Carstensen, 1992).

Hypervigilance: Threat of Illness As a Window for Self-Appraisal

Is the adoption of a risk aversion strategy a consequence of the growing ambiguity of somatic change, or is there more to it? It seems highly likely that multiple factors contribute to this strategy shift. As we indicated in the section, The Aging Self and Self-Regulation, there is an increasing awareness of the limitations of one's physical strength and resources, voiced in comments such as "I can't do what I used to do" or "I just don't have the energy I used to have." The experience of a decline in physical resources is accompanied by an increase in chronic conditions, some minor (e.g., loss of dentition, hearing, and visual acuity), some of intermediate value (e.g., mild hypertension, early stages of osteoarthritis), and others life-threatening and major (e.g., stroke, heart attack, breast cancer, and prostate cancer).

In addition to reductions in one's own sense of strength and vigor and the presence of chronic conditions, the older person participates in events surrounding the mortality and morbidity of spouses, family members, and peers. Social observations of this sort, in combination with the change in vigor and increasing chronic conditions in self, are likely to create a sense of increased nonspecific vulnerability, thus defining the self as mortal and susceptible to unforeseen calamity. Internal somatic changes, bolstered by observation of self and others, may lead to the cognitive reorganization of the self system, bringing questions of one's physical well-being to the fore. Thus, internal cues produced by either emotional stresses and/or short- or long-term physical and physiological change are increasingly likely to be interpreted in light of somatic risk, with cognitions dominated by questions such as "Am I stressed, am I ill, or am I just getting old?" "Am I physically able or am I declining in strength?" Physical soundness and longevity are issues central to each of these questions.

We hypothesize, therefore, that aging is associated with an increasing focus on physical well-being, a consequence of which is an increased tendency to interpret physical sensations, changes in physical function, and speed and vigor of intellectual and emotional reactions as possible signs of illness and/or decline in physical health. The hypothesis is consistent with data showing that major determinants of older adults' self-assessments of their health include physical function (Johnson & Wolinsky, 1993, 1994) and affective experience (Levkoff, Cleary, & Wetle, 1987; Tessler & Mechanic, 1978). Older adults who report problems with daily physical function and high levels of anxious and/or depressed affect are more likely to rate their health as poor (Benyamini, H. Leventhal, & E. A. Leventhal, 1997; Johnson, Stallones, Garrity, & Marx, 1990). Self-assessment of health has proven to be a strong predictor of mortality after controlling for medical history, age, and gender (Idler & Benyamini, 1997).

The hypothesis that age is associated with increases in the frequency with which somatic changes are interpreted as physical illness implies an increase in somatization and a decrease in reporting of emotional activation with increasing age. Age-related declines in emotional intensity are well documented (Diener et al., 1985; E. A. Leventhal & Prohaska, 1986), and the hypotheses that have been offered to account for it range from the purely psychological (i.e., that it reflects age-related withdrawal from daily life) to the purely biological (i.e., that it reflects an overall decline in physical and mental vigor). Although likely to be multiply determined, the hypothesis that the decline in strength of reported affect reflects an increased focus on illness threats leading to the categorization and experience of emotional distress as somatic (i.e., health) events fits with a number of mechanisms presumably involved in aging. For instance, although they report lessened intensity of affect in general, older adults do not report less fear in response to life-threatening illnesses such as heart disease (Brownlee, 1997; E. A. Leventhal & Prohaska, 1986), and age-related declines in inhibition of emotional expressiveness are frequently observed in older adults leading to assertions that they are irritable and uninhibited. The general decline in inhibitory processes with advancing age (e.g., weakening of the parasympathetic control of the sympathetic system; Schwartz, Gibb, & Tran, 1991) may prolong sympathetically driven somatic activation in response to environmental stressors, thereby muddying the perceived link between emotionally evocative stressors and the somatic activity they generate. The lack of specificity of somatic reactions to specific stressors may encourage older adults to interpret such somatic activity as indicators of relatively stable, illness-related changes (see H. Leventhal, Patrick-Miller, E. A. Leventhal, & Burns, 1998). The combination of observable increase in risk with age, increasing somatic symptoms, declining vigor, and attribution of affectively induced somatic changes to weakening of the physical system provides sufficient motivation for increased risk aversion, swift care seeking, and adherence to recommended treatment.

CONCLUSIONS

How individuals conceptualize or represent a disease threat can have a major impact on the use of self-care, seeking professional care, the type of care sought, and adherence to various aspects of treatment protocols in response to somatic or health changes. Defining the various attributes of procedures (e.g., negative medication beliefs that deter adherence) and exploring the links between representations and procedures defined as IF-THEN-ELSE rules represent an important advance in the conceptualization of the self-regulation process. It is also clear that the processes involve change as a function of historical or cohort factors and chronological and experiential age. Chronological age affects care seeking and adherence to treatment because it is associated with changes: in the way in which disease is experienced, in the older person's implicit view of the vulnerability of older persons to disease threats, and in strategies for self-appraisal and care seeking that compensate for the increased ambiguity of somatic cues and increased risk of life-threatening illness. In many Western nations today, older adults live near one another with a substantial degree of separation from their middle-aged children and young grandchildren. This social context provides the opportunity for a high frequency of social comparison allowing not only for the evaluation of one's overall health status, but also for information leading to a variety of potentially false inferences of the meaning of specific symptoms and of the procedures effective for their management, which, in turn, affect decisions regarding the need and value of professional care. The extensive investigation of social comparison processes often ignores, however, the factors affecting the choice of comparison object (H. Leventhal, Hudson, & Robitaille, 1997).

At present, we are merely at the threshold of illness cognition and adherence research. The self has been included as an explicit part of the self-regulation model, and only a limited number of self attributes have been defined and even fewer yet studied. Effective prevention programs depend upon developments in this area as do therapeutic interventions designed to maximize adaptation and minimize the cost of chronic and life-threatening illnesses. This latter challenge is great indeed, as life-threatening diseases are basic constituents of the human condition. The need for improved conceptualization of the context is also clear. How do people represent practitioners and the health care system? Are these representations independent of their views of health threats and their bodies? Understanding the links between these multilayered belief structures will represent a major step toward improving the quality, humaneness, and efficiency of care delivered to our older citizens by our health care system.

REFERENCES

Anderson, J. L. (1993). *The adaptive character of thought.* Hillsdale, NJ: Lawrence Erlbaum Associates.

Anderson, L. A., & Zimmerman, M. A. (1993). Patient and physician perceptions of their relationship and patient satisfaction: A study of chronic disease management. *Patient Education and Counseling, 20*(1), 27–36.

Baltes, P. B., & Baltes, M. M. (1990). Psychological perspectives on successful aging: The model of selective optimization with compensation. In P. B. Baltes & M. M. Baltes (Eds.), *Successful aging: Perspectives from the behavioral sciences* (pp. 1–34). New York: Cambridge University Press.

Bennett, R. L., Batenhorst, R. L., Bivins, B. A., Bell, R. M., Graves, D. A., Foster, T. S., Wright, B. D., & Griffen, W. O. (1982). Patient-controlled analgesia. *Annals of Surgery, 195,* 700–705.

Benyamini, Y., Leventhal, H., & Leventhal, E. A. (1997). *Self-assessments of health: What do people know that predicts their mortality.* Paper presented at the mmeeting of the Gerontological Society of America, Cincinnati, OH.

Bertakis, K. D., Helms, L. J., Callahan, E. J., Azari, R., & Robbins, J. A. (1995). The influence of gender on physician practice style. *Medical Care, 33*(4), 407–416.

Bishop, G. D. (1987). Lay conceptions of physical symptoms. *Journal of Applied Social Psychology, 17,* 127–146.

Bishop, G. D. (1991). Understanding the understanding of illness: Lay disease representations. In J. A. Skelton & R. T. Croyle (Eds.), *Mental representation in health and illness* (pp. 32–59). New York: Springer-Verlag.

Brownlee, S. (1997). Perceived vulnerability to illness. Dissertation Abstracts International, 58–07B. (University Microfilms No. 9800237)

Burgoon, J. K., Pfau, M., Parrott, R., Birk, T. S., Coker, R., & Burgoon, M. (1987). Relational communication, satisfaction, compliance-gaining strategies, and compliance in communication between physicians and patients. *Communication Monographs, 54*(3), 307–324.

Cameron, L. C., Leventhal, E. A., & Leventhal, H. (1995). Seeking medical care in response to symptoms and life stress. *Psychosomatic Medicine, 57,* 37–47.

Carstensen, L. L. (1992). Social and emotional patterns in adulthood: Support for the socioemotional selectivity theory. *Psychology and Aging, 7,* 331–338.

Croyle, R. T., & Jemmott, J. B. I. (1991). Psychological reactions to risk factor testing. In J. A. Skelton & R. T. Croyle (Eds.), *Mental representation in health and illness* (pp. 85–107). New York: Springer-Verlag.

D'Andrade, R. G., Quinn, N. R., Nerlove, S. B., & Romney, A. K. (1972). Categories of disease in American-English and Mexican-Spanish. In A. K. Romney, R. N. Shepard, & S. B. Nerlove (Eds.), *Multidimensional scaling: Theory and application in the behavioral sciences* (pp. 9–54). New York: Seminar Press.

Diener, E., Sandvik, E., & Larsen, R. J. (1985). Age and sex effects for emotional intensity. *Developmental Psychology, 21*(3), 542–546.

DiMatteo, M. R. (1993). Expectations in the physician-patient relationship: Implications for patient adherence to medical treatment recommendations. In P. D. Blank (Ed.), *Interpersonal expectations: Theory, research, and applications. Studies in emotional and social interaction* (pp. 296–315). New York: Cambridge University Press.

Easterling, D. V., & Leventhal, H. (1989). The contribution of concrete cognition to emotion: Neutral symptoms as elicitors of worry about cancer. *Journal of Applied Psychology, 74,* 787–796.

Feinstein, A. R. (1976). "Compliance bias" and the interpretation of therapeutic trials. In D. L. Sackett & R. B. Haynes (Eds.), *Compliance with therapeutic regimens* (pp. 152–166). Baltimore, MD: Johns Hopkins University Press.

Frankel, R. M. (1995). Emotion and the physician-patient relationship. *Motivation & Emotion, 19*(3), 163–173.

Furedy, J. J., & Riley, D. M. (1987). Human Pavlovian autonomic conditioning and the cognitive paradigm. In G. Davey (Ed.), *Cognitive processes and Pavlovian conditioning in humans* (pp. 1–25). New York: Wiley.

Giere, R. N. (1988). *Explaining science: A cognitive approach.* Chicago: University of Chicago Press.

Hale, W. E., Perkins, L. L., May, F. E., Marks, R. G., & Stewart, R. B. (1986). Symptom prevalence in the elderly: An evaluation of age, sex, disease, and medication use. *Journal of the American Geriatrics Society, 34*(5), 333–340.

Hall, J. A., & Roter, D. L. (1988). Meta-analysis of correlates of provider behavior in medical encounters. *Medical Care, 26,* 657–675.

Hankin, J. R., Steinwachs, D. M., Regier, D. A., Burns, B. J., Goldberg, I. D., & Hoeper, E. W. (1982). Use of general medical care services by persons with mental disorders. *Archives of General Psychiatry, 39,* 225–231.

Harver, A., & Mahler, D. A. (1997). Dyspnea: Sensation, symptom, and illness. In D. A. Mahler (Ed.), *Dyspnea.* New York: Marcel Dekker.

Heszen-Klemens, I., & Lapinska, E. (1984). Doctor–patient interaction, patients' health behavior and effects of treatment. *Social Science & Medicine, 19*(1), 9–18.

Heidrich, S. M., Forsthoff, C. A., & Ward, S. E. (1994). Psychological adjustment in adults with cancer: The self as mediator. *Health Psychology, 13,* 346–353.

Holt, W. S. (1991). Factors affecting compliance with screening sigmoidoscopy. *Journal of Family Practice, 32*(6), 585–589.

Horne, R. (1997). Representations of medication and treatment: Advances in theory and measurement. In J. A. Wienman & K. Petrie (Eds.), *The patients's perception of illness and treatment: Current research and applications* (pp. 155–188). London: Harwood Academic.

Idler, E. L., & Benyamini, Y. (1997). Self-ratings of heath and mortality: A review of 27 community studies. *Journal of Health and Social Behavior, 38*, 21–37.

Jamison, K. R. (1995). *An unquiet mind.* New York: Knopf.

Johnson, R. J., & Wolinsky, F. D. (1993). The structure of health status among older adults: Disease, disability, functional limitation, and perceived health. *Journal of Health and Social Behavior, 34*(2), 105–121.

Johnson, R. J., & Wolinsky, F. D. (1994). Gender, race, and health: The structure of health status among older adults. *The Gerontologist, 34*(1), 24–35.

Johnson, T. P., Stallones, L., Garrity, T. F., & Marx, M. B. (1990). Components of self-rated health among adults: Analysis of multiple data sources. *International Quarterly of Community Health Education, 11*(1), 29–41.

Kaesberg, P. R., & Ershler, W. B. (1989). The importance of immunoessence in the incidence and malignant properties of cancer in hosts of advanced age. *Journals of Gerontology: Biological Sciences, 44*(6), 63–66.

Kaplan, S. H., Greenfield, S., Gandek, B., Rogers, W. H., & Ware, J. E., Jr. (1996). Characteristics of physicians with participatory decision-making styles. *Annals of Internal Medicine, 124*(5), 497–504.

Kart, C. (1981). Experiencing symptoms: Attribution and misattribution of illness among the aged. In M. Haug (Ed.), *Elderly patients and their doctors* (pp. 70–78). New York: Springer.

Kulik, J. A., & Mahler, H. I. M. (1987). The effects of preoperative roommate assignment on preoperative anxiety and postoperative recovery from bypass surgery. *Health Psychology, 6*, 525–543.

Lau, R. R., & Hartman, K. A. (1983). Common sense representations of common illnesses. *Health Psychology, 2*(2), 167–185.

Lazarus, R. S., & Launier, R. (1978). Stress related transactions between person and environment. In L. A. Pervin & M. Lewis (Eds.), *Perspectives in interactional psychology* (pp. 287–327). New York: Plenum.

Lerman, C., Narod, S., Schulman, K., Hughes, C., Gomex-Caminero, A., Bonney, G., Gold, K., Trock, B., Main, D., Lynch, J., Fulmore, C., Snyder, C., Lemon, S. J., Conway, T., Tonin, P., Lenoir, G., & Lynch, H. (1996). BRCA1 testing in families with hereditary breast-ovarian cancer. *Journal of the American Medical Association, 275*, 1885–1892.

Leventhal, E. A., & Crouch, M. (1997). Are there differences in perceptions of illness across the lifespan? In J. A. Wienman & K. Petrie (Eds.), *The patients's perception of illness and treatment: Current research and applications* (pp. 77–102). London: Harwood Academic.

Leventhal, E. A., Easterling, D. V., Leventhal, H., & Cameron, L. D. (1995). Conservation of energy, uncertainty reduction, and swift utilization of medical care among the elderly: Study II. *Medical Care, 33*(10), 988–1000.

Leventhal, E. A., Leventhal, H., Schaefer, P., & Easterling, D. V. (1993). Conservation of energy, uncertainty reduction, and swift utilization of medical care among the elderly. *Journal of Gerontology, 48*(2), 78–86.

Leventhal, E. A., & Prohaska, T. (1986). Age, symptom interpretation, and health behavior. *Journal of the American Geriatrics Society, 34*, 185–191.

Leventhal, H. (1970). Findings and theory in the study of fear communications. *Advances in Experimental Social Psychology, 5*, 119–186.

Leventhal, H. (1975). The consequences of depersonalization during illness and treatment: An information-processing model. In J. Howard & A. Strauss (Eds.), *Humanizing health care* (pp. 119–161). New York: Wiley.

Leventhal, H. (1984). A perceptual-motor theory of emotion. In L. Berkowitz (Ed.), *Advances in experimental social psychology* (Vol. 17, pp. 117–182). New York: Academic Press.

Leventhal, H., & Cameron, L. D. (1987). Behavioral theories and the problem of compliance. *Patient Education and Counseling, 10,* 117–138.

Leventhal, H., Diefenbach, M., & Leventhal, E. A. (1992). Illness cognition: Using common sense to understand treatment adherence and affect cognition interactions. *Cognitive Therapy and Research, 16,* 143–163.

Leventhal, H., Easterling, D. V., Coons, H., Luchterhand, C., & Love, R. R. (1986). Adaptation to chemotherapy treatments. In B. Andersen (Ed.), *Women with cancer* (pp. 172–203). New York: Springer-Verlag.

Leventhal, H., Hudson, S., & Robitaille, C. (1997). Social comparison and health: a process model. In B. P. Buunk & F. X. Gibbons (Eds.), *Health, coping, and well-being: Perspectives from social comparison theory* (pp. 411–432). Mahwah, NJ: Lawrence Erlbaum Associates.

Leventhal, H., Leventhal, E. A., & Contrada, R. (in press). Self regulation, health, and behavior: A perceptual-cognitive approach. *Psychology and Health: The International Review of Health Psychology.*

Leventhal, H., Leventhal, E. A., & Schaefer, P. (1991). Vigilant coping and health behavior: A life span problem. In M. G. Ory & R. Abeles (Eds.), *Aging, health, and behavior* (pp. 109–140). Baltimore, MD: Johns Hopkins University Press.

Leventhal, H., Meyer, D., & Nerenz, D. (1980). The common sense representation of illness danger. In S. Rachman (Ed.), *Contributions to medical psychology* (Vol. 2, pp. 7–30). New York: Pergamon.

Leventhal, H., Nerenz, D., & Strauss, A. (1982). Self-regulation and the mechanisms for symptom appraisal. In D. Mechanic (Ed.), *Monograph series in psychosocial empidemiology 3: Symptoms, illness behavior, and help-seeking* (pp. 55–86). New York: Neale Watson.

Leventhal, H., & Niles, P. (1964). A field experiment on fear arousal with data on the validity of questionnaire measures. *Journal of Personality, 32,* 459–479.

Leventhal, H., Patrick-Miller, L., Leventhal, E. A., & Burns, E. A. (1998). Does stress-emotions cause illness in elderly people? In K. W. Schaie & M. P. Lawton (Eds.), *The annual review of gerontology and geriatrics* (Vol. 17, pp. 138–184). New York: Springer.

Leventhal, H., & Scherer, K. R. (1987). The relationship of emotion to cognition: A functional approach to semantic controversy. *Cognition and Emotion, 1,* 3–28.

Leventhal, H., Zimmerman, R., & Gutmann, M. (1984). Compliance: A self-regulation perspective. In W. D. Gentry (Ed.), *Handbook of behavioral medicine* (pp. 369–436). New York: Guilford.

Levkoff, S. E., Cleary, P. D., & Wetle, T. (1987). Differences in the appraisal of health between aged and middle-aged adults. *Journals of Gerontology, 42,* 114–120.

Lorig, K., Chastain, R. L., Ung, E., Shoor, S., & Holman, H. (1989). Development and evaluation of a scale to measure perceived self-efficacy in people with arthritis. *Arthritis and Rheumatism, 32,* 37–44.

Mazen, R., & Leventhal, H. (1972). The influence of communicator–recipient similarity upon the beliefs and behavior of pregnant women. *Journal of Experimental Social Psychology, 8,* 289–302.

Meichenbaum, D., & Turk, D. C. (1987). *Facilitating treatment adherence: A practitioner's guidebook.* New York: Plenum.

Meyer, D., Leventhal, H., & Gutmann, M. (1985). Common-sense models of illness: The example of hypertension. *Health Psychology, 4,* 115–135.

Millar, M. G., & Millar, K. U. (1995). Negative affective consequences of thinking about disease detection behaviors. *Health Psychology, 14*(2), 141–146.

Myers, R. E., Ross, E., Jepson, C., Wolf, T., Balshem, A., Millner, L., & Leventhal, H. (1994). Modeling adherence to colorectal cancer screening. *Preventive Medicine, 23,* 142–151.

National Center for Health Statistics. (1995). *Health United States, 1994.* Hyattsville, MD: U.S. Public Health Service.

Nisbett, R., & Ross, L. (1980). Human inference: Strategies and shortcomings of social judgment. Englewood Cliffs, NJ: Prentice-Hall.

Ory, M., & DeFreis, G. (1988). *Self-care in later life: Research, programs and policy perspectives.* New York: Springer.

Park, D. C. (1992). Applied cognitive aging research. In F. I. M. Craik & T. A. Salthouse (Eds.), *The handbook of aging and cognition* (pp. 449–493). Hillsdale, NJ: Lawrence Erlbaum Associates.

Park, D. C. (1994). Self-regulation and control of rheumatic disorders. In S. Maes & H. Leventhal (Eds.), *International review of health psychology* (pp. 189–217). Chichester, England: Wiley.

Park, D. C. (1996). Aging, health, and behavior: The interplay between basic and applied science. [References]. In R. J. Resnick & R. H. Rozensky (Eds.), *Health psychology through the life span: Practice and research opportunities* (pp. 59–75). Washington, DC: American Psychological Association.

Park, D. C., & Jones, T. R. (1997). Medication adherence and aging. In A. D. Fiske & W. A. Rogers (Eds.), *Handbook of human factors and the older adult* (pp. 257–287). San Diego, CA: Academic Press.

Park, D. C., Morrell, R. W., Frieske, D., & Kincaid, D. (1992). Medication adherence behaviors in older adults: Effects of external cognitive supports. *Psychology and Aging, 7*(2), 252–256.

Pennebaker, J. W. (1982). *The psychology of physical symptoms.* New York: Springer-Verlag.

Prohaska, T. R., Keller, M. L., Leventhal, E. A., & Leventhal, H. (1987). Impact of symptoms and aging attribution on emotions and coping. *Health Psychology, 6,* 495–514.

Prohaska, T. R., Leventhal, E. A., Leventhal, H., & Keller, K. L. (1985). Health practices and illness cognition in young, middle aged, and elderly adults. *Journal of Gerontology, 40,* 569–578.

Robitaille, C. (1998). *Effects of practitioner attributes on care-seeking decisions.* Doctoral dissertation in preparation, Rutgers University.

Scherer, K. R. (1984). On the nature and function of emotion: A component process approach. In K. R. Scherer & P. Ekman (Eds.), *Approaches to emotion* (pp. 293–317). Hillsdale, NJ: Lawrence Erlbaum Associates.

Schwartz, J. B., Gibb, W. J., & Tran, T. (1991). Aging effects on heart rate variation. *Journal of Gerontology: Medical Sciences, 46,* M99–M106.

Stoller, E. P. (1998). Medical self care: Lay management of symptoms by elderly people. In M. Ory & G. DeFreis (Eds.), *Self-care in later life: Research, programs, and policy perspectives* (pp. 24–61). New York: Springer.

Tessler, R., & Mechanic, D. (1978). Psychological distress and perceived health status. *Journal of Health and Social Behavior, 19*(3), 254–262.

Widmer, R. B., Cadoret, R. J., & Troughton, E. (1983). Compliance characteristics of 291 hypertensive patients from a rural Midwest area. *Journal of Family Practice, 17*(4), 619–625.

Willis, S. L. (1996). Everyday cognitive competence in elderly persons: Conceptual issues and empirical findings. *The Gerontologist, 36*(5), 595–601.

Wood, J. V. (1989). Theory and research concerning social comparisons of personal attributes. *Psychological Bulletin, 106,* 231–248.

10

Cognition and Affect in Medication Adherence

Odette N. Gould
North Dakota State University

It is well established that medication adherence is a complex behavior and that much more than simple memory processes determine adherence performance (Park & Mayhorn, 1996; Pesznecker, Patsdaughter, Moody, & Albert, 1990; Rudd, 1993). In this chapter, I attempt to illustrate the complexity of medication adherence by portraying this task as a process that involves many steps in which subjective and objective influences intertwine to affect behavior.

Figure 10.1 shows a model of the medication adherence process that is similar to the model of adherence developed by Park and her colleagues (e.g., Park & Kidder, 1996; Park & Mayhorn, 1996) but that emphasizes the relationship between the physician and the patient as a core part of the adherence process. It should be made clear at the outset that this model is in no way meant to represent the complete set of factors that influence medication adherence. This model has the more modest goal of highlighting some junctures in the process where the interaction between affective and cognitive variables seems particularly clear at this point in time. Not surprisingly, the model emphasizes select relationships between adherence variables that my colleagues and I have investigated during the past few years.

In general, this model proposes that the adherence process begins even before the physician and patient first meet. The beliefs that each holds about the illness symptoms, the medical condition, and each other's characteristics (gender, age, ethnicity) will have an ongoing effect on their relationship and on the patient's

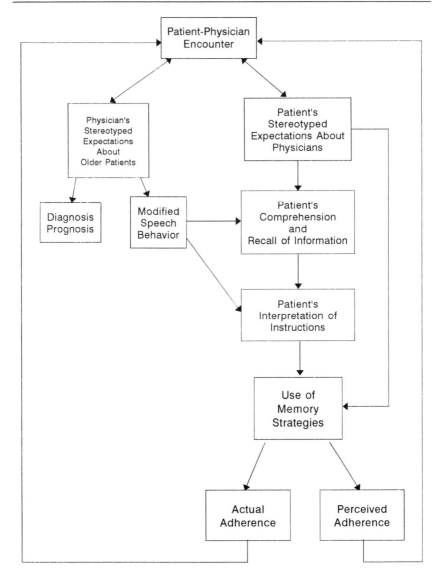

FIG. 10.1. Adherence process model emphasizing subjectivity influences on medication adherence.

adherence to the medical regimen. Moreover, the physician and patient's subjective reactions to each other are hypothesized to affect not only the relationship between them, but also the quality of the information exchanged during their meeting. This includes background information provided by the patient and necessary for diagnosis and care as well as medical information offered by the physician. Thus, the affective and social dimensions of the relationship continue to have an effect on the adherence process through patients' willingness and ability to follow the regimen prescribed by the physician. The model therefore highlights how cognitive and social factors interact. For example, a negative relationship with a physician may lead to an unwillingness to use the cognitive strategies that would ensure adherence to the medical regimen.

Next, assuming that the patient wishes to adhere (at least partly), the patient is faced with the cognitively demanding tasks of (a) interpreting the medication instructions accurately, and (b) remembering to carry out the appropriate behaviors. As pointed out by Park and her colleagues, medication adherence is a very complex cognitive task and is not simply a prospective memory challenge. The cognitive components of the adherence process may be particularly challenging for older adults, given the well-established patterns of age-related cognitive losses in working memory, episodic memory, and problem solving (see Salthouse & Babcock, 1991; Craik & Jennings, 1992; and Denney, 1989, respectively, for reviews). Park and colleagues also showed that metamemory variables, situational variables such as busyness, and belief variables related to the illness condition are all important aspects of the adherence process. They proposed, as I do here, that adherence is not simply a cognitive task.

Finally, the patient must monitor his or her adherence performance. The adherence process model as proposed here adopts the view presented in Gould, McDonald-Miszczak, and King (1997) that perceived adherence is an important variable. It is well established that self-reports of adherence are likely to be inaccurate (Park & Kidder, 1996; Rudd, 1993). However, we feel that self-reported adherence rates (or perceived adherence) is nonetheless an extremely important variable. Indeed, as Fig. 10.1 shows, we believe that this variable may be used by the patient to calibrate the use of (and need for) memory strategies. Also, self-reports of medication adherence are likely to be an important piece of information used by the physician to adjust the medication regimen prescribed. Indeed, physicians may not be as aware as are medication adherence researchers that perceived adherence is an inaccurate predictor of actual adherence behaviors. Thus, these self-reports of adherence are being used by both physician and patient to monitor medical care. We believe that it is therefore important to gain a better understanding of how these (inaccurate) perceived adherence rates are arrived at by young and old medication-takers.

In the next sections, I describe empirical evidence from different research teams—including mine—that have addressed the variables described in Fig. 10.1.

PATIENT–PHYSICIAN ENCOUNTERS: BELIEFS, EXPECTATIONS AND STEREOTYPES

Stereotypes are used by all of us to reduce the mass of information in social encounters to manageable levels (Hummert, Shaner, & Gartska, 1995). Many have proposed that physicians hold fairly negative views of their older patients (Fineman, 1994; Greene, Adelman, Charon, & Hoffman, 1986; Kreps, 1990). Others posit that age-related stereotypes may be too complex for a simple positive/negative categorization to be helpful (Hummert et al., 1995). Haug (1996; Haug & Ory, 1987) pointed out that gender, ethnicity, social class, and religion of both patient and physician may play an important role in determining the nature of the interaction. Whatever age-related stereotypes physicians may hold, the relationship between a young, female, African-American physician and her older, White male patient of lower socioeconomic status may be very different than any other combination of these variables. Furthermore, there are indicators that patients' reactions to physicians' behaviors are influenced by patients' personality traits (Musialowski, 1988) and the severity of the illness being treated. Buller and Buller (1987) found that communicative styles were more important in determining young adults' satisfaction with health care when the illness being treated was less severe. Given the large number of older adults receiving treatment for chronic (possibly less severe) illnesses, the communicative aspect of the medical interaction may be particularly important for older patients.

The relationship between the physician and patient affects adherence to medication regimens in at least two ways. First, the quantity and quality of information provided to the patient will vary across conversations. Patients who know less about their medication are likely to adhere less well to their regimen (e.g., Garrity & Lawson, 1989; German, Klein, McPhee, & Smith, 1982; Hulka, Cassel, Kupper, & Burdette, 1976). Second, when patients perceive their relationship with their physician as a positive one, adherence levels are also more likely to be higher (Garrity & Lawson, 1989; German et al., 1982; Kreps, 1990; Musialowski, 1988; Street, 1991).

The importance of age in determining the quality of medical interactions has received an increase in empirical attention. For example, Berlowitz, Du, Kazis, and Lewis (1995) found that physicians and nurses significantly underestimated nursing home residents' health-related quality of life self-reports. Fineman (1994) pointed out that when physicians have negative and inaccurate views of older adults' health and quality of life, their diagnoses and prognoses may be less sound.

Greene and her colleagues carried out a series of studies in which actual patient–physician interactions were analyzed. Greene et al. (1986) developed the Geriatric Interaction Analysis (GIA), which is a coding scheme that scores each topic raised as well as global dimensions of the interaction on a series of scales. Both the behaviors of the physician and the patient are rated. Using the GIA, Greene et al. (1986) rated the physicians as less egalitarian, less patient, less engaged and less respectful with older adults than with younger adult patients. Moreover, the physician gave their older patients poorer quality information with regard to both doctor- and patient-initiated topics. Morris, Grossman, Barkdoll, Gordon, and Soviero (1984) carried out a national survey and found that older patients reported being given directions for medication use only one half or one fourth as often as younger adults. Garrity and Lawson (1989) suggested that physicians may reduce the amount of information they present because they believe that older persons are not cognitively able to comprehend or recall the information. In medical settings, where short, hurried interactions with mostly frail and ailing older adults are common, it may be more likely that interactional styles will be based on stereotypical beliefs (Ryan & Cole, 1990), and ageism may be common (Greene et al., 1986).

Coupland, Robinson, and Coupland (1994) also carried out microanalyses of physician–older patient dyads and emphasized that dyadic interactions are a cocreation of the physician and the patient. Indeed, reactions to the physician may be due more to stereotypes held by the patient than to the actual behaviors of the physician (Ditto, Moore, Hilton, & Kalish, 1995).

McDonald-Miszczak and I carried out a survey to explore older adults' perceptions of ageism in health care professionals (Gould & McDonald-Miszczak, 1996). The survey was distributed to 58 older adults ($M = 75.9$ years of age) and 62 younger adults ($M = 19.6$ years of age). All participants were taking at least one prescription medication. Each participant was asked how the following three groups perceive older adults: (a) the general public, (b) health professionals, and (c) his or her own personal physician. Perceived attitudes in two domains are of particular interest here: (a) the general health of older adults and (b) the memory ability of older adults. Also, each participant judged the accuracy of the views about older people.

The pattern of results was quite similar in the two domains. Both age groups considered society at large to have a more negative view of older adults than do health professionals. Furthermore, older adults rated their own physicians as being (a) more positive about older adults' health and cognitive ability and (b) more accurate in these judgments than society in general or health professionals in general. It should be noted, however, that, even when older adults rated their own physician's accuracy about health issues, the average rating did not fall within the *very accurate* range. Thus, our results extend studies such as that of Berlowitz et al. (1995) who found that physicians and nurses underestimate older adults' health functioning. We show that older adults are aware of this bias in their health care professionals.

At least three conclusions can be drawn from our results. First, older adults do not rate their doctors, and neither age group rate health care professionals, as particularly accurate in making judgments about older adults. Second, health care professionals were not judged by older adults to be any more accurate than the general public in their judgments of older adults' cognitive or health status. Finally, older adults did perceive their own physicians as more accurate than other health care professionals. This last finding is particularly intriguing. One possibility is that, through trial and error, these individuals have found a physician who truly is less ageist than other professionals. Alternatively, the older adult may be exhibiting face-saving self-deception in holding these beliefs. In other words, they may not be admitting that they would seek the advice of an ageist doctor.

Thus, the results from this exploratory study suggest that in settings where older adults are interacting with unfamiliar health care professionals, their negative perceptions of this person's attitudes about old age may very well color the interaction. The relationship between older adults' stereotyped expectations about their health professionals and their willingness to adhere to the medical regimens prescribed by these professionals is an area that deserves more attention.

MEDICATION INSTRUCTIONS:
PATIENTS' RECALL OF MEDICAL INFORMATION

Speech Accommodation Theory proposes that people adjust their speaking style to their perception of the needs of their conversation partner (Ryan, Giles, Bartolucci, & Henwood, 1986; Ryan, Hummert, & Boich, 1995). When the abilities of a conversation recipient are underestimated, the resulting speaking style is described as overaccommodative speech or secondary babytalk. *Overaccommodative speech* contains "slower speech rate, exaggerated intonation, use of high pitch, increased loudness, more repetitions, tag questions, altered pronoun use, and simplification of vocabulary and grammar" (Ryan & Cole, 1990, p. 173). The resulting interaction is likely to be unsatisfying for both conversational partners, with the older person receiving overly simplified and patronizing speech and the younger speaker involved in a boring and uncomfortable conversation. Furthermore, the older person is faced with the Communication Predicament of Aging in that he or she is left with the unenviable options of (a) living down to the low expectations of their partner or (b) complaining or protesting and thereby being perceived as a cranky and demanding older person.

Most research on overaccommodative speech has focused on individuals' subjective reactions to this speaking style and finds that older adults, particularly those with high cognitive functioning, find it disrespectful and unwelcome (Ryan & Cole, 1990). Very little work has addressed the effectiveness of the speaking style for the transmission of information. This issue is of particular interest in the domain of medication instructions because health care professionals have been found to use overaccommodative speech (Ashburn & Gordon, 1981; Hummert & Mazloff, 1993, cited in Ryan et al., 1995) and to believe that its use is helpful (Caporael, Lukaszewski, & Culbertson, 1983; Shadden, 1988). Although more and more patients are receiving written prescription instructions, it remains that written instructions are much more effective when combined with individual counseling (Pesznecker et al., 1990).

In 1997, Gould and Dixon investigated the usefulness of overaccommodative speech using the following methodology. An actor was hired to produce videotapes of a physician presenting somewhat complex instructions for taking a new prescription. The physician used overaccommodative speech in one condition and neutral speech in the other. Eighty-two older women ($M = 71$ years of age) who responded to a newspaper advertisement and 40 younger women ($M = 21$ years of age) were tested on both their recall of the medication instructions and their subjective reactions to the speaker and to the speech. Furthermore, we used a composite score of three working memory measures to identify high and low ability groups among the older participants (i.e., the top and bottom thirds of the sample). The Alpha Span (Craik, 1986), the Reading Span (Salthouse & Babcock, 1991), and the Sentence Repetition test (Kemper, 1986) were used to create this composite score.

The results in this study were unexpected. We had hypothesized that only older adults with less working memory ability would benefit from the simplified speech. However, when we tested the speaking style effect within each group, it was the older women with higher working memory who recalled more information in the overaccommodation condition than the neutral speech condition. It is important to interpret these results within the context of the subjective reactions also measured in this project. First, younger adults, older adults with higher working memory ability, and older adults with lower working memory ability were similar in their ratings of the speaker (i.e., how respectful, nurturing, patronizing, dominant, and kind he was) and the speech (i.e., how slow, clear, simple, organized, detailed, and helpful it was). In general, all participants preferred the speaker characteristics of neutral speech and the speech characteristics of the overaccommodative speech. Participants in all three groups were also more likely to want the videotaped physician as their own physician if they had seen the neutral speaker rather than the overaccommodative speaker.

One final analysis performed in the Gould and Dixon (1997) study is particularly relevant in the context of the present chapter. A hierarchical multiple regression (on the entire sample) indicated that subjective ratings of the videotaped speaker were significant predictors of recall performance over and above the composite working memory score. This relationship was present for the older but not the younger sample.

Of course, findings from the Gould and Dixon (1997) study need replication (and such a study is being carried out). However, the results suggest some interesting issues. First, a paradox is present in that older adults do not necessarily prefer the speaking style that is most beneficial to their recall performance. (Similar findings were obtained by Kemper, Vandeputte, Rice, Cheung, & Gubarchuk, 1995, in another context.) This creates a difficult decision for the clinician who must choose between one speaking style that enhances recall and jeopardizes the physician–patient relationship—and possibly the motivation to adhere. A second speaking style may foster a more positive physician–patient relationship, but result in a decreased understanding and recall of the medical regimen itself. A third possibility is that clinicians could be trained to use an optimal speaking style that enhances comprehension without creating negative subjective reactions. However, this ideal style may be difficult to achieve if, as Gould and Dixon (1997) suggested, the same stylistic devices that increase recall also appear disrespectful.

A second key feature of these results is the highlighting of the intricacy of the relationship between cognitive and subjective features of the adherence process. Cognitive abilities seem to influence whether overaccommodative speech is helpful, but does not distinguish groups in terms of their subjective reactions to this speech. On the other hand, subjective reactions to the speaker is a strong predictor of recall performance in older, but not younger, adults. Thus, as hypothesized in the present model, the cognitive and subjective components seem to be interacting—particularly for older adults.

PROBLEM SOLVING:
INTERPRETING THE MEDICATION INSTRUCTIONS

After medication instructions have been transmitted to the older patient, there is no assurance that these recommendations will be carried out. As elaborated by Park and her colleagues (Park & Kidder, 1996; Park & Mayhorn, 1996) and others (e.g., Pesznecker et al., 1990), a vast number of variables are involved in predicting adherence. Physical constraints (e.g., difficult bottle caps) and illness variables (e.g., perceived seriousness of the illness) as well as psychosocial variables (e.g., health locus of control) have all been shown to play a role in adherence.

One issue that has received relatively less attention is how medication instructions are interpreted by older patients. Morrow, Leirer, and Sheikh (1988) described many problems that older adults may have when interpreting pill bottle labels. For example, when told to take three pills a day, they might plan to take the pills at equal intervals during their waking hours rather than over a 24-hour period.

We explored the question of how older adults interpret medication instructions using a very different approach (Gould, 1997; Gould & Malpert, 1995). We created a medication-taking dilemma and explored how different people went about solving this problem. In this dilemma story, the protagonist is faced with uncertainty about how to follow medication instructions. Our participants gave advice to the person experiencing the dilemma.

In this study, we interviewed 30 female college students ($M = 20.6$ years of age) and 27 older female adults from the community ($M = 69.4$ years of age). Fifty percent of the younger and 75% of the older women were taking medication at the time of the study. It is surprising that the younger and older adults reported similar numbers of medications during their lifetime (37% from both age groups had taken one to five medications in the past, and 63% from both age groups had received six or more prescriptions in the past).

First, participants were provided with background information about a fictitious medication, and then with a vignette describing an individual experiencing a dilemma involving the medication. The two manipulations of interest were the age of the advice giver and the amount of background information provided. Specifically, half of the participants were in the limited background condition and only received a pill bottle that was labeled with the physician's name, the medication name, and the dosage amount and time. The participants in the extensive background condition received a two-page text giving detailed instructions on how to take the medication. These instructions explained how the medication worked, what to do if a dose was forgotten, what foods, beverages, and over-the-counter medications to avoid, and what side effects to watch for.

Both groups of participants received the same dilemma in the form of a half-page narrative describing a woman who was taking the fictitious medication. In the story, she is experiencing cold symptoms and is trying to decide whether she should stop taking her prescription to take over-the-counter cold medicine, or whether she should take both at the same time. The readers in the extensive background information had situation-specific information that would suggest that the patient in the dilemma story is actually experiencing an allergic reaction to the pills, rather than a simple cold. All participants were asked to give advice to the person in the story, and this advice was audiotaped.

Two main questions were addressed with these data. First, we were interested in whether younger and older adults differentially depended on situation-specific background information when they give advice. Second, we were interested in the more general question of whether the advice-giving style of the two age groups differed.

To test the first hypothesis, we began by identifying each grammatical clause in the advice transcripts. Then, we counted the recommendations for action (e.g., see your doctor right away), and the justification for the recommendation (e.g., because you might be having an allergic reaction to your pills). For participants who had received the extensive background (the medication instructions) this was essentially a memory measure. In other words, we were testing whether the participant used relevant information from the background information to solve everyday problems. For participants who did not receive extensive background information (the pill bottle condition) this task was a measure of their use of relevant world knowledge to solve everyday problems.

In preliminary analyses, we have found that older women performed more similarly across the two conditions than did younger women (in other words, a significant Age × Background condition interaction was present). Thus, the older women had relevant facts at hand to justify their recommendations whether or not they were given situation-specific background information. This suggests that older adults have an extended knowledge network available about medication taking and may use this knowledge to extend or, possibly, replace their physician's instructions.

Similar findings were obtained by Rice and Okun (1994) using a very different paradigm. These authors also showed that this schema-based knowledge may be a great liability to older adults because it seems to hinder their ability to recall new information that contradicts their existing (possibly inaccurate) knowledge. Meyer, Russo, and Talbot (1995) also found proportionally more top-down processing when they studied how older women make decisions about breast cancer treatment options. However, they suggest the very intriguing possibility that this decision-making style may be an adaptive one for these older women to adopt, given declining cognitive resources.

The organization, accuracy, and extent of use of semantic knowledge about medication certainly deserves empirical attention. Such research is bound to be challenging however, given that considerable individual and cohort differences are likely to be present. We were surprised in our study to find extensive agreement between young and old raters when a second group of participants rated the quality of the advice given. Both young and old participants judged the older adults' advice to be of equally high quality whether or not the advice giver had received background information. For younger adults, however, it was only in the extensive background condition that their advice was judged to be as good as that offered by older adults.

In conclusion, these data support the notion that adherence is not simply a prospective memory task. Furthermore, these data may underline the usefulness of thinking about the interpretation of medication instructions as a problem-solving task, which may be a very useful perspective to adopt in future research. For example, we may discover that older patients are not only attempting to adapt a medication regimen to their daily activities, but also are, at the same time, (a) integrating the prescription medication regimen with their use of over-the-counter medications (Smith, Cunningham, & Hale, 1994) and (b) making judgments about the possibility that nonadherence (or imperfect adherence) may be adaptive. The latter issue should not be dismissed as a motivation problem, given the lack of training that many physicians have about medicating older adults (Pesznecker et al., 1990). For some older adults, imperfect adherence may be a sound decision.

METAMEMORIAL PROCESSES: STRATEGY USE AND PROSPECTIVE MEMORY

Medication adherence has often been described as an example of an everyday prospective memory task (Einstein & McDaniel, 1990; Park & Kidder, 1996), where *prospective memory* is memory for actions to be performed in the future. However, as is proposed here, and as has been argued and demonstrated by others, medication adherence involves much more than simple prospective memory. It remains, however, that prospective memory is clearly a key component in the task of medication adherence.

The study of prospective memory in old age is particularly interesting because in many studies, older adults outperform younger adults (e.g., Devolder & Pressley, 1992; West, 1988) through the use of memory aids (Maylor, 1990). Within the domain of medication taking, researchers have evaluated the usefulness of aids such as pill boxes and pill bottle alarms (e.g., Mackowiak et al., 1994; Park, Morrell, Frieske, & Kincaid, 1992), memory training (Leirer, Morrow, Pariente, & Sheikh, 1988), voice mail reminders (Leirer, Morrow, Tanke, & Pariente, 1991) or organizational charts (Park et al., 1992). Most of these studies have shown that these strategies are effective in increasing adherence, but very little attention has been paid to the strategies being used spontaneously by older adults.

In Gould et al. (1997) my colleagues and I carried out a survey to explore three main issues. First, we were interested in discovering which, if any, memory strategies older adults use in everyday life.

To investigate this issue, we developed the Prospective Memory for Medications Questionnaire (PMMQ), which is a 28-item survey. Each item lists a memory strategy that could be used to facilitate adherence to a prescribed medication regimen, and participants are asked to indicate how often they use each strategy on a scale ranging from 0 (*never*) to 4 (*always*). After indicating how often each strategy is used, participants are asked to rate whether the strategy is likely to increase adherence on a scale ranging from 0 (*very much disagree*) to 4 (*very much agree*).

The PMMQ includes both internal and external strategies. *External strategies* involve making changes in the environment to enhance memory performance (e.g., using alarm clocks, being reminded by others how much medication to take). *Internal strategies* involve purely mental activity that is used to enhance recall performance (e.g., mentally repeating regimen instructions, associating pill-taking times with daily activities). Items deal with remembering to take the medication on time as well as recall of the information needed for the medical regimen to be carried out. The strategies used often or always by more than one half of the sample are presented in Table 10.1.

We were surprised to find that older adults used external strategies significantly less than internal strategies to remember to take their medications correctly. In contrast, when we and others (e.g., Loewen, Shaw, & Craik, 1990) used questionnaires that tapped strategy use across domains of everyday life, external strategies were found to be used to a greater extent. This is an intriguing finding in that most work on the effectiveness of strategies for medication adherence has been done using external strategies (e.g., Leirer et al., 1991; Park et al., 1992).

One possible interpretation is that when older adults have been taking medications for a long time, they discover that certain external strategies lose their effectiveness with time. Thus, the choice and (perceived) effectiveness of a memory strategy may change across time. These results suggest at least two possible research questions. First, perhaps a useful direction to take would be to study the effectiveness of the strategies that older adults are likely to adopt spontaneously. If effective, such strategies may be much easier to train for, especially because older adults may be made anxious by having to learn new

TABLE 10.1
Strategy Used by a Majority of Older Adults

Strategy	% Used (Often or Always)
External Strategies	
Leaving pills in prominent place	76.5
Internal Strategies	
Concentrating hard when receiving instructions orally	90.2
Trying hard to learn amounts to be taken when receiving new prescription	88.2
Planning pill times around activities of the day at the beginning of the day	72.6
Rereading regimen instructions to increase recall	72.6
Reading regimen instructions very slowly to increase recall	72.6
Relating pills to usual activities	70.6
Concentrating hard to learn medication times when receiving new prescriptions	60.8
Mentally repeating medication instructions	56.9

strategies (Yesavage, Lapp, & Sheikh, 1989). Second, a longitudinal approach should be used to determine the dynamic process of memory strategy use. In order to optimally train for the use of strategies, we need to know which strategies are most effective, when, and for how long.

In the Gould et al. (1997) study, we were also interested in looking at what predicts the use of memory strategies by older adults. We compared the relative importance of three groups of variables as predictors of strategy use in a series of block-wise hierarchical regressions. In the first block in the equation, we entered variables related to the medical situation, namely (a) objective ratings of the seriousness of the condition, (b) objective ratings of the discomfort experienced without the medication, and (c) the number of prescriptions as an indicator of the cognitive complexity of the medication regimen. In a second block, we entered a metacognitive variable highly related to the adherence task, namely the self-rated importance of adherence to one's medication regimen. Finally, we entered scores from the Capacity and Anxiety scales of the Metamemory in Adulthood (MIA) questionnaire, (Dixon & Hultsch, 1984). *Metamemory* can be defined as including "knowledge, perceptions, and beliefs about the demand characteristics of particular tasks or situations, the availability and employability of relevant strategies and aids, and other memory-relevant characteristics of the persons themselves" (Dixon, 1989, p. 396). The Capacity scale measures respondents' perception of their memory performance across a multitude of everyday situations, in other words, memory self-efficacy. The Anxiety scale measures the influence of emotional states on cognitive performance and the influence of cognitively demanding tasks on emotional states (Dixon, 1989). In summary, these scales provide an indication of individuals' attitudes and feelings about their general memory performance in everyday life.

The results of these analyses indicated that, overall, metamemorial variables (self-efficacy and anxiety) were much better predictors of strategy use than were variables that offered a more objective measure of the medical situation. Moreover, high levels of general memory anxiety predicted the use of internal strategies, and a trend pointed to low levels of general memory self-efficacy as a predictor of the use of external memory strategies. Many programs attempting to increase medication adherence have aimed at increasing knowledge about the medication and the illness. Our findings suggest that perhaps the assessment of patients' beliefs and attitudes about their general memory beliefs and attitudes should also be integrated into such programs. A better understanding of the relationship between the use of internal memory strategies and general memory anxiety is particularly interesting and requires more research attention. Indeed, it may well be that individuals who are highly anxious about their memory performance are perseverating unwillingly on their medication instructions. Alternatively, the process may be an adaptive one, in that people decide to adopt effective strategies as an adaptive way to deal with their concerns over their own memory performance.

METAMEMORIAL PROCESSES
AND PERCEIVED ADHERENCE

The final question addressed in the Gould et al. (1997) project concerned an investigation of the factors related to perceived adherence. We use the term *perceived adherence* to describe self-reported adherence levels across indefinite time periods. As mentioned earlier, we propose that perceived adherence, although probably not a good measurement of actual adherence, is itself an interesting construct. Indeed, patients have a view of their own adherence levels, and it is this view, and not actual adherence levels, that is most often used by physicians, pharmacists, and patients in planning health care.

Our investigation of perceived adherence was carried out using a block-wise hierarchical multiple regression. The criterion variable was a composite variable formed from five different aspects of adherence: (a) taking the medication at the correct time, (b) taking the medication in the correct amount, (c) recall of side effects and foods/beverages/medications to avoid, (d) recall of medication name, and (e) a general rating of adherence. (Participants rated each of these aspects as very important and felt that taking one's medication at the exact time prescribed was less important than taking it in the exact amount. Other specific aspects of adherence were all judged equally important by our participants. Similar results were obtained by Gardner, Rulien, McGhan, and Mead (1988) with a young adult sample.

The first block of variables entered into the regression equation consisted of objective indicators of the medical situation, namely (a) the seriousness of the condition, (b) the discomfort felt when nonadherent, and (c) the number of medications prescribed. In the second block, we entered internal and external memory strategy use, and in the third block, we entered perceived effectiveness of the memory strategies used. Finally, we entered the metamemory variables of general (non-domain-specific) memory self-efficacy and anxiety from the MIA.

The results of this analysis revealed that the only block of variables that significantly increased the variance explained in perceived adherence was the last one, namely the individuals' beliefs and feelings about their general memory performance. It is surprising that patients do not seem to give substantial weight to such variables as the complexity of the cognitive task (i.e., number of medications), their use of memory strategies, or even their perception of how effective these strategies are. These findings may provide an explanation for the low accuracy of self-reports of medication adherence: Patients seemingly base these judgments not on their behaviors, but on their beliefs about memory.

This interpretation, if true, suggests that it would be very important in future research to investigate whether questions other than self-reported adherence could be used by health care workers to get a better estimate of actual adherence. There is convincing evidence that at least some external strategies are effective in reducing adherence errors (e.g., Leirer et al., 1991; Park et al., 1992). For example, asking older adults to list (or endorse) the memory strategies that they actually use may better describe adherence levels than do simple self-reports. Such research may have very useful clinical applications.

Finally, as pertains to the model portrayed in Fig. 10.1, the influence of both perceived and actual adherence levels is hypothesized to create a feedback loop. Indeed, actual and perceived adherence levels, as well as actual and perceived success of the medical treatment, are hypothesized to influence subsequent interactions between patient and physician. If patients believe that they have faithfully adhered to a medication regimen (whether they actually have), and their condition has not improved, their attitudes about their physician, their medical condition, and their medical treatment are likely to be affected. At the same time, if the physician is making conclusions about the effectiveness of a medical regimen based on incorrect adherence information, the quality of health care may be threatened.

CONCLUSION

In this chapter, I have attempted to provide an overview of a series of studies that my colleagues and I carried out. These studies are linked in their focus on showing that not only "classic" cognitive variables are important in determining adherence. Indeed, we consistently find that social beliefs, subjective reactions, and beliefs and feelings about memory in general are also important factors in the adherence process. Many of the findings described here are of an exploratory nature; replication, elaboration, and specification of constructs are very much needed. At the very least, I hope that the presentation of these findings in this context will help other researchers avoid the weaknesses and pitfalls of these exploratory studies.

In this chapter, I have also attempted to present adherence as a process with many phases. Park and her colleagues have done an excellent job of making us realize that there is more to adherence than "simple" prospective memory. Although the model represented in Fig. 10.1 is necessarily incomplete, it is hoped that this chapter will help to ensure that subjectivity, affect, and metamemory issues are given more importance in the future. Sinott stated in a review of the general prospective memory literature, that "students of the history of psychology will be aware that psychology is once again, after a long hiatus, putting subjectivity and the person back into objective studies" (1989, p. 363). The same integration may be required in the adherence literature. Whether conceptualized as (a) metamemorial variables such as memory self-efficacy or anxiety, (b) communicative variables such as overaccommodation, or (c) learning variables such as motivation, the integration of subjectivity into adherence models may be vital to understanding health behaviors in older adults.

ACKNOWLEDGMENTS

I would like to express my gratitude to Roger Dixon and Leslie McDonald-Miszczak for many fruitful discussions and collaborations over the past few years.

REFERENCES

Ashburn, G., & Gordon, A. (1981). Features of a simplified register in speech to elderly conversation-alists. *International Journal of Psycholinguistics, 8,* 7–31.

Berlowitz, D. R., Du, W., Kazis, L., & Lewis, S. (1995). Health-related quality of life of nursing home residents: Differences in patient and provider perceptions. *Journal of the American Geriatrics Society, 43,* 799–802.

Buller, M. K., & Buller, D. B. (1987). Physicians' communication style and patient satisfaction. *Journal of Health and Social Behavior, 28,* 375–388.

Caporael, L. R., Lukaszewski, M. P., & Culbertson, G. H. (1983). Secondary babytalk: Judgments by institutionalized elderly and their caregivers. *Journal of Personality and Social Psychology, 44,* 746–754.

Coupland, J., Robinson, J. D., & Coupland, N. (1994). Frame negotiation in doctor–elderly patient consultations. *Discourse & Society, 5,* 89–124.

Craik, F. I. M. (1986). A functional account of age differences in memory. In F. Klix & H. Hagendorf (Eds.), *Human memory and cognitive capabilities* (pp. 409–422). Amsterdam: Elsevier.

Craik, F. I. M., & Jennings, J. M. (1992). Human Memory. In F. I. M. Craik & T. A. Salthouse (Eds.), *The handbook of aging and cognition* (pp. 51–110). Hillsdale, NJ: Lawrence Erlbaum Associates.

Denney, N. W. (1989). Everyday problem solving: Methodological issues, research findings, and a model. In L. W. Poon, D. C. Rubin, & B. A. Wilson (Eds.), *Everyday cognition in adulthood and late life* (pp. 330–351). Cambridge, England: Cambridge University Press.

Devolder, P. A., & Pressley, M. (1992). Causal attributions and strategy use in relation to memory performance differences in younger and older adults. *Applied Cognitive Psychology, 6,* 629–642.

Ditto, P. H., Moore, K. A., Hilton, J. L., & Kalish, J. R. (1995). Beliefs about physicians: Their role in health care utilization, satisfaction, and compliance. *Basic and Applied Social Psychology, 17,* 23–48.

Dixon, R. A. (1989). Questionnaire research on metamemory and aging: Issues of structure and function. In L. W. Poon, D. C. Rubin, & B.A. Wilson (Eds.), *Everyday cognition in adulthood and late life* (pp. 394–415). Cambridge, England: Cambridge University Press.

Dixon, R. A., & Hultsch, D. F. (1984). The Metamemory in Adulthood (MIA) instrument. *Psychological Documents, 14,* 3.

Einstein, G. O., & McDaniel, M. A. (1990). Normal aging and prospective memory. *Journal of Experimental Psychology: Learning, Memory, and Cognition, 16,* 717–726.

Fineman, N. (1994). Health care providers' subjective understandings of old age: Implications for threatened status in late life. *Journal of Aging Studies, 8,* 255–270.

Gardner, M. E., Rulien, N., McGhan, W. F., & Mead, R. A. (1988). A study of patients' perceived importance of medication information provided by physicians in a health maintenance organization. *Drug Intelligence and Clinical Pharmacy, 22,* 596–598.

Garrity, T. F., & Lawson, E. J. (1989). Patient–physician communication as a determinant of medication in older, minority women. *The Journal of Drug Issues, 19,* 245–259.

German, P. S., Klein, L. E., McPhee, S. J., & Smith, C. R. (1982). Knowledge of and compliance with drug regimens in the elderly. *Journal of the American Geriatrics Society, 30,* 568–571.

Gould, O. N. (1997). *Advice-giving by young and old adult women.* Unpublished manuscript.

Gould, O. N., & Dixon, R. A. (1997). Recall of medication instructions by young and elderly adult women: Is overaccommodative speech helpful? *Journal of Language and Social Psychology, 16,* 50–69.

Gould, O. N., & Malpert, J. (1995, November). Advice-giving by young and old adult women. In E. B. Ryan (Chair), *Intergenerational communication.* Symposium presented at the 48th Annual Meeting of the Gerontological Society of America, Los Angeles, CA.

Gould, O. N., & McDonald-Miszczak, L. (1996, May). *Perceptions of ageism in health care workers.* Poster session presented at The Third International Conference on Communication, Aging, and Health, Kansas City, MO.

Gould, O. N., McDonald-Miszczak, L., & King, B. (1997). Metacognition and medication adherence: How do older adults remember? *Experimental Aging Research, 23,* 315–342.

Greene, M. G., Adelman, R., Charon, R., & Hoffman, S. (1986). Ageism in the medical encounter: An exploratory study of the doctor–elderly patient relationship. *Language & Communication, 6,* 113–124.

Haug, M. R. (1996). Elements in physician/patient interactions in late life. *Research on Aging, 18,* 32–51.

Haug, M. R., & Ory, M. G. (1987). Issues in elderly patient–provider interaction. *Research on Aging, 9,* 3–44.

Hulka, B. S., Cassel, J. C., Kupper, L. L., & Burdette, J. A., (1976). Communication, compliance, and concordance between physicians and patients with prescribed medications. *American Journal of Public Health, 66,* 847–853.

Hummert, M. L., Shaner, J. L., & Gartska, T. A. (1995). Cognitive processes affecting communication with older adults: The case for stereotypes, attitudes, and beliefs about communication. In J. F. Nussbaum & J. Coupland (Eds.), *Handbook of communication and aging research* (pp. 105–132). Mahwah, NJ: Lawrence Erlbaum Associates.

Kemper, S. (1986). Imitation of complex syntactic constructions by elderly adults. *Applied Psycholinguistics, 7,* 277–288.

Kemper, S., Vandeputte, D., Rice, K., Cheung, H., & Gubarchuk, J. (1995). Speech adjustments to aging during a referential communication task. *Journal of Language and Social Psychology, 14,* 40–59.

Kreps, G. I. (1990). A systematic analysis of health communication with the aged. In H. Giles, N. Coupland, & J. M. Wiemann (Eds.), *Communication, health, and the elderly* (pp. 135–154). London: Manchester University Press.

Leirer, V. O., Morrow, D. G., Pariente, G. M., & Sheikh, J. I. (1988). Elders' nonadherence, its assessment, and computer assisted instruction for medication recall training. *Journal of the American Geriatrics Society, 36,* 877–884.

Leirer, V. O., Morrow, D. G., Tanke, E. D., & Pariente, G. M. (1991). Elders' nonadherence: Its assessment and medication reminding by voice mail. *The Gerontologist, 31,* 514–520.

Loewen, E. R., Shaw, R. J., & Craik, F. I. M. (1990). Age differences in components of metamemory. *Experimental Aging Research, 16,* 43–48.

Mackowiak, E. D., O'Connor, T. W., Jr., Thomason, M., Nighswander, R., Smith, M., Vogenberg, A., Weissberger, F., & Wilkes, W. (1994). Compliance devices preferred by elderly patients. *American Pharmacy, NS34,* 47–52

Maylor, E. A. (1990). Age and prospective memory. *Quarterly Journal of Experimental Psychology, 42A,* 471–493.

Meyer, B. J. F., Russo, C., & Talbot, A. (1995). Discourse comprehension and problem solving: Decisions about the treatment of breast cancer by women across the life span. *Psychology and Aging, 10,* 84–103.

Morris, L., Grossman, R., Barkdoll, G., Gordon, E., & Soviero, C. (1984). A survey of patient sources of prescription drug information. *The American Journal of Public Health, 74,* 1161–1162.

Morrow, D., Leirer, V., & Sheikh, J. (1988). Adherence and medication instructions: Review and recommendations. *Journal of the American Geriatrics Society, 36,* 1147–1160.

Musialowski, D. M. (1988). Perceptions of physicians as a function of medical jargon and subjects' authoritarianism. *Representative Research in Social Psychology, 18,* 3–14.

Park, D. C., & Kidder, D. P. (1996). Prospective memory and medication adherence. In M. Brandimonte, G. Einstein, & M. McDaniel (Eds.), *Prospective memory: Theory and applications* (pp. 369–396). Mahwah, NJ: Lawrence Erlbaum Associates.

Park, D. C., & Mayhorn, C. B. (1996). Remembering to take medications: The importance of nonmemory variables. In D. Herrmann, M. Johnson, C. McEvoy, C. Hertzog, & P. Hertel (Eds.), *Research on practical aspects of memory* (Vol. 2, pp. 95–110). Mahwah, NJ: Lawrence Erlbaum Associates.

Park, D. C., Morrell, R. W., Frieske, D., & Kincaid, D. (1992). Medication adherence behaviors in older adults: Effects of external cognitive supports. *Psychology and Aging, 7*, 252–256.

Pesznecker, B. L., Patsdaughter, C., Moody, K. A., & Albert, M. (1990). Medication regimens and the home care client: A challenge for health care providers. *Home Health Care Services Quarterly, 11*, 9–68.

Rice, G. E., & Okun, M. A. (1994). Older readers' processing of medical information that contradicts their beliefs. *Journal of Gerontology: Psychological Sciences, 49*, P119–P128.

Rudd, P. (1993). The measurement of compliance: Medication taking. In N. A. Krasnegor, L. Epstein, S. Johnson, S. J. Yaffe (Eds.), *Developmental aspects of health compliance behavior* (pp. 185–213). Hillsdale, NJ: Lawrence Erlbaum Associates.

Ryan, E. B., & Cole, R. (1990). Evaluative perceptions of interpersonal communication with elders. In H. Giles, N. Coupland, & J. Wiemann (Eds.), *Communication, health, and the elderly* (pp. 172–190). Manchester, England: Manchester University Press.

Ryan, E. B., Giles, H., Bartolucci, G., & Henwood, K. (1986). Psycholinguistic and social psychological components of communication by and with the elderly. *Language and Communication, 6*, 1–24.

Ryan, E. B., Hummert, M. L.,& Boich, L. H. (1995). Communication predicaments of aging: Patronizing behavior toward older adults. *Journal of Language and Social Psychology, 14*, 144–166.

Salthouse, T. A., & Babcock, R. L. (1991). Decomposing adult age differences in working memory. *Developmental Psychology, 27*, 763–776.

Shadden, B. B. (1988). Perceptions of daily communicative interactions with older people. In B. B. Shadden (Ed.), *Communication behavior and aging: A sourcebook for clinicians* (pp. 12–37). Baltimore, MD: Williams & Wilkins.

Sinnott, J. (1989). Prospective/intentional memory and aging: Memory as adaptive action. In L. W. Poon, D. C. Rubin, & B. A. Wilson (Eds.), *Everyday cognition in adulthood and late life* (pp. 352–372). Cambridge, England: Cambridge University Press.

Smith, D. H., Cunningham, K. G., & Hale, W. E. (1994). Communication about medicines: Perceptions of the ambulatory elderly. *Health Communication, 6*, 281–295.

Street, R. L., Jr. (1991). Accommodation in medical consultations. In H. Giles, J. Coupland, & N. Coupland (Eds.), *Contexts of accommodation: Developments in applied sociolinguistics* (pp. 131–156). Cambridge, England: Cambridge University Press.

West, R. L. (1988). Prospective memory and aging. In M. M. Gruneberg, P. E. Morris, & R. N. Sykes (Eds.), *Practical aspects of memory* (Vol. 4, pp. 119–125). Chichester, England: Wiley.

Yesavage, J. A., Lapp, D., & Sheikh, J. I. (1989). Mnemonics as modified for use by the elderly. In L. W. Poon, D. C. Rubin, & B. A. Wilson (Eds.), *Everyday cognition in adulthood and late life* (pp. 598–614). Cambridge, England: Cambridge University Press.

11

Issues in the Measurement of Medication Adherence

Roger W. Morrell
The University of Georgia

Kim Shifren
The University of Michigan

Medication adherence may be defined as "the accurate use of medication, that is, taking the appropriate number of doses at the right time in the amount prescribed by a physician" (Park & Mayhorn, 1996, p. 95). Failure to take medication as prescribed has often been described as a major reason for failed therapy (Cramer, 1995). Furthermore, mistakes in taking medication may cost billions of dollars per year in the United States in lost productivity and increased annual medical costs (Park & Jones, 1997).

Because of grave health-related and financial consequences, medication nonadherence has been widely studied. In 1979, Haynes identified 185 articles that contained original data concerning adherence from more than 300 citations on the topic. Many of these articles were dated in the early 1960s. In 1995, Buckalew and Buckalew accounted for 225 articles that incorporated the search terms of "medication or patient noncompliance" in their titles and that had been published since 1985. No review is available on how many publications might be available in total on the topic in the late 1990s. What is clear is that the study of adherence to prescribed medical regimens is not new.

Despite the large number of articles published, many researchers remain unconvinced that the problem of medication nonadherence is well understood (see Park & Jones, 1997). Cramer notes that "no reliable methods have been developed to date for predicting which patients will comply with prescribed medical regimens" (1995, p. 25). A majority of the early studies focused on single constructs as possible determinants of nonadherence, such as the demographic features of patients (i.e., age, race, or gender) or aspects of the therapeutic regimen (i.e., number of dosages to be taken; Haynes, 1979). A number of researchers have suggested that medication adherence is an extremely complex behavior and it is likely that no single variable can account for the rates of nonadherence that have been observed in various populations. Instead, only by examining an intermix of medication, disease, and psychosocial and cognitive variables can one begin to understand what factors might drive medication-taking behaviors (Park, 1992).

Therefore, the purpose of this chapter is to identify several issues related to the study of medication adherence. Our discussion is guided by theoretical conceptualizations of how this problem might be viewed. We seek to answer two questions in this chapter and thus suggest alternative methods of how this type of research might be conducted in order to isolate the determinants of nonadherence.

1. What factors influence medication adherence? In the first section of this chapter we explore the complexity of medication-taking behavior by briefly presenting the social-cognitive model developed by Park and colleagues, including C. Hertzog, H. Leventhal, R. W. Morrell, E. Leventhal, M. Martin, and D. Birchmore. This model was used to guide an extensive interdisciplinary research project, which was funded by the National Institute on Aging. In this discussion, we focus on the cognitive component of the model and emphasize how specific laboratory measures of cognition have been successfully used to assess the impact of cognition on adherence.

2. How can the adherence data be examined? In the last section of this chapter we outline methodological problems that may be encountered when designing this type of research and also suggest types of statistical procedures that can be used to examine adherence data.

WHAT FACTORS INFLUENCE MEDICATION ADHERENCE?

As noted, most early researchers in this area did not utilize a comprehensive conceptual framework that incorporates a multidimensional view of medication-taking behavior to guide their research. Other investigators, however, suggest that medication adherence is a multifaceted behavior. Park and her colleagues (Park, 1992, 1994; Park & Jones, 1997) have developed a conceptual model for understanding medication adherence that proposes that medication adherence is governed by both beliefs and cognitive factors. This model integrates the Leventhal and Cameron (1987) self-regulatory view of medication adherence with basic cognitive psychology. The model has been named the social-cognitive model of medication adherence and is further described by Park (1994; see also Park & Jones, 1997; Park & Mayhorn, 1996).

According to the social-cognitive model, it is important to understand two types of beliefs patients may hold. The first type of beliefs is individuals' personal beliefs about illness. According to Leventhal and Cameron (1987), medication adherence is a self-regulatory behavior. An individual chooses to be adherent or nonadherent to a medication, and this choice is dependent upon what the individual believes to be true about a disease and how successful a particular medication is in the management of the disease. An individual's illness representation is dynamic and may change over the course of a disease.

In addition to illness beliefs, the social-cognitive model emphasizes that it is also important to understand beliefs about specific medications or a patient's medication representation. People will not take medication if they do not consider it useful or if a decision is made to use the medication only when symptoms occur (Park & Mayhorn, 1996). According to the social-cognitive model, other medication and disease variables, individual difference factors, and external cues are also expected to influence adherence in addition to beliefs and cognition (see Park & Jones, 1997).

Although many researchers insist that forgetting to take one's medications is a primary factor affecting adherence, there is little systematic evidence available to document this assertion. The social-cognitive model is novel in that it specifies the underlying cognitive mechanisms (above and beyond the broad terms of *forgetting* or *lapses in memory*) that might be responsible for nonadherence. According to Park (1992), remembering to take medications involves a number of cognitive processes. *Working memory* has been conceptualized as the amount of cognitive resource available to store and process new or recently accessed information (Salthouse, 1991). *Perceptual speed* has been defined as the speed at which mental operations are performed (Salthouse, 1996). An individual must use working memory to integrate and develop a medication plan for taking multiple medications. The effectiveness of this plan might be compromised by declines in perceptual speed as early information concerning how the regimen should be taken might be lost during the planning process if these mental operations are performed too slowly (Salthouse, 1996). The ability of an individual to reason how to combine and coordinate how to take a number of different medications at different times of the day and night may also influence this process (Salthouse, 1991).

Medication adherence also involves long-term memory because patients must remember the plan they have devised (Park, 1992). Finally, taking medication at the prescribed time is essentially a prospective memory task (Park & Kidder, 1996). That is, *prospective memory* may be defined as remembering to remember to do something (Park & Kidder, 1996). Patients must remember to remember to actually take the medication at the proper time in order to be adherent.

Other aspects of cognition may also influence an individual's ability to adhere to a prescribed medical regimen. Most prescription information is presented via the prescription signature on the medicine bottle or in written form (Morrell, Park, & Poon, 1989, 1990). Thus, the ability of patients to comprehend text and/or their level of vocabulary may influence whether they initially understand how they are to take their medications. If instructions are misunderstood, chances are that the medication will not be taken correctly.

Age-related declines in some of these underlying cognitive mechanisms (working memory, perceptual speed, long-term memory with recall measures, and reasoning) are well documented and may contribute substantially to older adults forgetting to take medication or not understanding how to properly take medication (see Salthouse, 1991). Age-related trends in prospective memory, vocabulary, and text comprehension are not as clear (see Salthouse, 1991; Park, Hertzog, Kidder, Morrell, & Mayhorn, 1997). Therefore, it is possible that these cognitive factors may not have differential influences on older adults' medication-taking behaviors.

Results from two studies conducted by Park and colleagues suggest that cognitive factors that have reliably shown age-related declines are related to nonadherence. In one study, with patients diagnosed with hypertension, the findings from the correlational analyses suggest that working memory capacity may play a role in one's ability to adhere to a medical regimen. In this study, scores on the Listening Span Task (Salthouse & Babcock, 1990; a version of the Reading Span Task) were significantly correlated with nonadherence for the prescribed medications the individuals were taking for conditions other than hypertension (Morrell, Park, Kidder, & Martin, 1997). Furthermore, findings from a large-scale study with 121 Rheumatoid Arthritis patients indicated that a combination of cognitive factors may be predictive of nonadherence (Park et al., 1998). In this study, an aggregate cognitive measure, composed of scores from instruments that measured speed of processing, working memory, long-term memory, and reasoning was shown to be related to nonadherence. (Descriptions of the instruments used to measure these constructs are outlined in Table 11.1.) In general, these results suggested that individuals with low cognitive function do show poorer adherence.

Thus, there appears to be a number of factors that might affect how an individual takes his or her medication. In the preceding section, we emphasized the role that cognition might play in adherence. Results from two studies suggest that measures of cognition that have shown age-related declines may be the best predictors of nonadherence in older adults relative to measures of other cognitive aspects. We also presented evidence that the measurement of these underlying cognitive factors is an important research component in order to determine which of these cognitive variables (or combinations thereof) might influence adherence above what is usually termed forgetting.

HOW CAN THE ADHERENCE DATA BE EXAMINED?

The discussion of the factors that might influence adherence leads us to another important question. What is the best time frame to assess medication adherence behaviors? Park and others who study medication adherence behavior often assess

TABLE 11.1
Instruments for Measuring Cognitive Factors Related to Nonadherence

Cognitive Factor and Instrument	Description
Perceptual Speed	
Letter Comparison Task (Salthouse & Babcock, 1991)	Participants determine if two strings of letters are the same or different. Three sets of comparisons are made, each comprised of either three, six, or nine letters. Participants have 30 sec. to complete as many of the comparisons in each set as possible. The dependent measure is the total number of correct decisions made.
Pattern Comparison Task (Salthouse & Babcock, 1991)	This task is identical to the letter comparison task, except that participants determine if geometric figures are the same or different.
Working Memory	
Reading Span Task (Salthouse & Babcock, 1990)	Participants read aloud a simple sentence presented on a computer screen. They answer a related question while simultaneously remembering the last word in the sentence they just read. Participants begin with a set of items requiring the recall of one word and progress in complexity (up to seven words) over sets of trials until an entire set is missed. The task ends when three consecutive errors are made. The dependent measure is the number of trials in which both the processing and storage components are correctly completed by the participant.
Computation Span Task (Salthouse & Babcock, 1990)	This task is identical to the reading span test, except participants are presented with equations (i.e., $2 + 4 = ?$) on the screen.
Long-term recall	
Free Recall (Park, et al, 1996)	Two sets of 25-word lists are presented to participants on a computer. Within each list of words, five categories of words with five exemplars per category are presented. After the final screen for each list, participants recall as many items as they can in any order. The main dependent variables are the number of words recalled and the number of categories.
Reasoning	
Letter Sets Test (Ekstrom et al., 1976)	Each problem has five sets of letters with four letters in each set. Four of the sets of letters are alike in some way (i.e., in alphabetical order). Participants find the rule that makes the four sets alike and draw an "X" through the set of letters that is different. The participants have 7 minutes to complete 15 sets. The dependent measure is the number of sets completed correctly.

this behavior daily, with studies ranging from a few weeks to eight weeks of daily assessments (Kim & Lagakos, 1994; Kruse, Eggert-Kruse, Rampmaier, Runnebaum, & Weber, 1993; Morrell et al., 1997; Park, Morrell, Frieske, & Kincaid, 1992). Researchers argue that to best understand the pattern that may exist for

behaviors such as medication adherence, daily assessments of behavior are necessary (e.g., Larsen & Cutler, 1996; Stone, Kennedy-Moore, & Neale, 1995; Usala
& Hertzog, 1991). This is because daily assessments of medication adherence
capture both stability and change in this behavior.

The lability in the taking of medication is an important issue because nonadherence for taking medications is assumed to deter the effects of treatment regimens
prescribed by physicians, ultimately rendering the treatment ineffective (Haynes,
McKibbon, & Kanani, 1996; Mengden, Binswanger, Spuhler, Weisser, & Vetter,
1993). Thus, obtaining an accurate assessment of medication adherence is important
in determining health outcomes. Therefore, we turn now to issues that are involved
in designing a study with daily assessments of medication adherence. After a
discussion of important methodological considerations, we will address the statistical approaches that best capture the pattern to medication adherence behaviors.

Methological Considerations

The methodological issues discussed below are not intended to be an all inclusive
discussion of methodological issues in daily design research. Instead, the focus is
issues that are specific to research on medication adherence. Methodological issues
in the daily assessment of medication adherence include the type of disease studied
and the number of medications monitored.

Type of Disease.   First, let us discuss an issue of central importance in
medication adherence research, the type of disease selected for study. Researchers
and practitioners have learned that there can be much variability across diseases
(Charmaz, 1991). Chronic diseases vary depending on a number of characteristics
including the biological system involved in the disease, the speed of progression,
and the symptomatic expression of the disease. For example, musculoskeletal
disorders show persistent signs or symptoms over time; however, epilepsy shows
discrete symptomatic episodes. Thus, monitoring medication adherence behaviors
in arthritis patients can be done on a daily basis, but it may not be worthwhile to
design a daily study for epilepsy.

In addition, some diseases show on/off periods in which the symptoms return
during the off periods related to medication adherence behavior (i.e., nighttime for
Parkinson's disease; Nissenbaum, Quinn, Brown, & Toone, 1987). Thus, it may be
important to design a daily assessment with multiple assessment periods throughout
each day rather than once a day (Larsen & Kasimatis, 1991). Therefore, it is
important to be aware of the variability present across diseases when studying
medication adherence behaviors on a daily basis. Otherwise, variability in medication adherence behavior over time can be confounded with the variability present
in the symptomatic expression of different kinds of diseases.

One way that researchers have attempted to control for this variability is by
examining only one disease group over time (Shifren, Hooker, Wood, & Nessel-

roade, 1997). For example, individuals who conduct research on arthritis know that the types of Rheumatic diseases vary in their expression of symptoms (Zautra et al., 1995). In particular, the expression of symptoms for rheumatoid arthritis and osteoarthritis differ over time (Park, 1994). Park et al., in their series of studies, designed one study to assess rheumatoid arthritis and a second study to assess osteoarthritis. This method allowed these researchers to examine the level of variability in medication adherence over time without confounding temporal variation with symptomatic expression of disease symptoms that may influence variability in medication adherence.

Number of Medications. A second important issue in the daily assessment of medication adherence behavior is the number of medications included in the assessment. The presence of multiple medications in an individual's medication regimen can make it difficult to monitor medication adherence behaviors on a daily basis (Morrell, Park, & Poon, 1989, 1990). In terms of cognitive resources, multiple medications can also be taxing on individuals' memories (Park, 1994).

In addition to limitations in personal cognitive resources, a lack of communication between the participant and the researchers can result in misleading information about medication adherence. For example, an individual being monitored for his or her medication adherence for 28 days may be asked by a physician to stop or increase the amount of times he or she takes one or more medications. Not only is this disruptive for those taking more than one medication, but also it may decrease researchers ability to accurately assess changes in medication-taking behavior over time (Park, 1994). Researchers who are monitoring individuals' medication adherence behaviors may be mislead by changes in the medication taking behavior of individuals who have forgotten to inform them of changes to their medication regimen. This is especially true for daily design studies in which both the timing of medication and correct dosage have been considered important aspects of medication adherence behaviors (White & Sanders, 1985).

Statistical Issues

From the discussion, it is clear that taking medication can often be a complex behavior requiring individuals to remember to take their medications at various times throughout the day (Park, 1994). Daily design studies capture the complex nature of this behavior, and they can provide information on the frequency and duration of adherence to medications. However, there are a number of statistical issues that need to be addressed before researchers conduct a daily assessment of medication adherence. These include (a) missing data, (b) stability or perfect adherence, (c) aggregating data, and (d) time-series analyses.

Missing Data. After methodological issues have been considered, researchers need to address some statistical issues that are likely to arise after data collection is complete. One such issue is missing data. Daily design studies of medication adherence, more than any other kind of design, are likely to have at least some missing data for each individual in the sample (Stone, Kessler, & Haythornthwaite, 1991). How does one deal with missing data? This is no trivial question, because data are not always missing in a random pattern (Raymond & Roberts, 1987). Nonrandom patterns to missing data need to be determined before researchers try to replace the values for missing data points.

One way to determine if data are missing in a nonrandom pattern is recording daily events. Researchers suggest that individuals involved in daily design studies keep diaries or record unusual events (Stone et al., 1991). Recording of daily events can help researchers determine if specific events precipitated the lack of responses at certain intervals. For example, an individual with Parkinson's disease who completed a daily design study did not complete questionnaires on days in which a daughter arrived for a visit (Shifren, 1996). In Park et al.'s series of studies, individuals with arthritis recorded in a daily diary any unusual events that occurred that disrupted their medication adherence. For example, an individual who was going on a trip took out all the medications that would be needed for several days on the morning before the trip. The recorded information on the electronic medication monitor was compared with the diary information to determine the actual adherence rates of that particular individual.

Another way to determine whether there is a pattern to the missing data is to look at graphs of the data with the medication adherence responses plotted over time. Linear or nonlinear trends in the plotted data can be determined with the use of regression analyses. Regression analyses can be performed on each individual's data with medication adherence responses as the dependent variable and day or time as the independent variable (Gottman, 1984). If there is no trend in the data (i.e., no significant pattern of increase or decrease in medication adherence behavior over time), then it is likely that missing data do not have a distinct nonrandom pattern.

A number of statistical approaches for dealing with missing data in both cross-sectional and longitudinal data have been tested including deletion or replacement of missing data values (Huberty & Julian, 1995; Kromrey & Hines, 1994). In particular, the following methods for dealing with missing data values have been assessed: (a) deletion of cases with missing data, (b) replacement of missing data values with the mean value for a series of cases, (c) replacement of missing data values with the values established from regression, and (d) replacement of missing data values with the values from iterated multiple regression (Raymond & Roberts, 1987). In the late 1990s, the preference of researchers and statisticians is the use of regression analyses to help determine the value of missing data. In daily design studies, the time order of the missing data is best determined from regression analyses rather than simple replacement of missing data with the mean value.

Perfect Adherence.   Another important issue in analyzing data is stability. Researchers who perform analyses on daily design data usually have defined specific criteria for determining "stability" in their data (cf. Hooker, 1991). For example, a number of prior studies have defined stability in data responses as any item that has 80% to 90% of responses in one category (e.g., Shifren et al., 1997). For example, if responses to an item could fall into five categories (1, *not at all* to 5, *all the time*) and an individual responds to that item with "five" 90% of the time, then that individual shows stability for that item.

Any kind of statistical analyses chosen to analyze data requires at least some variability in the data. Without variability in the data, data cannot be analyzed (Wei, 1990). For example, an individual from one of the Park et al. adherence studies showed more than 90% stability for taking medications for hypertension. This individual's medication-taking behavior data could not be used in statistical analyses; the behavior was viewed as adherent. Thus, complete adherence in medication adherence studies (i.e., 80% to 90% adherence rates) eliminates the inclusion of such stable data in analyses. If medication adherence shows no variance, then researchers cannot analyze the relationship between medication adherence and other variables, such as physical or mental health outcomes. This can limit researchers ability to determine whether medication adherence predicts future well-being or physical health, an important concern within the psychological literature (Park, 1994).

Aggregate Data. Let us continue our discussion of daily design studies with the assumptions that missing data has been dealt with properly and that there is sufficient variability to perform analyses. How do researchers correctly analyze daily design data? One method to analyzing multiple data points is to aggregate the data into larger variables (i.e., creating a weekly variable by summing data from a 7-day period). Aggregating data is an important issue because there is evidence that aggregating data increases the likelihood that relationships between variables will be bigger simply because more data points are included in the analyses (Stone et al., 1991).

Researchers may end up with an inflated set of results, not because the results really reflect such strong relationships, but because of aggregated data. This can have some consequences for those proposing interventions for medication adherence behaviors. Interventions based on aggregated data may show a stronger relationship to improved medication adherence than interventions not based on aggregated data.

Time-Series Analysis. What is the best way to analyze daily design data? This final issue, time-series analysis, addresses how to analyze daily design data without aggregating the data points for analyses. Time-series analysis allows researchers to examine data over time, rather than clumping or aggregating certain numbers of days into one large variable or sets of variables. With time-series analysis, researchers can analyze *autocorrelation,* how a variable relates to itself over time, and *cross-correlation,* how one variable relates to another variable over time (Gottman, 1984; Larsen, 1987).

Autocorrelation is the correlation of a variable on itself over time. Two common forms of autocorrelation are autoregressive (AR) and moving average (MA) models. When individuals display an autocorrelation in the form of an AR model, then this means their responses yesterday predict their responses today and gradually decay over time. If an individual displays an AR model of lag one for medication adherence, then medication adherence behavior yesterday predicted adherence behavior today and predictability of adherence gradually diminishes after the one-day lag. An individual from one of the Park et al. studies on adherence showed medication-taking behavior that had an AR model of lag one, indicating that forgetting medications on one day was predictive of forgetting medications the next day and gradually diminished over time. An individual with an MA model of lag one for medication adherence has data that show a discrete drop-off of predictability. Current medication adherence observations and portions of the one preceding adherence observation contain "random shock" that impacts on the variable (Schmitz, 1990). There is no gradual decay in predictability of adherence; instead predictability abruptly ends.

Cross-correlation is the correlation of two variables on each other over time. A variable's correlation on itself can influence the variance accounted for in the relationship between two variables over time. Time-series analysis can control for autocorrelation and display the cross-correlation between two variables not accounted for by a variable's relationship to itself over time. Thus, time-series analysis allows researchers to obtain a clearer picture of the relationship between variables such as medication adherence for two medications over time.

Time-series analysis was specifically designed to examine the time dimension, and it is more sensitive to possible trending in the data than ordinary linear regression (Wei, 1990). On the one hand, time-series analysis can show when data are slowly diminishing over time, a pattern that is often not detected in simple linear regression. On the other hand, time-series analysis can determine when there is a random pattern to the data (i.e., no autocorrelation). Shifren (1996) demonstrated the ability of time-series analysis to determine "white noise" from real patterns to the data in a study on optimism in Parkinson's patients. Ordinary regression analyses often do not detect slowly diminishing data patterns over time or white noise. Time-series analysis can provide the most stringent test for the kind of pattern that may occur for medication adherence behavior in one or more medications being monitored over time.

Researchers have found that both psychosocial and health variables can show trend, autocorrelation, and cross-correlations (Affleck, Tennen, Urrows, & Higgins, 1991; Larsen & Kasimatis, 1991; Shifren, 1996). Half of a sample of arthritis patients showed a trend in their reports of pain over a 75-day period (Affleck et al., 1991), with some showing an increase in pain and others showing a decrease in pain over time. An young adult sample showed autocorrelation in mood such that mood, was related to itself over short time periods (i.e., hours), but the relationship diminished over longer time periods (i.e., days; Larsen & Kasimatis, 1991). A number of individuals with Parkinson's disease showed a short period of autocorrelation for perceived symptom severity, such that perceived symptom severity was related to itself over a one-day period but diminished over longer time periods (i.e., two or more days; Shifren, 1996). Cross-correlations can also be informative. For example, Larsen and Kasimatis (1991) found that individuals' moods lead their symptoms over time much more than individuals' symptoms predicted their moods.

In terms of medication adherence, time-series analyses can reveal the following: (a) increases or decreases in adherence over time (trend), (b) whether prior levels of adherence predict future adherence (autocorrelation; if so, for how long?), (c) duration of adherence (Larsen & Kasimatis, 1991), and (d) whether adherence predicts psychological and physical health outcomes over time (i.e., cross-correlations).

However, a critical aspect of performing time-series analysis is the assumption that data are collected at regular time intervals. For example, individuals in a chronic illness study must complete measures of their behavior each day before they go to bed. If individuals record their behaviors at varying times on each day, then the assumption of regular time intervals has been violated. To examine medication adherence in a given individual, medications must be taken at the same time each day. If this is not possible, then results for each day of monitoring must be summed into a daily adherence variable to proceed with a time-series analysis. The use of time series for analysis of social science data is still not common. However, the richness of the information it can provide about medication adherence makes it a worthwhile statistical approach for medication adherence research.

SUMMARY

In this chapter, we have focused on issues that pertain to the study of medication adherence. In doing so, we have attempted to provide alternative ways in which adherence research might be conducted. First, we demonstrated how aspects of cognition can be measured in an adherence research project and presented some findings that suggested which cognitive factors (or combinations of factors) may be the most important to measure with older adults. In our final section, we provided an overview of methodological and statistical problems that might be encountered when conducting this type of research. Most important, we have tried to emphasize that medication adherence is a multifaceted behavior. Only through the examination of a number of different factors can the true determinants of nonadherence be isolated.

ACKNOWLEDGMENTS

This chapter was supported by Grant 3RO1-AG09868 awarded to Denise C. Park (principal investigator), Daniel Birchmore, and Christopher Hertzog from the National Institute on Aging. The research team conducting this research is composed of Denise C. Park, The University of Michigan; Christopher Hertzog, The

Georgia Institute of Technology; Daniel Birchmore, VA Hospital, Wilmington, Delaware; Howard Leventhal, Rutgers University; Roger W. Morrell, The University of Georgia; Mike Martin, University of Mainz; Elaine Leventhal, University of Medicine & Dentistry of New Jersey; and Kim Shifren and Joan Bennett, The University of Michigan.

REFERENCES

Affleck, G., Tennen, H., Urrows, S., & Higgins, P. (1991). Individual differences in the day-to-day experience of chronic pain: A prospective daily study of rheumatoid arthritis patients. *Health Psychology, 10*(6), 419–426.

Buckalew, L. W., & Buckalew, N. M. (1995). Survey of the nature and prevalence of patients' noncompliance and implications for intervention. *Psychological Reports, 76*(1), 315–321.

Charmaz, K. (1991). *Good days, bad days: The self in chronic illness and time.* New Brunswick, NJ: Rutgers University Press.

Cramer, J. A. (1995). Optimizing long-term patient compliance. *Neurology, 45,* 25–28.

Ekstrom, R. B., French, J. W., Harman, H. H., Dermen, D. (1976). *Kit of Factor-Referenced Cognitive Tests.* Princeton, NJ: Educational Testing Service.

Gottman, J. (1984). *Time-Series Analysis: A Comprehensive Introduction for Social Scientists.* Cambridge, England: Cambridge University Press.

Haynes, R. B. (1979). Strategies to improve compliance with referrals, appointments, and prescribed medical regimens. In R. B. Haynes, D. W. Taylor, & D. L. Sackett (Eds.), *Compliance in health care.* Baltimore, MD: Johns Hopkins University Press.

Haynes, R. B., McKibbon, K. A., & Kanani, R. (1996). Systematic review of randomized trials of interventions to assist patients to follow prescriptions for medications. *Lancet, 348,* 383–386.

Hooker, K. (1991). Change and stability in self during the transition to retirement: An intraindividual study using P-technique factor analysis. *International Journal of Behavioral Development, 14,* 209–233.

Huberty, C. J., & Julian, M. W. (1995). An ad hoc analysis strategy with missing data. *Journal of Experimental Education, 63,* 333–342.

Kim, H. M., & Lagakos, S. W. (1994). Assessing drug compliance using longitudinal marker data, with application to AIDS. *Statistical Medicine, 13,* 2141–2153.

Kromrey, J. D., & Hines, C. V. (1994). Nonrandomly missing data in multiple regression: An empirical comparison of common missing-data treatments. *Educational & Psychological Measurement, 54,* 573–593.

Kruse, W., Eggert-Kruse, W., Rampmaier, J., Runnebaum, B., & Weber, E. (1993). Compliance and adverse drug reactions: A prospective study with ethinylestradiol using continuous compliance monitoring. *Clinical Investigation, 71,* 483–487.

Larsen, R. J. (1987). The stability of mood variability: A spectral analytic approach to daily mood assessments. *Journal of Personality and Social Psychology, 52,* 1195–1204.

Larsen, R. J., & Cutler, S. E. (1996). The complexity of individual emotional lives: A within-subject analysis of affect structure. *Journal of Social and Clinical Psychology, 15,* 206–230.

Larsen, R. J., & Kasimatis, M. (1991). Day-to-day physical symptoms: Individual differences in the occurrence, duration, and emotional concomitants of minor daily illnesses. *Journal of Personality, 59,* 387–423.

Leventhal, H., & Cameron, L. (1987). Behavioral theories and the problem of compliance. *Patient Education and Counseling, 10,* 117–138.

Mengden, T., Binswanger, B., Spuhler, T., Weisser, B., & Vetter, W. (1993). The use of self-measured blood pressure determinations in assessing dynamics of drug compliance in a study with amlodipine once a day, morning versus evening. *Journal of Hypertension, 11,* 1403–1411.

Morrell, R. W., Park, D. C., Kidder, D. P., & Martin, M. (1997). Adherence to antihypertensive medications across the life span. *The Gerontologist, 37,* 609–619.

Morrell, R. W., Park, D. C., & Poon, L. W. (1989). Quality of instructions on prescription drug labels: Effects on memory and comprehension in young and old adults. *The Gerontologist, 29,* 345–353.

Morrell, R. W., Park, D. C., & Poon, L. W. (1990). Effects of labeling techniques on memory and comprehension of prescription information in young and older adults. *Journal of Gerontology: Psychological Sciences, 45,* 166–172.

Nissenbaum, H., Quinn, N. P, Brown, R. G., & Toone, B. K. (1987). Mood swings associated with the "on-off" phenomenon in Parkinson's disease. *Psychological Medicine, 17,* 899–904.

Park, D. C. (1992). Applied cognitive aging research. In F. I. M. Craik & T. A. Salthouse (Eds.), *The handbook of aging and cognition* (pp. 449–493). Hillsdale, NJ: Lawrence Erlbaum Associates.

Park, D. C. (1994). Self-regulation and control of rheumatic disorders. *International Review of Health Psychology, 3,* 189–217.

Park, D. C., Hertzog, C., Kidder, D. P., Morrell, R. W., & Mayhorn, C. B. (1997). The effect of age on event-based and time-based prospective memory. *Psychology and Aging, 12,* 314–327.

Park, D. C., Hertzog, C., Leventhal, H., Morrell, R. W., Leventhal, E., Birchmore, D., Martin, M., & Bennett, J. (1998). [Medication adherence in rheumatoid arthritis patients: Older is wiser.] Unpublished raw data.

Park, D. C., & Jones, T. R. (1997). Medication Adherence and Aging. In A. D. Fisk & W. A. Rogers (Eds.), *Handbook of human factors and the older adult* (pp. 257–288). Mahwah, NJ: Lawrence Erlbaum Associates.

Park. D. C., & Kidder, D. P. (1996). Prospective memory and medication adherence. In M. Brandimonte, G. O. Einstein, & McDaniel, M. A. (Eds.), *Prospective memory theory and applications* (pp. 369–390). Mahwah, NJ: Lawrence Erlbaum Associates.

Park, D. C., & Mayhorn, C. B. (1996). Remembering to take medications: The importance of nonmemory variables. In D. Herrmann, M. Hohnson, C. McEnvoy, C Hertzog, (Eds.), *Research on practical aspects of memory* (Vol. 2, pp. 95–110). Mahwah, NJ: Lawrence Erlbaum Associates.

Park, D. C., Morrell, R. W., Frieske, D. & Kincaid, D. (1992). Medication adherence behaviors in older adults: Effects of external cognitive supports. *Psychology and Aging, 7,* 252–256.

Park, D. C., Smith, A. D., Lautenschlager, G., Earles, J., Frieske, D., Zwahr, M., & Gaines, C. L. (1996). Mediators of long-term memory performance across the life span. *Psychology and Aging, 11,* 621–637.

Raymond, M. R., & Roberts, D. M. (1987). A comparison of methods for treating incomplete data in selection research. *Educational & Psychological Measurement, 47,* 13–26.

Salthouse, T. A. (1991). *Theoretical perspectives in cognitive aging.* Hillsdale, NJ: Lawrence Erlbaum Associates.

Salthouse, T. A. (1996). General and specific speed mediation of adult age diffences in memory. *Journal of Gerontology: Psychological Sciences, 51B*(1), P30–P42.

Salthouse, T., & Babcock, R. (1990). *Computation span and listening span tasks.* (Tech. Rep.). Atlanta, GA: Georgia Institute of Technology.

Salthouse, T., & Babcock, R. (1991). Decomposing adult age differences in working memory. *Developmental Psychology, 27,* 763–776.

Schmitz, B. (1990). Univariate and multivariate time-series models: The analysis of intraindividual variability and intraindividual relationships. In A. Van Eys (Ed.), *Statistical methods in longitudinal research: Vol. 2. Time-series and categorical longitudinal data* (pp. 351–386). New Yoerk: Academic Press.

Shifren, K. (1996). Individual differences in the perception of optimism and disease severity: A study among individuals with Parkinson's disease. *Journal of Behavioral Medicine, 19,* 241–271.

Shifren, K., Hooker, K., Wood, P., & Nesselroade, J. R. (1997). The structure and variation of mood in individuals with Parkinson's disease: A dynamic factor analysis. *Psychology and Aging, 12*(2), 328–339.

Stone, A. A., Kennedy-Moore, E., & Neale, J. M. (1995). Association between daily coping and end-of-day mood. *Health Psychology, 14,* 341–349.

Stone, A. A., Kessler, R. C., & Haythornthwaite, J. A. (1991). Measuring daily events and experiences: Decisions for the researcher. *Journal of Personality, 59,* 575–607.

Usala, P. D., & Hertzog, C. (1991). Evidence of differential stability of state and trait anxiety in adults. *Journal of Personality and Social Psychology, 60,* 471–479.

Wei, W. W. (1990). *Time series analysis: Univariate and multivariate methods.* New York: Addison-Wesley.

White, B., & Sanders, S. H. (1985). Differential effects on pain and mood in chronic pain patients with time- versus pain-contingent medication delivery. *Behavior Therapy, 16,* 28–38.

Zautra, A. J., Burleson, M. H., Smith, C. A., Blalock, S. J., Wallston, K. A., DeVellis, R. F., DeVellis, B. M., & Smith, T. W. (1995). Arthritis and perceptions of quality of life: An examination of positive and negative affect in rheumatoid arthritis patients. *Health Psychology, 14*(5), 399–405.

12

Problem Solving on Health-Related Tasks of Daily Living

Sherry L. Willis
Melissa M. Dolan
Rosanna M. Bertrand
The Pennsylvania State University

Older adults' maintenance of independence is closely associated with their ability to perform critical tasks of daily living. Competence in seven domains commonly referred to as instrumental tasks of daily living (i.e., taking medications, telephone use, preparing meals, managing finances, shopping, using transportation, and housekeeping [IADLs; Lawton & Brody, 1969]) have been found to be necessary for an independent lifestyle. This chapter addresses issues related to the cognitive demands involved in carrying out instrumental activities of daily living (IADLs) with particular attention to two domains—taking medications and meal preparation. Three broad questions are considered: What health outcomes have been found to be associated with cognitively demanding activities of daily living? What specific components or tasks related to taking medications and meal preparation have been found to be problematic for older adults? What particular cognitive abilities and processes have been reported to be associated with these health behaviors?

To address these questions, three distinct literatures on functional health and older adults are selectively reviewed. Each of the three perspectives has addressed a unique link in the Cognition–Health Behaviors–Health Outcomes triad. We begin with a brief review of the findings from survey and epidemiological studies on advanced cognitive IADLs and health outcomes associated with functional impairment in these domains. The second section of the chapter reviews the prior literature in experimental and health psychology on older adults' performance on medication and meal preparation tasks. In the third section, we identify contributions from prior research within cognitive aging that have guided our study of everyday problem solving in health-related domains. In a fourth section of the chapter, a qualitative analysis of types of errors made in everyday problem solving related to taking medications and meal planning, based on findings in our own research, is presented.

ADVANCED COGNITIVE IADLS: FINDINGS FROM SURVEY RESEARCH

Many disciplines, such as epidemiology, public health, and medical sociology have provided insights into the cognitive functioning of older adults in their everyday lives. Evaluation of functional competence in old age has focused on two broad activity domains: physical activities of daily living (PADLs), such as dressing, toileting, and bathing, and more behaviorally complex instrumental activities of daily living (IADLs), such as managing finances and taking medications. Much of the literature on instrumental tasks has arisen from an epidemiological, survey-based approach to functional competence in older adults. The focus of such research has been on global, self-report measures of competency or difficulties in functioning, rather than on objective assessment of specific components of instrumental tasks. Although this perspective may lack a differentiating view of functioning, one of its strengths is a focus on the relationship between functional ability in instrumental activities and distal health outcomes, such as hospitalization or nursing home placement.

The survey and clinical literature on functional competence indicates that limitations occur earlier in both normal and pathological aging for instrumental activities of daily living than for physical activities of daily living (Ashford, Hsu, Becker, Kuman, & Bekian, 1986; Reisberg, Ferris, de Leon, & Crook, 1982). Due to the earlier loss of functioning in instrumental domains, IADLs have become a major focus in evaluating whether an older adult can live independently in the community. In cases of suspected pathology such as dementia, it is often the person's inability to perform instrumental tasks that motivates spouses and adult children to seek assessment and diagnosis.

IADLs: Cognitive Versus Physical Demands

In the functional competence literature, distinctions have been made between cognitively advanced IADLs and other instrumental activity domains. Wolinsky and colleagues (Wolinsky, Callahan, Fitzgerald, & Johnson, 1992; Wolinsky & Johnson, 1991) suggested a hierarchical relationship among categories of instrumental activities, defining *household activities of daily living* (ADLs; i.e., light and heavy housework, shopping, etc.) as difficulties with daily chores that likely stem from physical impairment and *advanced cognitive ADLs* (i.e., taking medications, managing finances, using the phone) as those tasks that rely less on physical activity and represent cognitively directed everyday tasks. Advanced cognitive ADLs are seen as a set of activities that focus on the underlying mental functioning and cognitive capacity of older adults and often serve as early predictors of poor outcomes, such as institutional placement. Although this literature does not specifically address the cognitive demands inherent in such advanced ADLs, working memory, language, comprehension, and planful behavior appear to be necessary components of such activities (Wolinsky & Johnson, 1991). For example, the ability to take medications requires an individual to comprehend the instructions on the label, remember these instructions, and then remember to comply with the dosage guidelines (Morrell, Park, & Poon, 1989).

Older adults' reports of limitations in advanced ADLs have been found to be more closely related to global measures of cognitive functioning than limitations in either self-maintenance (i.e., basic self-care) or household domains (Fitzgerald, Smith, Martin, Freedman, & Wolinsky, 1993; Johnson & Wolinsky, 1993). In a large-scale epidemiological study of older adults, difficulties in advanced cognitive ADLs contributed significant unique variance to the prediction of several health outcomes including number of disability days, hospital visits, and mortality (Wolinsky & Johnson, 1991). Such results illustrate the importance of examining the advanced ADL categories for their separate impact on functioning and outcomes and suggest that impairments in self-maintenance, household, and advanced cognitive ADLs may represent varying degrees of functional dependence. Although difficulties in household ADLs, such as housework, certainly contribute to risk of nursing home placement and other negative outcomes (Wolinsky et al., 1992), limitations in more cognitively challenging advanced ADLs appear earlier and may be more useful in detection of impairment in its formative stages.

Specifically, Wolinsky and colleagues have found the presence of limitations in advanced cognitive ADLs to be predictive of a lower consumption of physician and hospital resources in the subsequent 6 years. The authors hypothesize that early cognitive limitations in select instrumental domains in many cases may be indicative of disorders of cognition and may result in older adults being placed earlier in care facilities such as nursing homes and, hence, being less likely to be hospitalized or to receive independent physician care (Wolinsky, Callahan, & Johnson, 1994; Wolinsky, Stump, & Johnson, 1995). Crimmins and Saito (1993) reiterated these hypotheses, suggesting that deficits in such advanced cognitive ADLs may not be caused by the same disease conditions as the health conditions limiting functioning in other less cognitive and more physically demanding instrumental domains. In a similar vein, Barberger-Gateau et al. (1992) suggested that limitations in certain cognitively demanding instrumental domains may be useful early predictors of cognitive pathologies. They found that self-reported difficulties in four specific IADL domains (i.e., telephone use, transportation, medication use, and finances) were associated with cognitive impairment.

Self-Reported Limitations in IADLs

Due to the cognitive demands of advanced ADLs (e.g., meal planning and preparation, remembering to take medications) as well as the crucial importance of these activities to the maintenance of independence, it is particularly salient to examine self-reported difficulties in these domains.

Myers (1992) utilized 50 IADL items intended to assess both physical and cognitive limitations among a sample of senior apartment residents in Canada between the ages of 60–95. Although 93% of the sample reported no difficulty in preparing light meals, only 76% were able to meet the demands of a more complex menu involving a full meal. Further, 44% of older adults in this study had difficulty remembering shopping items and 25% reported problems in performing regular shopping activities. Clearly, low levels of functional competence in shopping activities could significantly impact success in meal preparation as well. In the domain of medication, 85% of participants in this investigation reported no difficulty in remembering to take medications, but 34% had difficulty reading the pill labels on those drugs. In this case, sensory impairment (i.e., reading the label) may impact an older adults' competence in the more cognitively complex task (i.e., taking the medication at the correct time).

Findings from large-scale epidemiological studies of older adults have also yielded estimates of self-reported limitations with regard to nutrition and medication use. Estimates indicate that the number of older adults reporting such limitations increases with age. Using data from the Longitudinal Study of Aging (LSOA), a nationally representative sample of community-dwelling older adults 70 years old or older, Crimmins and Saito (1993) examined difficulty in instrumental tasks over a 2-year interval. At baseline, 4.8% of participants reported limitations in meal preparation, although this proportion increased to 8.7% at follow-up. Similarly, difficulty in shopping tasks affected 9.3% of the sample, and this incidence rose to 13.8% after 2 years. Although the initial incidence rates are not substantial, rates of disability in these areas rose fairly rapidly, at an approximate rate of 4% over a 2-year period. Furner, Rudberg, and Cassel (1995) also investigated disability in the LSOA sample, but examined only those older adults who reported no IADL limitations at the baseline interview. Among this initially well functioning sample, reported disability in the areas of meal preparation and shopping increased from approximately 3% to 5% over a 6-year interval.

A smaller proportion of old-old adults (i.e., age 75 and older) are capable of functioning independently, with estimates of 40% to 45% of adults reporting difficulties with daily tasks, particularly in the domains of shopping, transportation, and housekeeping (Cassel, Rudberg, & Olshansky, 1992; Fillenbaum, 1985). The ability to function independently decreases with age, with the greatest decline occurring between ages 80 and 85 (Fillenbaum, 1985). A study of functional competency among the oldest-old adults in Sweden further illustrates this age effect, finding increases in new IADL disability over 2-year and 4-year intervals among adults age 84 to 90 (Zarit, Johansson, & Malmberg, 1995).

IADLs and Distal Health Outcomes

Functioning in instrumental domains has also been linked to mortality. Findings from the LSOA indicate that survival rates for older adults depended on the extent of instrumental limitations present at baseline. In this study, 65% of those receiving ADL assistance were alive 2 years later, as compared to 78% of those receiving only IADL assistance and 86% of those without functional difficulties (Kovar & Lawton, 1994). Fillenbaum (1985) found that older adults with disability in five IADL domains had a mortality rate 5.4 times greater than that of the entire sample, and Manton (1988) reported a 4.5 times greater risk for a similarly impaired subsample. Further, the presence of impairments often leads to adverse outcomes, such as greater service use, hospitalization, and even institutional placement (Branch & Jette, 1982; Kemper, 1992; Wolinsky et al., 1992).

MEDICATIONS AND NUTRITION BEHAVIORS: EXPERIMENTAL FINDINGS

In this section, we move from a review of findings with regard to global IADL functioning to an examination of the experimental literature on medication and nutrition-related health behaviors among older adults. Functioning in these domains is considered from a component task analysis perspective.

Reading Food Labels

Food labels are the most widely read source of nutritional information (Bender & Derby, 1992; National Dairy Council, 1986). They conveniently provide consumers with the information necessary to make the correct dietary selection. It appears, however, that many older adults are making inadequate dietary choices. For example, Thomas, Kendrick, and Eddy (1990) wrote that, although older adults indicate that dietary practices are very important for good health, nutritional deficiencies among this segment of the population are quite common. Ability to read a nutrition label does not necessarily result in correctly interpreting the information. Some older adults lack the ability to process and interpret the written materials presented on food labels and thus cannot utilize this information in making food choices.

In a study examining the relevance of behavioral principles to older consumers' food-buying practices, Friedman (1990) proposed that the older consumer's knowledge, understanding, and ability to use food label information is lacking. He argues, for example, that comparing labels on different brands of the same food taxes the older consumer's short-term memory, rendering the task overwhelming. Although Friedman discusses this as a problem of short-term memory, the integration and synthesis of information provided on food labels probably also burdens working memory. As a result, older consumers may take a limited problem-solving approach to their grocery selections (Friedman, 1990). Older adults may depend on the use of familiar products or base their buying decision on only one factor, such as price. For example, in an investigation examining nutrition, cancer prevention, and adults' willingness to make dietary changes, Cotugna, Subar, Heimendinger, and Kahle (1992) reported that more than 65% of their sample had never made dietary changes because of health. The most frequently offered response for not making dietary changes (i.e., 76%) was that respondents were happy with the food they were presently eating. This response suggests that adults may be depending on prior experience rather than searching food labels for more nutritionally appropriate choices. In addition, Cotugna et al. (1992) noted that unwillingness or inability to make dietary changes increases with age, but decreases with higher income and education levels.

Difficulty performing simple arithmetic may also impact the older adults' ability to correctly interpret nutrition labels. Longitudinal research has revealed that decrements in number ability are evident in the young-old adult (Schaie, 1996). Because at least a moderate amount of arithmetic skill is necessary to interpret food labels, particularly when multiple dietary considerations and cost are being made, it is likely that errors in this domain contribute to ineffective label reading.

Researchers (Bender & Derby, 1992; Guthrie, Fox, Cleveland, & Welsh, 1995) have reported several characteristics that are believed to influence the use of food labels. In their study examining the use and dietary significance of nutrition labeling, Guthrie et al. (1995) found that having a higher level of education (i.e., at least some college) was associated with an increase in the likelihood of being a label user. On the other hand, being a male, a main meal-planner/preparer, and living alone were among the variables associated with a decreased likelihood of being a label user. Bender and Derby (1992) found similar results in their food label study. Their results revealed that consumers who are the most likely to use ingredient lists and nutritional labels are younger (i.e., 25–34 years of age), White, female, and better educated. Among their sample of adults, older (i.e., 55 years or older), non-White, less-educated (i.e., high school or less) males were most likely to ignore both ingredient lists and nutrition labels. Finally, in their study of nutrition and cancer prevention, Cotugna et al. (1992) reported that education level is associated with attitudes about receiving many different types of dietary recommendations. Those participants with a high school education or less reported being too confused to make recommended adjustments to their diet. These reports of confusion support prior findings of less frequent use of food labels among adults with a low level of education.

Medication Comprehension

Increased problems with prescription and over-the-counter (OTC) medication usage have been reported by several researchers (Gien & Anderson, 1989; Park, Morrell, Frieske, & Kincaid, 1992; Salzman, 1991). Of particular concern is the increased use of OTC medications with age, especially for women (Crawley, 1993). Investigators examining self-medication (i.e., OTC drugs) have found that older adults are significantly more likely than younger adults to use OTC medications (Gien & Anderson, 1989) and may use up to twice as many OTC medications as prescription medications (Conn, 1991). Given these findings and the fact that older adults have been found to make more prescription drug errors than younger adults (Morrell, Park, & Poon, 1989, 1990), it can be argued that OTC medication dosage errors occur more frequently than prescription medication errors. With the likelihood of an older adult being on a regimen of multiple medications, the possibility of drug interactions with OTC and/or prescription medications pose potentially serious health risks for this growing segment of the population.

Examining factors that contribute to medication adherence errors is an important first step in designing medical interventions to assist older adults in maintaining a safe drug regimen. Several reports have addressed this issue and reveal possible causes for compliance problems (Ascione, 1994; Morrell et al., 1989, 1990; Murray, Darnell, Weinberger, & Martz, 1986; Park, Morrell, Frieske, Blackburn, & Birchmore, 1991). Specifically, in an article reviewing the literature on medication compliance, Ascione (1994) wrote that compliance decreases in proportion to the complexity of the medical regimen. Because older adults generally take more medications over longer periods of time than younger adults, the task becomes more difficult, increasing the likelihood of compliance errors. This notion is supported by the work of Murray et al. (1986) who reported that in their study of older tenants of public housing, noncompliance was significantly associated with taking more than five prescribed medications. The investigation by Park et al. (1991) examining the utility of medical organizers also revealed that subjects who were taking many drugs (i.e., 7 or more) had more difficulties comprehending their complex regimen.

Interpreting Dosage

Morrell et al. (1989, 1990) found medication errors involving inaccurate interpretation of dosage and special instructions on medicine labels in their samples of older adults. The authors noted that a major cause of noncompliance in these investigations is cognitively related. Specifically, they found that interpretation errors occurred because older adults spent less time than younger adults reading and studying the labels. It is possible that older adults are not sufficiently processing or reading the smaller print or the material placed at the end of the text such as warning labels, special instructions, and/or auxiliary labels. In their study examining correlates of medication noncompliance, Murray et al. (1986) revealed that a significantly larger percentage of the older adults in their sample could not read auxiliary labels (i.e., 39%) as compared to primary labels (i.e., 24%).

Morrell et al. also noted that older adults have difficulty interpreting dosages because many medication instructions require the patient to make inferences, an area where older adults display a disadvantage (1990; Park et al., 1991). These findings are supported in the cognitive literature by Dixon, Hultsch, Simon, and von Eye (1984) who reported age-related differences in recalling details versus main ideas in a short text (i.e., 98 words). In addition, in a similar way to the impact of computational skill on interpreting nutrition and cost information in food products, the decline in numeric ability, observed as early as age 50 (Schaie, 1996), is hypothesized to inhibit correct dosage interpretation and to contribute to medication noncompliance.

COGNITIVE AGING AND EVERYDAY PROBLEM SOLVING

One of the most intriguing issues in the study of applied cognitive aging is the manner in which older adults employ the wealth of knowledge and prior experience acquired over many years in dealing with instrumental tasks of daily living. When applied in appropriate situations, the older adults' prior knowledge would be expected to facilitate everyday problem solving. The older adult must determine in what problem situations it is expeditious to base decisions on prior experience. There is the danger that due to deficits in processing resources, rigidity, or lack of psychological energy the older adult may rely on prior knowledge in inappropriate problem-solving situations.

In this section, we briefly review some of the major concepts and findings from the problem-solving literature in cognitive aging that we have found relevant to our own research. For the purposes of this discussion, *problem solving* involves assessing the present state of a situation, defining the desired state, and finding ways to transform the former to the latter (Reese & Rodeheaver, 1985). *Decision making* refers to the evaluation of these possible solutions and the selection of one for implementation.

Declarative Knowledge Developed Through Prior Experience

As older adults go about solving everyday problems, they employ both declarative and procedural knowledge. Our reference to the terms declarative and procedural knowledge are based on their use and conceptualization in cognitive science and in the study of expertise. *Declarative knowledge* is defined as knowing certain facts and determining whether they are relevant in a particular situation (Chi, 1985). Novices and experts differ in both the amount of declarative knowledge they possess and the organization of the knowledge. Experts' declarative knowledge is stored in larger, more abstract units and is organized hierarchically with information indexed in terms of meaningful interrelations, which allows experts to recall their memory of a topic quickly and efficiently (Hershey, Walsh, Read, & Chulef, 1990).

A major distinction between experts and novices is that experts attend to fewer pieces of information in a problem-solving situation, but the information chosen is often at a higher order within the information hierarchy.

Given their lifetime of experiences, older adults might be expected to have hierarchically organized knowledge bases that were well integrated and to use less information in solving problems. However, findings from research on older adults problem solving with respect to real-life problems only partially support these hypotheses. In problem-solving research varying widely in the substantive domain of the problem, older adults have been found to reach a problem solution based on a more limited set of information than that sought by younger adults (Meyer, Russo, & Talbot, 1995; Streufert, Pogash, Piasecki, & Post, 1990). Similar to the approach of experts, older adults also engaged in a less extensive information search than younger adults before reaching a solution. In contrast to findings with experts, however, older adults did not necessarily have a greater body of prior declarative knowledge, nor was their knowledge base better integrated or hierarchically organized. These deficits in organization and usage of declarative knowledge may be attributed to limited memory and information processing resources. Because of limited cognitive resources, the declarative knowledge has been poorly stored or organized and thus, efficient retrieval and usage is difficult.

Procedural Knowledge and Information Processing Resources

Procedural knowledge represents the individual's understanding of how to go about solving a particular problem—determining what declarative knowledge is relevant to the current problem and deciding how to integrate and manipulate information to produce a solution (Chi, 1985). Procedural knowledge has been characterized as involving both a game plan and a set of rule-based mental operations into which the relevant parameters for a particular problem can be inserted (Abelson, 1981; Hershey et al., 1990). From the perspective of clinical psychology and neuropsychology, procedural knowledge is often referred to as involving executive functioning. In the study of psychometric abilities, procedural knowledge has been related to fluid intelligence, whereas declarative knowledge has been associated with crystallized intelligence. Procedural knowledge involves cognitive resource capacity and allocation. In advancing age, there is the potential that limitations in information processing and resource allocation will limit the older adults' ability to carry through the multiple steps often involved in a game plan or rule-based problem solving. Although most problem solutions require both declarative and procedural knowledge, limitations in procedural knowledge are considered more serious.

Several researchers have described age-related changes in procedural knowledge or processing styles (Labouvie-Vief & Hakim-Larson, 1989; Sinnott, 1989). These researchers differ, however, in their view of the nature of the changes in processing style and whether these changes are viewed positively.

Labouvie-Vief and colleagues described two modes of thinking and know-ing—an abstract and objectified approach versus a more pragmatic, concrete, and subjective manner. The former approach is said to characterize young adulthood, whereas the later approach becomes more common in middle and later adulthood. With age and experience, the adult's approach to thinking and solving problems is said to reflect greater sensitivity to the interpersonal context and to focus on personal experience as a way of thinking and knowing. The age-related change is not exclusively from an abstract, objectified approach to a subjective, personalized approach. Rather, with age and experience, the individual reaches a balance between the two approaches; in adulthood, there is the unique potential to integrate the optimal use of both modes of thinking. Labouvie-Vief and colleagues suggested that the study of cognitive aging has focused primarily on youthful modes of thinking and has characterized the subjective, more personalized approach as regressive. She stated that "as individuals acquire expertise, their knowledge becomes too complex and richly organized to conform to a simple rule-oriented system and flexible functioning is enhanced by a less explicit and more intuitive approach" (Labouvie-Vief & Hakim-Larson, 1989, p. 80).

Sinnott (1989) also described age-related modes of problem solving, but sug-gested that the optimal approach is reached in middle age, rather than old age. Similar to Labouvie-Vief characterizations, Sinnot's *youthful style* is characterized by a bottom-up approach; younger adults lack relevant knowledge and compensate by gathering large amounts of information and focusing on data rather than prior experience. In contrast, the *old style* represents primarily a top-down approach. Older adults are seen as using, somewhat indiscriminately, the extensive knowledge acquired through a lifetime of experience. Procedural knowledge or heuristics developed through prior experience are used with little consideration of whether these procedures are relevant to the problem at hand. Sinnott stated that the old styles are suited for "rapid, low energy-demand solutions done by the experienced solver with many available structures of knowledge. It was top-down in style with little attention to data, probably because of poor memory capacities" (1989, p. 96). The *mature style* is characterized as the optimal approach and is said to be more evident in midlife. It represents a balance of the bottom-up and top-down approaches—rec-ognizing in what problem situations each approach is most efficacious.

Personalized Knowledge

In the study of health decision making, the Leventhals and colleagues (H. Leventhal & Cameron, 1987; E. A. Leventhal, H. Leventhal, Schaefer, & Easterling, 1993) suggested that a distinct type of knowledge is relevant to problem solving in later adulthood. They distinguish between *semantic* memories, which represent the individual's conceptual knowledge about the problem and *episodic* memories, or autobiographical information, based on the subject's prior experiences with respect to a particular problem domain. Semantic memories are somewhat similar to the form of declarative knowledge described earlier. In contrast, episodic memories represent personalized knowledge and may be especially salient in the study of problem solving with older adults. Personalized knowledge would appear to be relevant to the second mode of thinking discussed by Labouvie-Vief (Labouvie-Vief & Hakim-Larson, 1989) and characterized by Sinnott's (1989) old processing style.

H. Leventhal further suggested that solutions to health problems may vary depending on the salience of semantic versus episodic memories in the problem-solving process. For example, with respect to medical problem solving, semantic memories may inform the person that certain diseases (e.g., heart disease) are asymptomatic and hence one cannot rely on how one feels in deciding on the efficacy of a medication or when to see a doctor. Personalized knowledge, however, may lead an individual to conclude that, in the past, illness was related to not feeling well and hence, if one has no symptoms, one is not sick. Research by E. Leventhal indicates that personalized knowledge rather than semantic memories is more predictive of compliance in health problems. Personalized knowledge becomes particularly salient and persuasive when the problem is not clearly defined or understood and the individual lacks procedural knowledge for how to go about solving the problem.

PROBLEM SOLVING ON HEALTH-RELATED TASKS: A QUALITATIVE ANALYSIS

In our Adult Cognitive Development Laboratory, we are examining older adults' ability to solve cognitively demanding instrumental tasks of daily living associated with each of the IADL domains. In prior work, we took primarily a quantitative approach, examining level of performance on mental abilities and everyday problem tasks and described age-related change in level of performance over time (Willis, Jay, Diehl, & Marsiske, 1992). A major focus of our more recent work has become the qualitative analyses of the specific types of errors that older adults make as they solve everyday cognitive tasks. Of particular interest is whether errors made by older adults reflect the types of knowledge and processing styles discussed in the preceding section. Because qualitative research is concerned with describing patterns and processes of behavior and inferring the meanings behind such behavior (Reinharz & Rowles, 1988), it is a useful tool for understanding age-related functional changes.

In addition, we are examining the relationship between error patterns made on instrumental tasks of daily living and performance on clinical batteries traditionally used to examine limitations in cognitive functioning associated with early dementia and age-associated memory loss. For the purposes of this chapter, we limit our discussion to two IADL domains most closely related to health-related tasks of daily living—taking of medications and planning of nutritionally adequate meals. In this section, we present some of our work and findings.

Description of the Study

Since 1996, we have been studying everyday problem solving in a sample of community dwelling older adults of lower socioeconomic status living in a rural county in southwest Pennsylvania. The sample was drawn from the Monongahela Valley Independent Elders Survey (MoVIES), a community-based, longitudinal, prospective study of cognitive impairment and dementia directed by Ganguli (Ganguli et al., 1991). Adults, ages 65 years and older, were selected through age-stratified random sampling from voter registration lists. The mean age of the 596 participants studied was 78 years (range, 70–94), at the time the data to be reported was collected. All participants had been screened for dementia on the Clinical Dementia Rating Scale (CDR; Hughes, Berg, Danziger, Cohen, & Martin, 1982).

At the time of assessment, subjects were first administered the MoVIES protocol, involving an extensive interview and a battery of clinical and neuropsychological measures. The MoVIES clinical and neuropsychological test battery (Ganguli et al., 1991) is an expansion of the protocol defined by the Consortium to Establish a Registry for Alzheimer's Disease (CERAD; Morris et al., 1989). The battery includes the Mini-Mental State Examination (MMSE; Folstein, Folstein, & McHugh, 1975) and Temporal Orientation (Benton, Hamsher, Varney, & Spreen, 1983). Broadly speaking, the test battery assesses the domains of verbal ability (e.g., verbal fluency), memory (e.g., immediate and delayed recall of components of a story or a word list), and executive functioning (e.g., trailmaking, coping figures, clock drawing). Following the MoVIES battery, subjects were invited to respond to a measure of everyday problem solving. Subjects were paid $10 for their participation in the MoVIES project and an additional $10 for testing on the everyday problems measure.

Everyday problem solving was assessed by the Everyday Problems for Cognitively Challenged Elderly (EPCCE) test, a measure of older adults' cognitive ability to solve tasks associated with everyday activities (Willis et al., 1998). The test was developed to assess everyday problem solving competence in normal older adults with low levels of education and early stage Alzheimer's patients—representing potentially cognitively challenged portions of the older adult population. Participants were shown 16 printed stimulus materials that represent real-world stimuli encountered in tasks of daily living, such as an itemized phone bill, directions for over-the-counter medication, or a nutrition label. Upon viewing each stimuli, subjects are asked to solve two problems related to the information presented (e.g., "For how many days should the laxative be taken?"). In this study, a subset of 12 items focusing on health and nutrition was used. These items assess complex cognitive functioning in the IADL domains of medications, meal preparation and nutrition, and health care.

EPCCE Errors: A Qualitative Approach

A hierarchical taxonomy representing a qualitative classification of error types on the EPCCE was developed. The complete error hierarchy represents four levels, but the current presentation will focus primarily on the first two levels of the hierarchy. Error types at each level are mutually exclusive; each error was coded in only one category at a particular level.

The first level of the hierarchy involves the total number of errors on the EPCCE. The second level involves four error categories: inappropriate use of prior experience, incomplete processing, random, and no attempt errors. Examples of the errors in this second level of the hierarchy are shown in Table 12.1.

Prior experience errors involve inappropriate use of prior knowledge and life experience. We were interested in the extent to which deficits in use of declarative knowledge and Sinnott's old style of problem solving would be manifest in solving everyday problems. The old style would be characterized by application of knowledge and problem-solving strategies developed through prior experience with little consideration of whether this knowledge or approach was relevant to the problem at hand. Sinnott suggests that this approach may reflect poor memory capacities. In a somewhat similar vein, inappropriate use of prior experience may reflect Leventhal's description of personalized knowledge. Personalized knowledge becomes more salient in problem solving when relevant procedural knowledge is not available or its application is limited due to information processing and resource deficits.

Incomplete processing errors would be expected to be the most common type of error, given the extensive prior research on older adults' limitations in memory and cognitive resources. Incomplete processing errors would be expected to repre-

TABLE 12.1
Description of Error Types With Examples

Error Type	Description	Example	Incorrect Response
Level I			
Total errors	All incorrect responses.		
Level II			
Prior experience	Inappropriate use of prior knowledge in solving the problem	To get the most benefit, for how many days should you use this product?	Subject responds based on prior experience.
Incomplete processing	Shallow processing—subject does not take into account all the information needed to solve the problem.	If you are concerned about both low cost and low calories, which product would be the best choice?	Considers only information regarding price. Does not consider price and calories.
Random response	Errors that can not be classified according to the established coding scheme.	Any question on the test.	Response makes no logical sense in the context of the question.
No attempt	Subject makes no attempt to answer the question.	Any question on the test.	For example, "I don't know."

sent inadequate application of procedural knowledge for solving the problem. For example, the subject may have failed to execute all mathematical steps necessary to solve the problem. In other items, a shallow level of processing may have been used; the subject stopped the search process before all relevant information needed to solve the problem was acquired, often focusing solely on information presented early in the stimuli (Johnson, 1990; Leventhal et al., 1993; Meyer et al., 1995; Walsh & Hershey, 1993).

Random errors are the type of incorrect response that do not appear to be related to the stimuli or question and make no logical sense in the context of the question.

No attempt errors represent instances in which the participant made no attempt or was unable to formulate a response.

Findings From the Study

On average, older adults made errors on more than one fourth (28%) of the health-related tasks. Almost all participants (95%) made at least one error on the measure. Participants whose educational attainment was below the high school level made significantly more errors in health-related problems than those with education at or beyond high school. Further, old-old (i.e., 75 years and older) participants made significantly more errors on such items than did the young–old (i.e., 70-74 years of age).

Individual Differences and Errors.   At the second level of the hierarchy (see Table 12.1), the total number of errors were decomposed into four error types. Ninety percent of the total errors made were classified as incomplete processing, 8% involved prior experience responding, 1% were considered random responses, and 1% represented no attempt to answer the item.

The vast majority of errors (90%) involved instances of incomplete processing of information. Nearly every participant (93%) made at least one error of incomplete processing. Inappropriate use of prior experience represented 8% percent of the errors made. Approximately 22% of participants generated one or more errors categorized as based on prior experience. As expected, errors classified as random or no attempt were far less common. Fewer than 1% of incorrect responses involved no response or random responding.

The effects of age, educational level, and gender on Level II errors were examined. Age and education effects were found for prior experience errors, with age showing a higher level of significance. The young-old adult group made significantly fewer errors attributable to the inappropriate use of prior experience than did the old-old adult group.

With regard to educational level, findings demonstrate a particular disadvantage among participants without a high school education. This group made significantly more prior experience errors than those with trade school or college and a significantly higher percentage of incomplete processing and random errors than all other educational levels.

Relation of Errors to Cognitive Processes. Correlational analyses revealed highly significant associations for total number of errors and measures in the cognitive battery. The total number of errors was significantly related to scores on the MMSE (Folstein et al., 1975), memory, verbal ability, and executive functioning. Total errors were also significantly related to education and age.

Considering the Level II error types, incomplete processing errors exhibited a similar pattern of relationship to the cognitive battery as was reported for total errors. However, prior experience, random, and no attempt errors displayed associations with only a limited subset of cognitive measures. Prior experience errors were more highly related to scores on memory and verbal fluency as well as the MMSE (Folstein et al., 1975). Only random errors were significantly associated with Temporal Orientation (Benton et al., 1983). Both no attempt and prior experience errors had significant associations with age and education, whereas random and incomplete processing errors were related only to education level.

SUMMARY AND IMPLICATIONS

In this chapter, we have considered everyday health-related tasks as a subset of those instrumental activities of daily living considered essential for maintenance of an independent lifestyle in our society. Recent work based on survey and epidemiological studies suggest that everyday health-related tasks, such as taking medications and meal planning, are included in a set of instrumental tasks known as advanced cognitive ADLs. The advanced cognitive ADLs are of particular interest because it has been shown that reports of limitations in these domains are associated with lower cognitive functioning as well as subsequent patterns of health service utilization that differ from basic or household ADLs (Wolinsky et al., 1994; Wolinsky et al., 1995). The advanced cognitive ADLs are of interest both to those studying cognitive aging and to clinicians because decline in competence on cognitively complex tasks of daily living occurs relatively early in normal aging and also may be among the earliest indicators of neurological pathologies.

Error Patterns

Meal preparation and medication use are included among advanced cognitive ADLs critical for the maintenance of an independent lifestyle. We have suggested links between a qualitative examination of error patterns on such cognitively demanding, health-related IADLs and prior work on problem solving within cognitive aging. Our research has indicated two major error types made by older adults in solving everyday problems involving health information—incomplete processing of information and inappropriate use of prior experience.

The most common type of error involved incomplete processing of the information required to solve the task. Deficits in combining and integrating information and in determining the types of mental operations needed in problem solution most likely reflect difficulties with procedural knowledge. Incomplete processing errors took several different forms. In problems requiring one or more mathematical computations for a solution, some older adults had difficulty formulating the series of computations required or forgot to perform one or more of the computations. For example, subjects had difficulty computing the total number of teaspoons of cough syrup to be taken in 24 hours if each dose involved 2 teaspoons, and a maximum of four doses could be taken in 24 hours.

Another type of incomplete processing error that reflected procedural knowledge deficits involved comparing products on several criteria. Subjects were asked to compare four cereal brands and determine the brand lowest in calories and cost. A common error was to examine products taking into account only one of the two criteria on which labels were to be compared. This finding supports the work of Friedman (1990) who suggested that processing and interpreting labels may overburden the older adult's memory resources, resulting in a limited problem-solving approach. Furthermore, medication compliance research demonstrates an increased likelihood of dosage errors stemming from more complex regimens involving multiple medications (Ascione, 1994; Murray et al., 1986; Park et al., 1991).

A third common type of incomplete processing error involved failure to take into account specialized information that was particularly relevant to the immediate problem. In determining the appropriate medication dosage for a patient with a smoker's cough, subjects failed to recognize the relevance of a supplementary warning label for patients with this condition. Instead, subjects recommended that a patient with a smoker's cough take the standard dosage. These results reiterate previous research indicating that older adults may not be attending to auxiliary labels (e.g., warning labels, special instructions) when interpreting appropriate dosage (Morrell et al., 1989, 1990; Murray et al., 1986). In many errors involving incomplete processing, subjects ended the information search process too early and formulated an answer based on information occurring early in the stimulus material rather than searching the entire document for relevant information. Thus, as was found in prior text processing research (Meyer et al., 1995), subjects reduced their information search and sought less information before reaching a decision.

Relation of Cognition to Error Patterns

Findings on incomplete processing and deficits in procedural knowledge complement cognitive aging research on age-related decline in abilities and processes such as inductive reasoning and working memory (Salthouse, 1990; Schaie, 1996). These abilities are among the earliest abilities to exhibit normative age-related decline and have been shown to be associated with incomplete processing errors. With respect to the clinical cognitive battery used in our research, all of the clinical measures were associated with incomplete processing errors, indicating the global nature of these errors.

Of particular interest are errors associated with inappropriate use of prior experience. Twenty-two percent of subjects in our research made at least one error based on inappropriate use of prior experience. This type of error appears to be associated with personalized knowledge described by the Leventhals (H. Leventhal & Cameron, 1987; E. A. Leventhal et al., 1993) and to styles of processing discussed by Sinnott (1989) and Labouvie-Vief (Labouvie-Vief & Hakim-Larson, 1989). Inappropriate use of prior experience is most closely related to Sinnott's old processing style. Rather than searching for relevant information within the stimulus material, the subject answers the problem by reporting how they solved other problems in their past. Prior research suggests that this type of error is more likely to occur when the problem is ill structured and solution of the problem requires making inferences based on the information presented (Morrell et al., 1990; Park et al., 1991). Although prior problem-solving research has focused on the association of age and use of prior experience, our analyses indicate that education is a salient individual difference variable. Older adults with less than a high school education were particularly likely to base their responses inappropriately on prior experience.

One striking example of this error type in our own research was older adults' response to a question on how much of an adult laxative should be given to children. Many subjects responded that they gave children one half of an adult dosage. There are a number of possible explanations regarding older adults reliance on prior experience. Responses based on prior experience may reflect the subject's deficits in procedural knowledge or their lack of psychological energy to process the information required to solve the problem; as a result, they rely on prior experience to formulate an answer. Of particular concern is that the Leventhals (H. Leventhal & Cameron, 1987; E. A. Leventhal et al., 1993) found personalized knowledge, the type most likely used in prior experience errors, more closely associated with patient compliance in health concerns than with declarative knowledge.

Two findings from our study with regard to prior experience errors are noteworthy. First, the old-old participants were significantly more likely to make prior experience errors than the young-old participants. Second, prior experience errors were significantly related to only a few of the clinical measures studied. The significant relationship to Story Recall, Delayed Story Recall, and Verbal Fluency suggests deficits in verbal memory associated with prior experience errors. Sinnott hypothesized an association between old style processing and memory deficits. Given the salience of memory deficits in dementia, it would be of interest to examine prior experience errors as indicators of early dementia.

Instrumental activities play a major role in the lives of older adults and may become increasing influential in determining an individual's ability to continue living independently. Assessing the extent to which older adults have difficulties with cognitively challenging everyday activities may aid in determining how well persons are able to function in the environment as well as their need for services or interventions. It may be particularly salient to examine difficulties in the specific domains of nutrition and medication due to the high cognitive demands of such tasks (e.g., remembering to take medications, planning meals, etc.) as well as the crucial importance of these activities and their impact on chronic illness and overall health.

Qualitative analysis of specific types of errors in these domains may further our understanding of the cognitive processes involved in approaching as well as solving health-related everyday problems. Identification of the underlying cognitive processes involved in incomplete processing and prior knowledge errors may allow us to differentiate true cognitive deficits from cognitive rigidity or educational disadvantage. It is possible that this information may aid in identifying potential areas for cognitive training and contribute to food and medication labeling that is more sensitive to the cognitive processing difficulties that may accompany old age and educational limitations. Although charts and directions on labels are designed to reduce memory load, our qualitative results suggest that the individual is responsible for integrating the information. For example, the auxiliary warning on the directions for cough syrup is placed at the end of the label, forcing the individual to integrate this caution with the preceding dosage information in making a decision. Interventions for older adults that simply increase the print size or darken warnings on labels may not be sufficient to achieve adequate comprehension. Instead, the focus should be to reduce working memory load and promote the integration of information. Interventions designed to improve understanding of labels, directions, or forms pertinent to health-related instrumental activities may reduce the risk of excess disabilities.

ACKNOWLEDGMENTS

The research reported in this chapter was supported by funding from the National Institute on Aging (AG11032) to Sherry L. Willis. Support for funding of the MoVIES project has been provided by the National Institute on Aging to Dr. Mary Ganguli at the University of Pittsburgh (AG06782; AG07562; AG00312). Melissa Dolan received predoctoral funding by Training Grant #5 T32 MH18904-09 from the National Institute of Mental Health. We thank Mary Ganguli and the entire MoVIES project staff for their dedication to this research. Thanks also to Roger Morrell and an anonymous reviewer for their comments on an earlier draft.

REFERENCES

Abelson, R. P. (1981). Psychological status of the script concept. *American Psychologist, 36,* 715–729.

Ascione, F. (1994). Medication compliance in the elderly. *Generations, Summer, 18*(2), 28–33.

Ashford, J., Hsu, L., Becker, M., Kuman, V., & Bekian, C. (1986). Mini-mental status and activities of daily living: Cross validation by scalogram and item analysis techniques. *The Gerontologist, 26,* 143A.

Barberger-Gateau, P., Commenges, D., Gagnon, M., Letenneur, L, Sauvel, C., & Dartigues, J. (1992). Instrumental activities of daily living as a screening tool for cognitive impairment and dementia in elderly community dwellers. *Journal of the American Geriatrics Society, 40,* 1129–1134.

Bender, M. M., & Derby, B. M. (1992). Prevalence of reading nutrition and ingredient information on food labels among adult Americans: 1982–1988. *Journal of Nutrition Education, 24*(6), 292–297.

Benton, A. L., Hamsher, K. deS., Varney, N. R., Spreen, O. (1983). *Contributions to neuropsychological assessment.* New York: Oxford University Press.

Branch, L., & Jette, A. M. (1982). A prospective study of long-term care institutionalization among the aged. *American Journal of Public Health, 72,* 1373–1379.

Cassel, C. K., Rudberg, M. A., & Olshansky, S. J. (1992). The price of success: Health care in an aging society. *Health Affairs, 11*(2), 87–99.

Chi, M. T. H. (1985). Interactive roles of knowledge and strategies in the development of organized sorting and recall. In S. Chipman, J. Segal, & R. Glaser (Eds.), *Thinking and learning skills: Current research and open questions* (Vol. 2, pp. 457–483). Hillsdale, NJ: Lawrence Erlbaum Associates.

Conn, V. S. (1991). Older adults: Factors that predict the use of over-the-counter medication. *Journal of Advanced Nursing, 16,* 1190–1196.

Cotugna, N., Subar, A. F., Heimendinger, J., & Kahle, L. (1992). Nutrition and cancer prevention knowledge, beliefs, attitudes and practices: The 1987 national health interview survey. *Journal of the American Dietetic Association, 92*(8), 963–968.

Crawley, B. (1993). Self-medication and the elderly. In E. M. Freeman (Ed.), *Substance abuse treatment: A family systems perspective* (pp. 217–238). Newbury Park, CA: Sage.

Crimmins, E. M., & Saito, Y. (1993). Getting better and getting worse. *Journal of Aging and Health, 5*(1), 3–36.

Dixon, R. A., Hultsch, D. F., Simon, E. W., & von Eye, A. (1984). Verbal ability and text structure effects on adult age differences in text recall. *Journal of Verbal Learning and Verbal Behavior, 23,* 569–578.

Fillenbaum, G. G. (1985). Screening the elderly: A brief instrumental activities of daily living measure. *Journal of the American Geriatrics Society, 33,* 698–706.

Fitzgerald, J. F., Smith, D. M., Martin, D. K., Freedman, J. A., & Wolinsky, F. D. (1993). Replication of the multidimensionality of activities of daily living. *Journal of Gerontology: Social Sciences, 48*(1), S28–S31.

Folstein, M. F., Folstein, S. E., & McHugh, P. R. (1975). Mini-mental state: A practical method for grading the cognitive state of patients for the clinician. *Journal of Psychiatric Research, 12,* 189–198.

Friedman, M. (1990). The recommended food-buying principles of consumer educators: A behavioral science assessment of their feasibility for older consumers. *Journal of Nutrition for the Elderly, 9*(3), 17–46.

Furner, S. E., Rudberg, M. A., & Cassel, C. K. (1995). Medical conditions differentially affect the development of IADL disability: Implications for medical care and research. *The Gerontologist, 35*(4), 444–450.

Ganguli, M., Ratcliff, G., Huff, F. J., Belle, S., Kancel, M. J., Fischer, L., Seaberg, E. C., Kuller, L. H. (1991). Effect of age, gender, and education on cognitive tests in a rural elderly community sample: Norms from the Monongahela Valley Independent Elders Survey. *Neuroepidemiology, 10,* 42–52.

Gien, L., & Anderson, J. A. (1989). Medication and the elderly: A review. *Journal of Geriatric Drug Therapy, 4*(1), 59–89.

Guthrie, J. F., Fox, J. J., Cleveland, L. E., & Welsh, S. (1995). Who uses nutrition labeling, and what effects does label use have on diet quality? *Journal of Nutrition Education, 27*(4), 163–172.

Hershey, D. A., Walsh, D. A., Read, S. J., & Chulef, A. S. (1990). The effects of expertise on financial problem solving: Evidence for goal directed problem solving scripts. *Organizational Behavior and Human Decision Processes, 46,* 77–101.

Hughes, C., Berg, L., Danziger, W., Cohen, L., & Martin, R. (1982). A new clinical scale for the staging of dementia. *British Journal of Psychiatry, 140,* 566–572.

Johnson, M. M. (1990). Age differences in decision making: A process methodology for examining strategic information processing. *Journal of Gerontology, 45,* 75–78.

Johnson, R. J., & Wolinsky, F. D. (1993). The structure of health status among older adults: Disease, disability, functional limitation, and perceived health. *Journal of Health and Social Behavior, 34*(2), 105–121.

Kemper, P. (1992). The use of formal and informal home care by the disabled elderly. *Health Services Research, 27,* 421–451.

Kovar, M. G., & Lawton, M. P. (1994). Functional disability: Activities and instrumental activities of daily living. In M. P. Lawton & J. A. Teresi (Eds.), *Annual review of gerontology and geriatrics: Vol. 14. Focus on assessment techniques* (pp. 57–75). New York: Springer.

Labouvie-Vief, G., & Hakim-Larson, J. (1989). Developmental shifts in adult thought. In S. Hunter & M. Sundel (Eds.), *Midlife myths* (pp. 69–96). Newbury Park, CA: Sage.

Lawton, M. P. & Brody, E. (1969). Assessment of older people: Self maintaining and instrumental activities of daily living. *The Gerontologist, 9,* 179–185.

Leventhal, E. A., Leventhal, H., Schaefer, P. M. & Easterling, D. (1993). Conservation of energy, uncertainty reduction, and swift utilization of medical care among the elderly. *Journal of Gerontology: Psychological Sciences, 48,* P78–P86.

Leventhal, H., & Cameron, L. (1987). Behavioral theories and the problem of compliance. *Patient Education and Counseling, 10,* 117–138.

Manton, K. G. (1988). A longitudinal study of functional change and mortality in the United States. *Journal of Gerontology: Social Sciences, 43,* S153–S161.

Meyer, B. J. F., Russo, C., & Talbot, A. (1995). Discourse comprehension and problem solving: Decisions about the treatment of breast cancer by women across the life-span. *Psychology and Aging, 10,*(1), 84–103.

Morrell, R. W., Park, D. C., & Poon, L. W. (1989). Quality of instructions on prescription drug labels: Effects on memory and comprehension in young and old adults. *Gerontologist, 29,* 345–354.

Morrell, R. W., Park, D. C., & Poon, L. W. (1990). Effects of labeling techniques on memory and comprehension of prescription information on young and old adults. *Journal of Gerontology, 45,* 166–172.

Morris, J. C., Heyman, A., Mohs, R. C., Hughes, J. P., van Belle, G., Fillenbaum, G., Mettits, E. D., & Clark, C. (1989). The Consortium to Establish a Registry for Alzheimer's Disease (CERAD): Part I. Clinical and neuropsychological assessment of Alzheimer's disease. *Neurology, 39,* 1159–1165.

Murray, M. D., Darnell, J., Weinberger, M., & Martz, B. L. (1986). Factors contributing to medication noncompliance in elderly public housing tenants. *Drug Intelligence and Clinical Pharmacy, 20,* 146–151.

Myers, A. M. (1992). The clinical Swiss army knife: Empirical evidence on the validity of IADL functional status measures. *Medical Care, 30*(5), MS96–MS111.

National Dairy Council. (1986). Nutrition labeling and health claims. *Dairy Council Digest, 57*(6), 31–36.

Park, D. C., Morrell, R. W., Frieske, D., Blackburn, A. B., & Birchmore, D. (1991). Cognitive factors and the use of over-the-counter medication organizers by arthritis patients. *Human Factors, 33*(1), 57–67.

Park, D. C., Morrell, R. W., Frieske, D., & Kincaid, D. (1992). Medication adherence behaviors in older adults: Effects of external cognitive supports. *Psychology & Aging, 7*(2), 252–256.

Reese, H. W., & Rodeheaver, D. (1985). Problem solving and complex decision making. In J. E. Birren & K. W. Schaie (Eds.), *Handbook of the psychology of aging* (pp. 606–625). New York: Van Nostrand Reinhold.

Reinharz, S. & Rowles, G. D. (1988). *Qualitative gerontology.* New York: Springer.

Reisberg, B., Ferris, S. H., de Leon, M. J., & Crook, T. (1982). The Global Deterioration Scale for assessment of primary degenerative dementia. *American Journal of Psychiatry, 139*(9), 1136–1139.

Salthouse, T. A. (1990). Working memory as a processing resource in cognitive aging. *Developmental Review, 10*(1), 101–124.

Salzman, C. (1991). Geriatric psychopharmacology. In A. J. Gelenberg, E. L. Bassuk, & S. C. Schoonover (Eds.), *The practitioner's guide to psychoactive drugs* (3rd ed., pp. 319–339). New York: Plenum Medical Book Co.

Schaie, K. W. (1996). *Intellectual development in adulthood: The Seattle longitudinal study.* New York: Cambridge University Press.

Sinnott, J. D. (1989). A model for solution of ill-structured problems: Implications for everyday and abstract problem solving. In J. D. Sinnott (Ed.), *Everyday problem solving: Theory and applications* (pp. 72–99). New York: Praeger.

Streufert, S., Pogash, R., Piasecki, M., & Post, G. M. (1990). Age and management team performance. *Psychology and Aging, 5,* 551–559.

Thomas, S. E., Kendrick, O. W., & Eddy, J. M. (1990). Modification of a nutritional questionnaire for older adults and the ability of its knowledge and attitude evaluations to predict dietary adequacy. *Journal of Nutrition for the Elderly, 9*(4), 35–63.

Walsh, D. A., & Hershey, D. A. (1993). Mental models and the maintenance of complex problem-solving skills in old age. In J. Cerella, J. M. Rybash, W. Hoyer, & M. L. Commons (Eds.), *Adult information processing: Limits on loss* (pp. 553–584). San Diego, CA: Academic Press.

Willis, S. L., Allen-Burge, R., Dolan, M. M., Bertrand, R. M., Yesavage, J., & Taylor, J. L. (1998). Everyday problem solving among individuals with Alzheimer's disease. *The Gerontologist, 38,* 569–577.

Willis, S. L., Jay, G. M., Diehl, M., & Marsiske, M. (1992). Longitudinal change and prediction of everyday task competence in the elderly. *Research on Aging, 14*(1), 68–91.

Wolinsky, F. D., Callahan, C. M., Fitzgerald, J. F., & Johnson, R. J. (1992). The risk of nursing home placement and subsequent death among older adults. *Journal of Gerontology: Social Sciences, 47*(4), S173–S182.

Wolinsky, F. D., Callahan, C. M., & Johnson, R. J. (1994). Subjective health status and mortality in the elderly. In B. Vellas, J. L. Albarede, & P. J. Carry (Eds.), *Facts and research in gerontology 1994: Epidemiology and aging* (pp. 13–27). New York: Springer.

Wolinsky, F. D., & Johnson, R. J. (1991). The use of health services by older adults. *Journal of Gerontology: Social Sciences, 46*(6), S345–357.

Wolinsky, F. D., Stump, T. E., & Johnson, R. J. (1995). Hospital utilization profiles among older adults over time: Consistency and volume among survivors and decedents. *Journal of Gerontology: Psychological and Social Sciences, 50B*(2), S88–S100.

Zarit, S. H., Johansson, B., & Malmberg, B. (1995). Changes in functional competency in the oldest old. *Journal of Aging and Health, 7*(1), 3–23.

IV

Human Factors

13

How Do I Work This Thing?
Cognitive Issues in Home
Medical Equipment Use
and Maintenance

Marilyn Sue Bogner
Institute for the Study of Medical Error

The ever-expanding capability of medicine to increase longevity through interventions such as immunizations, antibiotics, management of chronic diseases, and prosthetic implants (e.g., hip replacements) has led to an aging population dependent on medically related activities for their well-being. Some of these activities are familiar because people of all ages engage in them; other activities are not so familiar.

The most familiar medically related activity is taking over-the-counter and prescription medication. This tends to be quite common in the elderly who, because of the exigencies of physiological aging as well as disease, have health problems. Given the pervasiveness of medication in the elderly and the cognitive and information processing aspects of appropriate self-medication, an important literature on issues related to self-medication has developed (e.g., Morrow, Leirer, Adrassy, Tanke, & Stine-Morrow, 1996). Other less familiar types of medically related activities that are becoming increasingly evident in contemporary life are associated with providing home care to a person with a serious health problem. Those activities, which include using heath care procedures and medical devices, also involve information-processing issues—many of which have yet to be addressed by research.

Home care, although pervasive in self-care, is becoming more common in providing care for another person, particularly for the aging population. Within home care, both in self-care and especially in providing care for another, the use of medical equipment is becoming increasingly evident. The use of medical equipment in the home care environment—often complex and sophisticated equipment—can be an intimidating if not threatening responsibility to most lay persons. Providing health care and operating the medical equipment have cognitive and information-processing implications, particularly for older individuals.

To identify cognitive and information-processing issues that impact on the use of home medical equipment by the largest category of users, elderly, the following discussion first presents a brief overview of home care. Next, cognitive information-processing tasks involved in the lay person, particularly the older person, providing health care using home medical equipment are discussed. Then, implications are drawn for research that applies cognitive and information processing knowledge to home health care activities by elderly.

OVERVIEW

Traditionally, the home was the locus of health care. Childbirth occurred in the home; people died at home, and in the interval between those events, health care occurred at home with physicians making visits. This was supplanted by the locus of health care being outside the home at the office of the physician or a hospital. In the late 1960s, childbirth involved a 5- to 7-day hospital stay for both the infant and mother. Surgery required a hospital stay of a number of days, often a week or more. Among the factors that contributed to lengthy hospital stays were the lack of people at home to assist during convalescence. This no longer is a consideration. Health care as it has been known since the 1970s is changing markedly.

The change in the provision of health care is a reaction to the magnitude of the financial costs incurred by what has been considered as excessive medical treatment including extended hospital stays. This has lead to a reduction in length of hospital stays, some of which have been radical. For example, the length of stay for childbirth can be as brief as less than 24 hours. Conditions that, in recent decades had received hospital care, in the 1990s are treated at home by the patients themselves or by lay care providers who typically are family or friends (Daatland, 1996). Because dismissal from the hospital and even from professional care typically occurs soon after the acute phase of a health problem, patients are returning home "quicker and sicker." The home once again is becoming to a large extent the locus of health care. Also, many terminally ill people—who in recent decades were maintained in a hospital on life support for extended periods—now complete their lives at home.

Because of the brevity of the period of facility-based professional medical treatment, conditions treated in home care range from chronic health problems with severe disease-related conditions such as diabetes and renal disease through recuperation from an illness, accident, surgery, or medical procedure to home hospice care. Although the injuries and illnesses treated by home care in the 1990s are analogous to those treated when the home was the locus of health care in the 1930s, the contemporary home situation is not the same as then nor are the means by which care is provided. Homes have become smaller; extra bedrooms to be dedicated to care of the sick are not common. People to provide care are not readily available; the extended family home rarely exists in contemporary society. Adult family members capable of providing care typically live in various locales unavailable to assist on a regular basis or give respite for the care provider. Funds for such services from social agencies no longer are available.

People are not available to provide care even in the nuclear family. Many if not most women, the traditional caregivers, work outside the home. When home health care of a family member is necessary, only a retired or otherwise unemployed older relative, partner, or friend is available to help. It is relatively common for an old-old parent to receive home care from a late middle-aged or older child. The obverse also occurs—an elderly child receives care from a very old parent (Applegate, 1994). Thus, home care of others as well as self-care most often is provided by older individuals whose physical and cognitive functioning may be compromised by the aging process and by the medication for the ills that accompany that process.

An advantage of home care, in addition to cost savings, is the quality of life for the care recipient, which is enhanced by the familiar home environment—a quality of life unattainable in a health care facility. The quality of life experienced by the care recipient often entails a decrement in the quality of life of the care provider. Although the strain of making multiple trips to a facility for visits is avoided in home care, that does not compensate for the stress and fatigue incurred from unfamiliar health care activities, the concern for doing the right thing, and the lack of social support that can contribute to illness particularly for the older care provider (Grundy, Bowling, & Farquhar, 1996).

Home care often involves treating the patient using sophisticated medical equipment placed in the home, which can be anxiety inducing and add to the decrement in quality of life for the care provider. That anxiety can reflect concern for one's ability to use the medical equipment in providing care—an activity that involves a number of information-processing tasks.

INFORMATION-PROCESSING TASKS

It is necessary that a person who is providing health care to another person or to themselves accurately determine when the health condition is appropriate for medication or a procedure and safely and effectively provide that care. Information-processing tasks inherent to such determination are central to effective home care. Those tasks reflect complex cognitive processes that involve the integration of several sets of cognitive cues. For optimal care, the provider must understand and integrate information about the psychological as well as physical characteristics of the care recipient, the disease process or injury for which the person is receiving care, how the physiological insult interacts with patient characteristics, the procedures by which the treatment is given (e.g., the way the medical devices function), and the anticipated result of the treatment (S. Swayze, personal communication, 1997). Lay care providers cannot be expected to participate in those cognitive tasks the same as highly skilled clinicians; however, it is necessary that a modicum of those cues be incorporated in home care.

How information-processing tasks can enhance home care by the elderly is addressed in the subsequent discussion. First, information-processing tasks in determining when care is appropriate are described. Next, cognitive tasks in the operation of medical devices are considered. Then, the impact of medication, illness, and aging on the cognitive processes of the elderly home care provider are presented. It should be noted that, although the discussion is targeted for the elderly, the issues pertain to home health care providers of any age.

Information-Processing Tasks
to Determine When Care Is Appropriate

When to use a home care device is not always apparent. The onset of illness may be masked by its symptoms occurring incrementally over time. A person may feel peculiar one day and become accustomed to that feeling. Later, the person feels peculiar again, and again becomes accustomed to that feeling. Subsequent experiences of feeling peculiar each represent a decrement in health from the previously compromised status. Unless people reflect on how they currently feel with respect to their typical sense of well-being before the onset of the peculiar feelings, they neglect symptoms until the disease has progressed to the point that, when they feel they should use a home care device or seek professional health care, the optimal time to treat the problem has passed (Bogner, 1997).

Interpreting cues as indicative of illness is important in providing appropriate health care. It is difficult to identify and interpret the cues of changing health status of a care recipient or as previously discussed, oneself. For example, a person who experiences shortness of breath and chest tightness may explain away those symptoms as reflecting lack of exercise. Based on that, the care provider would not use a broncho-dilator inhaler. When the symptoms become asthmatic bronchitis, the person uses the inhaler. The effectiveness of such treatment, which is targeted for prevention, is severely diminished at that stage of the illness. Because of lack of processing information provided by the cues, it is necessary to obtain treatment appropriate for the advanced stage of the illness. This incurs costs in terms of the care recipient's ill health as well as cost for professional care.

Some home care providers, particularly the elderly, may be perceptive to changes in their personal health status and to that of family members with whom they are most familiar, such as a spouse of many years, sibling, or other close relative. Such perceptiveness cannot be assumed, however, because it may be compromised by factors associated with medication, illness, or the aging of the care provider.

Cognitive Tasks in the Operation of Medical Devices

Once the condition of the care recipient has been identified as requiring the use of a medical device, the care provider must confront the cognitive and information-processing demands inherent in the procedure to operate the device and interpret the information it provides. The ability to perform those tasks is presumed to be conveyed prior to the need to use the device via a demonstration, which often is referred to as training. Written instructions may accompany the device.

Instructions may be targeted to the lay user, using a font size to accommodate vision problems and simplified sentence structure and terminology. Even with those considerations, the information presented in the instructions may not be what the lay care provider needs. Written instructions may be supplemented by a demonstration on video. It cannot be assumed that users will read the instructions or watch the video, or if they do, that the information will be assimilated and useful.

Information-processing problems occurred in the following experience expressed by an energetic 45-year-old woman who provides home care for her husband. Undoubtedly, her feelings are shared by elderly home health care providers.

> Obtaining and using home medical equipment carries a great deal of emotional stress, and that affects how we learn about the equipment and how we use and maintain it. Before Leonard was discharged from the hospital, we had a training session. I tried to listen carefully, but it was overwhelming—so many procedures to remember, so much terminology. And as the hospital nurse was talking, I was very aware of Leonard's feelings. I think it really sank in then that he was going to depend on a machine for the rest of his life and that much of the load would fall on me. When I got home, I realized I hadn't absorbed half of what I'd been told. (National Research Council, 1996, p. 6)

The preceding quotation illustrates the pervasiveness of the presumption that training is an effective means of enabling a person to provide care using medical devices. That presumption may not be valid; training may not be effective, particularly for activities that are contrary to cognitive processes manifest in well-established habits. An example is a procedure that incudes a task after completion of the primary task—this is contrary to the cognitive trait identified as "closure" by perceptual psychologists (Wertheimer, 1959). The potency of that trait is evidenced by research on postcompletion tasks conducted by Bryne and Bovair (1997).

Bryne and Bovair (1997) reported that postcompletion tasks are not executed even after the people were instructed to do so. An example of a postcompletion task is pressing the "Enter" key after a change has been programmed in a medical device—an activity similar to changing television channels using an early model remote control. (Although television remote controls no longer include that activity, medical devices do.) These findings illustrate the difficulty in conforming a cognitive process to a procedure and suggest that activities, in this discussion health care and medical device procedures, should be developed to accommodate the cognitive processes of the provider.

Health care procedures that conflict with the providers' cognitive processes can induce error and lead to adverse outcomes, such as serious injury or death. To reduce the likelihood of such error, particular consideration should be made to accomodate cognitive processes that have been found to differ for older and younger persons in the development of home health protocols for elderly care providers.

Age-related declines have been reported in the ability to do more than one task concurrently. From their review of the dual-task and multitask performance literature, McDowd, Vercruyssen, and Berrin (1991) concluded that older adults have greater difficulty in dual-task performance than younger adults. This difficulty was reported for tasks that require attention to be spread over multiple sense modalities, such as auditory monitoring of a medical device while visually checking its functioning, and across cognitive activities.

In the case of multiple cognitive or motor processes, older adults tends to conduct activities in a serial rather than a concurrent manner. A potentially serious problem could occur if the lead activity was to attend to household distractions and the nonlead activity, which is conducted after completion of the lead activity, was critical in detecting a problem with the device or the care recipient. Such a problem can be compounded by decreases in attention resulting from anxiety, fatigue, loss of sleep, and depression (McDowd, Vercruyssen, & Berrin, 1991)—factors that are present in a home care situation.

Training on the operation of complex medical devices, even training that has been successful with young adults, can not be presumed to be successful with older individuals. Operating equipment such as medical devices is not a unitary process; it can involve familiar tasks as well as tasks that are new to the user. The importance of familiarity of a task or subtask differs with the age of the individual. New tasks are more difficult for older adults to learn than for younger people; however, well-learned tasks can be performed by older adults without decrement (Fisk & Rogers, 1991). From this and the findings from the dual-task and multi-task literature, it is apparent that age-related task performance must be considered in training older adults to provide home care and operate medical devices. Those differences also should be accommodated in the design and development of procedures for providing home health care, including medical devices that will be used extensively by the elderly.

Cognitive processes that differ between younger and older adults are not the only age-related characteristic that influences on the provision of home health care. Older care providers are likely to be taking medication, have a chronic health condition, and experience infirmities associated with aging that affect their cognitive and information processing abilities.

Impact of Medication, Illness, and Aging on Cognitive Processes

The effects of medication may compromise a person's cognitive functioning and information-processing ability. These effects can be manifest in behavioral aberrations such as forgetting that medication has been taken and taking it again, thus escalating the effect, leaving the stove on, or wandering. This is a particularly dangerous situation when a caregiver is involved in self-care as well as in caring for another—a likely scenario for the elderly population.

The use of a device in treatment of a disease can be affected by the disease process as well as by cognitive functioning and the physical characteristics of the user. Technological advances have enabled the miniaturization of medical devices, which has allowed many of them to be portable and used in self-care. Examples include blood glucose meters (BGM) that enable diabetics to test the sugar content of their blood to guide their diet, exercise, and use of insulin. For the BGM, miniaturization raises a number of use issues that pertain to the characteristics of the user, especially the older user, and the process of the disease for which the device was developed.

Small objects are difficult to manipulate by older individuals who have arthritis. This compounds the problem that diabetes causes decreased manual dexterity—a very small device is difficult to use with impaired manual dexterity—a user with advanced disease has difficulty grasping and manipulating a credit card size BGM. It is difficult to insert the test strip with the drop of blood into the very small opening on the left side of the monitor. Diabetes also can cause failing eyesight (diabetic retinopathy). Because the BGM is so small, the display that presents the blood glucose level is by necessity quite small, with small numbers that are difficult to read with disease-compromised eyesight. Misread numbers can result in inappropriate self-medication with insulin, which could lead to a diabetic coma.

For older adults with diabetes, people who for years might have assessed their glucose level using the color of the urine test strips, the numerical information provided by the BGM presents a cognitive and information-processing challenge. That challenge is the translation of the numbers into a more familiar indication for altering insulin dose, changing diet, or modifying an exercise program.

As in lay home caregivers of any age, elderly care providers initially are anxious and frightened. These feelings are exacerbated in the elderly because of their sense of diminished resources stemming in part from compromised physical strength, endurance, and perceptual acuity that accompanies aging. The findings that older people compensate for compromised abilities by modifying their behavior to reduce risk taking and increase vigilance when driving an automobile (Szlyk, Seiple, & Viana, 1995) may suggest a tendency to be overly cautious that may cause problems when providing health care. Risk in changing behavior is necessary to treat a care recipient's rapidly deteriorating condition. If being overly cautious indeed is a characteristic of older caregivers, then it should be accommodated in procedures and protocols for providing care by explicitly stating behaviors that could reduce the perception of risk.

In home care by and for the elderly, their cognitive processes are compromised by distorted sensory input from age-impaired sensory functioning. Diminished visual acuity and hearing loss hinder care givers from perceiving changes in skin tone and raspiness of breath indicative of impending need for medication or use of a medical device. The impaired sensory functioning also influences caregivers' ability to comprehend numbers necessary to program a device and on their ability to attend to warnings and alarms. Although such impairment might be corrected with changes in eyeglasses, hearing aids, and increases in the volume of alarms, it often is dismissed as evidence of cognitive decline (Vroman, Cohen, & Volkman, 1994). Such misinterpretation has serious implications for the elderly care provider and consequently for the care recipient. The implications also are serious for the elderly engaged in self-care.

Despite impairment, it is necessary for the caregiver to make decisions regarding the health status of the care recipient, which could, if inaccurate, have serious consequences. The experiences of the 45-year-old home caregiver again provides an example:

> If something seems amiss—if Leonard is overly tired or has a fever or the fluid balance doesn't look quite right—we have to decide whether it's something that can be taken care of by adjusting the technology or whether there's another cause. Twice we have gone to the hospital emergency room, only to discover that we could have taken care of the problem at home. (National Research Council, 1996, p. 6)

For most older persons, success in providing home care is more than merely keeping the person needing care out of the hospital or even treating one's own chronic disease. Home care often is the critical factor that enables older persons to live independently. Central to success in providing home care by the elderly is home medical equipment that accommodates the cognitive functioning and information-processing needs of older persons. That accommodation helps insure the safe and effective use of the equipment by the elderly careprovider and contributes to the ability to live independently.

Living independently not only increases the individuals' quality of life but also reduces the time and money (often public money) spent for long-term, nursing home care. To accomplish this, it is necessary that a concerted effort be made to develop the procedures and medical devices that are to be used by elderly home care providers to be in concert with all aspects of those providers. Unlike nearly all other consumer products, the general public, including design engineers, has little if any experience in using medical devices even in self-care. Neither have we experienced chronic disease that necessitated self-care beyond medication, so we are not sensitized to the problems of using such equipment. In addition, the design engineers, almost by definition because they are employed, are not elderly, so are not aware of the ways age-related cognitive and physical characteristics affect the operation of medical devices in the complex, home care setting. This has implications for research.

IMPLICATIONS FOR RESEARCH

Success in home health care provided by and for the elderly is important not only to those directly involved but also to society. Success in such a complex activity does not happen by chance. As home health care became more prevalent, organizations to assist the providers grew and proliferated. In the 1990s environment of constrained resources, funding for services provided by those organizations is becoming significantly reduced to the extent that services must be curtailed. Telephone contact is supplanting face-to-face services.

Research that applies existing knowledge of the cognitive functioning and information processing of the elderly to the activities, protocols, and operation of medical devices can enhance the provision of home health care by lay persons. A precedent exists for the application of research findings to medical issues in the research on medication reminders described in the chapters of this book.

Research that applies knowledge about tasks in operating equipment that is similar to medical devices (Cushman & Rosenberg, 1991), when tailored by the findings of research on the cognitive and information characteristics of older people, could contribute significantly to success in home health care by and for the elderly.

Also, research by the manufacturers of medical devices is needed to determine if the design of a device is viable for the least able potential user, the elderly home health care provider. A preponderance of current medical equipment is computer-based and its operation often is nonintuitive with opaque feedback (Obradovich & Woods, 1996). Devices with those characteristics are used for providing chemotherapy or analgesia in home care. Using those devices is problematic for health care professionals; problems in their use by lay care providers, especially the elderly, is a certainty. Whether using medical equipment to care for another or to treat one's own health problem, home health care devices are predominately operated by nonprofessional, older lay care providers and must be designed for that use if home health care is to be successful.

Home care is the fastest growing industry in the United States and the elderly comprise the fastest growing age group of the population. Self-care and home care of the elderly and the associated use of medical devices are becoming ubiquitous. For home care to be safe and effective, information-processing issues in the use of home medical devices must be addressed.

REFERENCES

Applegate, M. H. (1994). Diagnosis-related groups: Are patients in jeopardy? In M. S. Bogner (Ed.), *Human error in medicine* (pp. 349–371). Hillsdale, NJ: Lawrence Erlbaum Associates.

Bogner, M. S. (1997). Naturalistic decision making in health care. In C. E. Zsambok & G. Klein (Eds.), *Naturalistic decision making* (pp. 61–70). Mahwah, NJ: Lawrence Erlbaum Associates.

Byrne, M. D., & Bovair, S. (1997). A working memory model of a common procedural error. *Cognitive Science, 21*(1), 31–61.

Cushman, W. H., & Rosenberg, D. J. (1991). *Human factors in product design.* Amsterdam: Elsevier.

Daatland, S. O. (1996). Formal and informal care: New approaches. In G. Caselli & A. D. Lopez (Eds.) *Health and mortality among elderly populations* (pp. 315–330). Oxford, England: Clarendon.

Fisk, A. D., & Rogers, W. A. (1991). Development of skilled performance: An age-related perspective. In D. L. Damos (Ed.), *Multiple-task performance* (pp. 415–443). London: Taylor & Francis.

Grundy, E., Bowling, A., & Farquhar, M. (1996). Social support, life satisfaction, and survival at older ages. In G. Caselli & A. D. Lopez (Eds.), *Health and mortality among elderly populations* (pp. 135–156). Oxford, England: Clarendon.

McDowd, J., Vercruyssen, M., & Berrin, J. E. (1991). Aging, divided attention, and dual-task performance. In D. L. Damos (Ed.), *Multiple-task performance* (pp. 387–414). London: Taylor & Francis.

Morrow, D. G., Leirer, V. A., Adrassy, J. M., Tanke, E. D., & Stine-Morrow, E. A. L. (1996). Medication instruction design: Younger and older adult schemas for taking medication. *Human Factors, 38*(4), 556–573.

National Research Council. (1996). *Safe, comfortable, attractive, and easy to use: Improving the usability of home medical devices.* Washington, DC: National Academy Press.

Obradovich, J. H. & Woods, D. D. (1996). Users as designers: How people cope with poor HCI design in computer-based medical devices. *Human Factors, 38*(4), 574–592.

Szlyk, P. P., Seiple, W., & Viana, M. (1995). Relative effects of age and compromised vision on driving performance. *Human Factors, 37*(3), 430–437.

Vroman, G., Cohen, I., & Volkman, N. (1994). Misinterpreting cognitive decline in the elderly: Blaming the patient. In M. S. Bogner (Ed.), *Human error in medicine* (pp. 349–371). Hillsdale, NJ: Lawrence Erlbaum Associates.

Wertheimer, M. (1959). *Productive thinking.* New York: Harper & Row.

14

What Does It Say?
Text Design,
Medical Information,
and Older Readers

James Hartley
University of Keele

This chapter is divided into three parts. In the first part, I discuss, in the context of medical information, those features of text design that make printed information easier to read and understand. In the second part, I indicate what research can tell us about the effects of aging in connection with these features. And in the third part, I discuss the implications of the findings reported in the second part. The basic, underlying theme throughout this chapter is that legibility matters for everyone, but that cognitive loads have to be reduced for older adults.

TEXT DESIGN AND MEDICAL INFORMATION

When considering issues of text design, I like to focus on three overlapping areas. These involve (a) the appearance of the text—in particular, its typography and layout; (b) the language of the text—how easy it is to read and understand; and (c) the effectiveness of the text—how well it does its job.

233

.

Typography and Layout

I have tried to encapsulate in Table 14.1 some of the main issues concerning typography and layout that designers might consider when they are designing medical information.

Key issues here are the choice of page size, line length, typefaces, type sizes, and, most critical, how space is used to convey the structure of the text. Other concerns lie with how this structure can be further clarified by typographic devices such italic, bold, or colored typefaces. There is, in fact, a considerable research literature on most of these issues (e.g., see J. Hartley, 1994a; Misanchuk, 1992; Shriver, 1997).

The Language of Text

There is also considerable literature on the language of text. Suffice it to say here that it is generally accepted that text is easier to read and to understand when authors use simple wording and short—but varied—sentence lengths. Numerous authors offer advice on how to produce clear text. The following suggestions are typical:

- Write relatively short paragraphs.
- Write few sentences containing two or more subordinate clauses.
- Use concepts and words that readers will understand.
- Delete unnecessary words.
- Use the active rather than the passive voice.
- Use positive rather than negative formulations.
- Avoid negatives, especially double or triple ones.
- Consider personalizing the text for interest.
- Provide introductory summaries and, possibly, interim and concluding ones.
- Convey structure by using main and secondary headings.
- Space out and itemize listed points (e.g., as here, with bullets).

Guidelines such as these have been fleshed out in more detail in books and articles for people writing medical text (e.g., see Albert & Chadwick, 1992; Morrow & Leirer, chap. 15, this volume; Reece, 1995; Wogalter & Sojourner, chap. 17, this volume). Such guidelines are often contravened and this may cause difficulties for some readers—particularly older ones. Furthermore, some guidelines might be criticized for being based upon opinion rather than evidence as far as older adults are concerned—hence the need for evaluation studies.

Evaluating Text

There are numerous techniques for evaluating the effectiveness of text. Schriver (1989) distinguished between (a) methods using experts (e.g., peer review), (b) methods using readers (e.g., comprehension tests), and (c) methods focusing on the

TABLE 14.1
Guidelines for Design Decisions When Planning Medical Text

Characteristic	Guideline
Page size	The choice (and orientation) of the page size determines many of the subsequent decisions shown in this table. In Europe, there are internationally agreed on page sizes (see J. Hartley, 1994a). Large page sizes are useful for providing variations in column widths and for presenting good size tables, graphs, and illustrations. Small page sizes present particular difficulties in these respects. However, books with large page sizes are difficult to shelve and to use on a desk with other materials.
Margins	Both the inner and outer margins of text need to be about 25mm to allow for binding and photocopying (because the text is usually printed on both sides). The top and bottom margins may be a little narrower than this.
Column widths	A single column of text on a large page size may be too wide. Two columns of equal width may work well but it may be better to think of one narrow (say one third) and one wider column (say two thirds of the width). This structure allows one to use larger illustrations set to the inner margin. Column widths should be used consistently and not vary from page to page.
Type sizes	Type size measurement is complicated and confounded by the fact that different typefaces with the same designated type size actually differ in size. (See J. Hartley, 1994a, for illustrations and an explanation.) However, text is normally measured in *points,* and a text set in 10-point type on a 12-point line feed is quite common. The Royal National Institute for the Blind in the United Kingdom recommends the use of 12-point type because most people, even if they are visually impaired, can read type of this size.
Type faces	Conventional type faces are more suitable than exotic ones. It is good practice not to use more than two typefaces in a document—one face for the text and one for the table captions and so forth is quite adequate. This may seem restrained, but it is less confusing for the reader.
Inter-line	Interline spacing depends on the line length. But a rule of thumb for spacing is to use spacing about 125% of the type size as the line space. As noted previously, 10-point type is often set with 12-point line feed. In word-processed text, some people recommend a line feed of one-and-a-half.
Justification	This text in this paragraph is set *unjustified*: it has a ragged right-hand edge. *Justified* text, in contrast, has straight left- and right-hand edges. Research suggests that there is little to choose between the two systems, and it is largely a matter of style. Unjustified text has everything starting from the left: justified text is balanced about a central axis. Unjustified text is probably more flexible for information leaflets. In either style, wrapping text around an illustration should be avoided.
Paragraphs	One unit of line feed, without indentation, helps paragraphs to stand out. If such a system is used, this amount of space must be used consistently and not vary from page to page.
Space above and below items	Measures of internal spacing must be decided for above and below items in advance and adhered to throughout a text. Proportional systems can be considered: for example, one space between paragraphs; two spaces above and one space below a secondary heading; four spaces above and two spaces below a main heading, etc. Similarly, one might have two spaces above a caption and one below it throughout a text.

Table 14.1, Continued

Characteristic	Guideline
Number of lines per page	This need not be fixed but can vary according to the spacing system used in the text and concerns over meaningful stopping points. New paragraphs need not start on the last line of a page just to fill in the space, nor need the last line of a paragraph appear on the top of a new column or page.
Cueing headings	Heading levels can be differentiated by typographic cues: for example, capital letters for main headings; upper and lower case bold for secondary headings; italic for tertiary ones. Color can also be used to distinguish headings in text, but this color should not be varied from page to page.
Emphasis	Avoid the use of all capital letters for emphasis. Bold and italic typefaces can be used, but preferably not together. Sometimes color is used as well as larger letters, but such multiple cueing systems can be confusing.
Color	Black print on white paper has the best contrast value. Legibility is impaired when dark text is printed on a strongly colored background and pale text is printed on pale backgrounds.
Overprinting	Legibility is badly impaired when the text is printed over differently colored illustrations and/or black-and-white photographs. Such over printing should be avoided.

Note. These guidelines are expanded in Hartley (1994a).

text itself (e.g., the application of readability formulae, or computer-based stylistic analysis programs). These different methods can be used separately or in combination to evaluate the effectiveness of a piece of text and to provide information that can be used to improve it (e.g., see J. Hartley, 1995; Ley & Llewelyn,1995).

Some Problems

Medical texts, of course, come in all shapes and sizes. Indeed, within each type of text, there is enormous variety. To illustrate this, I once analysed the main typographic features of 100 patient information leaflets (i.e., leaflets provided with medicine packs). These were sampled from a compendium of 430 such leaflets provided by 47 pharmaceutical companies in Europe in 1995 (Walker, 1995). The results showed that more than two thirds of the leaflets were printed in a *portrait* style layout (where the length is longer than the width), and that most of these used a justified single-column format. The data suggested however, that *landscape* versions (where the width is longer than the length) were more likely to be used when there was a need for diagrams, illustrations, and two-column text.

However, this summary does not convey the variety of page sizes, typefaces, type sizes, and use of color that exists within information leaflets. In addition, a variety of methods were used (a) to show how the information was sequenced, (b) to help people keep track of when to take their medicines, (c) to convey numbered information, and (d) to list ingredients. Each of these topics could benefit from more detailed research in this context. Research on patient leaflets is described by Morrow and Leirer (chap. 15, this volume) and by Wogalter and Sojourner (chap. 17, this volume).

AGING AND TEXT DESIGN

The research literature on the effects of aging on learning and memory is even larger than the typographic literature described so far. Following Bond, Coleman, and Peace (1993), I distinguish here between three overlapping areas of research in this context: physiological, cognitive, and social. *Physiological* research looks at the biology of aging and its physiological correlates. Most people, for example, experience with age a decline in eyesight and other senses (see, e.g., Kosnik, Winslow, Kline, Rasinski, & Sekuler, 1988; Pirkl, 1994). *Cognitive* research on aging focuses on changes in memory, learning, and judgment (e.g., see Salthouse, 1982; Schaie, 1994). Such cognitive changes also have implications for text design, as we shall see. *Social* research on aging examines how, for example, societies expect their older members to function. Studies of ageism, for example, focus on how attitudes and beliefs about what old people should and should not do determine to a considerable extent what, in fact, they do (e.g., see Hess, 1994). Such beliefs might affect how people use medical information.

It is not possible to summarize in a few lines the main findings of these multifaceted studies of aging and their implications for text design. The picture is complex, and the research in this field is expanding rapidly. Nonetheless, I think that there are two main points to bear in mind when thinking about text design for older readers: (a) working memory capacity (i.e., information held and used in ongoing tasks) declines as people get older (e.g., see Babcock & Salthouse, 1990; Baddeley, 1986) and (b) the more difficult the task and the older the person, then the more disproportionately difficult that task becomes (e.g., see Salthouse, 1982). Thus, for example, older people recall narrative texts relatively well but find expository texts more difficult (J. T. Hartley, 1989; Tun, 1989). But summarizing expository text is even more difficult for older compared to younger adults (Byrd, 1985).

Meyer, Young, and Bartlett (1989) and Meyer (in press) suggested that it is important to consider three overlapping variables in studies of older people learning from text:

- Reader variables, such as verbal ability and prior knowledge.
- Text variables, such as text structure, genre, difficulty, and so forth.
- Task variables, such as remembering, following instructions, and so forth.

Thus, one might not expect differences between older and younger readers when the verbal ability of the readers is high, when they have good prior knowledge, when the texts are well presented, and when the tasks are relatively straightforward. Differences, however, might be expected to emerge with less able readers, less familiar materials, poorly designed text, and more complex tasks.

Generally speaking, studies on the effects of aging suggest that text will be easier for older people to use when their perceptual and memory processing cognitive loads are reduced. One would imagine, therefore, that this might be achieved by, for example, using larger type-sizes; using clearer layouts; using more readable text; and clarifying the structure of the text by, perhaps, using summaries, headings, and signals.

In the first part of this section, I outline some of the results from studies specifically carried out with older users in these respects. These studies have mainly used what I call typographically simple text—that is, continuous expository prose. I discuss studies with typographically complex text in the next section (see also J. Hartley, 1994b).

The Effects of Improving Typographically
Simple Texts for Older Readers

When preparing to write this chapter, I reviewed 15 studies that had examined various aspects of text design with older users. Table 14.2 shows the number of studies found for each aspect of text design.

Unfortunately, as shown in Table 14.2, there was an insufficient number of studies in each category to allow any clear generalizations from their conclusions. Furthermore, these studies varied in the kinds of tasks they used and in how they defined old age.

Type Sizes.   All five studies on type size, however, did suggest that larger type sizes were more suitable for older readers and that 12- or 14-point type seemed reasonable (Poulton, 1967, 1969; Prince, 1967; Shaw, 1969; Vanderplas & Vanderplas, 1980).

Unjustified Text.   The three studies concerning unjustified text suggested that there were advantages for unjustified text with older readers when the line lengths were short (seven to eight words long) (Gregory & Poulton, 1970, 2 studies; Zachrisson, 1965).

TABLE 14.2
The Number of Studies Found on Aspects of Text Design With Older Readers

Number of studies	Aspect
5	Type size
3	Unjustified text
2	Underlining
2	Advanced organizers
1	Signals
1	Questions in text
1	Text structure and organization

Underlining.   The two studies on underlining had mixed results—one neutral (Taub, 1894) and one positive—about whether underlining helped older readers (Taub, Sturr, & Monty, 1985).

Advance Organizers.   The two studies on advance organizers also had mixed results—one neutral (Thompson & Diefenderfer, 1986) and one positive—about whether advanced organizers helped older readers (Charness, Schumann, & Boritz, 1992).

Signals, Questions, and Text Structure.   Finally, studies with signals (Meyer & Rice, 1989), embedded questions (Woods & Bernard, 1987), and variations in text structure (Rice, Meyer, & Miller, 1989) were carried out with older readers (but not always with control groups of younger ones). *Signals* have been defined as words and phrases used to enhance the structure of the text. For example, comparisons can be signalled by the word *however* or the phrase *on the other hand.* Some researchers also include headings in their definition of a signal.

These individual studies all suggested that these various devices helped their older readers. And, in this group of studies, the one by Rice, Meyer, and Miller (1989) utilized medical materials. Here 70 older people (more than 65 years in age) read and recalled two passages containing medical information about hypertension and arthritis. Half the participants read the original passages and the other half read the passages in which the text structure had been revised so that the target ideas identified as important by medical consultants were located at higher levels in the content structure.

The results showed that the participants reading the revised passages did significantly better on free recall measures than did the participants reading the original passages, but that this effect was not found with a cloze-type comprehension test. (The cloze test involves filling in missing words; see J. Hartley, 1995.) It was also found that the participants with the revised passages recalled more main points but less details than did the participants with the original passages. And, as in other studies, educational level was important, with better educated participants doing better in both conditions.

Conclusions.   I concluded several things from reviewing these studies:

1. There were few studies of any one variable involving older participants.
2. Some of the studies just used one group of older people, so that direct comparisons with younger participants were not possible.
3. However, larger type sizes did seem to be helpful for older readers.
4. Half of the studies showed ability effects: high-ability respondents did better than low-ability respondents, irrespective of age.

5. Six of the studies showed interactions between conditions and ability. Three of these studies showed that the conditions helped the more able participants (Meyer & Rice, 1989; Rice et al., 1989; Taub, 1984), and three of them showed that the conditions helped the less able ones (Gregory & Poulton, 1970; Thompson & Diefenderfer, 1986; Zachrisson, 1965.)

6. Finally, and most devastating, few of the studies reported here actually used materials specifically designed to take into account the visual problems of their older readers. Thus, one might possibly argue that many of the older participants in these studies were reading with an additional handicap.

The Effects of Improving Typographically Complex Text for Older Readers

So far I have discussed research with texts that have had relatively simple typographic settings. I now turn to studies of older people using materials that are more complex, both typographically and literally. Such materials include, for example, bus and train schedules, labels on medicine bottles, food packaging, and government forms. Willis, Dolan, and Bertrand (chap. 12, this volume) summarized the evidence that shows that many older adults perform poorly on everyday tasks with materials such as these.

Table 14.3 lists the 10 studies that I have found in this connection.

In this section, I focus on the four examples with medical text because limitations of space prevent me from discussing all of the examples listed in Table 14.3.

Medical Insurance Policies.   Walmsley, Scott, and Lehrer (1981) assessed how good and poor readers over 60 years old ($N = 52$) fared on three versions of four documents that outlined U.S. medical insurance policies. The average length of the four original texts was 1,635 words, and their average estimated reading age level was 15 to 16 years. Two revised versions of each document were produced. The first revision simplified the texts by routinely shortening sentences and substituting easier words. The second revision was made by skilled writers aiming to clarify the text for older readers. The average estimated reading age level of the texts after the first revision was 14 to 15 years, and after the second, 12 to 13 years.

Readers were asked to read one version of each of three of the four passages for five minutes and then to answer comprehension questions without the passages being available to them. The results indicated that good readers did significantly better than poor readers, but that for only one of the four documents (the longest and the most highly simplified) was comprehension improved by using the skilled writers' version.

Informed Consent Forms.   Taub, Baker, and Sturr (1986) investigated the effects of re-writing a patient's informed consent form. The original document (283 words long) had a Flesch readability score of 45, which, according to the

TABLE 14.3
The Results of Studies Using Complex Texts with Older Readers

Topic	Main results
Readability of medical insurance policies (Walmsley et al. 1981)	Few differences (old participants only). (See text)
Readability of informed consent (Taub et al. 1986)	Slight, nonsignificant differences between forms for older and younger readers. (See text)
Medicine labels (Morrell et al. 1989)	Recall of older participants worse than that of younger ones. Marginal differences in comprehension. (See text)
Prescription information (Morrell et al. 1990)	Recall of older participants worse than that of younger ones. Older participants hindered by visual presentation; younger ones helped by it. (See text)
UK income tax forms (James, Lewis, & Allison, 1987).	Older people responded positively to changes in forms design.
Visual advance organiser (Caplan & Schooler, 1990)	Without the organizer, older and younger participants did equally well. With the organizer, older participants did worse than younger ones.
Flow charts (Michael & Hartley, 1991)	School children solved artificial problems more quickly with flowcharts than with contingency statements (if . . . then . . .). Older persons were much slower, and took the same amount of time for flowcharts and statements. Older people were confused by flowcharts.
Diagrams (Lipman & Caplan, 1992)	Older participants did worse than younger ones. The diagram improved the performance of younger participants and worsened the performance of the older ones.
Procedural instructions for assembly tasks (Morrell & Park, 1993)	Older participants did worse than younger ones. Visual instructions helped. The greater the difficulty of the task, the worse the effect on the older participants.
Food labels (Cole & Balasubramanian, 1993)	Older participants had greater difficulties than younger ones in integrating several pieces of information in order to make a decision.

formula, requires 13 to 18 years' reading skills. A revised version was produced by shortening sentences and simplifying the technical vocabulary. This version had a Flesch score of 76, now deemed suitable for 12-year-old readers.

Three groups of readers, ages 27 to 49 years ($N = 30$), 50 to 59 years ($N = 84$), and 60 to 69 years ($N = 74$), took part, and the last two groups were further subdivided into three groups in terms of their years of education. Half of the respondents in each age group were assigned to the original information sheet (low readability) and half to the revised version (high readability). After reading their passage, participants completed a 10-item multiple choice test on the contents with the passage freely available to them. The results showed that the changes in readability had no significant effects but that the readers between 60 to 69 years of age had greater difficulties than did readers between 50 to 59 years, and that these readers in turn had greater difficulties than those between 27 to 49 years. These differences were statistically significant. Furthermore, the results were affected by years of education, in that participants with more education did significantly better than those with less.

Medicine Bottle Labels.   Morrell, Park, and Poon (1989) examined both comprehension and memory for information on medicine bottles in three separate experiments with different groups of old and young participants (with an average age of 70 and 20, respectively, in each experiment). The labels were taped to the sides of the medicine bottles and were typed single-spaced on a standard 10-pica typewriter. In the first two experiments, the labels were carefully organized but, in the third experiment, real-world organizations were used by copying the layouts from actual prescription labels. In this third experiment, care was taken to ensure that all the participants had at least 20/30 corrected binocular vision.

In the first experiment, the participants listened to descriptions of how to take the appropriate medications and then, after a fixed period of study time (20 seconds), the bottles were removed and the participants were tested on their recall of the instructions. After this, with the bottles placed again in front of them, participants wrote plans describing how they would take the medicine. Thus, these procedures measured recall and comprehension. In the second and third experiments, the fixed study time was replaced by allowing the participants to pace themselves for the study period. The results indicated that in all three studies the recall of the older participants was worse than that of the younger ones and that the recall of both groups was worse as the amount of information to be recalled was increased. In experiments one and two, there were few comprehension errors for either group, but in experiment three, with the real-world labels, comprehension errors increased substantially: to 14% for the young participants and to 21% for the old participants. However, this difference between young and old participants was not statistically significant.

Prescription Information.   Morrell, Park, and Poon (1990) studied the effects of presenting prescription information in two different formats to 32 participants (average age of 71 years) and 32 more (average age of 19 years). The participants studied the labels provided on medicine bottles in one of two formats: verbal labels only and verbal labels with pictorial information (see Fig. 14.1).

The results indicated the following:

- Overall, the older participants recalled this information less well than did the younger ones.
- The younger participants recalled *more* with the illustrated format than they did with the plain text.
- The older participants recalled *less* with the illustrated format than they did with the plain text.

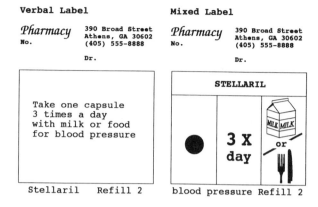

FIG. 14.1. An example of the materials used in the study by Morrell et al. (1990). From "Effects of Labelling Techniques on Memory and Comprehension of Prescription Information in Young and Old Adults," by R. W. Morrell, D. C. Park, and L. W. Poon, 1990. *Journal of Gerontology, 45*(4), p. 168. Copyright © 1990 by The Gerontological Society of America. Reprinted with permission.

Conclusions. Some conclusions can be drawn from this review:

1. There are few studies of any one variable involving older participants.
2. Two of the ten studies report data for older participants only.
3. The remaining eight studies all report that older participants do worse than younger ones (although these differences are not always significant).
4. Two studies that report ability data show that high-ability participants do better than low-ability ones, irrespective of age.
5. Three studies show that devices introduced to help the participants actually hindered the older ones.
6. Only three studies specifically report ensuring that their older participants could read the relevant materials.

The results of these studies thus suggest that the producers of complex medical text for older adults will need to give careful thought to the design of such materials. Morrell and Park (1993) pointed out that the older people could do the tasks in their study, but that they needed additional help. They suggested, in the context of their experiment, that additional subsets of instructions need to be prepared for older people. Cole and Balasubramanian (1993) found that their older participants were helped in their laboratory study if they were allowed to write down the information that they found during their search tasks.

SOME CONCLUDING REMARKS

I would like to draw three main ideas from the analyses:

1. Changes made to improve typographically simple medical information may help older readers.
2. Changes made to improve typographically complex medical information may help younger readers but, at the same time, may hinder older readers. Certainly more research needs to be conduced with older adults on their use and comprehension of diagrams, charts, and tables, to see if this is the case.
3. Methods of text production that might, inadvertently, hinder the comprehension of younger readers (e.g. printing text over photographs, the inappropriate use of colored print on colored backgrounds, and the use of 3-D rather than 2-D graphs, e.g., see Carswell, Frankenberger, & Bernhard, 1991; Siegrist, 1996) might cause even greater confusion for older adults, but this hypothesis remains to be tested.

Why should these things occur? Amongst the proffered explanations for the effects described, I would like to consider two: the "experience" or "practice" hypothesis and the "cognitive-overload" explanation.

The experience or practice hypothesis might explain the better performance of younger readers and the poorer performance of older ones reading complex texts. Modern typography is very different from that of 20 or more years ago. There has been a dramatic increase in the use of color, overprinting, and graphics in magazines and textbooks since the advent of computer-based technology. Older readers have had far more experience with traditional materials, whereas younger readers are more familiar with modern techniques. We might not therefore expect great differences between the performance of old and young readers with simple texts, but we might expect them with more complex texts.

The cognitive-overload hypothesis is connected with the decline in working memory capacity discussed earlier. Here, we might expect difficulties with reading typographically simple expository text with older readers, despite the fact that they are well practised in reading it. Kemper (1986) and Kemper and Rash (1988) provided some interesting data in this respect. Kemper and Rash showed that both in adults' speech patterns and in their written diaries, the number of clauses used within each sentence declined with age. Clearly, such data are consistent with the argument that limitations in working memory affect older adults' production and comprehension of the complex syntactic structures involved in prose comprehension and recall. Kemper, Jackson, Cheung, and Anagnopoulos (1993) discussed the instructional implications of these findings.

Basically, however, the argument of the cognitive overload theory is that material is difficult to understand when many elements must be held together in working memory (Marcus, Cooper, & Sweller, 1996). If the number of elements to be processed exceeds working memory capacity, then some elements must be combined into "chunks" or schemas before that material can be understood. Diagrams, for example, may help in this respect. But, of course, they may hinder the reader if, to understand the diagram, one has to switch one's attention to a different method of processing (see Mousavi, Low, & Sweller, 1995). The idea presented here thus suggests that older readers (with reduced memory capacity) will have greater difficulty with complex materials because these materials require more divided attention between different elements. Numbered among these elements must be the various typographical devices designers add to improve the text.

Whatever the reasons for the difficulties of older people with more complex text, there are clear implications for the production of medical texts:

- It cannot hurt to keep text simple.
- It cannot hurt to avoid fancy techniques of production.
- It cannot hurt to include some older readers when evaluating first drafts of medical texts.

Designing medical text for older persons is not likely to produce text that will confuse the young reader, but designing medical text for younger persons may well produce text that confuses older readers.

REFERENCES

Albert, T., & Chadwick, S. (1992). How readable are practice leaflets? *British Medical Journal, 305,* 1266–1268.

Babcock, R. A., & Salthouse, T. A. (1990). Effects of increased processing demands on age differences in working memory. *Psychology and Aging, 5,* 421–428.

Baddeley, A. D. (1986). *Working memory.* Oxford, England: Oxford University Press.

Bond, J., Coleman, P., & Peace, S. (Eds.). (1993). *Ageing in society: An introduction to social gerontology* (2nd ed.). London: Sage.

Byrd, M. (1985). Age differences in the ability to recall and summarize textual information. *Experimental Aging Research, 11*(2), 87–91.

Caplan, L. J., & Schooler, C. (1990). The effects of analogical training models and age on problem-solving in a new domain. *Experimental Aging Research, 16*(3), 151–154.

Carswell, C. M., Frankenberger, S., & Bernhard, D. (1991). Graphing in depth: perspectives on the use of three-dimensional graphs to represent lower-dimensional data. *Behaviour and Information Technology, 10*(6), 459–474.

Charness, N., Schumann, C. E., & Boritz, G. M. (1992). Training older adults in word processing : Effects of age, training technique, and computer anxiety. *International Journal of Technology and Aging, 5*(1), 79–106.

Cole, C. A., & Balasubramanian, S. K. (1993). Age differences in consumers' search for information: Public policy implications. *Journal of Consumer Research, 20,* 157–169.

Gregory, M., & Poulton, E. C. (1970). Even versus uneven right-hand margins and the role of comprehension reading. *Ergonomics, 13*(4), 427–434.

Hartley, J. (1994a). *Designing instructional text* (3rd ed.). London: Kogan Page.

Hartley, J. (1994b). Designing instructional text for older readers: A review. *British Journal of Educational Technology, 25*(3), 172–188.

Hartley, J. (1995). Is this chapter any use? Methods for evaluating text. In J. R. Wilson & E. N. Corlett (Eds.), *Evaluation of human work* (2nd ed., pp. 285–309). London: Taylor & Francis.

Hartley, J. T. (1989). Memory for prose: Perspectives on the reader. In L. W. Poon, D. C. Rubin, & B. A. Wilson (Eds.), *Everyday cognition in adulthood and later life* (pp. 135–156). Cambridge, England: Cambridge University Press.

Hess, T. M. (1994). Social cognition in adulthood: Aging-related changes in knowledge and processing mechanisms. *Developmental Review, 14,* 373–412.

James, S., Lewis, A., & Allison, F. (1987). *The comprehensibility of taxation: A study of taxation and communications.* Aldershot, England: Avebury.

Kemper, S. (1986). Imitation of complex syntactic constructions by elderly adults. *Applied Psycholinguistics, 7,* 277–288.

Kemper, S., Jackson, D., Cheung, H., & Anagnopoulos, C. A. (1993). Enhancing older adults' reading comprehension. *Discourse Processes, 16,* 405–428.

Kemper, S., & Rash, D. J. (1988). Speech and writing across the life-span. In M. M. Gruneberg, P. E. Morris, & R. N. Sykes (Eds.), *Practical aspects of memory* (Vol. 2, pp. 107–112). Chichester, England: Wiley.

Kosnik, W., Winslow, L., Kline, D., Rasinski, K., & Sekuler, R. (1988). Visual changes in daily life throughout adulthood. *Journal of Gerontology: Psychological Sciences, 43*(3), P63–P70.

Ley, P., & Llewelyn, S. (1995). Improving patients' understanding, recall, satisfaction and compliance. In E. Broome & S. Llewelyn (Eds.), *Health psychology* (2nd ed., pp. 75–98). London: Chapman and Hall.

Lipman, P. D., & Caplan, L. J. (1992). Adult age differences in memory for routes: Effects of instruction and spatial diagram. *Psychology and Aging, 7*(3), 435–442.

Marcus, N., Cooper, M., & Sweller, J. (1996). Understanding instructions. *Journal of Educational Psychology, 88*(1), 49–63.

Meyer, B. J. F. (in press). The importance of text structure in everyday reading. In A. Ram (Ed.), *Understanding language understanding: Computational models of reading.* Cambridge, MA: MIT Press.

Meyer, B. J. F., & Rice, G. E. (1989). Prose processing in adulthood: The text, the reader, and the task. In L. W. Poon, D. C. Rubin, & B. A. Wilson (Eds.), *Everyday cognition in adulthood and later life* (pp. 259–267). Cambridge, England: Cambridge University Press.

Meyer, B. J. F., Young, C. J., & Bartlett, B. J. (1989). *Memory improved: Reading and memory enhancement across the life-span through strategic text structures.* Hillsdale, NJ: Lawrence Erlbaum Associates.

Michael, D., & Hartley, J. (1991). Extracting information from flowcharts and contingency statements: The effects of age and practice. *British Journal of Educational Technology, 22*(2), 84–98.

Misanchuk, E. R. (1992). *Preparing instructional text: Document design using desktop publishing.* Englewood Cliffs, NJ: Educational Technology Publications.

Morrell, R. W., & Park, D. C. (1993). The effects of age, illustrations, and task variables on the performance of procedural assembly tasks. *Psychology and Aging, 8*(3), 389–399.

Morrell, R. W., Park, D. C., & Poon, L. W. (1989). Quality of instructions on prescription drug labels: Effects on memory and comprehension in young and old adults. *The Gerontologist, 29*(3), 345–354.

Morrell, R. W., Park, D. C., & Poon, L. W. (1990). Effects of labelling techniques on memory and comprehension of prescription information in young and older adults. *Journal of Gerontology, 45*(4), 166–172.

Mousavi, S. Y., Low, R., & Sweller, J. (1995). Reducing cognitive load by mixing auditory and visual presentation modes. *Journal of Educational Psychology, 87*(2), 319–334.

Pirkl, J. (1994). *Transgenerational design: Products for an aging population.* New York: Van Nostrand Reinhold.

Poulton, E. C. (1967). Skimming (scanning) news items printed in 8 point and 9 point letters. *Ergonomics, 10*(6), 713–716.

Poulton, E. C. (1969). Skimming lists of food ingredients printed in different sizes. *Journal of Applied Psychology, 53*(1), 55–58.

Prince, J. H. (1967). Printing for the visually handicapped. *Journal of Typographic Research, 1*(1), 31–47.

Reece, D. (Ed.). (1995). *How to do it. Vol. 3* (3rd ed.). London: British Medical Journal Publishing Group.

Rice, G. E., Meyer, B. J. F., & Miller, D. C. (1989). Using text structure to improve older adults' recall of important medical information. *Educational Gerontology, 15,* 527–542.

Salthouse, T. (1982). *Adult cognition: An experimental psychology of human aging.* New York: Springer-Verlag.

Schaie, K. W. (1994). The course of adult intellectual development. *American Psychologist, 49*(4), 304–313.

Schriver, K. A. (1989). Evaluating text quality: The continuum from text-focused to reader-focused methods. *I.E.E.E. Transactions on Professional Communication, 32*(4), 238–255.

Schriver, K. A. (1997). *Dynamics in document design.* New York: Wiley.

Shaw, A. (1969). *Print for partial sight.* London: Library Association.

Siegrist, M. (1996). The use or misuse of three-dimensional graphs to represent lower-dimensional data. *Behaviour and Information Technology, 15*(2), 96–100.

Taub, H. A. (1984). Underlining prose material for elderly adults. *Educational Gerontology, 10,* 401–405.

Taub, H. A., Baker, M. T., & Sturr, J. F. (1986). Informed consent for research: Effects of readability, patient age and education. *Journal of the American Geriatrics Society, 34,* 601–606.

Taub, H. A., Sturr, J. F., & Monty, R. A. (1985). The effect of underlining cues upon memory of older adults. *Experimental Aging Research, 11*(4), 225–226.

Thompson, D. N., & Diefenderfer, K. (1986). The use of advance organisers with older adults of limited verbal ability. Unpublished manuscript, Georgia State University, Department Educational Foundations, Atlanta.

Tun, P. A. (1989). Age differences in processing expository and narrative text. *Journal of Gerontology: Psychological Sciences, 44*(1), P9–P15.

Vanderplas, J. M., & Vanderplas, J. H. (1980). Some factors affecting legibility of printed materials for older adults. *Perceptual and Motor Skills, 50,* 923–932.

Walker, G. (Ed.). (1995). *Compendium of patient information leaflets 1995–6.* London: Datapharm Publications.

Walmsley, S. A., Scott, K. M., & Lehrer, R. (1981). Effects of document simplification on the reading comprehension of the elderly. *Journal of Reading Behavior, 8*(3), 237–248.

Woods, J. H., & Bernard, R. M. (1987). Improving older adults' retention of text: A test of an instructional strategy. *Educational Gerontology, 13,* 107–120.

Zachrisson, B. (1965). *Legibility of printed text.* Stockholm: Almqvist & Wiksell.

15

Designing Medication Instructions for Older Adults

Daniel Morrow
University of New Hampshire

Von O. Leirer
Decision Systems

Medication adherence is a complex set of behaviors that is influenced by a range of patient, medication, and other factors. According to some models of adherence (e.g., Park & Jones, 1997), cognitive factors such as understanding and remembering how to take medication are important components of adherence (although noncognitive factors are also important, see Park & Mayhorn, 1996). Because these components depend on getting accurate information, communication about taking medication is also critical for adherence (Morrow, Leirer, & Sheikh, 1988). Cognitive components are becoming more important as health organizations provide more complete or expanded information to patients about their medications. For example, the majority of pharmacy patients in the United States report receiving some form of expanded written instructions that augment medication labels with information such as purpose and possible side effects (U.S. Food and Drug Administration, 1995). Expanded information is also provided by automated telephone messaging systems, which are now used by many organizations to remind people to take their medications or to attend health service appointments (e.g., Tanke & Leirer, 1994). This expanded communication is partly a response to federal legislation mandating pharmacist consultation with patients in the United States (Drug Store News for the Pharmacist, 1992). It is also a response to more general federal guidelines for providing medication information to patients. For example, there is a call for the private sector to distribute "useful" expanded information about new prescribed medications to 95% of all pharmacy patients by the year 2006 (U.S. Department of Health & Human Services, 1996). However, in order to support adherence, this expanded communication must be easy to understand and remember.

The present chapter has four parts: (a) we first describe a cognitive approach to designing expanded medication instructions; (b) this is followed by a summary of several laboratory studies intended to successively refine the design of expanded instructions; (c) we then describe a preliminary study that examined the impact of expanded instructions on older adults' adherence in a simulated medication-taking task; and (d) we discuss implications of the findings for health care communication and adherence.

DESIGNING EXPANDED MEDICATION INSTRUCTIONS

Communication and Adherence

Communication is a precondition for adherence. Patients must integrate several types of information in order to create a plan for taking medication (an adherence plan). For example, they need to know what to take (name of medication), why to take it (purpose), how much and when to take it, and what warnings to keep in mind. Moreover, when taking multiple medications, patients must integrate information about these medications in order to create a daily or weekly schedule. Effective communication helps patients understand how to take their medication in the first place by providing the information needed to create an adherence plan (e.g., Morrow et al., 1988). This point is made by some models of medication adherence (Park, 1992) and by more general models of prospective memory (Einstein, Holland, McDaniel, & Guynn, 1992). According to these models, comprehension and retrospective memory are preconditions for prospective memory tasks such as remembering to take medication. Because the ability to understand and remember new information depends on cognitive resources such as working memory capacity (e.g., van Dijk & Kintsch, 1983), adherence should also depend on individual differences in these resources (Park & Jones, 1997).

Although our approach focuses on cognitive factors, we recognize that other factors play an important role in adherence. Park and her colleagues (e.g., Park & Jones, 1997; Park & Mayhorn, 1996) suggested that beliefs about the illness or the medication can influence adherence. For example, patients may understand how to take a medication, but fail to do so because they think it will not work or because they believe the costs of taking the medication (e.g., side effects) outweigh the benefits. Patients also have to integrate their adherence plan with their daily routines at work and home. Thus, adherence also depends on situational factors such as level of daily activity—people may forget to take medication because other activities compete for limited cognitive resources (Park & Mayhorn, 1996; Wilkins & Baddeley, 1988). Adherence may also depend on beliefs about cognitive abilities. Because creating and carrying out an adherence plan may require a high level of cognitive resources, successful adherence may depend on beliefs about one's ability to accomplish the task (i.e., self-efficacy beliefs, see Bandura, Cioffi, Taylor, & Brouillard, 1988). Adherence may also depend on beliefs about memory abilities, which can influence actual memory performance (Hertzog, Dixon, & Hultsch, 1990). Locus of control beliefs can also influence complex task performance. Adults with more externally directed locus of control beliefs about health care (e.g., belief in the role of powerful others or fate in determining health status) may depend more on external support for creating adherence plans (e.g., Robinson-Whelan & Storandt, 1992). To sum up, a wide range of beliefs about the medication, illness, or one's own cognitive abilities may play a role in adherence. Although our research focuses on cognitive components of adherence, we have made some preliminary attempts to link them to noncognitive components.

Aging, Communication, and Adherence

Cognitive factors may play an especially important role for adherence by older adults because of age-related declines in cognitive resources such as working memory capacity or speed of processing (Salthouse, 1991). Working memory is often viewed as a mental work space for storing and processing new information (Baddeley, 1986). Thus, it is necessary for understanding instructions or other kinds of discourse (e.g., van Dijk & Kintsch, 1983). Older adults may have trouble understanding instructions that require inferring or reorganizing information, which impose heavy demands on working memory. They may also have difficulty integrating multiple medication information into an adherence plan (Park & Jones, 1997). Therefore, older adults may particularly benefit from well-designed medication communication. Such communication may provide an environmental support that simplifies the adherence task (Craik & Jennings, 1992).

Age differences in health-related beliefs may also influence adherence. Older adults tend to hold more negative views of their memory abilities (Hertzog et al., 1990) as well as more externally oriented beliefs about health care (e.g., Robinson-Whelan & Storandt, 1992). Thus, they may depend more on external forms of support in order to create adherence plans. In short, communication is particularly likely to influence older adult adherence by either supporting or undermining cognitive and other components of adherence. This is important because older adults are more likely to use health services (e.g., World Health Organization, 1981) and thus often are likely to receive expanded instructions from their pharmacist or other forms of expanded health communication. Our goal is to help design expanded medication instructions that are more complete than typical labels. Because these instructions also present more information than most labels, they must be well designed so that they are also easier to understand and remember than labels. We also hope to improve on pharmaceutical inserts that often accompany medications or on current forms of expanded instructions provided by many pharmacies, which vary widely in terms of content and organization (U.S. Food and Drug Administration, 1995).

An Approach to Instruction Design

Levels of Discourse.   Medication instructions (like other types of discourse) can be analyzed on several levels. Instructions should have appropriate content (e.g., complete information about taking the medication), organization (e.g., the content must be arranged to create an effective instruction set), form (e.g., explicit, nontechnical terminology), and presentation medium (visual instructions, for example, text or graphic icons, or spoken instructions). We have focused on the impact of instruction content, organization, and medium on comprehension and recall of medication information (for a more general model of discourse levels, see Brewer & Lichenstein, 1981).

Situation Model Approach to Comprehension.   To fully understand instructions, narratives, or other types of text, readers must create a situation model (or mental model) that represents the described situations rather than the text itself (van Dijk & Kintsch, 1983). This involves interpreting the text in terms of prior knowledge about these situations. Readers would create a situation model of the medication-taking task by interpreting the medication instructions in terms of what they already know about the adherence task, the illness, or other topics. Thus, the ability to draw inferences by combining information in the text with knowledge provides an important type of evidence for situation models (e.g., van Dijk & Kintsch, 1983). The ability to draw inferences from medication instructions may also be important for adherence. For example, people may need to integrate dose information ("take two pills") and time information ("take at noon and in the evening") in order to create a daily or weekly adherence plan. At the same time, the process of drawing inferences can impose heavy demands on working memory because readers must keep information from the text and from long-term memory in working memory while drawing the inference (e.g., van Dijk & Kintsch, 1983).

Aging and Instruction Comprehension.   Age differences in understanding medication information may increase as comprehension becomes more difficult because of declines in working memory capacity among older adults. Older adults are more likely than younger adults to misunderstand medication labels that require inferences about medication dose or duration (Diehl, Willis, & Schaie, 1995). More general discourse research shows that age differences tend to increase for more complex discourse (e.g., faster speech rates, less predictable text), although this is not always the case (for a review, see Tun & Wingfield, 1997). Thus, well-designed instructions should reduce age differences by providing environmental support. According to Craik and Jennings (1992), environmental support in the form of external aids (e.g., pictures) or externally provided organizational strategies can simplify processing and reduce the demands of encoding or retrieving new information for older adults (also see Bäckman, Mäntylä, & Herlitz, 1990).

LABORATORY STUDIES
OF INSTRUCTION COMPREHENSION

We conducted a set of studies that examined the influence of instruction content, organization, and presentation medium on older and younger adults' comprehension of expanded medication instructions. We focused on two general ways in which instructions can support comprehension and memory. First, organizing instructions in terms of knowledge about the medication task should help older adults create a situation model by reducing the steps needed to integrate the instructions with this knowledge. Second, making instructions more explicit should reduce the amount of inferencing required to create the situation model. In both cases, the instructions should be more compatible with how readers mentally represent medication information, such as dose and time. Understanding such instructions should place fewer demands on working memory. Findings from each study also allowed us to successively refine the design of the instructions. For example, after we identified how to organize medication information to create an instruction set, we investigated how to best signal this organization.

Instruction Content

Instructions should provide enough information so that readers can create an accurate situation model for taking medication. Based on a review of the adherence literature, Morrow et al. (1988) identified at least 10 types of information that expanded instructions should contain (e.g., medication purpose, dose, time, warnings, duration, possible side effects; see Fig. 15.1 for an example). Several of these items usually are not found on medication container labels (e.g., purpose, side effects). In addition to providing information that explains how to take medication, instructions may be more effective if they present information that targets incorrect beliefs about the illness or medication. Rice and Okun (1994) included information in passages that was consistent or inconsistent with older adults' beliefs about arthritis and found that the consistent information was better remembered. Inconsistent information was better recalled when it was more explicitly presented in the passage. Carter, Beach, and Inui (1986) found that reminder messages for flu vaccinations improved clinic attendance when they contained information that addressed incorrect beliefs about side effects of the immunization. Such findings suggest that health-related beliefs influence comprehension of health information

White Pills

Identifying your medicine
   1. Name of doctor:
      Your doctor is Dr. Farley. You can call Dr. Farley at (603) 436-2200.

   2. Name of medicine:
      The name of your medicine is White Pills.

   3. Purpose of medicine:
      Your White Pills are for relief of symptoms from seasonal allergies.
How to take your medicine
   4. Dose:
      Take two pills each time.

   5. Time to take medicine:
      Take the White Pills four times each day. You should take your medicine
      at 8 a.m. in the morning, 12 noon, 4 p.m. in the afternoon, and 8 p.m. in
      the evening.

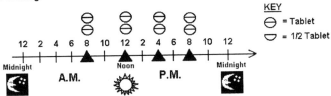

   6. How long to take medicine:
      Take your White Pills for two weeks.

   7. Warnings:
      Take with a full glass of water. If you miss a dose, take immediately upon
      remembering.

Possible side effects
   8. Mild side effects:
      Continue to take your medicine even if you experience an increase in
      appetite or feel weak. Consult your doctor only if these symptoms persist.

   9. Dangerous side effects:
      Stop taking the White Pills and call Dr. Farley if you experience heart
      palpitations or perspire excessively.

   10. In case of emergency, use your telephone and dial 911.

FIG. 15.1. Sample expanded instruction set (with time line icon).

and that instructions may need to target incorrect beliefs that undermine adherence. More generally, these studies emphasize the connections between cognitive and belief-based components of adherence.

Instruction Organization

After we identified information needed for expanded instructions, we investigated how to organize this content into an instruction set.

Schemas for Organizing Medication Instructions.   The situation model approach to comprehension emphasizes that people understand instructions in terms of what they already know about the task. This prior knowledge is represented in the form of schemas, or long-term memory structures (e.g., van Dijk & Kintsch, 1983). This may also be true for medication instructions because taking medication is often a familiar task.

If people share a schema for taking medication, they should organize medication information in similar ways. More specifically, we examined the question of whether people agree on how to order (e.g., dose should come before side effect information in instructions) and how to group information (e.g., dose and time information should be presented together). Indeed, we found that older adults (Morrow, Leirer, Altieri, & Tanke, 1991) and younger adults (Morrow, Leirer, Andrassy, Tanke, & Stine-Morrow, 1996) shared preferences for organizing medication information. These preferences suggested a schema with three categories: general information (e.g., name and purpose of the medication), how to take the medication (dose, time, duration, and warnings), and possible outcomes of taking the medication (side effects and what to do in case of an emergency). Instructions were recalled 13% to 20% more accurately when organized in terms of this medication-taking schema (i.e., information presented in a preferred order). We also examined whether age differences in health-related locus of control beliefs influenced recall (Morrow, Leirer, Andrassy, Tanke, et al., 1996). Although older adults reported more external beliefs about health care than did younger adults (also see Robinson-Whelan & Storandt, 1992), we found no evidence that age differences in these beliefs influenced instruction recall.

Signaling Organization.   Expanded instructions may be further improved if they contain cues that emphasize schema organization. These cues make instruction organization more explicit to readers. We examined whether instructions are better understood if presented as a list rather than a paragraph and if the instructions contained headers that labeled the schema categories (i.e., General Information About Your Medication; How to Take Your Medication; Possible Outcomes). These organizational cues should help readers to integrate new information from the instructions with the medication-taking schema. The list format segmented the instructions into parts because each item (e.g., medication purpose, dose) was presented on a separate line of the instruction. This format also emphasized sequential relationships between these parts. In addition, the headers emphasized the hierarchical grouping of items into larger categories.

Older adults (60–84 years of age) better understood and remembered lists than paragraphs, although headers did not improve memory (Morrow, Leirer, & Altieri, 1995). Morrow, Leirer, Andrassy, Hier, and Menard (1998) compared the impact of list formats on younger (20–30 years of age) and older (60–90 years of age) adults and found that the list format reduced age differences in comprehension time, with the list format particularly benefitting the oldest participants (more than 70 years of age). These findings suggest that the list format helps readers create a situation model because they are better able to integrate information in the instruction. More direct evidence for this conclusion comes from the finding that list formats especially improved comprehension of inferred information about the daily dose (which required integrating medication dose and time information).

Category headers did not improve instruction comprehension or memory. Headers might be more effective for instructions with more complex relationships among subsections, or if the section headers are more saliently presented in the instruction. These findings are important because many expanded instructions provided by pharmacies are organized as paragraphs rather than lists and contain a variety of headers that vary in terms of content and position in the instruction (U.S. Food and Drug Administration, 1995).

Presentation Medium

We also examined two issues related to presentation medium for medication instructions: Are instructions more effective when icon (pictorial) formats are added to text? Does organization improve recall of spoken reminders as well as printed medication instructions?

Icon and Text Formats. Instructions are often improved by adding icons that highlight important information (see Wickens, 1992, for a review). Icons may help readers construct a situation model from instructions because they are more compatible than text with how people represent spatial and temporal information (e.g., Glenberg & Langston, 1992). Icons can also be more explicit than text, reducing the need for inferences (Larkin & Simon, 1987). Older adults may especially benefit if icons reduce the amount of processing required to understand instructions. They can benefit as much as or more than younger adults when information is presented by both icon and text formats (Morrell & Park, 1993). Icons, however, have some drawbacks. For example, many concepts are not easily depicted by icons. Effective icons are difficult to create for some types of medication warnings (Wolff & Wogalter, 1993). Rather than try to develop icons for all information in expanded instructions, we examined whether expanded instructions would be improved by adding an icon that only depicted dose and time information.

The first step was to develop an icon that was easy to interpret. We investigated alternative icons that conveyed dose and time information, comparing a time line to various clock icons as well as a text-only condition (see Fig. 15.1 for an example of the time line). Older and younger adults better understood and remembered the time line than the clock icons. The time line was also interpreted as accurately as the text, although it was recalled less accurately. This may reflect the fact that the time line was a less familiar format than text for conveying medication dose and time information (Morrow, Leirer, & Andrassy, 1996).

We next investigated whether the time line icon improved comprehension of medication information when combined with text in expanded instructions. The time line may help readers create a situation model because it directly depicts information that is only implicit in the text. For example, the time line directly depicts the number of pills taken in a 24-hour period, whereas this information had to be inferred from the text. Older and younger adults were presented instructions either with or without the time line (see Fig. 15.1), and they answered questions about depicted information (dose and time) and nondepicted information (e.g., purpose, side effects).

The time line had a selective benefit, only improving comprehension of depicted information. Most important, icon benefits were greater for dose and time information that was implied rather than directly stated in the text (total daily dose), presumably because the icon reduced the amount of mental integration required to identify this information (Morrow, Hier, Menard, & Leirer, 1998).

A second experiment provided more direct evidence that the time line improves comprehension by reducing the mental integration involved in identifying dose and time information. It compared the same time line with a less integrated time line. This latter icon indicated medication-taking times on the time line, but it indicated dose information (take one or two pills each time) in a "dose per time" box that was segregated from the time line. Therefore, this version of the time line, like the text, required readers to integrate dose and time information in order to identify the total daily dose. We found that inferences about the total daily dose were drawn more quickly and accurately from the original time line than from either the less integrated time line or from the text-only instructions (Morrow, Hier, et al., 1998). This finding shows that the icon must directly or perceptually integrate dose and time information in order to improve comprehension. It also suggests that icons can help both older and younger adults create a situation model of the medication task and, more generally, that instructions are more effective when conveyed by multiple media (see also Morrell & Park, 1993; Wickens, 1992). However, the finding that the time line icon improved older as well as younger adult comprehension appears to conflict with Morrell, Park, and Poon (1990), who found that adding an icon to medication labels improved recall for younger but not older adults. This apparent discrepancy may reflect differences in the icons in the two studies. The icon in Morrell et al. (1990) consisted of three pictures that had to be integrated in order to understand the medication instructions. This icon may have increased rather than decreased the comprehension demands on older adults.

Spoken Medication Instructions.   We also investigated telephone reminder messages for taking medication. Many health organizations use automated telephone messaging systems to routinely deliver messages about medication, appointments, lab results, and other services to a wide range of patients (e.g., Tanke & Leirer, 1994). Participants in our study were presented the same information as in the printed medication instruction study (Morrow, Leirer, Andrassy, Tanke, et al., 1996) and were asked to create telephone medication reminder messages. Older and younger adults organized these reminders in much the same way that the printed medication instructions had been organized in the previous study, suggesting that they organized medication reminders and expanded instructions according to the same schema. In addition, both spoken and printed versions of the reminders were better recalled when the medication information was presented according to the schema (Morrow, Carver, Leirer, & Tanke, 1998).

Expanded Instructions and Medication Labels

The studies described to this point helped to identify appropriate content, organization, and presentation medium for expanded medication instructions. These instructions should present information in an order that matches readers' medication-taking schema, with the text formatted as a list and augmented by a time line icon (whether adding other icons would further improve expanded instructions is an open question). We then tested whether these expanded instructions were better remembered than instructions similar to medication container labels. Expanded instructions should be better remembered than labels (even though they are longer) because they are more explicit and are organized to match readers' schemas. We also varied the number of instructions that participants studied in order to examine the impact of memory load on recall. This issue is important because older adults often take multiple medications and therefore must keep track of several instructions at the same time (World Health Organization, 1981). Higher memory load may increase age differences in recall because of increased demands on working memory capacity, which tends to decline with age (Salthouse, 1991). We also wanted to know if increased memory load would eliminate the benefits of instruction organization on recall.

Older and younger participants studied either one or three instructions at a time and then recalled the instructions. These instructions were presented either as expanded instructions or as labels. The analyses focused on information that occurred on both expanded instructions and on labels (e.g., medication name, dose, time, warnings). Expanded instructions were recalled more accurately (Expanded = 49% items recalled, Label = 38% items recalled). Recall was also higher for the low memory load condition, that is, when one rather than three instructions were studied (Low Load = 63% items per instruction recalled, High Load = 49% items recalled), but this memory load effect did not diminish the benefit of the expanded instruction on recall. Although older participants recalled less overall (34% vs. 53%), the magnitude of the age difference was not increased by the high memory load condition. Similarly, Morrell, Park, and Poon (1989) found that memory load (number of medication labels studied for a recall test) reduced recall but did not increase the magnitude of the age difference. To sum up, our study established that older and younger adults better remembered expanded instructions than medication labels, even when multiple instructions were studied.

EXPANDED COMMUNICATION AND SIMULATED MEDICATION ADHERENCE

We investigated whether the comprehension and memory advantages of expanded instructions in the laboratory translate into improved adherence in a simulated medication-taking task. Instead of actually taking medication, participants used credit-card size "time wands" to scan bar codes corresponding to different medications. In this way, they recorded the date and time that they remembered to take medications. This technology has been used to measure simulated (Leirer, Morrow, Pariante, & Sheikh, 1988) and actual medication adherence (Park, Morrell, Frieske, & Kincaid, 1992). The simulated adherence task was fairly complex, with participants required to remember four medications with different schedules. We examined whether older adults would more accurately perform this simulated task when they used expanded instructions (including a daily calendar that summarized the four medication schedules) rather than medication labels. The expanded instructions should support adherence by helping people understand and remember how to take the medication, for example by eliminating errors related to violating warnings (e.g., combining incorrect medications).

As pointed out earlier, adherence may depend as much on noncognitive factors as on cognitive factors such as instruction comprehension (Park & Mayhorn, 1996). For example, people may understand and remember how to take their medication yet forget or choose not to do so because they are too busy or they decide that the task is less important than other plans. Thus, another goal of the study was to identify individual differences on a variety of demographic, situational, and cognitive variables that may predict adherence. We gathered information about participants' level of education and cognitive ability (vocabulary and sentence span working memory tests), their level of daily activity (e.g., hours per day devoted to work, volunteer activities, and hobbies), and reminding strategies that they used during the study. We also measured general beliefs about their memory ability (Lowen, Shaw, & and Craik, 1990), locus of control beliefs about health care (Robinson-Whelan & Storandt, 1992), and a specific measure of participants' confidence in their ability to perform medication-taking tasks (modeled after self-efficacy measures, see Bandura et al., 1988).

Forty older adults (mean age = 72.5 years) participated in the study for 2 weeks. Half used expanded medication instructions and half used typical medication labels (the two groups did not differ in age, education, cognitive ability, or amount of reported daily activity). Several types of errors in the simulated medication-taking task were examined, including omissions (missed medication times) and errors that reflected violations of warnings in the instructions (e.g., incorrect combination of medications). We analyzed the percentage of omissions (the most frequent type of error) by a Group (Expanded vs. Label instructions) × Schedule Complexity (medications taken 1–4 times per day) × Week (first or second week of study) analysis of variance (ANOVA), with the latter two variables repeated measures. The two instruction groups did not differ in errors (Expanded Instruction: 4.4% missed medication-taking times, Label: 6.3%, $p > .10$). Errors increased with complexity (4 medication times per day = 6.5% errors; 3 times = 7.3%; 2 times = 5.5%, 1 time = 2.2%, linear trend $p < .001$), but did not increase from week 1 to 2 (4.9% vs. 5.9%, $p > .10$).

There are several reasons why expanded instructions may not have improved adherence in this simulated task. First, participants in both instruction groups did very well—error rates were much lower than typical estimates of nonadherence (e.g., Leirer et al., 1988). This may reflect the fact that participants in the study were well-educated, healthy, and in their 60s and early 70s, an age group that may be particularly adherent (Park & Jones, 1997). Second, as we will see, the majority of participants in the label group created their own external memory aids, which they appeared to use in place of the label instructions to support adherence. Third, the low error rates may reflect the novelty of the bar code scanners, and more errors might have occurred over a longer data collection period (Park & Jones, 1997). Finally, we may not have successfully simulated important aspects of the medication-taking task. For example, because participants were not actually taking medication, we could not examine the possibility that expanded instructions would better explain what to do in case of side effects.

Adherence errors did relate to some individual difference variables. Those participants who reported higher levels of daily activity also had more omission errors ($r = .38$, $p < .05$). This relationship suggests that high levels of concurrent activity can compete with the prospective memory task for limited cognitive resources (Einstein et al., 1992; Wilkins & Baddeley, 1988).

Self-reported reminding strategies also influenced errors. After completing the study, participants were asked which of the following strategies they used: (a) memory (e.g., images, associations), (b) the instructions (Label or Expanded), (c) visual aids (e.g., calendars), (d) physical devices (e.g., beeper), or (e) another person (i.e., collaborative reminding). Forty-eight percent of the participants reported using a visual aid or physical device (for the Expanded group this was usually the calendar that we provided whereas participants in the Label group created their own aids). Some reported relying only on their memory (14%) or a combination of memory, instructions, or external strategies (38%). Participants in the two instruction groups did not differ in the frequency of these strategies.

A post hoc analysis of the influence of reminding strategies on omission errors compared participants who used external strategies (visual aids or physical devices, $n = 18$), participants who relied on their memory or on the instructions ($n = 7$), and those who used both external and memory strategies ($n = 12$). These three groups did not differ in age, education, cognitive ability, or amount of daily activity. Strategy type influenced errors. Participants who used external aids made fewer errors (3.3%) than those who relied on memory (6.6%) or a mix of strategies (8.3%), $p < .01$. Participants relying on their memory or on the instructions, on the other hand, did appear to make better use of the instructions. They recalled more information from the instructions during a cued recall test at the end of the study (37% items in the instruction correctly remembered) compared to the external group (22% items correct) or the mixed strategy group (29% correct). It is interesting that memory strategy participants also made fewer adherence errors that reflected violations of instruction warnings (Memory = 0.2% errors, External = 0.5% warning errors, Both = 1.4% errors). These findings converge with other studies to show that external aids such as calendars can improve adherence (e.g., MacDonald, MacDonald, & Phoenix, 1977; but see Park et al., 1992), although it is not clear if these aids improve comprehension, prospective memory, or both.

Finally, we found that participants in the two instructional groups differed in self-efficacy beliefs related to medication-taking. Both before and after the adherence study, we measured confidence (on a scale from 0–100%) in the ability to follow scenarios that described medication schedules of varying difficulty. The ratings were analyzed by an Instruction Group (Expanded vs. Label) × Scenario Difficulty (Low, Medium, or High) × Time (Before vs. After study) ANOVA, with the latter two variables repeated measures. A Group × Time interaction showed that confidence declined after the study for participants in the Label group (Before = 92.8, After = 87.5), but not for participants in the Expanded Instruction group (Before = 91.2, After = 92.7). Omission errors were related to both prestudy ratings (Label: $r = -.58$, $p < .01$; Expanded $r = -.54$, $p < .05$; higher ratings, fewer errors), and poststudy ratings (Label $r = -.35$, $p > .10$; Expanded $r = -.42$, $p < .10$; the correlations between errors and prestudy ratings, and between errors and poststudy ratings did not differ). Thus, self-efficacy beliefs may play a role in adherence, as suggested by Park's (1992) psychosocial model of medication adherence.

To summarize, we found that instructions had only a limited impact on adherence in this simulated medication-taking task, and this influence is best understood within the context of both cognitive and noncognitive factors. First, participants who reported using external aids in the study had fewer omission errors than those who reported relying on their memory or on the instructions. This fits with other evidence that older adults often rely on external reminding strategies (e.g., Lowen et al., 1990; but see Gould, chap. 10, this volume). However, there appeared to be a trade-off between using external aids and memory-based strategies in our study. Although those who reported relying on external aids had fewer missed medication times, they also remembered less information from the instructions and were more likely to commit specific adherence errors that reflected a failure to follow instruction warnings. Second, we found that the amount of participants' daily activity during the study (in both instruction groups) predicted adherence errors. Those who reported more hours of activity were more likely to miss medication times. Finally, expanded instructions appeared to influence participants' confidence in their ability to take medication correctly. Participants in the medication label but not the expanded instruction group were less confident in their ability to follow complex medication schedules after the 2-week study, suggesting that even though expanded instructions did not improve actual adherence, they may have supported older adults' beliefs about the ability to take medication.

HEALTH COMMUNICATION AND OLDER ADULT ADHERENCE

Our findings support several principles for designing medication instructions. These principles fit into a broader collaborative approach to health communication for older adults that encompasses face-to-face communication, automated telephone messages, and written materials such as instructions or educational pamphlets (Morrow, 1997). According to this approach, health professionals and patients work together to ensure messages are mutually understood. Professionals must produce messages that they think will be understood based on shared knowledge about the health service, the client, and other topics. They must also monitor the ongoing communication to make sure the message is understood. Patients in turn must indicate whether they understand the message (see Clark & Schaefer, 1989, for a general discussion of collaborative processes).

The following principles for improving expanded medication instructions may also improve collaboration in a variety of health communication contexts. First, instructions that are organized in terms of medication-taking schemas should help readers create a situation model from the instructions. This compatibility principle also applies to other types of health messages. For example, older and younger adults share preferences for organizing information about attending health service appointments, and telephone appointment messages are better remembered when organized to match these preferences (Morrow, Leirer, Carver, & Tanke, in press). Shared schemas about health-related information may also support face-to-face communication. Pharmacists may improve consultations with their clients by relying on shared schemas so that they present information in an order that makes sense to the client (Morrow, 1997).

Second, medication instructions should be explicit, which reduces the amount of inferencing necessary to construct situation models. Instructions were better understood and remembered when presented as a list rather than a paragraph, perhaps because the list format emphasized, or explicitly signaled, the schematic order of information. List formats also facilitated the ability of older and younger adults to draw inferences from the instructions, presumably by segmenting the instructions so that the information necessary for drawing the inference was easier to identify. Expanded instructions were also made more explicit by adding a time line icon to the text. This icon appeared to reduce inferring by directly depicting information that was only implicit in the text. Thus, it provided perceptual support for creating a situation model from the instructions.

We expected instructions embodying these principles to differentially benefit older adults by providing environmental support that simplified comprehension (e.g., Craik & Jennings, 1992). However, evidence for this prediction was limited. List formats reduced age differences for comprehension time (Morrow, Leirer, et al., 1998), but schema-compatible organization (Morrow, Leirer, Andrassy, Tanke, et al., 1996) and the presence of time line icons (Morrow, Hier, et al., 1998) equally benefited older and younger participants. Nonetheless, it is important that older adults benefited as much as younger adults from improved instructions.

We also predicted that well-designed instructions would help people remember to take medication because they improve comprehension and retrospective memory for medication information. The preliminary study of simulated adherence did not support this prediction, perhaps because of limitations of the study's procedure and sample. More positively, some findings from this study raise important issues about how to integrate medication instructions with other cognitive and noncognitive components of adherence. For example, many participants used external aids. These aids reduced omission errors, but they also appeared to increase errors that reflected violations of instruction warnings, suggesting that they focused attention on medication-taking times at the expense of warning information. Thus, it may be important to more fully integrate external aids and medication instructions by, for example, including warning as well as dose and time information on calendars or other aids.

More generally, different types of health communication can be viewed as multiple resources. If they are designed to be mutually reinforcing, patients and health professionals can more effectively achieve collaborative goals at each step of the health service process. For example, patients rely on face-to-face communication with doctors and other professionals when a medical problem is diagnosed and treatment prescribed. They rely on both spoken and written communication with pharmacists when filling prescriptions. At home, they use medication labels and expanded instructions in order to take the medication. They also may rely on live or automated telephone communication in order to be reminded of appointments for further care or to monitor the outcome of medical treatments. These various forms of communication will be more effective if they are explicitly integrated or coordinated so that there is a consistent flow of information between health organization and patient. Thus, consultations between patients and pharmacists can be organized around client schemas for taking medication, which will ensure that this communication is consistent with the expanded medication instructions used at home (Morrow, 1997). Automated telephone messages can be similarly organized. In addition to making different forms of health communication consistent, they also need to be integrated with noncognitive components of adherence. For example, adherence errors in the simulated adherence study increased with the level of participants' daily activity during the study. This suggests the importance of developing communication aids that help link adherence plans with other daily plans. For example, medication-taking times and health service appointments could be integrated with other important events in a daily or weekly planner. A more comprehensive approach to health communication that encompasses noncognitive and cognitive components of adherence will become even more important in the future as communication about health services continues to expand with new technology.

ACKNOWLEDGMENTS

Support provided by NIA grants R01 AGO9254 and R01 AG12163.

REFERENCES

Bäckman, L., Mäntyla, T., & Herlitz, A. (1990). The optimization of episodic remembering in old age. In P. B. Baltes & M. M. Baltes (Eds.), *Successful aging: Perspectives from the behavioral sciences* (pp. 118–163). Cambridge, England: Cambridge University Press.

Baddeley, A. D. (1986). *Working memory.* New York: Oxford University Press.

Bandura, A., Cioffi, D., Taylor, C., & Brouillard, M. (1988). Perceived self-efficacy in coping with cognitive stressors and opioid activation. *Journal of Personality and Social Psychology, 55,* 479–488.

Brewer, W., & Lichtenstein, E. (1981). Event schemas, story schemas, and story grammars. In J. Long & A. Baddeley (Eds.), *Attention & Performance IX* (pp. 363–379). Hillsdale, NJ: Lawrence Erlbaum Associates.

Carter, W., Beach, L., & Inui, T. S. (1986). The flu shot study: Using multiattribute utility theory to design a vaccination intervention. *Organizational Behavior and Human Decision Processes, 38,* 378–391.

Clark, H. H., & Schaefer, E. F. (1989). Contributing to discourse. *Cognitive Science, 13,* 259–294.

Craik, F. I. M., & Jennings, J. M. (1992). Human memory. In F.I.M. Craik & T.A. Salthouse (Eds.), *The handbook of aging and cognition* (pp. 51–110). Hillsdale, NJ: Lawrence Erlbaum Associates.

Diehl, M., Willis, S. L., & Schaie, W. (1995). Everyday problem solving in older adults: Observational assessment and cognitive correlates. *Psychology and Aging, 10,* 478–491.

Drug Store News for the Pharmacist. (1992, December). *1993 Pharmacist's reference for patient counseling [Special supplement],* 2.

Einstein, G., Holland, L., McDaniel, M., & Guynn, M. (1992). Age-related deficits in prospective memory: The influence of task complexity. *Psychology and Aging, 7,* 471–478.

Glenberg, A. M., & Langston, W. (1992). Comprehension of illustrated text: Pictures help to build mental models. *Journal of Memory and Language, 31,* 129–151.

Hertzog, C., Dixon, R. A., & Hultsch, D. F. (1990). Metamemory in adulthood: Differentiating knowledge, belief and behavior. In T. M. Hess (Ed.), *Aging and cognition: Knowledge organization and utilization* (pp. 161–212). Amsterdam: North-Holland.

Larkin, J. H., & Simon, H. A. (1987). Why a diagram is (sometimes) worth ten thousand words. *Cognitive Science, 11,* 65–99.

Leirer, V. O., Morrow, D. G., Pariante, G. M. & Sheikh, J. I. (1988). Elders' nonadherence, its assessment, and computer-assisted instruction for medication recall training. *Journal of the American Geriatrics Society, 36,* 877–884.

Loewen, E. R., Shaw, R. J., & Craik, F. I. M. (1990). Age differences in components of metamemory. *Experimental Aging Research, 16,* 43–48.

MacDonald, E. T., MacDonald, J. B., & Phoenix, M. (1977). Improving drug compliance after hospital discharge. *British Medical Journal, 2,* 618–621.

Morrell, R., & Park, D. (1993). The effects of age, illustrations, and task variables on the performance of procedural assembly tasks. *Psychology and Aging, 9,* 389–399.

Morrell, R., Park, D., & Poon, L. (1989). Quality of instructions on prescription drug labels: Effects on memory and comprehension in young and old adults. *The Gerontologist, 29,* 345–354.

Morrell, R., Park, D., & Poon, L. (1990). Effects of labeling techniques on memory and comprehension of prescription information in young and older adults. *Journal of Gerontology: Psychological Sciences, 45,* P166–P172.

Morrow, D. G. (1997). Improving consultations between health professionals and clients: Implications for pharmacists. *International Journal of Aging and Human Development, 44,* 47–72.

Morrow, D. G., Carver, L. M., Leirer, V. O., & Tanke, E. D. (1998). *Influence of schema organization on comprehension and recall of medication reminder messages.* Manuscript in preparation.

Morrow, D. G., Hier, C. M., & Leirer, V. O. (1998). Icons improve older and younger adult comprehension of medication information. *Journal of Gerontology: Psychological Sciences, 53B,* P240–P254.

Morrow, D. G., Leirer, V. O., & Altieri, P. (1995). List formats improve medication instructions for older adults. *Educational Gerontology, 21,* 163–178.

Morrow, D. G., Leirer, V. O., Altieri, P., & Tanke, E. D. (1991). Elders' schema for taking medication: Implications for instruction design. *Journal of Gerontology: Psychological Sciences, 48,* P378–P385.

Morrow, D. G., Leirer, V. O., & Andrassy, J. M., (1996). Using icons to convey medication schedule information. *Applied Ergonomics, 27,* 267–275.

Morrow, D. G., Leirer, V. O., Andrassy, J. M., Tanke, E. D., & Stine-Morrow, E. A. L. (1996). Age differences in schemes for taking medication. *Human Factors, 38,* 556–573.

Morrow, D. G., Leirer, V. O., Andrassy, J. M., Hier, C. M., & Menard, W. E. (1998). The influence of list format and category headers on age differences in understanding medication instructions. *Experimental Aging Research, 24,* 231–256.

Morrow, D. G., Leirer, V. O., Carver, L. M., & Tanke, E. D. (in press). Older and younger adult memory for memory for health appointment information: Implications for automated telephone messaging design. *Journal of Experimental Psychology: Applied.*

Morrow, D. G., Leirer, V. O., & Sheikh, J. (1988). Adherence and medication instructions: Review and recommendations. *Journal of the American Geriatric Society, 36,* 1147–1160.

Park, D. C. (1992). Applied cognitive aging research. In F. I. M. Craik & T. A. Salthouse (Eds.), *The handbook of aging and cognition* (pp. 449–493). Hillsdale, NJ: Lawrence Erlbaum Associates.

Park, D. C., & Jones, T. R. (1997). Medication adherence and aging. In A. D. Fisk & W. A. Rogers (Eds.), *Handbook of human factors and the older adult* (pp. 257–287). San Diego, CA: Academic Press.

Park, D. C., & Mayhorn, C. B. (1996). Remembering to take medications: The importance of nonmemory variables. In D. Hermann, C. McEvoy, C. Hertzog, P. Hertel, & M. Johnson (Eds.), *Basic and applied memory research* (Vol. 2, pp. 95–110). Mahwah, NJ: Lawrence Erlbaum Associates.

Park, D. C., Morrell, R. W., Frieske, D., & Kincaid, D. (1992). Medication adherence behaviors in older adults: Effects of cognitive interventions. *Psychology and Aging, 7,* 252–256.

Rice, G. E., & Okun, M. A. (1994). Older readers' processing of medical information that contradicts their beliefs. *Journal of Gerontology: Psychological Sciences, 49,* P119–P128.

Robinson-Whelen, S., & Storandt, M. (1992). Factorial structure of two health belief measures among older adults. *Psychology and Aging, 7,* 209–213.

Salthouse, T. (1991). Mediation of adult age differences in cognition by reductions in working memory and speed of processing. *Psychological Science, 2,* 179–183.

Tanke, E. D., & Leirer, V. O. (1994). Automated telephone reminders in tuberculosis care. *Medical Care, 32,* 380–389.

Tun, P. A., & Wingfield, A. (1997). Language and communication: Fundamentals of speech communication and language processing in old age. In A. D. Fisk & W. A. Rogers (Eds.), *Handbook of human factors and the older adult* (pp. 125–150). San Diego, CA: Academic Press.

U.S. Department of Health and Human Services. (1996). Prescription drug information for patients: Notice of request for collaboration to develop an action plan. *Federal Register, 6,* No. 166, 43769.

U.S. Food and Drug Administration. (1995). Prescription Drug Labeling; Medication Guide Requirements; Proposed Rule. *Federal Register, 60,* No. 164, Health and Human Services, Food and Drug Administration. CFR Parts 201, 208, 314, and 601.

van Dijk, T., & Kintsch, W. (1983). *Strategies of discourse comprehension.* New York: Academic Press.

Wickens, C. D. (1992). *Engineering psychology and human performance* (2nd Ed). New York: HarperCollins.

Wilkins, A. J., & Baddeley, A. D. (1988). Remembering to recall in everyday life: An approach to absentmindedness. In M. M. Gruneberg, P. E. Morris, & R. N. Sykes (Eds.), *Practical aspects of memory* (pp 27–34). New York: Academic Press.

Wolff, J. S., & Wogalter, M. S. (1993). Test and development of pharmaceutical pictorials. *Interface '93,* 187–192.

World Health Organization. (1981). Health care in the elderly: Report of the Technical Group on the use of medications by the elderly. *Drugs, 22,* 279–294.

16

Maximizing the Effectiveness
of the Warning Process:
Understanding the Variables
That Interact With Age

Wendy A. Rogers
Gabriel K. Rousseau
Georgia Institute of Technology

Nina Lamson
The University of Georgia

A perusal of any room in the house would reveal an array of warnings. For example, the medicine cabinet in the bathroom is filled with products that contain warnings. There are the obvious items, such as prescription and over-the-counter medicines, but also a variety of other types of warnings, such as those on nail polish remover (*Caution: Flammable, keep away from flame*); shaving cream (*Warning: Contents under pressure. Do not puncture or incinerate*); and even deodorant (*Warning: Do not use on broken skin. If a rash develops, discontinue use*). Other products in the bathroom, such as hair dryers, curling irons, and electric razors, also carry warnings. In addition, individuals with diabetes might have blood glucose monitors and hypodermic needles, asthmatics might have inhalers, people with glaucoma might have special eye drops, and so on. These products comprise only some of the items in the bathroom and, obviously, the bathroom is only one room in the house. Thus, we are faced with a large number of warnings in our daily lives.

The field of human factors is particularly relevant to the study of warnings, because one of its primary goals is to ensure the safety of individuals as they interact with products and systems. Consequently, human factors experts are concerned with determining when, where, and which warnings are attended to and complied with in an effort to design better warning systems and ensure the safety of consumers.

A *warning* is anything that alerts one's attention to a potentially dangerous situation. For example, a stop sign, a fire alarm, and a blinking light may all be considered types of warnings. However, an ideal warning is one that alerts to the hazard, describes the hazard, explains the consequences of the hazard, and instructs about what to do or not to do to avoid the hazard. For example, a sign that says *"Danger! Strong Undertow. You could drown. Do not swim or wade in this water."* contains all of the primary elements of a warning. Another example is *"Caution! Drug interacts with alcohol and will cause drowsiness. Do not drink alcohol while on this medication."* It is important to provide all of these elements in a warning: signal words (Danger, Warning, Caution) serve to alert a person to the level of the hazard; the description and explanation of the hazard enable a person to understand what might or will happen if the warning is ignored; and the instructions inform a person about how to avoid the hazard. Unfortunately, even if a warning label or sign has these elements, it still may not be heeded.

Whether a warning will successfully affect behavior is a complicated issue. Rogers, Lamson, and Rousseau (1998) described the warning process as having four major components: (a) Notice the warning—attention is directed to the warning; (b) Encode the warning—external information is translated into some internal representation through reading words, processing symbols, and so on; (c) Comprehend the warning—the meaning of the warning is understood; and (d) Comply with the warning—behavior is in accordance with the warning (see also DeJoy & Wogalter, 1993; Laughery & Brelsford, 1991; Purswell, Krenek, & Dorris, 1987; Sanders & McCormick, 1993; Wogalter & Laughery, 1996; Wogalter & Sojourner, chap. 17, this volume, for other classifications of the warning process). The Rogers et al. (1998) conceptualization is presented in Fig. 16.1.

A warning can only be effective if it is noticed, encoded, comprehended, and complied with. In addition, a warning is only considered effective if it results in a higher level of compliance than if it were not present (Adams & Edworthy, 1995). For example, if 60% of the users of a pesticide wear gloves and the provision of a warning resulted in 62% of the users wearing gloves, the warning would not be considered very effective.

The warning process is a complex, multifaceted system that can be influenced by a number of different variables. The Rogers et al. (1998) review of the warning literature revealed two major classes of variables that influence the warning process, namely, person variables and warning variables. *Person variables* are those that vary among the individuals encountering the warning, such as age, sex,

WARNING PROCESS

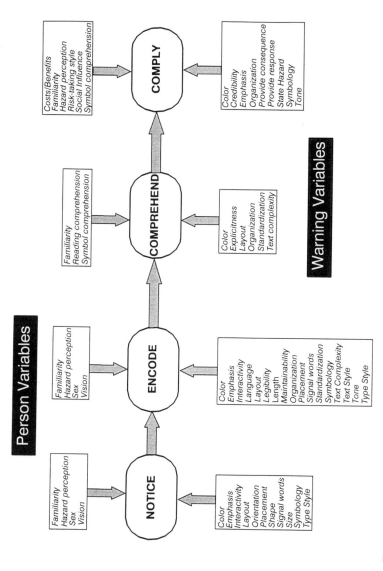

FIG. 16.1. Components of the warning process and the variables that have been empirically demonstrated to affect the process. Definitions of the components are as follows: *Notice*—attention is directed toward the warning; *Encode*—external information is translated into some internal representation through reading words, processing symbols, and so on; *Comprehend*—the meaning of the warning is understood; *Comply*—behavior is in accordance with the warning. The variable categories and definitions were adapted from Rogers, Lamson, and Rousseau (1998).

269

vision, familiarity, comprehension ability, and risk-taking style. *Warning variables* refer to characteristics of the warning itself, the context in which the warning is presented, and the characteristics of the product or task. As is evident in Fig. 16.1, both person and warning variables affect each component of the warning process. For example, a person with poor vision (a person variable) is not likely to notice and successfully encode a warning. However, the placement of the warning (a warning variable) influences whether it is noticed or encoded. Similarly, an individual's familiarity with a warning will influence the degree to which it is comprehended and complied with. On the warning side, comprehension will be influenced by the text complexity and compliance will depend on whether the warning provides the appropriate response for handling a product safely. The distinction between person and warning variables is critical for a thorough analysis of the effectiveness of the warning process.

OVERVIEW AND SCOPE OF CHAPTER

The goal of our chapter is to understand the variables in the warning process that may interact with aging and, consequently, have an effect on the warning process. That is, as individuals grow older, what are the physical, cognitive, and personality changes that might be affected and subsequently influence the components of the warning process? To that end, we focus on the person variables in Fig. 16.1. The variables included in the figure represent those variables that have been empirically demonstrated to influence the warning process (see Rogers et al., 1998). Clearly there are many more warning than person variables that have been investigated. This dearth of empirical research on person variables is the impetus for our chapter.

Table 16.1 presents the specific person variables that we focus on and shows their definitions and sources of age-relevant research. Several cognitive variables are not included, either in Fig. 16.1 or Table 16.1 because their influence on the warning process has not been empirically investigated. These include attention, working memory, and prospective memory. Although the importance of these variables is often mentioned in overviews of warning issues (e.g., Ayres et al., 1989; Laughery & Brelsford, 1991; Lehto & Miller, 1988; Purswell et al., 1987), their effects on warnings have not been studied, either for the general population or specifically for older adults. In addition, some of the variables represented in Table 16.1 have been investigated within the warning literature but not specifically with respect to older adults.

We have opted to focus on visually presented warnings to the exclusion of auditory warnings, primarily due to space considerations. However, the consequences of age-related hearing declines (see Kline & Scialfa, 1997) on the effectiveness of auditory warnings warrants investigation. For a general review of issues relevant to auditory warnings, see the excellent text by Adams and Edworthy (1995), and for issues relevant to older adults and auditory warnings, see Rousseau, Lamson, and Rogers (1998).

TABLE 16.1
Person Variable Definitions and Relevant Sources

Variable	Definition	Component Influenced	Relevant Sources
Vision	Visual capacity (e.g., contrast sensitivity, acuity)	notice, encode	Backinger and Kingsley (1993); Morrell and Echt (1997); Wogalter and Dietrich (1995)
Sex	Male, female	notice, encode	
Familiarity	Prior experience with products or warnings	notice, encode, comprehend, comply	Fincham (1986); Morrow et al. (1996); Ostrom et al. (1985); Rice and Okun (1994); Silver et al. (1993); Vigilante and Wogalter (1996); Wright et al. (1982)
Hazard perception	Subjective level of danger	notice, encode, comply	Fincham (1986); Wogalter et al. (1994)
Reading comprehension	The ability to understand textual information	comprehend	Meyer et al. (1993); Williams et al. (1995)
Symbol comprehension	Ability to understand what a symbol represents	comprehend	Collins (1983); Collins and Lerner (1982); Easterby and Hakiel (1981); Lambert and Fleury (1994); Morrell et al. (1990)
Costs/benefits	Advantages/disadvantages of compliance and noncompliance	comply	
Risk-taking style	Propensity to engage in dangerous behavior	comply	Zuckerman et al. (1978)
Social influence	Basing your behavior on the actions of others	comply	

NOTE: Definitions of the components are as follows: *Notice*—attention is directed toward the warning; *Encode*—external information is translated into some internal representation through reading words, processing symbols, and so on; *Comprehend*—the meaning of the warning is understood; *Comply*—behavior is in accordance with the warning. The variable categories and definitions were adapted from Rogers, Lamson, and Rousseau (1998). The sources listed here are studies that have specifically addressed the effects of aging on these person variables.

We also limit our scope to a discussion of healthy, cognitively intact older individuals (over age 60). There has been relatively little research on the warning process for older adults in general, much less for older individuals who are in poor physical or mental health. We can reasonably assume that the effects we report for healthy, cognitively intact older individuals will represent the best case scenario for the entire population of persons over age 60.

A general tenet of human factors design is that safety should be ensured through the design of the system; if the potential hazard cannot be designed out, then it should be guarded against; if guarding is not possible, then an adequate warning system should be developed (Sanders & McCormick, 1993). To illustrate within the domain of medical warnings, a home-based intravenous perfusion pump should be designed such that incorrect dosages cannot be administered. If this is not possible, then an automatic shutoff could be incorporated to guard against overdoses. Designers should rely on warnings to convey the potential dangers of the system only as a last resort.

Warnings on prescriptions or over-the-counter medicines often do not meet the first two tenets of human factors design. Consequently, warnings are the primary means to ensure safe usage by the consumers. Given that 75% of older adults report using prescription drugs and 82% report using over-the-counter drugs, understanding warnings on pharmaceuticals is particularly important for the health and safety of older adults (Kart, Dunkle, & Lockery, 1994). Kart et al. also reported that older Americans have been estimated to consume 30% of all prescription drugs. Moreover, 12% to 17% of acute hospital admissions for patients older than age 70 have been attributed to adverse drug reactions, indicating that warnings may be going unheeded for this population.

Samples from over-the-counter medicines are presented in Table 16.2 and are used at various points in the chapter to illustrate difficulties that might be encountered when trying to interpret warnings. These samples were selected from the classes of medicines most often used by older adults, such as analgesics and laxatives (Fleming, Pulliam, Perfetto, Hanlon, & Bowling, 1993).

We now present the variables we have identified that may interact with age and, consequently, have an effect on the warning process. In each section, we describe the importance of the variable for warnings in general (see Rogers et al., 1998, for additional details) followed by a review of the status of age-related research on that variable.

VISION

Age-related declines in visual functioning have been well documented. In their recent review, Kline and Scialfa (1997) reported that older adults have poorer visual acuity, contrast sensitivity, acuity for peripheral targets, and color discrimination than younger adults. Older individuals also have more difficulty with glare, yet they need stronger light sources to maximize their visual capability. These visual changes will affect the likelihood that an older person will first notice a warning sign or label as well as whether he or she will be able to read or encode the contents of the label.

Kline and Scialfa (1997) made some general recommendations for enhancing the visual performance of older adults, some of which are particularly relevant to the warning process (see also Charness & Bosman, 1992; Rousseau et al., 1998).

TABLE 16.2

Examples of Over-The-Counter Pharmaceutical Warnings

Product	Sample from Warning
Ibuprofen	WARNING:. . .Do not take for pain for more than 10 days or for fever for more than 3 days unless directed by a doctor. If pain or fever persists or gets worse, if new symptoms occur, or if the painful area is red or swollen, consult a doctor. These could be signs of serious illness. . . . If you experience any symptoms which are unusual or seem unrelated to the condition for which you took ibuprofen, consult a doctor before taking any more of it. . . . Although ibuprofen is indicated for the same conditions as aspirin and acetaminophen, it should not be taken with them except under a doctor's direction. Do not combine this product with any other ibuprofen containing product. . . . In case of accidental overdose, seek professional assistance or contact a poison control center immediately.
Naproxen Sodium	GENERAL WARNINGS: Do not take (brandname) for more than 10 days for pain, or for more than 3 days for fever unless directed by a doctor. Consult a doctor if: your pain or fever persists or gets worse, the painful area is red or swollen, you take any other drugs on a regular basis, you have had serious side effects from any pain reliever, you have any new or unusual symptoms, more than mild heartburn, upset stomach, or stomach pain occurs with use of this product or if even mild symptoms persist. Although naproxen sodium is indicated for the same conditions as aspirin, ibuprofen, and acetaminophen, it should not be taken with them or other naproxen-containing products except under a doctor's direction.
Analgesic for Arthritis	CAUTION: If pain persists for more than 10 days, or redness is present, or in arthritic or rheumatic conditions affecting children under 12 years of age, consult a physician immediately. WARNING: Children and teenagers should not use this medicine for chicken pox or flu symptoms before a doctor is consulted about Reye Syndrome. . . . In case of accidental overdose, contact a physician immediately.
Arthritis Pain Relieving Rub	WARNINGS: For external use only. Avoid contact with the eyes or mucous membranes. Do not use with a heating pad. Discontinue use if excessive irritation of the skin develops. If pain persists for 10 days or more, or in conditions affecting children under 12 years of age, consult a physician. Do not apply to wounds or damaged skin. Do not bandage tightly.
Sleep Aid	Warnings: Do not give to children under 12 years of age or use for more that 10 days unless directed by a doctor. Consult a doctor if symptoms persist or get worse, if new ones occur, or if sleeplessness persists continuously for more than two weeks because these may be symptoms of a serious underlying medical illness. . . . Avoid alcoholic beverages while taking this product. . . .
Fiber Therapy	WARNINGS: May cause allergic reaction in people sensitive to inhaled or ingested psyllium. . . . Taking this product without adequate fluid may cause it to swell and block your throat or esophagus and may cause choking. Do not take this product if you have difficulty in swallowing. If you experience chest pain, vomiting, or difficulty in swallowing or breathing after taking this product, seek immediate medical attention.

Note: The warning information is presented as it appears on actual warning labels, including the use of upper and lower case letters.

These include increasing contrast (especially for detailed stimuli), avoiding glare, avoiding subtle distinctions among colors, and minimizing the need to discriminate fine detail.

The limitations of the visual capabilities of older adults have been recognized in recent guidelines for the development of manuals and labeling. For example, Backinger and Kingsley (1993) admonished developers of home use instruction manuals to know their user population. For older adult users, manuals should use nonshiny or matte finish pages to reduce glare, use 14-point type, and avoid the use of the color blue which is difficult for older adults to see. Morrell and Echt (1997) provided useful tips for the most appropriate text characteristics to use when designing texts for older individuals.

Considering age-related visual declines, Wogalter and his colleagues have attempted to develop larger, easier to read labels for pharmaceutical products. For example, Wogalter and Dietrich (1995) provided additional warning information on an added cap label, and these labels were preferred by the older adults. In a follow-up study, Wogalter, Magurno, Scott, and Dietrich (1996) found that having additional information on a cap label also yielded higher knowledge scores in comparison to a control group. Future studies should determine whether these benefits were obtained because the label design minimized the effects of visual declines or if the benefits of the added label message were due to the information itself.

SEX

There is some evidence to suggest that males and females react differently to warnings. For example, if a product is perceived as hazardous, females are more likely to look for the warning message than are males (Godfrey, Allender, Laughery, & Smith, 1983). In a later study, LaRue and Cohen (1987) found females were more willing to read warnings, regardless of how dangerous they perceived the product to be. Researchers have also found that females are more likely to comply with warnings than males. For example, Goldhaber and deTurck (1989) found that adolescent males were more likely to behave in a risk-taking manner, especially when warning signs regarding swimming pools were present.

There have not been any investigations into whether the sex differences in warning behaviors are maintained as individuals grow older. One prediction might be that age has brought with it experience with warnings and dangerous situations, and older males would be as likely as older females to notice and encode warnings. Alternatively, the reported sex differences may be maintained throughout the life span. These possibilities remain to be empirically differentiated.

FAMILIARITY

Familiarity with the class of products, the specific product, or even the particular warning influences all components of the warning process from initially noticing the warning to compliance with the warning. We have divided the idea of familiarity into three subareas: general experience with the product or warning, schemata, and technical knowledge.

General Experience

Past experiences with a product may make the user either more or less likely to look for and encode a warning. For example, if prior experience with a product has been benign (i.e., has not led to any adverse consequences), then people are less likely to even look for a warning for that particular product (Godfrey & Laughery, 1984). Evidence suggests that the influence of general experience on the likelihood of reading instructions and warning information is consistent across age groups. For example, Wright, Creighton, and Threlfall (1982) assessed whether people thought they would read instructions for a range of household products. Their sample consisted of three age groups: young (under 30), middle-aged (30–50), and old (over 50). All age groups were much less apt to say that they would read instructions for familiar products, especially if they were nonelectrical items, such as garden shears, bleach, cough syrup, and cake mixes. People were more likely to claim that they would read the instructions for the electrical products, such as a hair dryer, steam iron, and an electric shaver. Thus, prior experience with products influenced whether warning materials would be read, and this was true for all three age groups. The few age differences observed seemed to be due to familiarity as well. For example, older adults were less likely to read the instructions for a hurricane lamp, presumably because they had more exposure to them. In addition, these data also provide evidence to suggest that experience influences one's perception of the hazard involved, which in turn influences noticing, encoding, and complying with the warning. Hazard perception is discussed in more depth later in the chapter.

Schemata

A *schema* is a knowledge structure used in explaining and predicting events in the world. For example, a schema about going to the doctor's office might include signing in at the reception window, sitting and waiting to have your name called, going to a room to have your blood pressure taken, and then going to another room to undress and wait for the doctor. This general knowledge structure allows you to explain the events that are happening in the doctor's office as well as to predict what will happen next. However, if you go to a new doctor that follows a different procedure, inconsistency with your preexisting schema might lead to inappropriate expectations. Thus, a schema can be helpful for interpreting information but may also be disruptive if the stimulus information is inconsistent with your schema.

Most people have a general schema for how medical information should be presented in instructions, and general schemata appear to be consistent across age groups (e.g. Morrow, Leirer, Andrassy, Tanke, & Stine-Morrow, 1996; Vigilante & Wogalter, 1996). For example, Morrow et al. (1996) had young and old participants arrange information into the optimal order for effective instructions. Older adults (ages 60–87) preferred the following order: medication name, purpose, dose, schedule, duration, warnings, mild side effects, severe side effects, doctor's name, and emergency instructions. The only departure for the young adults (ages 20–30) was in the location of the doctor's name, which came earlier in the list. In a second study, Morrow et al. showed that presenting information in an order that was compatible with the schema uncovered in the initial study improved recall for both age groups (although overall recall was superior for young adults).

In a variety of studies, Morrow and his colleagues have demonstrated the importance of presenting medical instructions in a manner that is compatible with the general schema that people have about the appropriate ordering of such information (e.g., Morrow et al., 1996; Morrow, Leirer, & Sheikh, 1988). Unfortunately, a sample of actual instructions reveals that even within a product, organization is internally inconsistent as well as inconsistent with the commonly preferred ordering of information. Table 16.3 presents two examples of how information is organized and presented on various components of the same medicine.

The naproxen sodium had different orderings (and somewhat different information) on the container itself, on the outside box, and on the patient package insert (PPI). The work of Morrow et al. (1988, 1996) suggests that this inconsistency would be particularly problematic for older adult users of the product. Notice that the general warnings are not even presented on the container and are presented in different orderings on the box and the PPI. In addition to the problem of inconsistent

TABLE 16.3
Examples of Inconsistent Information Presentation Within a Single Product

	Order of Information Presentation		
Product	*On Container*	*On Outside Box*	*On Patient Package Insert*
Naproxen	Indications	Allergy warning	Allergy warning
sodium	Directions	Alcohol warning	Alcohol warning
	Allergy warning	Indications	Indications
		General warnings	Directions
		Directions	General warnings
		Active ingredient	Active ingredient
		Inactive ingredient	Inactive ingredient
Arthritis	Caution	Dosage	(no insert)
analgesic	Active ingredients	Active ingredients	
	Inactive ingredients	Inactive ingredients	
	Dosage	Caution	
	Warning	Warning	

presentation, the lack of information on the container itself is a concern because this is likely to be the only information that will be retained by the user.

An important question is whether the schema that people have for instructions will yield the maximal effectiveness of the warning information. The empirical data show that compatibility of information with schemata is preferred more and improves recall. However, the optimal ordering reported by Morrow et al. (1996) has the warning information embedded in the middle of the list. If the goal is to increase recall and adherence to the warning information in particular, it may be better to place it either first or last in the list to capitalize on the well-established primacy and recency effects in human memory (Ashcraft, 1994). When required to remember a list of information, memory is superior for the items at the beginning of the list (primacy) and at the end of the list (recency). Consistent with this suggestion, Wogalter, Fontanelle, and Laughery (1985) demonstrated that warning information was better remembered when it was presented early in the instructions. Thus, presenting critical information early in the instructions may improve warning compliance, even if such a layout is incompatible with existing schemata.

However, warning information that is contrary to a user's beliefs may not be heeded. Rice and Okun (1994) showed that older adults had difficulty recognizing and recalling new information that was inconsistent with their prior beliefs about osteoarthritis, even though the new information was more accurate. They suggest that new, accurate, information may be discarded over time if it is inconsistent with preexisting schema. Thus, the importance of how information is ordered, and whether such ordering conflicts with prior schemata, requires further study.

Technical Knowledge

Issues relating to technical knowledge are twofold. The first issue is understanding how much knowledge the product user has, and the second is determining how much technical information needs to be provided to properly warn and instruct the user. For example, a common concern for the medical field involves the potentially dangerous interaction of medications. This is especially a concern for older adults who typically take a variety of medications at the same time. Fleming et al. (1993) surveyed 100 older adults and found that they were taking an average of nearly seven prescription medicines and three over-the-counter medicines. The average older adult probably does not know a great deal about which medicines will interact with which other medicines (Ostrom, Hammerlund, Christensen, Plein, & Kethley, 1985). Thus, in order to provide adequate warning, some technical information will have to be provided. The warnings in Table 16.2 for the ibuprofen and naproxen sodium samples both provide information about potentially dangerous interactions. The ibuprofen label warns against also taking aspirin and acetaminophen or any other product containing ibuprofen. However, Fincham (1986) suggested that there is a general lack of awareness that the same drug could have several names (e.g., Advil and Nuprin both contain ibuprofen) and such ignorance could lead to overuse and toxicity. In addition, the ibuprofen sample label does not specifically mention naproxen sodium. Thus the user would have to know that naproxen sodium should also be avoided when using ibuprofen.

Expecting older adults to comprehend detailed technical information presented on warning labels may be unreasonable. Williams et al. (1995) developed a test of "functional health literacy," which measures basic reading and numeracy abilities necessary to function in a health-care setting. They found that between 48% and 80% of patients over 60 years of age had inadequate functional health literacy. The range represents differences across samples of Caucasians, African Americans, and Spanish-speaking individuals. Hence, concerns for medical information providers will be whether and how much technical information to provide as well as whether older individuals will be able to comprehend and use that information.

In a more general sense, technical knowledge about warnings may refer to the use of signal words such as *danger, warning,* and *caution,* and here older individuals may actually have an advantage. The American National Standards Institute (ANSI) has provided guidelines for the use of these signal words:

> DANGER: Indicates an imminently hazardous situation which, if not avoided, will result in death or serious injury. This signal word is to be limited to the most extreme situations.
>
> WARNING: Indicates a potentially hazardous situation which, if not avoided, could result in death or serious injury.
>
> CAUTION: Indicates a potentially hazardous situation which, if not avoided, may result in minor or moderate injury. It may also be used to alert against unsafe practices. (ANSI Z535.4-1991, p. 3)

Although the differences among the three words are described quite clearly in the ANSI standard, such differences may not be clear to the average individual. Wogalter, Jarrard, and Simpson (1994) and Leonard, Matthews, and Karnes (1986) showed that young adults often do not differentiate appropriately between the terms *warning* and *caution.* However, a study by Silver, Gammella, Barlow, and Wogalter (1993) showed that older adults were actually better able to differentiate between *warning* and *caution* signal words.

HAZARD PERCEPTION

Human factors researchers make a distinction between the terms hazard and risk. *Hazard* refers to a condition that might cause injury or death, whereas a *risk* is the probability or likelihood of that injury or death (Sanders & McCormick, 1993, p. 675). For example, a toaster presents a hazard of electrocution but the level of risk is relatively low (unless of course you use a knife to extract a piece of toast that has lodged in the toaster). In the context of research on warnings, the effects of hazard and risk perception on the warning process are interrelated and difficult to separate. In addition, Young, Brelsford, and Wogalter (1990) found that participants do not differentiate the terms *hazard* and *risk*. Consequently, we will use the term hazard perception to refer to both hazard and risk perception.

Research suggests that people are more likely to notice, encode, and comply with a warning if their perception of hazard is high (Laughery & Brelsford, 1991). Direct assessments of compliance with warnings have shown that as hazard perception increases, so too does compliance with warnings (Friedmann, 1988; Wogalter & Barlow, 1990).

The role of hazard perception in warning compliance may be critically important for medical information processing because the hazards are typically not self-evident but may be accrued over time and exposure. As is evident in the samples presented in Table 16.2, warnings typically instruct people not to use the product for longer than a specified time (e.g., 10 days), presumably because complications may arise with extended exposure to the medication. In addition, Fincham (1986) argued that, because over-the-counter drugs are available without a prescription, people underestimate their potency and hence the hazard associated with them.

There is a some evidence to suggest that there are age-related differences in hazard perception. For example, Wogalter et al. (1994) found that older adults rated consumer products (e.g., fabric protector, drain opener, aspirin, hair mousse, contact lens cleaner) to be less hazardous than younger adults. Wogalter et al. argued that perhaps because the older adults have more experience with these products, they might perceive them to be less hazardous. However, the mean age of their older adult group was 42 years and these results may not generalize to an older sample.

READING COMPREHENSION

One of the main components of the warning process is the comprehension of the warning. Many warnings consist of both verbal and symbolic information; thus we discuss the influence of age-related differences in reading comprehension in this section and symbol comprehension in the following section.

Reading comprehension ability generally declines as a function of age. In a review of language and aging, Kemper (1992) reported that age-related declines in prose processing are especially evident when inferences are required or links must be made between disparate parts of a text (e.g., between a pronoun and its referent). This type of processing relies on working memory capacity which, as discussed later, declines with age. Increased working memory load and text complexity are likely to affect older adults' reading comprehension. Much of the research reviewed by Kemper assessed prose comprehension. However, age-related declines in reading comprehension have also been reported for tasks representative of typical reading. For example, as discussed earlier, older adults have been found to have inadequate functional health literacy, which is measured in part by reading comprehension (Williams et al., 1995).

Hill (1993) used the Adult Basic Learning Examination, which includes such tasks as reading newspaper advertisements, package labels, and letters. He found that a sample of college-educated older adults was reading below 12th grade level. Meyer, Marsiske, and Willis (1993) used a similar test, the Educational Testing Service's Test of Basic Skills that includes printed materials such as bus schedules, warranties, and labels, to assess age-related differences in everyday text processing. For their sample, ages 52–93, they found that performance on this test was correlated with memory span, which supports the idea that memory ability is directly related to reading comprehension, even for everyday textual materials.

The sample warnings presented in Table 16.2 provide some indication of how working memory might be overloaded by textual information. Consider for example the sleep aid warning "Consult a doctor if symptoms persist or get worse, if new ones occur, or if sleeplessness persists continuously for more than two weeks because these may be symptoms of a serious underlying medical illness." This is a long sentence, with many components. There are also multiple layers (if or, if, or if) that result in a high working memory load. Another example is the left-branching sentence at the end of the fiber therapy warning ("if you experience . . . seek immediate medical attention"). This type of syntactical structure is particularly difficult for older adults because it requires the storage of the initial part of the sentence in working memory until the main clause is reached (Kemper, 1992). These examples are representative of warnings on many over-the-counter medications and may help to explain why older adults often cannot fully comprehend the information presented. Moreover, warnings such as these may be difficult for people of all ages to read.

On the other hand, there is some encouraging information about reading comprehension. Age differences in reading comprehension are reduced for more highly educated individuals (e.g., Harris, Rogers, & Qualls, 1998; Meyer, Young, & Bartlett, 1989). In addition, reading comprehension can be improved through strategy training (Meyer et al.), even with the relatively simple strategy of rereading the text for better comprehension (e.g., Harris et al.). Thus, understanding that age-related differences in reading comprehension may influence warning comprehension and, consequently, compliance is an important first step. A perhaps equally important second step is determining which strategies for improving reading comprehension will be most beneficial for comprehension of warning information.

SYMBOL COMPREHENSION

In addition to age-related differences in reading comprehension, others, for example, individuals for whom English is a second language, children, and illiterates, may also have difficulty understanding written warnings. Consequently, research has been conducted on the use of symbols and pictorials to convey warnings, either in addition to or instead of verbal information. *Pictorials* refer to pictures that represent the concept of interest (e.g., a picture of a fire extinguisher). *Symbols* are more abstract representations of a concept, the meaning of which must be learned (e.g., skull and crossbones to denote poison). For our purposes, we combine pictorial and symbol comprehension. Much of the research in this area does not differentiate between the two and often includes examples of both pictorials and symbols in their stimulus array. Moreover, the ANSI standard for symbols combines the two in its definition of a symbol as "a configuration, consisting of an image . . . which conveys a message without the use of words. As used in this standard, the word symbol includes graphic art, such as pictograms, pictorials, and glyphs" (ANSI Z535.3-1991, p. 2).

Evidence for the benefits of symbols for young adults is somewhat mixed. Otsubo (1988) found that warning compliance was best for a verbal and symbol condition (50%), whereas the rate was only 22% for the symbol alone and 44% for the verbal alone. Jaynes and Boles (1990) also found a pictogram plus text condition yielded the best compliance, and Young and Wogalter (1990) found a comprehension benefit (compliance was not directly measured) when a symbol was used. These data suggest that text plus a symbol is better than either text or the symbol alone. However, Wogalter, Kalsher, and Racicot (1992) found a nonsignificant increase in compliance when a symbol was incorporated into the warning.

The picture is also blurred when age differences in symbol comprehension are considered. Mayer and Laux (1989) assessed participants' ability to recognize the hazard depicted by 16 different symbols (e.g., flammable, explosive, eye protection). They compared adults ages 17 to 40 to adults ages 41 to 83. Of the 16 symbols, 9 were recognized equally well by the two age groups, 4 were better for the younger group, and 2 were better for the older group (one was not recognized by either group). Thus, the degree to which there were age differences varied across symbols. However, there was not an analysis of what made particular symbols more or less recognizable for the different age groups. In addition, the age groupings in the Mayer and Laux study may provide a misrepresentation of the degree to which symbol comprehension declines with age. That is, the inclusion of 41- to 60-year-old adults in the older group may have provided an overestimate of comprehension for older adults, who are more typically defined as individuals over 60 years of age).

Even for symbols that were recognized by both age groups in the Mayer and Laux (1989) study, there were differences in the actual hazard associated with the symbol. Participants selected behaviors that were most appropriate for a particular warning symbol. Older adults were less likely to choose seemingly appropriate (and obvious) behaviors such as "wash hands after using" or "would not drink or eat" for a skull and cross bones symbol. Thus, although the older adults were capable of recognizing many of the symbols, it is not clear that they really comprehended their meaning.

Although the results are somewhat mixed, the preponderance of evidence suggests that symbol comprehension is impaired for older adults. Age-related differences favoring young adults have been found for information on a prescription medication label (Morrell, Park, & Poon, 1990), fire safety symbols (Collins & Lerner, 1982), traffic signs (Lambert & Fleury, 1994), mine safety symbols (Collins, 1983), and hazard symbols for household products (Easterby & Hakiel,

1981). Consequently, although the use of symbols in warning communication may have tremendous potential, symbols must be chosen that convey similar information to all age groups.

Much of the research on symbol comprehension only determines that certain symbols are better comprehended (or recognized) than other symbols. There has been little effort to determine the source of age differences. Recent research by Wolff and Wogalter (1993) is promising in that they are taking an iterative approach to the development of symbols to be used for medications. Those symbols that are not well comprehended are reworked until they can be comprehended by 85% of the population of interest, which is the minimum level suggested by ANSI (ANSI Z535.3-1991, p. 20). In addition, Wolff and Wogalter are including older adults in their population. Future research should help to determine those symbols that may be understood by people of all ages.

COSTS/BENEFITS OF COMPLIANCE

Whether a warning is heeded may depend on weighing the cost of the compliance and the benefit of noncompliance. If a warning label indicates that gloves should be used with an oven cleaner, but gloves are not readily available, there will be some cost associated with purchasing or finding the gloves before using the product. The benefit of noncompliance is that time and perhaps money is saved by not using the gloves. Other costs of compliance are discomfort (e.g., wearing goggles or ear plugs), the length of time required to follow the safety procedures, and so on. Reducing the cost of compliance will increase the compliance rate. For example, if safety gloves are attached to a cleaning solvent bottle, they are more likely to be used (Dingus, Hathaway, & Hunn, 1991; Wogalter, McKenna, & Allison, 1988).

Although we could find no empirical research on the relative effects of the costs of compliance for older adults, there may be situations in which compliance costs are more influential for this population. For example, having to go down to the basement or dig through a bottom drawer for safety gloves may be much more effortful or difficult (i.e., costly) for an older individual. Similarly, going to see a physician if certain symptoms appear after taking a particular medicine might be particularly costly for an older individual who does not drive or is on a limited budget. These and other pragmatic costs of compliance may be influential in the degree to which older adults choose to comply with warnings and should be investigated.

RISK-TAKING STYLE

There are individual differences in the degree to which individuals are willing to take risks. Even a well-designed warning that is noticed, encoded, and comprehended may not lead to compliance if the person is willing to take a risk. Purswell, Schegel, and Kejriwal (1986) found that scores on a risk-taking attitude questionnaire were correlated with risk-taking behavior—people more willing to take risks were less likely to behave safely. These data suggest that risk-taking style may contribute to the likelihood that an individual will comply with a warning. However, every indication suggests that older adults are not likely to be classified as risk-takers. Zuckerman, Eysenck, and Eysenck (1978) reported that scores on the Sensation Seeking Scale significantly declined as a function of age. Although there are individual differences even within an age group, risk-taking style is not apt to play a significant role in the warning process for an average group of older adults.

SOCIAL INFLUENCE

Whether an individual will choose to comply with a warning may be influenced by social factors. Wogalter, Allison, and McKenna (1989) showed that people were more likely to comply with a warning when they saw someone else complying. Racicot and Wogalter (1992) showed that the benefits of social influence could also be obtained via videotaped presentation of information. Unfortunately, there has not been any research to determine whether older adults are also susceptible to the pressures of social influence, especially via videotaped presentation of information. Videotapes of warning demonstrations could prove to be a valuable tool for older adults because they would minimize the need for both reading and symbol comprehension, would be relatively easy to provide, and could increase warning compliance.

INFLUENCE OF OTHER COGNITIVE VARIABLES

The person variables discussed thus far are those that have been demonstrated to have an influence on the warning process. As is evident from Table 16.1, the effects of aging have not yet been investigated for several of the variables and even when age-related differences have been considered, the amount of research is relatively small. Additional information about the effects of aging on the warning process may come from the cognitive aging literature. Certain cognitive functions have been shown to decline with age and these abilities may be important for noticing, encoding, comprehending, and complying with warnings (see Rousseau et al., 1998). Several cognitive variables have already been discussed, such as reading and symbol comprehension. However, others were not included in our review because their influence has not been investigated for either younger or older adults. Yet, these variables may be important to the process and should be considered for future research studies. We next provide a brief discussion of the importance of attention, working memory, and prospective memory.

Attention

Attention is a multifaceted construct that includes selection of information as well as focusing, dividing, and maintaining attentional resources. Most relevant to warnings are divided attention and selective attention. *Divided attention* literally means sharing your attention between two or more tasks. For example, in driving there are the specific driving-related tasks (steering, pressure on gas pedal) as well as the need to attend to warning information about upcoming road construction or sharp turns in the road. Laboratory tasks have revealed that older adults are at a distinct disadvantage on tasks that require divided attention (e.g., McDowd & Craik, 1988). However, the effects of age-related declines in divided attention on the processing of warnings have not been investigated.

Selective attention involves choosing the information from the environment that will receive further processing. Thus, product users must be able to selectively attend to warning information in sometimes cluttered environments (Wogalter & Laughery, 1996). Age differences have also been reported for laboratory-based selective attention tasks (for a review see Hartley, 1992). However, Hartley also reported the encouraging finding that older adults are able to benefit from cues to the relevant information. Thus, cues to warnings, such as color or highlighting, might prove especially beneficial for older adults.

Warnings researchers have discussed the importance of attention from the perspective of how well a warning captures attention. One way to capture attention in a warning environment is to use signal words such as *danger, warning,* or *caution* (Wogalter & Laughery, 1996). As suggested earlier, the degree to which such words are well learned and capture attention should be maintained for older adults.

Working Memory

Working memory refers to the simultaneous storage and processing of information in active memory (Baddeley, 1986). Declines in working memory for older adults have been documented frequently (Salthouse, 1991). As discussed earlier, reading warning labels such as those presented in Table 16.2 can be working memory intensive. Also, if part of the warning process requires step-by-step directions, the need to maintain the steps in working memory may cause difficulties for older adults. We suspect that working memory capacity can influence all of the components of the warning process. For example, if working memory is overloaded, the warning will not be noticed, nor will it likely be encoded even if it is noticed. In addition, working memory limitations may influence the comprehension of a complex warning as well as compliance with the warning.

There has been scant research on the influence of working memory declines in older adults in the context of either warnings or medical information processing. In one of the few studies, Morrell, Park, and Poon (1989) manipulated the number of medications in a hypothetical patient's regimen and found that the increased load (three to eight medications) was detrimental to the recall and comprehension performance of both younger and older adults. However, the decrement was not differentially greater for the older adults, as would be predicted on the basis of working memory declines. This single study may not be representative of the effects of working memory declines on the warning process because the focus was on recall and comprehension of medication instructions. Future research studies should investigate the importance of age-related working memory declines for the effectiveness of the warning process.

Prospective Memory

Prospective memory involves remembering to perform actions in the future. For example, an instruction manual might instruct you to take a certain precaution at a certain stage when using the product. However, you may not reach that stage until minutes, hours, or even days later. Prospective memory tasks can be classified as event-based tasks and time-based tasks. In an event-based task, some external event serves as a cue to perform a particular action ("When the nurse comes in, it is time to take my medicine"). In a time-based task, only the passage of time serves as a cue ("I must take my medicine every four hours"). Age-related differences are generally less evident for event-based tasks unless the task is relatively complex; however, age-related differences are typically observed for time-based tasks (see Smith, 1997).

There has been remarkably little research conducted on the importance of prospective memory to the warning process. However, it would seem to be of tremendous importance for warnings about medications. Individuals might read the warnings associated with a particular medicine the first time they take it. Every time thereafter, however, they would have to remember the instructions and warning-related information such as not to consume alcohol while taking the product or to take with food or milk. The act of remembering to take the medicine would be a time-based task, but remembering the warning information might be an event-based task, if the medicine itself served as the cueing event. If so, then we might not expect to find age differences. However, this supposition remains to be empirically determined.

MAXIMIZING WARNING EFFECTIVENESS

There are two main approaches to improving the effectiveness of the warning process. First is to try to influence the person variables, perhaps through training how to comply with warnings, exposure to the situation, education about the risks, or through prosthetics such as eyeglasses. Little is known about the degree to which education and training programs can influence the effectiveness of warnings. For example, the information provided in the ANSI standards could be developed into an educational program to aid individuals in understanding distinctions between signal words, as well as the use of particular colors, shapes, and symbols on warnings. In addition, individuals might benefit from education about the hazards involved when using products or systems.

Given the observation of age-related declines on many of the person variables (e.g., vision, reading and symbol comprehension, familiarity), perhaps a more fruitful approach would be to change the characteristics of the warnings themselves.

As is evident in Fig. 16.1, there are many warning variables that influence the components of the warning process. Design solutions may be drawn from these studies that might overcome age-related deficits (see Rousseau et al., 1998).

For example, in our discussion on visual deficits, we provided a number of suggestions for improving the visual quality of warning information, such as increasing type size, choosing optimum type styles, and so on. In addition, Pirkl (1994) suggested the idea of redundant cueing of warning information such that the warning information is provided in two modalities (visual and auditory). Similarly, warning information might be provided both in text format and symbol format to increase the likelihood that it will be comprehended by older adults. Warnings with both text and symbols have been shown to increase comprehension and compliance for young adults (e.g., Jaynes & Boles, 1990), and such benefits should be investigated for older adults. However, the fact that older adults have more difficulty comprehending symbols must be considered in the design of such instructions.

Design solutions may also be based on the abilities that remain intact for older adults. For example, older adults were able to differentiate between particular signal words (Silver et al., 1993). Signal words can be used to increase hazard perception, which can, in turn, increase compliance (Wogalter et al., 1994). Similarly, older adults are able to benefit from cues that direct their attention (Hartley, 1992) and from signals in texts that identify important information (e.g., Meyer et al., 1989). These maintained abilities should be considered when designing warnings. Lastly, older adults maintain schemata about how information should be presented that can aid them in understanding and remembering information. Morrow and his colleagues (e.g., Morrow et al., 1996) have taken advantage of these well-learned schemata for the presentation of medical information, and future research could assess schema benefits specifically for warning information.

CONCLUSION

The warning process is complex and multifaceted. Our review has shown that there are myriad factors that can affect whether a warning will ultimately be complied with. The warning must be noticed, encoded, comprehended, and then, perhaps, compliance will occur. However, at each stage of the process there are aspects of the individual (person variables) and of the warning itself (warning variables) that will influence the success of the process. Our goal in this chapter was to explore the effects of these different variables and to provide examples of how they may be influenced to improve warning compliance.

As human factors researchers, our goal is to maximize the effectiveness of the warning process to ensure the safety of individuals interacting with particular products or systems. The present focus has been on medically related products such as prescription and over-the-counter medications as well as medical technologies.

However, the basic principles will apply to warnings across domains. As is the case in most fields of study, more research is needed. However, we hope that our organization of the extant literature will provide direction for that future research.

ACKNOWLEDGMENTS

The authors were supported in part by a grant from the National Institutes of Health (National Institute on Aging) Grant No. P50 AG11715 under the auspices of the Center for Applied Cognitive Research on Aging (one of the Edward R. Roybal Centers for Research on Applied Gerontology). This chapter is based on a presentation given at the Medical Information Processing Conference in Destin, FL (February, 1997). The authors would like to thank the attendees at the conference for their input, and Dan Morrow, Roger Morrell, and Mike Wogalter for constructive criticisms on a draft of the chapter.

REFERENCES

Adams, A. S., & Edworthy, J. (1995). Quantifying and predicting the effects of basic text display variables on the perceived urgency of warning labels: Tradeoffs involving font size, border, weight, and color. *Ergonomics, 38,* 2221–2237.

American National Standards Institute. (1991). *Product Safety Signs and Labels.* ANSI Z535.3 and ANSI Z535.4. Washington, DC: National Electrical Manufacturer's Association.

Ashcraft, M. H. (1994). *Human memory and cognition.* New York: HarperCollins.

Ayres, T. J., Gross, M. M., Wood, C. T., Horst, D. P., Beyer, R. R., & Robinson, J. N. (1989). What is a warning and when will it work? *Proceedings of the Human Factors Society 33rd Annual Meeting* (pp. 426–430). Santa Monica, CA: Human Factors Society.

Backinger, C. L, & Kingsley, P. A. (1993). *Write it right: Recommendations for developing user instruction manuals for medical devices used in home health care.* Washington, DC: U.S. Department of Health and Human Services.

Baddeley, A. (1986). *Working Memory.* Oxford, England: Clarendon.

Charness, N., & Bosman, E. A. (1992). Human factors and age. In T. A. Salthouse & F. I. M. Craik (Eds.), *Handbook of aging and cognition* (pp. 495–552). Hillsdale, NJ: Lawrence Erlbaum Associates.

Collins, B. L. (1983). Evaluation of mine-safety symbols. *Proceedings of the Human Factors Society 27th Annual Meeting* (pp. 947–949). Santa Monica, CA: Human Factors Society.

Collins, B. L., & Lerner, N. D. (1982). Assessment of fire-safety symbols. *Human Factors, 24,* 75–84.

DeJoy, D. M., & Wogalter, M. S. (1993). Preface: Warnings and risk communication. *Safety Science, 16,* 565–568.

Dingus, T. A., Hathaway, J. A., & Hunn, B. P. (1991). A most critical warning variable: Two demonstrations of the powerful effects of cost on warning compliance. *Proceedings of the Human Factors Society 35th Annual Meeting* (pp. 1034–1038). Santa Monica, CA: Human Factors Society.

Easterby, R. S., & Hakiel, S. R. (1981). Field testing of consumer safety signs: The comprehension of pictorially presented messages. *Applied Ergonomics, 12,* 143–152.

Fincham, J. E. (1986). Over-the-counter drug use and misuse by the ambulatory elderly: A review of the literature. *Journal of Geriatric Drug Therapy, 1,* 3–21.

Fleming, B. B., Pulliam, C. C., Perfetto, E. M., Hanlon, J. T., & Bowling, J. M. (1993). Medication use by home health patients. *Journal of Geriatric Drug Therapy, 7,* 33–45.

Friedmann, K. (1988). The effect of adding symbols to written warning labels on user behavior and recall. *Human Factors, 30,* 507–515.

Godfrey, S. S., Allender, L., Laughery, K. R., & Smith, V. L. (1983). Warning messages: Will the consumer bother to look? *Proceedings of the Human Factors Society 27th Annual Meeting* (pp. 950–954). Santa Monica, CA: Human Factors Society.

Godfrey, S. S., & Laughery, K. R. (1984). The biasing effects of product familiarity on consumers' awareness of hazard. *Proceedings of the Human Factors Society 28th Annual Meeting* (pp. 483–486). Santa Monica, CA: Human Factors Society.

Goldhaber, G. M., & deTurck, M. A. (1989). A developmental analysis of warning signs: The case of familiarity and gender. *Proceedings of the Human Factors 33rd Annual Meeting* (pp. 1019–1023). Santa Monica, CA: Human Factors Society.

Harris, J. L., Rogers, W. A., & Qualls, C. D. (1998). Written language comprehension for younger and older adults. *Journal of Speech and Hearing Research, 41,* 603–617.

Hartley, A. A. (1992). Attention. In T. A. Salthouse & F. I. M. Craik (Eds.), *Handbook of aging and cognition* (pp. 3–49). Hillsdale, NJ: Lawrence Erlbaum Associates.

Hill, R. D. (1993). Predictors of reading performance in college-educated adults. *Educational Gerontology, 19,* 21–30.

Jaynes, L. S., & Boles, D. B. (1990). The effect of symbols on warning compliance. *Proceedings of the Human Factors 34th Annual Meeting* (pp. 984–987). Santa Monica, CA: Human Factors Society.

Kart, C. S., Dunkle, R. E., & Lockery, S. A. (1994). Self-health care. In B. R. Bonder & M. B. Wagner (Eds.), *Functional performance in older adults* (pp. 136–147). Philadelphia: Davis.

Kemper, S. (1992). Language and aging. In T. A. Salthouse and F. I. M. Craik (Eds.), *The handbook of aging and cognition* (pp. 495–552). Hillsdale, NJ: Lawrence Erlbaum Associates.

Kline, D. W., & Scialfa, C. T. (1997). Sensory and perceptual functioning: Basic research and human factors implications. In A. D. Fisk & W. A. Rogers (Eds.), *Handbook of human factors and the older adult* (pp. 27–54). New York: Academic Press.

Lambert, L. D., & Fleury, M. (1994). Age, cognitive style, and traffic signs. *Perceptual and Motor Skills, 78,* 611–624.

LaRue, C., & Cohen, H. H. (1987). Factors affecting consumers' perceptions of product warnings: An examination of the differences between male and female consumers. *Proceedings of the Human Factors Society 31st Annual Meeting* (pp. 610–614). Santa Monica, CA: Human Factors Society.

Laughery, K. R., & Brelsford, J. W. (1991). Receiver characteristics in safety communications. *Proceedings of the Human Factors Society 35th Annual Meeting* (pp. 1068–1072). Santa Monica, CA: Human Factors Society.

Lehto, M. R., & Miller, J. M. (1988). The effectiveness of warning labels. *Journal of Products Liability, 11,* 225–270.

Leonard, S. D., Matthews, D., & Karnes, E. W. (1986). How does the population interpret warning signals? *Proceedings of the Human Factors Society 30th Annual Meeting* (pp. 116–120). Santa Monica, CA: Human Factors Society.

Mayer, D. L., & Laux, L. F. (1989). Recognizability and effectiveness of warning symbols and pictorials. *Proceedings of the Human Factors Society 33rd Annual Meeting* (pp. 984–988). Santa Monica, CA: Human Factors Society.

McDowd, J. M., & Craik, F. I. M. (1988). Effects of aging and task difficulty on divided attention performance. *Journal of Experimental Psychology: Human Perception and Performance, 14,* 267–280.

Meyer, B. J. F., Marsiske, M., & Willis, S. L. (1993). Text processing variables predict the readability of everyday documents read by older adults. *Reading Research Quarterly, 28,* 234–249.

Meyer, B. J. F., Young, C. J., & Bartlett, B. J. (1989). *Memory improved: Reading and memory enhancement across the life span through strategic text structures.* Hillsdale, NJ: Lawrence Erlbaum Associates.

Morrell, R. W., & Echt, K. V. (1997). Designing written instructions for older adults to use computers. In A. D. Fisk & W. A. Rogers (Eds.), *Handbook of human factors and the older adult* (pp. 335–361). San Diego, CA: Academic Press.

Morrell, R. W., Park, D. C., & Poon, L. W. (1989). Quality of instructions in prescription drug labels: Effects on memory and comprehension in young and old adults. *The Gerontologist, 29,* 345–354.

Morrell, R. W., Park, D. C., & Poon, L. W. (1990). Effects of labeling techniques on memory and comprehension of prescription information in young and old adults. *Journal of Gerontology, 45,* 166–172.

Morrow, D. J., Leirer, V. O., Andrassy, J. M., Tanke, E. D., and Stine-Morrow, E. A. L. (1996). Medication instruction design: Young and older adults schemas for taking medication. *Human Factors, 38,* 556–573.

Morrow, D. J., Leirer, V. O., & Sheikh, J. (1988). Adherence and medication instructions. *Journal of the American Geriatrics Society, 36,* 1147–1160.

Ostrom, J. R., Hammerlund, E. R., Christensen, D. B., Plein, J. B., & Kethley, A. J. (1985). Medication usage in an elderly population. *Medical Care, 23,* 157–164.

Otsubo, S. M. (1988). A behavioral study of warning labels for consumer products: Perceived danger and use of pictographs. *Proceedings of the Human Factors Society 32nd Annual Meeting* (pp. 536–540). Santa Monica, CA: Human Factors Society.

Pirkl, J. J. (1994). *Transgenerational design: Products for an aging population.* New York: Van Nostrand Reinhold.

Purswell, J. L., Krenek, R. F., & Dorris, A. (1987). Warning effectiveness: What do we need to know? *Proceedings of the Human Factors Society 31st Annual Meeting* (pp. 1116–1120). Santa Monica, CA: Human Factors Society.

Purswell, J. L., Schegel, R. E., & Kejriwal, S. K. (1986). A prediction model for consumer behavior regarding product safety. *Proceedings of the Human Factors Society 30th Annual Meeting* (pp. 1202–1205). Santa Monica, CA: Human Factors Society.

Racicot, B. M., & Wogalter, M. S. (1992). Warning compliance: Effects of a video warning sign and modeling on behavior. *Proceedings of the Human Factors Society 36th Annual Meeting* (pp. 608–610). Santa Monica, CA: Human Factors Society.

Rice, G. E., & Okun, M. A. (1994). Older readers' processing of medical information that contradicts their beliefs. *Journal of Gerontology, 49,* 119–128.

Rogers, W. A., Lamson, N., & Rousseau, G. K. (1998). *Warning research: An integrative perspective.* Manuscript submitted for publication.

Rousseau, G. K., Lamson, N. & Rogers, W. A. (1998). Designing wanrings to compensate for age-related changes in perceptual and cognitive abilities. *Psychology and Marketing, 15,* 643–662.

Salthouse, T. A. (1991). *Theoretical perspectives on cognitive aging.* Hillsdale, NJ: Lawrence Erlbaum Associates.

Sanders, M. S., & McCormick, E. J. (1993). *Human factors in engineering and design* (7th ed.). New York: McGraw-Hill.

Silver, N. C., Gammella, D. S., Barlow, A. S., & Wogalter, M. S. (1993). Connoted strength of signal words by elderly and non-native English speakers. *Proceedings of the Human Factors and Ergonomics Society 37th Annual Meeting* (pp. 516–519). Santa Monica, CA: Human Factors and Ergonomics Society.

Smith, A. D. (1997). Memory. In J. E. Birren & K. W. Schaie (Eds.), *Handbook of the psychology of aging* (pp. 236–250). San Diego, CA: Academic Press.

Vigilante, W. J. & Wogalter, M. S. (1996). The ordering of over-the-counter pharmaceutical label components. *Proceedings of the Human Factors and Ergonomics Society 40th Annual Meeting* (pp. 141–145). Santa Monica, CA: Human Factors and Ergonomics Society.

Williams, M. V., Parker, R. M., Baker, D. W., Parikh, N. S., Pitkin, K., Coates, W. C., & Nurss, J. R. (1995). Inadequate functional health literacy among patients at two public hospitals. *Journal of the American Medication Association, 274,* 21.

Wogalter, M. S., Allison, S. T., & McKenna, N. A. (1989). Effects of cost and social influence on warning compliance. *Human Factors, 31,* 133–140.

Wogalter, M. S., & Barlow, T. (1990). Injury severity and likelihood in warnings. *Proceedings of the Human Factors Society 34th Annual Meeting* (pp. 580–583). Santa Monica, CA: Human Factors Society.

Wogalter, M. S., & Dietrich, D. A. (1995). Enhancing label readability for over-the-counter pharmaceuticals by elderly consumers. *Proceedings of the Human Factors and Ergonomics Society 39th Annual Meeting* (pp. 143–147). Santa Monica, CA: Human Factors and Ergonomics Society.

Wogalter, M. S., Fontanelle, G. A., & Laughery, K. R. (1985). Behavioral effectiveness of warnings. *Proceedings of the Human Factors Society 29th Annual Meeting* (pp. 679–683). Santa Monica, CA: Human Factors Society.

Wogalter, M. S., Jarrard, S. W., & Simpson, S. N. (1994). Influence of warning label signal words on perceived hazard level. *Human Factors, 36,* 547–556.

Wogalter, M. S., Kalsher, M. J., & Racicot, B. M. (1992). The influence of location and pictorials on behavior compliance to warnings. *Proceedings of the Human Factors Society 36th Annual Meeting* (pp. 1029–1033). Santa Monica, CA: Human Factors Society.

Wogalter, M. S., & Laughery, K. R. (1996). Warning! Sign and label effectiveness. *Current Directions in Psychological Science, 5,* 33–37.

Wogalter, M. S., Magurno, A. B., Scott, K. L., & Dietrich, D. A. (1996). Facilitating information acquisition for over-the-counter drugs using supplemental labels. *Proceedings of the Human Factors and Ergonomics Society 39th Annual Meeting* (pp. 143–147). Santa Monica, CA: Human Factors and Ergonomics Society.

Wogalter, M. S., McKenna, N. A., & Allison, S. T. (1988). Warning compliance: Behavioral effects of cost and consensus. *Proceedings of the Human Factors Society 32nd Annual Meeting* (pp. 901–904). Santa Monica, CA: Human Factors Society.

Wolff, J. S., & Wogalter, M. S. (1993). Test and development of pharmaceutical pictorials. *Interface '93,* 187–192.

Wright, P., Creighton, P., & Threlfall, S. M. (1982). Some factors determining when instructions will be read. *Ergonomics, 3,* 225–237.

Young, S. L., Brelsford, J. W., & Wogalter, M. S. (1990). Judgments of hazard, risk, and danger: Do they differ? *Proceedings of the Human Factors Society 34th Annual Meeting* (pp. 503–507). Santa Monica, CA: Human Factors Society.

Young, S. L., & Wogalter, M. S. (1990). Comprehension and memory of instruction manual warnings: Conspicuous print and pictorial icons. *Human Factors, 32,* 637–649.

Zuckerman, M., Eysenck, S., & Eysenck, H. J. (1978). Sensation seeking in England and America: Cross-cultural, age and sex comparisons. *Journal of Consulting and Clinical Psychology, 46,* 139–149.

17

Research on
Pharmaceutical Labeling:
An Information
Processing Approach

Michael S. Wogalter
Russell J. Sojourner
North Carolina State University

Various methods are employed to communicate pharmaceutical information to the general public. Information may be conveyed by a variety of sources including labeling on the product container itself, on enclosures such as patient product inserts (PPIs), on exterior packaging, through advertising, or via direct communication with medical professionals. In many instances, the printed material supplied with a pharmaceutical product may be the only medium used to educate consumers on information associated with the product. Using these printed materials to communicate pharmaceutical information to older adults is a practice that is receiving greater attention. Interest is due in large part to the fact that older adults tend to consume more medications than other population groups. This fact, combined with the onset of visual and cognitive difficulties that accompany the aging process, make the creation of effective methods of communicating medication information to adults in general, and older adults in particular, an important challenge.

Pharmaceutical labels are used to disseminate information about medication uses, indications, benefits, and potential hazards. Effective medication labels serve as both a source of information and as a method used to influence behavior. Both purposes are important, and a growing body of research has revealed various factors that influence label effectiveness.

Information Processing Model

Many of the processes associated with pharmaceutical labeling can be organized using one of several models of human information processing. This modeling approach categorizes people's mental activities into a coherent sequence of processing stages. Figure 17.1 depicts a simplified human information-processing model that is useful in organizing the factors that influence the effectiveness (or ineffectiveness) of pharmaceutical labeling. For a label to be effective at communicating information and influencing behavior, it must first capture attention and then maintain attention long enough for a person to adequately extract information from the material. Next, the material must be understood and needs to concur with the person's existing attitudes and beliefs; if it is in disagreement, the information should be adequately persuasive to evoke a change toward agreement. Finally, the message must motivate the consumer to perform proper compliance behavior. Each stage of the model can produce a bottleneck preventing information from being processed further. Accordingly, the model predicts that a label that is not noticed will not be read, a label that is not read will have little or no influence on beliefs and attitudes, and a poorly understood label will probably not motivate the appropriate behavior.

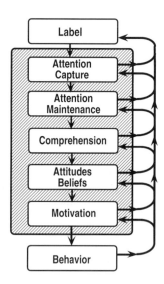

FIG. 17.1. An information processing model that describes a series of stages involved in successful communication and behavioral compliance.

This chapter is organized using this information-processing model. It is similar to the one described in Wogalter and Laughery (1996), except that in the earlier version Attention was described as a single stage. In the current model, Attention is separated into two stages, Attention Capture and Attention Maintenance. These stages delineate the process of noticing and then focusing atention to the warning.

In this chapter, each stage is described as it relates to warning labels in general, and next, research relating to pharmaceutical labels is emphasized. Research using adults of all ages will be cited, although studies involving older adults are mentioned where they exist.

ATTENTION CAPTURE

The first stage in the information-processing model concerns the capture of attention. An effective warning must initially attract the attention of persons at risk in the target audience. Because many environments are cluttered, the label must fight to grab attention in visual contexts. Thus, a label needs to be designed to adequately stand out from the background (i.e., be salient or conspicuous) in order to be noticed. This is particularly true when people are not actively seeking information concerning medication hazards and warnings. In situations like these, the "warnings have to look for people" (Laughery & Wogalter, 1997, p. 1181). Laughery and Wogalter (1997) proposed several basic human factors guidelines that can increase the saliency of displayed information:

Contrast. Printed information should have high contrast (light-dark difference) with the background; dark print on light background or vice versa increases its prominence or salience (Barlow & Wogalter, 1993). Certain color combinations (e.g., black and yellow) may facilitate adequate contrast.

Size. Within reasonable limits, bigger is generally better (Barlow & Wogalter, 1991, 1993). However, the absolute size of the label is not the only consideration. A label designer should also consider the relative size of the message components. For example, information on how to prevent injury should be allocated relatively more space than other, less important information (e.g., inert chemical composition).

Location. Because English-language users tend to scan left to right and top to bottom, important information should be located near the top or to the left if possible (Hartley, 1994). Warnings should not be buried within less important text (Strawbridge, 1986). Another consideration is sequencing of information. The preferred placement of warning statements is before rather than following usage instructions (Vigilante & Wogalter, 1997).

Signal words. Signal words can be used in labels to attract attention. The most common are CAUTION, WARNING, and DANGER, which are intended to denote increasing levels of hazard, respectively. In addition, fairly consistent perceptions of additional signal words have been found using diverse participant groups including older adults, elementary, middle-school, and college students; and non-native English speakers (Wogalter & Silver, 1995).

Pictorials. Pictured concepts can make labels more noticeable (Young & Wogalter, 1990). Laughery, Young, Vaubel, and Brelsford (1993) found that pictorials reduce reaction time and enhance eye movement toward warnings.

Habituation. Repeated and long term exposure to a label may result in a loss of attention-capturing properties over time (Wogalter & Laughery, 1996). Even a well-designed label that incorporates the features that facilitate attention capture will eventually become habituated—although habituation may be slowed by these features.

Application of Attention Capture to Pharmaceutical Labels

Recent research has specifically addressed the attention-capturing properties of pharmaceutical labels. Generally, drug labels contain considerable information restricted to a very small space, resulting in printed information being compacted and reduced to very small sizes, which can negatively affect attention capture. Type size is particularly important for older adults because age-related vision problems may preclude them from reading the material on many pharmaceutical labels. Four point type (i.e., 4/72 inch in height) is commonly found on over-the-counter pharmaceutical products.

Recent research has focused on ways to counteract the small print, cluttered nature of labels. One remedy is to increase the available surface area on small containers. Barlow and Wogalter (1991) developed six alternative label designs (tag, wings, cap, box, disc, and wraparound) on very small (0.3 fluid ounce) product containers and compared them to a conventional control label design. Depictions are shown in Fig. 17.2. Undergraduates (mean age = 19 years) and older adults (mean age = 76 years) evaluated the container labels on various dimensions including one relevant to attention capture, the likelihood of noticing the warning.

Results indicated that alternative label designs compared to the conventional design were judged to be more noticeable by both participant groups. The students rated the tag label significantly higher than the other labels. The older adults judged the tag and wings labels most noticeable.

A later study by Wogalter, Forbes, and Barlow (1993) focused on the tag, wings, and control labels and introduced a type size manipulation in which the information was printed in three different sizes. Both undergraduates (mean age = 19 years) and older adults (mean age = 72 years) perceived the control inferior in warning noticeability compared to the alternative labels. In addition, both groups indicated that larger print size made the warnings more likely to be noticed.

The noticeability measures cited thus far only involved subjective evaluations. To evaluate effects on behavior, Wogalter and Young (1994) performed a compliance study that investigated whether the tags and wings labels would promote safer behavior when attached to a product that participants actually used. Undergraduates

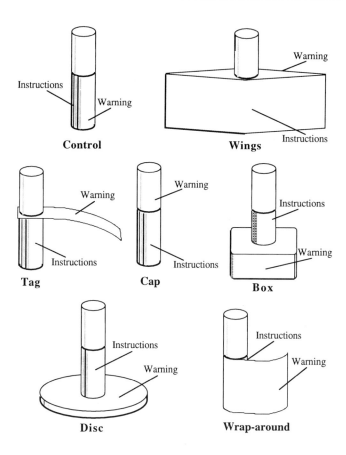

FIG. 17.2. Seven small container labeling methods. NOTE. From "Increasing the Surface Area on Small Product Containers to Facilitate Communication of Label Information and Warnings," by T. Barlow and M. S. Wogalter, 1991, in *Proceedings of Interface 91*, p. 90. Copyright 1991 by Human Factors Society. Reprinted with permission.

used a small glue bottle having either a control, wings, or tag label while performing a model airplane assembly task. Participants were not told that warnings design and compliance behavior were the main interests of the study (i.e., there was incidental exposure to the warning while doing the task). Although the content of the information printed on all labels was identical, the increased surface area of the tag and wings label enabled larger print (the font on the control label was 5-point type and, on both alternative labels, it was 9-point type). Whether or not participants wore protective gloves (as directed by a warning on the label) was measured. Participants complied significantly more often with the tag (80%) warning than with either the wings (36%) or control (13%) warning.

Kalsher, Wogalter, and Racicot (1996) continued to investigate the benefits of expanded surface area labels, but instead of using glue product labels, they used prescription medication containers. Undergraduates (mean age = 22 years) and older adults (mean age = 73 years) rated labels that varied by type (control, tag, fold-out), print size, and presence or absence of pictorials, on various dimensions including noticeability. A clear preference for the alternative labels was shown by both populations, and labels with pictorials were rated as more noticeable than labels without.

Wogalter and Dietrich (1995) also investigated the attention-getting aspects of medication labels. However, rather than using an alternative label design, they used an existing OTC easy open design. This type of OTC container, as shown in Fig. 17.3, has substantially more usable surface area than more conventional containers holding the same or similar medications. The easy open containers have space on the cap section for placing additional information.

In the Wogalter and Dietrich (1995) study, there were six label conditions, differing in color and placement of warning information. One control label was identical to a conventional OTC product commercially available at any pharmacy—having front, back, and side labels (but nothing of material relevance on the cap section). A second control label lacked the side, back, and cap labels (only the front label was used). The four experimental containers had the labels of the conventional control (with front, back, and side labels) but also included an additional label on the cap. All of the cap labels had the same information. It repeated some of the most important information from the back and side labels, plus it had larger print, a signal word (WARNING), and a signal icon (an exclamation point surrounded by a triangle). The four experimental cap conditions differed only by color (white, orange, both orange and white, and fluorescent green).

The results showed that participants (mean age 75 years) judged the containers with the added label on the cap more positively than the currently sold design without the cap information. Furthermore, participants preferred the colored cap

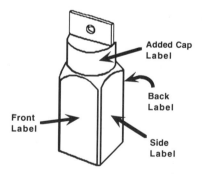

FIG. 17.3. OTC easy open cap container.

labels, ranking them higher than the white label. Thus it appears making use of existing surface space together with various conspicuity-enhancing features improves judged noticeability.

As we have seen, various methods derived from human factors principles can be used to increase the salience of printed information. However, the unique nature of pharmaceutical labels (e.g., a large amount of printed information on a small amount of space) make application of the principles difficult. Nevertheless, research indicates that using expanded surface area and conspicuity-enhancing features such as larger print, color, signal words, and pictorials can promote attention capture.

Attention capture is the initial requirement to get information processing underway, and thus it is the first hurdle. With the capture of attention, the information flow is allowed to continue to subsequent stages. Nevertheless, over time and repeated exposure, all labels, even ones with numerous attention-getting properties, will lose their ability to attract attention. Although there are no easy solutions to the problem of habituation, one approach is to intermittently vary the label appearance, structure, and content, making it look less familiar. This will retard habituation for a time, until the appearance must be altered again.

ATTENTION MAINTENANCE

Individuals might notice the presence of warnings and instructions on a label but not stop to examine them. If they do not examine it further, the effectiveness of the label will be limited only to knowing that a label is present, and there will be nothing conveyed regarding the content. Thus to proceed further with information processing, after the information on a label is noticed, attention must be maintained and focused on the material. At this stage, individuals decide to examine the information printed on a label. Many of the same design features that capture attention also appear to help maintain attention (Barlow & Wogalter, 1991; Wogalter, Forbes, et al., 1993). For example, large print not only attracts attention but also increases legibility, which lets users focus on the characters forming the message. Legible print and pictorials make reading less effortful and can make the material more desirable to read.

Factors that also influence attention maintenance include formatting and brevity. A label that is aesthetically pleasing in the way it is formatted will likely attract and hold attention during which the material is examined and information extracted (Hartley, 1994). Formatting can be based on many factors including the amount of "white space," information groupings, line spacing, and so forth. Material that is in an outline/list format is generally preferred to that in paragraph/prose style (Desaulniers, 1987). Furthermore, if the label contains large amounts of text, individuals may decide that it takes too much effort to read. Thus, brevity is desirable (Wogalter et al., 1987). See Hartley (1994) and his chapter in this volume (chap. 14) for more detail on formatting.

Application of Attention Maintenance to Pharmaceutical Labels

Older adults tend to consume more medications and have reduced vision capabilities relative to other population groups. Thus, the persons who most need the information may not be able to obtain it as they have difficulty reading the small print (Wogalter, Magurno, Scott, & Dietrich, 1996). As described earlier in the attention capture section, Barlow and Wogalter (1991) and Wogalter, Forbes, et al. (1993) found that alternative label designs with larger print increased noticeability ratings. They also found that these designs also increased participant's willingness to read the labels. Enhancements designed to attract attention (expanded surface area, etc.) also frequently promote attention maintenance such as reading behavior (Kalsher et al., 1996; Sojourner & Wogalter, 1997; Young & Wogalter, 1990).

Morris and Kanouse (1980) found that a moderate amount of information on drug leaflets is preferred. Too little and too much are negative features. This result reveals the conflict between brevity and completeness. Brief messages are more likely to be read but they may be incomplete. Message that are highly comprehensive in content may address all of the questions that individuals may have, yet reduce the likelihood that people will make the effort to read the material.

Labeling and communication of drug information more generally require systems consideration. The packaging, the on-product label, and the insert all have different roles. A more complete insert will allow health care professionals or interested consumers to acquire more detailed information. The exterior packaging serves to convey the drug's appropriateness during purchase decisions, whereas the on-product label conveys information on use, and so forth. Allocating different information components to different parts of the label system may permit brevity and larger print on the container label, thereby increasing people's willingness to read what is there.

COMPREHENSION

A person may notice a label and examine it, but if he or she does not understand the words and pictures, the information goes no further, and processing stops. This creates a bottleneck that fails to inform and, down the line, negatively affects compliance. In the comprehension stage, information coming in makes connections with existing knowledge related to the label's message. The incoming information acts as a cue, activating memory structure and elaborating on the label information; this information is relatively easily assimilated into memory. If the message contains information that is not known, then with sufficient time and effort, the new information may be accommodated into memory where new structure and connections are created (i.e., learning may take place).

As necessary as it is, research on the factors that make label wording comprehensible is surprisingly limited. There is research on signal words that shows that certain terms may be useful in producing understanding of the level of hazard involved. Some signal word studies (e.g., Wogalter & Silver, 1995) have examined understanding using subjective ratings, frequency of occurrence in the language, and readability indexes. Two novel approaches have used measures of variability (e.g., standard deviations) and missing (blank) evaluations as indications of understandability. The assumption is that if people's subjective evaluations are highly variable it indicates that people have different conceptions of what the word means (suggesting its use may not be appropriate if the intention is to communicate a particular level of hazard). When participants fail to evaluate the words (i.e., leave them blank), it is an indication that the terms are not well known (once again suggesting lack of viability as signal words). The tabled data in Wogalter and Silver (1995) could be used to select understandable terms spanning the entire hazard-level dimension as evaluated by older adults, young children, and recent U.S. immigrants.

Other than signals words, research on label wording is virtually nonexistent. Although there is considerable research testing label comprehension, this research does not necessarily test comprehension factors. For example, although Wogalter et al. (1996) found that knowledge acquired (using a comprehension test) differed depending on cap label conditions, this does not mean that the differences among conditions is a result of a direct impact on the comprehension factor. Instead, the difference between cap conditions was probably due to effects on the attention capture or attention maintenance phases. In other words, the earlier stages in the information-processing model may cause a bottleneck that shows up when a higher level stage is measured. Thus, although comprehension may be measured (i.e., the dependent variable), it does not mean that the manipulation (i.e., the independent variable) directly affects the comprehension stage.

A common (and sometimes unfortunate) misconception held by subject-matter experts is that certain kinds of hazards and the information conveyed on labels will be as well understood by less expert people as by themselves (Laughery, 1993). The knowledge held by experts is sometimes so ingrained that they may not realize that others may not understand it. Therefore, the resulting label may not do its job with respect to conveying clearly the needed information. In some cases, the target audience is well trained, for example, physicians and other professionals to whom the product may be restricted in its and application (e.g., prescription medications), and therefore some assumptions can be made concerning the extent of their knowledge. Frequently, however, the lay public is the intended target of the message. Thus the main concern are individuals who have lower (or different) reading skills and education about the particular hazards of concern. Reading comprehension in older adults with lower education levels tends to decline with age (Meyer, 1987). To have a better chance of reaching these groups, the label should be made understandable by the lowest practical level of readers. Consider the statement "low birth weight" found on the label of some cigarette warnings. This statement is intended to convey the warning that smoking is harmful to the baby. However, there is some anecdotal evidence that some women have interpreted the statement to be a benefit of continuing to smoke, such as making labor easier because the baby will be smaller, whereas others have interpreted it as a way to keep their own weight down. Had this warning been tested with a representative sample of the target population, in this case women of childbearing age, the wording could have been changed to avoid ambiguity.

Although there is not much research specifically on label language, other literatures (e.g., basic grammar, technical writing) point to factors that are likely to affect word comprehension. Some of these characteristics include the use of short, high-frequency words in the form of brief statements. In fact, computer-based readability indexes exist that are based on these criteria (e.g., the Flesch and Dale-Chall formulae) and that can automatically measure the grade level or percentage of the population that will understand the text. The readability indexes and the simplified language criteria are only starting points, however. Numerous research studies (e.g., Davison & Green, 1987; Klare, 1984) have shown that these criteria can provide misleading measures of comprehension and probably should be used only as a rough guide in the preliminary writing stages.

Other factors can also influence the understandability of text messages. A label that has headings and is logically organized (e.g., by content matter, ordered temporally or procedurally) and physically formatted (e.g., small chunks of text in a bulleted list format separated by white space) is likely to promote better comprehension than a single large chunk of disorganized prose. Guidelines on these characteristics can be found in the technical writing literature and are likely to benefit the construction of preliminary label prototypes (Hartley, 1994). However, to really assure label understandability, variants of the warning message should undergo usability evaluations using a representative sample of the target population. Iterative label redesign may be necessary if the tested message does not meet adequate comprehension (Hartley, 1995).

Although there is not much research on the specific factors influencing the word understandability of label text, there is a larger literature on pictorials. Pictorials are a potentially useful way to facilitate understanding. Well-designed pictorials can be worth a thousand words (more or less) and potentially communicate large amounts of information in a glance (Dewar, in press). Also there are benefits for people who have difficulty reading text because of low literacy levels, lack of familiarity with the language, or vision problems that make reading very small print difficult. However, although standards organizations like the American National Standards Institute (1991) and the International Standards Organization (1984) have specific testing methods to assure understanding is at adequate levels, most pictorials in common use today probably have not been tested and many may not be understood by the intended targets.

Application of Comprehension to Pharmaceutical Labels

The purpose of having understandable medication labels is to provide individuals with use, benefit, and risk information. Understandable labels enable informed decisions and promote safe actions by users of pharmaceutical products. As mentioned earlier, the text needs to be sufficiently salient and large to get people to notice and read it. We have reviewed a number of studies that have tested alternative label designs that appear to reduce the print size problem. Enlarging the label surface area allows one to increase text size, to reprint the most important textual material in a salient manner, and to provide space for pictorials.

The general characteristics of word and statement simplification are likely to benefit text comprehension. Comprehensibility can also be enhanced by organizing the information on labels. In a study on label organization, Vigilante and Wogalter (1997) had students, community volunteers, and older adults arrange component text sections of four actual OTC medications. They found that participants arranged the four labels in a consistent order, preferring that, after the medication brand name, that labels have information in the following order:

1. Drug indications.
2. Warnings (cautions and precautions) and use (directions).
3. Active ingredients.
4. Inactive ingredients.
5. Safety-sealed designation.
6. Storage instructions.
7. Manufacturer information.
8. Bar code.

All three groups had similar orderings, although the older adults' assignments were somewhat more variable. These results are similar to those found by Morrow, Leirer, Altieri, and Tanke (1991) who had seniors arrange sections of a prescription drug label. See chap. 15 by Morrow and Leirer in this volume for a more extensive discussion of this topic.

Recent research has shown that some kinds of pictorials are successful at communicating important pharmaceutical-related information and warnings effectively. For example, Magurno, Wogalter, Kohake, and Wolff (1994) tested a diverse population group on the meanings of 30 pharmaceutical pictorials developed by the U.S. Pharmacopoeia Convention (USPC) and found that 18 of the pictorials met or exceeded the ANSI (1991) standard comprehension criterion of 85%. Furthermore, upon redesign, six more pictorials met the 85% correct comprehension criterion. Wolff and Wogalter (1993) performed similar testing using 28 of the 30 USPC pictorials and found that all but five of the pictorials surpassed the ANSI criterion. Ringseis and Caird (1995) tested comprehension for a set of pharmaceutical pictorials developed by the Pharmex Company and found that 9 of 10 pictorials tested (either original or redesigned pictorials) surpassed the ISO (1984) criteria of 67% correct comprehension.

Morrell, Park, and Poon (1990) developed and tested a unique pharmaceutical dosing pictorial. Medication label instructions were presented in either a traditional text format or in a format which combined text and pictorials. After studying a medication bottle label, participants were asked to recall the instructions. The results showed that for younger adults, the mixed text and pictorials instructions were comprehended and remembered better than the plain text instructions, but older adults did worse when pictorials were present compared to text instructions alone.

Wogalter, Sojourner, and Brelsford (1997) found that even when some pharmaceutical pictorials were not well understood, brief exposure to the verbal referent (its name in words) can significantly raise and then maintain comprehension over an extended period. In this study, participants were exposed to 20 pharmaceutical and 20 industrial safety pictorials. Participants were initially tested on the meaning of each pictorial. Later, a verbal description (either its simple verbal referent or a more detailed explanation) of each pictorial was given. Later, comprehension tests were given at different points in time. Results showed that brief exposure to the verbal referent substantially increased comprehension and that high levels were retained over time.

Pharmaceutical pictorials are also preferred by consumers. For example, Kalsher et al. (1996) demonstrated that consumers believe pharmaceutical pictorials are helpful and should be included on medication labels. Ratings showed that consumers strongly preferred drug labels with pictorials over those labels without pictorials.

Unfortunately, depicting pharmaceutical information by pictorials can be difficult. As described earlier, several commercially available pharmaceutical pictorials fail to meet the ANSI or ISO acceptability criteria (Magurno et al., 1994; Ringseis & Card, 1995; Wolff & Wogalter, 1993). The difficulty is partly due to the concepts being depicted. Abstract, less visible concepts (e.g., the passage of time for the concept "Take until gone") tend to be more difficult to design. Concrete, visible concepts (e.g., "Take with water") are much easier to design and generally perform well on comprehension tests.

Moreover, by their very nature, many medication instructions are often highly complex, comprising multiple ideas. Consider the seemingly simple instruction "Take two hours after meals." This instruction is actually an abstract, multiple-component concept that relates to the consumption of medication after the passage of a specific time duration relative to food intake. As might be expected, representing this concept with a highly understandable pictorial (without any text) would be difficult. In fact, various pictorials depicting this concept have been found to be poorly understood (Magurno et al., 1994)

In extreme cases, poor comprehension can lead to "critical confusions," resulting in people understanding the opposite of what they should, and possibly prompting people to perform the wrong behaviors. These confusions are of particular concern when dealing with potentially hazardous medicines. ANSI (1991) allows no more than 5% critical confusions in pictorial comprehension tests.

In recognition of the need to avoid using pictorials that inadequately or incorrectly convey the intended message, printed material accompanying prescription medications is likely to contain only an incomplete set of pictorials. That is, each and every textual instruction item may not be supplemented by an accompanying pictorial. Concrete concepts may be represented by pictorials, whereas the complex and abstract instructions may be represented by text alone.

The effect of using an incomplete set of pharmaceutical pictorials was recently examined by Sojourner and Wogalter (1997). Five prescription medication information sheets (similar to commercially available Drug Information Leaflets) were created containing medication instructions that specified the directions and warnings for drug use. There were five instruction sheet conditions: (a) text only, (b) pictorials only, (c) simultaneous text and redundant pictorials, (d) text with one half of the statements being accompanied by a redundant pictorial (incomplete pictorials), and (e) a no instruction control. On one of the evaluated dimensions, undergraduates rated how easy it was to understand the instructions on the drug information sheet. The results showed that text with a full set of pictorials was rated as easiest to understand, followed by the partial pictorials condition. Apparently, pharmaceutical instructions with both text and pictorials allows people to process information in the form they prefer—as a verbal (text) code or a nonverbal (pictorial) code.

However, pictorials should probably not be used as a sole source of pharmaceutical information. In the Sojourner and Wogalter study, the drug information sheets that contained only pictorials were rated lowest in both comprehension dimensions compared to any of the information sheets with text. Apparently, pictorials are considered beneficial in augmenting text, not replacing it.

Morrow, Leirer, and Andrassy (1996) performed two experiments that showed the detrimental effect of not using highly understandable pictorials and accompanying text. Three medication schedule pictorials were developed: a time line, a pair of 12-hour clocks (one each for AM and for PM hours), and a 24-hour clock. The pictorials were compared with text instructions using younger (mean age = 26 years) and older (mean age = 70 years) adult participants. In the first experiment, participants paraphrased and then recalled schedules that were conveyed by the different instructional methods. Text was paraphrased more quickly than any of the pictorials, and text and time line schedules were paraphrased more accurately than the two clock pictorials. In the second experiment, free and cued recall after limited study time was assessed. Again, text instructions were associated with highest performance and were recalled more accurately than any pictorial. Morrow and his colleagues explained that the superior performance associated with text is due to people's greater familiarity with textual instructions. Another reason may be the quality of the pictorials used. See Morrow and Leirer's chapter (chap. 15) in this volume for a more extensive review of this topic.

BELIEFS AND ATTITUDES

Given that a warning captures attention, is read, and is understood, then the next stage in the information-processing model concerns beliefs and attitudes. *Beliefs* refer to an individual's knowledge of a topic that is accepted as true (regardless of actual truth) and which is used to form opinions, expectations, and judgments. *Attitudes* are similar to beliefs but have more emotional involvement. Because of their similarity, beliefs and attitudes are grouped together in the model.

Although beliefs and attitudes follow comprehension in the model, their effect on human information processing could occur at earlier stages. For example, individuals who believe a product is safe may not look for a warning, and even when a warning is noticed, the individual may elect not to examine it further. The fact that later stages influence decisions at earlier stages points to the fact that there are backward or feedback effects among the stages of the information-processing model.

When people are familiar with a product, the probability of looking at, reading, and complying to the label is lower than if the product is unfamiliar (e.g., Godfrey, Allender, Laughery, & Smith, 1983; Wogalter, Brelsford, Desaulniers, & Laughery, 1991). Repeated use generally increases product knowledge, which can reduce the propensity to seek additional information about the product. Also, it could produce overconfidence about how to use a product, or lead to erroneously low levels of perceived risk, and, as a consequence, unsafe behavior may be produced. However, this does not necessarily mean that familiarity breeds unsafe behavior. When going from being unfamiliar to familiar, the information gained could include knowledge of how a product is used as well as possible side effects and warnings, which in turn, could result in safer behavior. Familiarity beliefs are detrimental when they cause people to not read labels for similar-appearing, but more hazardous, products.

Related to familiarity, an important factor associated with people's beliefs and attitudes is hazard perception. Familiar products tend to be less hazardous. Persons who do not perceive a product as hazardous will be less likely to notice or read an associated label (Wogalter et al., 1991; Wogalter, Brems, & Martin, 1993). And even if they do read the label, people may not comply with the directives on a product if they believe the hazard is low.

Another related factor is injury severity or the extent to which people think they may be hurt. People are more likely to consider injury severity than injury likelihood when forming their hazard perceptions (Wogalter et al., 1991; Woglater, Forbes, et al., 1993).

Assuming that individuals do read the information on a label, if it does not conform to, or is discrepant with, an individual's existing beliefs and attitudes, then the information will likely be disregarded. The information conveyed must then be sufficiently persuasive to change the person's beliefs and attitudes to concur with the appropriate ones to assure safety. Although bringing about change to someone's belief structure is not an easy task, it is facilitated by first presenting information in a form that will be noticed, read, and understood using the facilitating charac- teristics discussed earlier—so it has a chance to affect beliefs and attitudes by giving a persuasive presentation of the critical information. In some cases, it might need to be strong enough to override people's preexisting knowledge and experience.

Application of Beliefs and Attitudes
to Pharmaceutical Labels

Some people are under the misconception that if a drug store can sell a medication over the counter, or if a physician is willing to prescribe a medication, than it must be safe. This "safety complacency" creates problems when people do not believe there are any risks and ignore the labeling.

Moreover, when individuals become familiar with a medication, they are less likely to look at or read the label information. Repeated use can produce overconfidence and may lead to incorrect administration of the drug. Familiarity can also cause a problem when people do not read labels of similar-appearing pharmaceutical products or of new (possibly more hazardous) versions of older products. However, as mentioned earlier, familiarity is not always detrimental; over time, the individual may learn why and how the medication is used as well as possible side effects and, as a consequence, produce safer behavior.

Clearly, then, when people have certain beliefs and attitudes that are discrepant with realities of medication consumption and risks, it creates a problem. The label must correct those beliefs and attitudes, but at the same time people may not look for or read the label. In such cases, the label design must ensure attention capture and maintenance and the vital importance of heeding the label. This can accomplished in part by changing or altering the characteristics of the product label packaging so that it appears substantially different.

Recently, there have been proposals calling for standardized pharmaceutical label formats. Standardization could increase label usability, allowing consumers quickly to locate and extract important information from consistently organized pharmaceutical labels. Research has begun to examine characteristics of standardized labels. Morrow et al. (1991) and Vigilante and Wogalter (1997) found that people tended to consistently order components of labels for prescription and OTC medications, respectively. However, with standardization, labels will look very similar and may falsely promote familiarity beliefs and habituation across different kinds of drugs. Because standardization of medication labels will have both positive and negative outcomes, there still needs to be some flexibility so that critically important information can be conveyed in a salient fashion, particularly in cases where the medication has greater risks than consumers assume.

MOTIVATION

If pharmaceutical instructions are noticed, read, understood, and agree with a person's beliefs and attitudes (or are sufficiently strong to change beliefs and attitudes), the process moves to the motivation stage of the information processing model. To be effective at this stage, the instructions must motivate or "energize" the desired behavior. In this context, motivation takes two primary forms. First, individuals must be sufficiently motivated to read the label. Here, motivation feeds back to the attention maintenance stage in the information processing model. Motivation may derive from the person desiring to maintain safety (internally generated) or from the information on the product label, which, if designed well, should grab and hold attention (externally generated).

Second, individuals must be motivated to perform the correct behavior. One factor affecting compliance motivation is the message wording. In particular, information on injury severity can motivate people because few want to get hurt. A warning that says "Consuming alcohol within 2–3 hours of taking this drug can cause liver failure, which can produce death" is more likely to motivate compliance than a simple "Ask your doctor before using this drug if you consume alcohol." The former is also more explicit than the latter. Explicit statements clearly state the dangers of noncompliance. For example, Laughery, Vaubel, Young, Brelsford, and Rowe (1993) showed that the more explicit statement "Do not exceed recommended dosages because nervousness, dizziness, or sleeplessness may occur" raised hazard perceptions more than the less explicit statement "Do not exceed recommended dosages because undesirable effects may occur." Similarly, other wording characteristics may motivate behavior, including statements from a more authoritative source (e.g., U.S. Food and Drug Administration) than a less authoritative source (e.g., a sports figure or an actor) (Wogalter, Kalsher, & Rashid, in press).

Another factor affecting motivation is the cost (any expenditure of effort, time, or money) of complying and not complying. When people perceive the cost of compliance to be greater than the benefits, they are less likely to take proper actions. The requirement to expend even a minimal amount of extra time or effort can dramatically reduce motivation to comply (Wogalter, Allison, & McKenna, 1989; Wogalter et al., 1987). One way of reducing the cost of compliance is to make the directed behavior easy to perform (Wogalter et al., 1987, 1989).

The costs of noncompliance can also have a powerful influence on compliance motivation. These costs include injury, reprimands, and fines. Information on these aspects need to be known or communicated. Explicit consequence statements (e.g., the extent of potential injury) provides such information. Such statements have the power to motivate because they express outcomes that people wish to avoid.

Other variables also affect motivation. Time pressure reduces compliance likelihood (Wogalter, Magurno, Rashid, & Klein, 1998). Also, social influence influences motivation. If people see others comply, they are more likely to comply, and, if they see others not comply, they are less likely to comply (Wogalter et al., 1989).

Application of Motivation to Pharmaceutical Labels

One factor playing a critical role for eliciting motivation is the message content. Labels should have direct, explicit statements that communicate the consequences of not complying so that users can appreciate the costs of noncompliance (usually in terms of warnings/cautions and contraindications). To reduce compliance costs, the label should contain step-by-step instructions and if possible should include all the materials necessary for safe use of the product. For example, if a bulb syringe, rubber gloves, or measuring instrument is to be used with some kinds of medications, they might be included with the product. Likewise, providing a 24-hour toll-free number to address medication-related questions might also decrease compliance costs. See chap. 13 by Bogner in this volume for more information on these issues.

SUMMARY AND FINAL COMMENTS

There are numerous issues involved in the design of pharmaceutical label information. An information processing approach has served as a framework to analyze the steps involved in attention capture, attention maintenance, comprehension, beliefs and attitudes, and motivation. Furthermore, this approach has been used to highlight the factors influencing label effectiveness. Several recommendations can be made:

1. Pharmaceutical labels should be designed so that they will be noticed and examined. Enhancing salience and visual interest will benefit attention capture and maintenance. The small size of most pharmaceutical containers makes application of good design principles a challenge, but as we have seen, there are ways to increase the surface area of labels which allow the use of attention-enhancing features such as pictorials and legible print. Particular consideration should be given to older adults who tend to take more medications than other age groups and who may have age-related vision problems.

2. Pharmaceutical information should be understandable by as large a portion of the intended audience as possible. Factors that would benefit understanding of the label material includes simplified wording, organization of the material using headings, and pictorials.

3. Pharmaceutical information should contain persuasive, assertive statements to ensure that readers have or form the correct beliefs and attitudes. Changing the appearance of labels may be useful in countering familiarity beliefs that might prevent a person from reading the persuasion attempt.

4. Information contained in pharmaceutical labels should motivate people to comply. Cost of compliance needs to be low, and the consequences of noncompliance should be communicated explicitly.

How does the designer of a pharmaceutical label know whether the pharmaceutical label has the correct combination of desirable features? Inevitably, trade-offs have to be made. For example, explicit warnings are recommended, yet they also require more space than less explicit warnings—space that could be used for larger print or the inclusion of a signal word. Consider also the case regarding label standardization, where consistency across drugs will enable quick and easy location of desired information, but may also promote habituation. How to make decisions on the importance of trade-off principles in pharmaceutical label applications will require further research. In the mean time, answers to questions on adequacy of particular pharmaceutical labels require testing using a representative sample of the target population.

Testing may use many methods including subjective ratings, legibility assessments, comprehension tests, and actual behavioral compliance. There are also techniques using initial label prototypes in usability and market testing. Compliance testing is best, but sometimes can not be employed because of ethical and time constraints. Unfortunately, most pharmaceutical labels probably have not been tested at all, which is probably the main reason for their low quality. We believe that some testing is better than none at all, even if the tests do not use compliance measures or large numbers of test participants. Quite a number of improvements can be made with limited testing. Ideally, this testing should be an iterative process, requiring multiple label redesigns in order to find the right mix of adequate design factors. These data will help to confirm (or disconfirm) whether appropriate tradeoffs are successful.

Finally, testing can be directed at specific stages in the human information-processing model and may identify potential bottlenecks in the intermediate stages leading up to behavior. For example, if it is noted that people do not have the correct beliefs regarding a medication, enhancing label noticeability may not have any effect. Thus, the model also serves as a means of performing detective work when a warning is less effective than desired. By using the model as a basis for investigation, bottlenecks in the processing can be identified and appropriate steps taken to eliminate the barriers leading to safe behavior. This will be especially relevant to older adults who will surely benefit the most from advances in pharmaceutical label design.

REFERENCES

American National Standards Institute. (1991). *American National Standard for Safety Warnings, Z535.1 to .5.* Arlington, VA: National Electrical Manufacturers Association.

Barlow, T., & Wogalter, M. S. (1991). Increasing the surface area on small product containers to facilitate communication of label information and warnings. In *Proceedings of Interface 91* (pp. 88–93). Santa Monica, CA: Human Factors Society.

Barlow, T., & Wogalter, M. S. (1993). Alcoholic beverage warnings in magazine and television advertisements. *Journal of Consumer Research, 20,* 147–155.

Davison, A., & Green, G. (Eds.). (1987). *Linguistic complexity and text comprehension: A re-examination of readability with alternative views.* Hillsdale, NJ: Lawrence Erlbaum Associates.

Desaulniers, D. R. (1987). Layout, organization, and the effectiveness of consumer product warnings. In *Proceedings of the Human Factors Society 31st Annual Meeting* (pp. 56–60). Santa Monica, CA: Human Factors Society.

Dewar, R. (in press). Design and evaluation of graphic symbols. In H. J. G. Zwaga, T. Boersema, & H. C. M. Hoonhout (Eds.), *Visual information for everyday use: Design and research perspectives.* London: Taylor & Francis.

Godfrey, S. S., Allender, L., Laughery, K. R., & Smith, V. L. (1983). Warning messages: Will the consumer bother to look? In *Proceedings of the Human Factors Society 27th Annual Meeting* (pp. 950–954). Santa Monica, CA: Human Factors Society.

Hartley, J. (1995). Is this chapter any use? Methods for evaluating text. In J. R. Wilson & E. N. Corlett (Eds.), *Evaluation of human work* (pp. 285–309). London: Taylor & Francis.

Hartley, J. (1994). *Designing instructional text* (3rd ed.). London: Kogan Page.

International Standards Organization. (1984). *International Standard for Safety Colours and Safety Signs: ISO 3864.* Geneva, Switzerland: Author.

Kalsher, M. J., Wogalter, M. S., & Racicot, B. M. (1996). Pharmaceutical container labels: Enhancing preference perceptions with alternative designs and pictorials. *International Journal of Industrial Ergonomics, 18,* 83–90.

Klare, G. R. (1984). Readability and comprehension. In R. S. Easterby & H. J. G. Zwaga (Eds.), *Information design: The design and evaluation of signs and printed material* (pp. 479–495). New York: Wiley.

Laughery, K. R. (1993) Everybody knows: or do they? *Ergonomics in Design, 1,* 8–13.

Laughery, K. R., Vaubel, K. P., Young, S. L., Brelsford, J. W., & Rowe, A. L. (1993). Explicitness of consequence information in warnings. *Safety Science, 16,* 597–613.

Laughery, K. R., & Wogalter, M. S. (1997). Warnings and risk perception. In G. Salvendy (Ed.), *The handbook of human factors* (2nd ed., pp. 1174–1197). New York: Wiley.

Laughery, K. R., Young, S. L., Vaubel, K. P., & Brelsford, J. W. (1993). The noticeability of warnings on alcoholic beverage containers. *Journal of Public Policy and Marketing, 12,* 38–56.

Magurno, A. B., Wogalter, M. S., Kohake, J. R., & Wolff, J. S. (1994). Iterative test and development of pharmaceutical pictorials. In *Proceedings of the 12th Triennial Congress of the International Ergonomics Association, 4,* 360–362.

Meyer, B. (1987). Reading comprehension and aging. In W. Schaie (Ed.), *Annual review of gerontology and geriatrics* (pp. 93–115). New York: Springer.

Morrell, R. W., Park, D. C., & Poon, L. W. (1990). Effects of labeling techniques on memory and comprehension of prescription information in young and old adults. *Journal of Gerontology, 45,* 166–172.

Morris, L. A., & Kanouse, D. E. (1980). Consumer reactions to differing amounts of written drug information. *Drug Intelligence and Clinical Pharmacy, 14,* 531–536.

Morrow, D., Leirer, V., Altieri, P., & Tanke, E. (1991). Elder's schema for taking medication: Implications for instruction design. *Journal of Gerontology: Psychological Sciences, 46,* P378–P385.

Morrow, D. G., Leirer, V. O., & Andrassy, J. M. (1996). Using icons to convey medication schedule information. *Applied Ergonomics, 27,* 267–275.

Ringseis, E. L., & Caird, J. K. (1995). The comprehensibility and legibility of twenty pharmaceutical warning pictograms. In *Proceedings of the Human Factors Society 39th Annual Meeting* (pp. 974–978). Santa Monica, CA: Human Factors Society.

Sojourner, R. J., & Wogalter, M. S. (1997). The influence of pictorials on evaluations of prescription medication instructions. *Drug Information Journal, 31,* 963–972.

Strawbridge, J. A. (1986). The influence of position, highlighting, and imbedding on warning effectiveness. In *Proceedings of the Human Factors Society 30th Annual Meeting* (pp. 716–720). Santa Monica, CA: Human Factors Society.

Vigilante, W. J., & Wogalter, M. S. (1997). The preferred order of over-the-counter (OTC) pharmaceutical label components. *Drug Information Journal, 21,* 973–988.

Wogalter, M. S., Allison, S. T., & McKenna, N. A. (1989). The effects of cost and social influence on warning compliance. *Human Factors, 31,* 133–140.

Wogalter, M. S., Brelsford, J. W., Desaulniers, D. R., & Laughery, K. R. (1991). Consumer product warnings: The role of hazard perception. *Journal of Safety Research, 22,* 71–82.

Wogalter, M. S., Brems, D. J., & Martin, E. G. (1993). Risk perception of common consumer products: Judgments of accident frequency and precautionary intent. *Journal of Safety Research, 24,* 97–106.

Wogalter, M. S., & Dietrich, D. A. (1995). Enhancing label readability for over-the-counter pharmaceuticals by elderly consumers. In *Proceedings of the Human Factors and Ergonomics Society 39th Annual Meeting* (pp. 143–147). Santa Monica, CA: Human Factors and Ergonomics Society.

Wogalter, M. S., Forbes, R. M., & Barlow, T. (1993). Alternative product label designs: Increasing the surface area and print size. In *Proceedings of Interface 93* (pp. 181–186). Santa Monica, CA: Human Factors Society.

Wogalter, M. S., Godfrey, S. S., Fontenelle, G. A., Desaulniers, D. R., Rothstein, P. R., & Laughery, K. R. (1987). Effectiveness of warnings. *Human Factors, 29,* 599–612.

Wogalter, M. S., Kalsher, M. J., & Rashid, R. (in press). Effect of signal word and source attribution on judgments of warning credibility and compliance likelihood. *International Journal of Industrial Ergonomics.*

Wogalter, M. S., & Laughery, K. R. (1996). WARNING: Sign and label effectiveness. *Current Directions in Psychology, 5,* 33–37.

Wogalter, M. S., Magurno, A. B., Rashid, R., & Klein, K. W. (1998). The influence of time stress and location on behavioral compliance with warnings. *Safety Science, 29,* 143–158.

Wogalter, M. S., Magurno, A. M., Scott, K. L., & Dietrich, D. A. (1996). Facilitating information acquisition for over-the-counter drugs using supplemental labels. In *Proceedings of the Human Factors and Ergonomics Society 40th Annual Meeting* (pp. 732–736). Santa Monica, CA: Human Factors and Ergonomics Society.

Wogalter, M. S., & Silver, N. C. (1995). Warning signal words: Connoted strength and understandability by children, elders, and non-native English speakers. *Ergonomics, 11,* 2188–2206.

Wogalter, M. S., Sojourner, R. J., & Brelsford. (1997). Comprehension and retention of safety pictorials. *Ergonomics, 40,* 531–542.

Wogalter, M. S., & Young, S. L. (1994). The effect of alternative product-label design on warning compliance. *Applied Ergonomics, 25,* 53–57.

Wolff, J. S., & Wogalter, M. S. (1993). Test and development of pharmaceutical pictorials. In *Proceedings of Interface 93* (pp. 187–192) Santa Monica, CA: Human Factors Society.

Young, S. L., & Wogalter, M. S. (1990). Comprehension and memory of instruction manual warnings: Conspicuous print and pictorial icons. *Human Factors, 32,* 637–649.

Author Index

A

Abelson, R. P., 207, 216
Aberdeen, J. S., 6, 22
Adams, A. S., 268, 270, 287
Adelman, R., 169, 170, 171, 182
Adham, M., 73, 91
Adrassy, J. M., 223, 232
Affleck, G., 194, 196
Albert, D., 60, 66
Albert, M., 112, 120, 124, 125, 167, 172, 174, 176, 183
Albert, T., 234, 245
Alexander, M., 110, 111, 117, 124
Allen-Burge, R., 210, 219
Allender, L., 274, 288, 304, 308
Allison, F., 241, 246
Allison, S. T., 282, 283, 290, 306, 309
Altieri, P., 134, 143, 255, 264, 301, 305, 309
Altman, W. M., 56, 66
Anagnopoulos, C. A., 244, 246
Anderson, J. A., 205, 217
Anderson, J. L., 150, 161
Anderson, J. R., 47, 52
Anderson, L. A., 151, 161
Andrassy, J. M., 250, 253, 255, 256, 257, 262, 264, 265, 271, 275, 276, 277, 286, 289, 303, 309
Annas, G. J., 58, 66
Ansell, J., 24, 28
Appelbaum, P. S., 56, 62, 63, 66, 110, 113, 124
Applegate, M. H., 225, 231

Arenberg, D., 41, 53
Arocha, J. F., 130, 132, 133, 138, 139, 142, 143
Aschenbrenner, M., 60, 66
Ascione, F. J., 15, 22, 205, 214, 216
Ash, A., 56, 66
Ashburn, G., 172, 181
Ashcraft, M. H., 277, 287
Ashcroft, J. J., 70, 73, 74, 88
Ashford, J., 200, 216
Austin, D. F., 70, 71, 72, 74, 75, 82, 85, 86, 90
Avorn, J., 24, 28
Ayres, T. J., 270, 287
Azari, R., 151, 161

B

Babcock, R. A., 237, 245
Babcock, R. L., 6, 22, 37, 54, 134, 143, 169, 172, 183, 188, 189, 197
Backe, B., 59, 67
Backinger, C. L., 271, 274, 287
Bäckman, L., 128, 142, 253, 263
Baddeley, A. D., 63, 66, 97, 107, 237, 245, 251, 260, 263, 265, 284, 287
Baider, L., 72, 88
Baker, D. W., 271, 278, 279, 289
Baker, M. T., 240, 241, 247
Balasubramanian, S. K., 241, 243, 245
Balshem, A., 158, 164
Baltes, M. M., 157, 161
Baltes, P. B., 47, 52, 157, 161

Bandura, A., 251, 259, 263
Barberger-Gateau, P., 201, 216
Bargh, J. A., 7, 12, 19
Barkdoll, G., 170, 182
Barlow, A. S., 271, 278, 286, 289
Barlow, T., 279, 290, 293, 294, 295, 297, 298,
        304, 308, 309
Baron, J., 35, 52
Bartlett, B. J., 237, 246, 280, 286, 288
Bartolucci, A., 116, 118, 125
Bartolucci, G., 172, 183
Batenhorst, R. L., 151, 161
Baugh, D. K., 27, 28
Baum, A., 56, 67
Bauman, W. S., 47, 54
Bayne, J. R., 9, 20
Beach, L., 253, 264
Beach, S. R., 72, 88
Becker, M., 200, 216
Beisecker, A. E., 56, 60, 66, 71, 74, 85, 89
Beisecker, T. D., 60, 66, 71, 85, 89
Bekian, C., 200, 216
Bell, R. M., 151, 161
Belle, S., 210, 217
Belson, W. A., 95, 107
Bender, M. M., 203, 204, 216
Bennett, J., 14, 15, 16, 21, 188, 197
Bennett, R. L., 151, 161
Benson, D., 110, 112, 124
Benton, A., 120, 124, 210, 213, 216
Benyamini, Y., 159, 161, 163
Ben Zur, H., 51, 52
Berg, G., 120, 124
Berg, L., 112, 124, 210, 217
Bergman, U., 14, 15, 19
Berlowitz, D. R., 170, 171, 181
Bernard, R. M., 247
Bernhard, D., 244, 245
Berrin, J. E., 228, 232
Berry, J. M., 141, 143
Bertakis, K. D., 151, 161
Bertrand, R. M., 210, 219
Bettman, J. R., 34, 49, 52, 53
Beyer, R. R., 270, 287
Bienias, J., 99, 105, 108
Bilodeau, B. A., 56, 60, 66
Binswanger, B., 190, 197
Birchmore, D., 9, 14, 15, 16, 21, 188, 197, 205,
        206, 214, 215, 218
Birk, T. S., 151, 162
Bishop, G. D., 146, 149, 161, 162
Bivins, B. A., 151, 161
Blackburn, A. B., 9, 21, 205, 206, 214, 215, 218
Blalock, S. J., 191, 198
Bless, H., 102, 108
Blichert-Toft, M., 69, 70, 89

Blood, R. O., 72, 89
Blum, T. C., 72, 88
Bluming, A. Z., 87, 91
Bockenholt, U., 60, 66
Bogner, M. S., 226, 231
Bohner, G., 102, 108
Boich, L. H., 172, 183
Boles, D. B., 281, 286, 288
Bondi, M., 112, 125
Bonney, G., 153, 155, 163
Boritz, G. M., 239, 245
Boshuizen, H. P. A., 132, 143
Bosman, E. A., 42, 52, 272, 287
Botwinick, J., 112, 124
Bourke, R. S., 120, 124
Bovair, S., 227, 231
Bowling, A., 225, 232
Bowling, J. M., 272, 277, 287
Bradburn, N., 94, 97, 104, 105, 107, 108
Branch, L., 203, 217
Brandstatter, V., 17, 19
Branstetter, A. D., 87, 90
Brelsford, J. W., 268, 270, 278, 279, 288, 294,
        302, 304, 306, 309, 310
Brems, D. J., 304, 309
Brewer, W., 252, 264
Breznitz, S. J., 51, 52
Brody, D. S., 56, 66, 67
Brody, E., 199, 218
Bromiley, P., 50, 52
Brouillard, M., 251, 259, 263
Brown, G. W., 72, 89
Brown, H., 72, 90
Brown, R. G., 190, 197
Brown, R. V., 35, 52
Brownlee, S., 153, 155, 156, 160, 162
Buchner, D., 25, 28
Buckalew, L. W., 185, 196
Buckalew, N. M., 185, 196
Buehler, R., 44, 52
Buller, D. B., 170, 181
Buller, M. K., 170, 181
Burdette, J. A., 170, 182
Burgoon, J. K., 151, 162
Burgoon, M., 151, 162
Burke, R. J., 72, 89
Burleson, M. H., 191, 198
Burns, B. J., 151, 160, 162
Burns, E. A., 160, 164
Burrows, L., 12, 19
Butkovich, S. L., 9, 20
Butters, M., 110, 112, 119, 124
Butters, N., 110, 112, 119, 124, 125, 126
Byrd, M., 6, 19, 237, 245
Byrne, M. D., 227, 231
Byrne, M. J., 60, 68

C

Cadoret, R. J., 151, *165*
Cady, B., 87, 89
Caird, J. K., 301, 302, *309*
Calderwood, R., 41, *53*
Calhoun, R. E., 39, *52*
Califf, R. M., 24, *28*
Callahan, C. M., 201, 203, *219*
Callahan, E. J., 151, *161*
Caltagirone, C., 120, *125*
Cameron, L., 15, *20*, 145, 153, 158, 162, *163*, *164*, 186, 187, *196*, 208, 215, *218*
Caplan, L. J., 241, *245*, 246
Caporael, L. R., 172, *181*
Caputo, G. C., 56, 57, 66, 67
Carbone, P. P., 69, 71, 72, 82, 85, 88, 90
Carstensen, L. L., 159, *162*
Carswell, C. M., 244, *245*
Carter, W., 253, *264*
Carver, C. S., 73, 77, 87, 89, 90, 91
Carver, L. M., 258, 262, *264*, 265
Cassel, C. K., 202, *217*
Cassel, J. C., 170, *182*
Cassileth, B. R., 12, *19*, 56, 57, 60, 63, 66
Cebul, R. D., 34, 35, *53*
Cella, D. F., 70, 71, 72, 74, 86, *91*
Chadwick, S., 234, *245*
Chaglassian, T., 73, *90*
Chalmers, T. C., 24, *28*
Chapman, J. P., 44, *52*
Chapman, L. J., 44, *52*
Charles, G., 56, 60, 68
Charmaz, K., 190, *196*
Charness, N., 42, *52*, 135, *142*, 239, *245*, 272, *287*
Charon, R., 169, 170, 171, *182*
Chase, W. G., 136, 137, *142*
Chassein, B., 96, *108*
Chastain, R. L., 146, *164*
Chatterjee, A., 110, 114, 115, 116, 117, 122, *124*
Chen, M., 12, *19*
Chen, V. W., 70, 71, 72, 74, 75, 82, 85, 86, *90*
Chenery, H. J., 112, *125*
Cherry, K. E., 6, *21*
Cheung, H., 173, *182*, 244, *246*
Chi, M. T. H., 206, 207, *217*
Choodnovskiy, I., 24, *28*
Chrischilles, E. A., 25, *28*
Christensen, D. B., 271, 277, *289*
Chulef, A. S., 206, 207, *217*
Cioffi, D., 251, 259, *263*
Cjifer, E., 134, *142*
Clark, C., 210, *218*
Clark, H. H., 262, *264*

Clark, K. C., 73, *90*
Cleary, P. D., 159, *164*
Cleveland, L. E., 204, *217*
Clifford, E., 71, 73, 87, 89
Coates, W. C., 271, 278, 279, *289*
Coben, L., 112, *124*
Cody, H., 35, *53*, 109, 110, 111, 114, 115, 116, 117, *125*
Cohen, G., 6, *19*, 64, 66, 134, *142*
Cohen, H. H., 274, *288*
Cohen, I., 230, *232*
Cohen, L., 210, *217*
Cohen, S., 77, 89
Coker, R., 151, *162*
Cole, C. A., 241, 243, *245*
Cole, R., 171, 172, *183*
Collins, B. L., 271, 281, *287*
Commenges, D., 201, *216*
Conn, V. S., 205, *217*
Connolly, T., 42, *54*
Contrada, R., 149, 150, *164*
Conway, T., 153, 155, *163*
Coons, H., 149, *164*
Cooper, M., 244, 246
Copland, S., 110, *125*
Correa, P., 70, 71, 72, 74, 75, 82, 85, 86, 90
Costa, P. T., Jr., 41, *53*
Cotugna, N., 204, *217*
Coughlin, L. D., 136, 137, *142*
Coupland, J., 171, *181*
Coupland, N., 171, *181*
Coyne, J. C., 72, 89
Cracchiolo-Caraway, A., 72, 85, *90*
Craik, F. I. M., 6, *19*, 133, *142*, 169, 172, 177, *181*, *182*, 251, 253, 259, 261, 262, *264*, 284, *288*
Cramer, J. A., 185, 186, *196*
Craven, B., 70, 71, 74, *90*
Crawley, B., 205, *217*
Creighton, P., 271, 275, *290*
Crimmins, E. M., 201, 202, *217*
Crook, T., 200, *218*
Crouch, M., 147, 157, *163*
Croyle, R. T., 150, *162*
Culbertson, G. H., 172, *181*
Cummings, J., 110, 112, *124*
Cunningham, K. G., 176, *183*
Curley, S. P., 38, 39, 50, *52*
Cusack, B. J., 25, *28*
Cushman, W. H., 231, *232*
Cutler, S. E., 190, *196*

D

Daatland, S. O., 224, *232*
Dakof, G. A., 72, *91*
D'Andrade, R. G., 149, *162*

Danis, C., 104, *107*
Danziger, W., 112, *124*, 210, *217*
Darnell, J., 205, 214, *218*
Dartigues, J., 201, *216*
Dean, C., 73, *89*
Deber, R. B., 39, *52*
Deeg, D. J. H., 99, *107*
DeFreis, G., 147, *165*
Degner, L. F., 56, 59, 60, 66, 71, 74, *89*
DeJoy, D. M., 268, *287*
de Leon, M. J., 200, *218*
DeLongis, A., 72, *89*
DeMaio, T. J., 104, *107*
Denney, N. W., 135, *142*, 169, *181*
Dennis, A. R., 42, *54*
Densberber, J. E., 58, *66*
Derby, B. M., 203, 204, *216*
Derhagopian, R. P., 77, *89*
Dermen, D., 189, *196*
Desaulniers, D. R., 297, 304, 306, *308*, *309*
deTurck, M. A., 274, *288*
Deutsch, B., 98, *108*
DeVellis, B. M., 191, *198*
DeVellis, R. F., 191, *198*
Devolder, P. A., 176, *181*
Dewar, R., 300, *308*
Diefenbach, M., 149, 150, *164*
Diefenderfer, K., 239, 240, *247*
Diehl, M., 110, 121, *124*, 209, *219*, 252, *264*
Diener, E., 154, 160, *162*
Dietrich, D. A., 271, 274, *290*, 296, 298, 299, *309*, *310*
DiMatteo, M. R., 151, *162*
Dingus, T. A., 282, *287*
Ditto, P. H., 171, *181*
Dixon, R. A., 64, 66, 128, 133, 135, *142*, 172, 173, 178, *181*, 206, *217*, 251, *264*
Doherty, M. E., 47, *53*
Dolan, M. M., 210, *219*
Dorris, A., 268, 270, *289*
Dorris, G., 72, 85, *90*
Dosik, G. M., 87, *91*
Du, W., 170, 171, *181*
Dunkle, R. E., 272, *288*
Dyck, D. G., 71, 74, *89*
Dymek, M., *125*

E

Earles, J., 6, 7, *22*, 64, 67, 189, *197*
Easterby, R. S., 271, 281, *287*
Easterling, D., 11, 20, 71, 85, *89*, 149, 153, 157, 158, *162*, *163*, *164*, 208, 212, 215, *218*
Eaton, T. A., 9, 10, *21*, *22*
Echt, K. V., 271, 274, *289*
Eddy, J. M., 203, *219*

Edelstein, B., 110, *124*
Edwards, B. K., 70, 71, 72, 74, 75, 82, 85, 86, *90*
Edworthy, J., 268, 270, *287*
Eggert-Kruse, W., 189, *196*
Einstein, G. O., 6, 14, *19*, 176, *181*, 250, 260, *264*
Eisenhardt, K. M., 40, *52*
Ekstrom, R. B., 189, *196*
Eley, J. W., 70, 71, 72, 74, 75, 82, 85, 86, *90*
Elwork, A., 109, *125*
Ende, J., 56, *66*
Engelhardt, N., 27, *28*
Ennis, K., 110, *125*
Eraker, S. A., 38, 39, *52*
Ericsson, K. A., 128, 132, 133, *142*
Ershler, W. B., 157, *163*
Eson, M. E., 120, *124*
Evans, D. A., 130, 139, *142*, *143*
Eysenck, H. J., 283, *290*
Eysenck, S., 283, *290*

F

Fahrenberg, J., 97, *107*
Farber, J. M., 60, *66*
Farquhar, M., 225, *232*
Farrow, D. C., 70, *89*
Feinstein, A. R., 146, *162*
Ferris, S. H., 200, *218*
Fillenbaum, G., 202, 203, 210, *217*, *218*
Fincham, J. E., 271, 277, 279, *287*
Fineman, N., 169, 170, *181*
Fischer, L., 210, *217*
Fischhoff, B., 45, *53*, 60, *68*
Fisk, A. D., 6, *19*, 228, *232*
Fitten, L. J., 62, 63, *66*
Fitzgerald, J. F., 201, 203, *217*, *219*
Fleissner, D., 47, *54*
Fleming, B. B., 272, 277, *287*
Fleury, M., 271, 281, *288*
Folstein, J., 65, *66*
Folstein, M., 110, 114, *124*, 210, 213, *217*
Folstein, S., 65, *66*, 114, *124*, 210, 213, *217*
Fontanelle, G. A., 277, *290*, 297, 306, *309*
Forbes, R. M., 294, 297, 298, 304, *309*
Forsthoff, C. A., 146, *162*
Foster, T. S., 151, *161*
Fox, J. J., 204, *217*
Fozard, J. L., 99, *107*
Frankel, R. M., 151, *162*
Frankenberger, S., 244, *245*
Franzosi, M. G., 24, *28*
Frederiksen, C. H., 134, 136, *143*
Fredrickson, B. L., 46, *52*
Freedman, J. A., 201, *217*
French, J. W., 189, *196*
Fresco, C., 24, *28*

Friedland, R., 120, *124*
Friedman, K., 279, *288*
Friedman, M., 204, 214, *217*
Frieske, D., 6, 7, 9, 14, 15, *21, 22,* 64, 67, 146,
    155, *165,* 176, 177, 179, *183,* 189,
    197, 205, 206, 214, 215, *218,* 259,
    260, *265*
Frost, R. O., 34, *52*
Fulmore, C., 153, 155, *163*
Furedy, J. J., 153, *162*
Furner, S. E., 202, *217*

G

Gadd, C. S., 130, *142*
Gado, M., 112, *124*
Gagnon, M., 201, *216*
Gaines, C., 6, 7, *22,* 64, 67, 189, *197*
Gainotti, G., 120, *125*
Gammella, D. S., 271, 278, 286, *289*
Gandek, B., 151, *163*
Ganguli, M., 210, *217*
Gardner, M. E., 179, *181*
Garrity, T. F., 159, *163,* 170, *181*
Gartska, T. A., 169, 170, *182*
Gaskell, G. D., 96, *107*
Gerard, D., 73, *89*
German, P. S., 170, *181*
Gibb, W. J., 160, *165*
Gien, L., 205, *217*
Giere, R. N., 149, *162*
Giese-Davis, J., 72, 85, *89*
Giles, H., 172, *183*
Gilweski, M. J., 134, *143*
Given, B., 59, *68*
Glasgow, R. E., 87, *90*
Glenberg, A. M., 256, *264*
Godfrey, S. S., 274, 275, *288,* 297, 304, 306,
    308, 309
Gogate, J., 59, *68*
Gold, K., 153, 155, *163*
Goldberg, I. D., 151, *162*
Goldhaber, G. M., 274, *288*
Gollwitzer, P. M., 17, *19, 20*
Gomex-Caminero, A., 153, 155, *163*
Goodman, R. L., 70, 73, 74, *89*
Goodwin, J. S., 70, *90*
Gordon, A., 172, *181*
Gordon, E., 170, *182*
Gottlieb, M. S., 70, *90*
Gottman, J., 192, 193, *196*
Gould, O. N., 169, 171, 172, 173, 174, 176, 178,
    179, *181, 182*
Gouthro, T. A., 27, *28*
Grady, C., 120, *124*
Graham, D., 71, 74, *89*

Graves, D. A., 151, *161*
Greenberg, R. S., 70, 71, 72, 74, 75, 82, 85, 86,
    90
Greenblatt, D. J., 27, *28*
Greene, M. G., 169, 170, 171, *182*
Greenfield, S., 151, *163*
Gregory, M., 238, 240, *245*
Grice, H. P., 95, *107*
Griffen, W. O., 151, *161*
Griffin, D., 44, *52*
Griffin, M. R., 27, *28*
Grisso, T., 56, 62, 63, 66, 109, 110, 113, 116,
    124
Groen, G. J., 132, 134, 136, 138, *142, 143*
Gross, M. M., 270, *287*
Grossman, R., 170, *182*
Grundy, E., 225, *232*
Gubarchuk, J., 173, *182*
Gurwitz, J. H., 24, *28*
Guthrie, J. F., 204, *217*
Gutmann, M., 145, 149, 153, *164*
Guynn, M., 250, 260, *264*

H

Hack, T. F., 59, 66, 71, 74, *89*
Hailey, B. J., 60, *66*
Hait, H. I., 57, 63, *66*
Hakiel, S. R., 271, 281, *287*
Hakim-Larson, J., 207, 208, 209, 215, *218*
Hale, W. E., 157, *162,* 176, *183*
Hall, J. A., 151, *162*
Hamann, C., 62, 63, *66*
Hammel, B., 59, *67*
Hammerlund, E. R., 271, 277, *289*
Hamsher, K., 120, *124,* 210, 213, *216*
Hankin, J. R., 151, *162*
Hanlon, J. T., 272, 277, *287*
Hannum, J. W., 72, 85, *89*
Harding, K., 72, 85, *89*
Harker, J., 60, *68*
Harlacher, U., 102, *108*
Harman, H. H., 189, *196*
Harmatz, J. S., 27, *28*
Harrell, L., 35, *53,* 109, 110, 111, 114, 115, 116,
    117, 118, 119, 120, 121, 122, *124,*
    125
Harris, J. L., 280, *288*
Harris, S. D., 73, 77, *89, 90*
Harris, T. O., 72, *89*
Hartley, A. A., 284, 286, *288*
Hartley, J., 234, 235, 236, 237, 238, 239, 241,
    245, 246, 293, 297, 300, *308*
Hartman, K. A., 146, *163*
Hartman-Stein, P., 110, *125*
Harver, A., 146, *162*

Hasher, L., 6, 20, 22, 42, 43, 52
Hastie, R., 49, 53
Hatfield, A. K., 72, 85, 89
Hathaway, J. A., 282, 287
Haug, M. R., 56, 67, 170, 182
Hawkins, L., 110, 116, 118, 119, 120, 121, 125
Haxby, J., 120, 124
Hay, J. F., 7, 20
Haynes, R. B., 185, 186, 190, 196
Haythornthwaite, J. A., 192, 193, 198
Heckhausen, H., 17, 20
Heglin, H. J., 38, 52
Heidrich, S. M., 146, 162
Heimendinger, J., 204, 217
Helmig, L., 71, 74, 89
Helms, L. J., 151, 161
Henderson-Laribee, D., 110, 125
Henwood, K., 172, 183
Herlitz, A., 253, 263
Hershey, D. A., 206, 207, 212, 217, 219
Hertzog, C., 6, 14, 15, 16, 20, 21, 188, 190, 197,
        198, 251, 264
Hess, T. M., 237, 246
Heszen-Klemens, I., 151, 162
Heyman, A., 112, 119, 126, 210, 218
Hier, C. M., 250, 253, 255, 257, 262, 264, 265
Higgins, P., 194, 196
Hill, R. D., 280, 288
Hilton, J. L., 171, 181
Hines, C. V., 192, 196
Hippler, H. J., 95, 98, 106, 108
Hitch, G. J., 97, 107
Hoberman, H. M., 77, 89
Hodges, J. R., 112, 124
Hodges, S. D., 47, 54
Hodgkins, S., 17, 21
Hodne, C. J., 63, 67
Hoeper, E. W., 151, 162
Hoffman, S., 70, 71, 74, 90, 169, 170, 171, 182
Hogan, B., 60, 66
Holland, J. C., 73, 90
Holland, L., 250, 260, 264
Holliday, S. G., 50, 52
Holman, H., 146, 164
Holmes, M., 59, 68
Holt, W. S., 151, 163
Hooker, K., 190, 192, 193, 196, 198
Horne, R., 146, 151, 163
Horst, D. P., 270, 287
Horwitz, B., 120, 124
House, W. C., 56, 68
Howard, D. V., 7, 20
Hsu, L., 200, 216
Huberty, C. J., 192, 196
Hudson, S., 150, 154, 161, 164
Huff, F. J., 210, 217

Hughes, C., 112, 124, 153, 155, 163, 210, 217
Hughes, J., 112, 119, 126, 210, 218
Hughes, K. K., 74, 89
Hulka, B. S., 170, 182
Hultsch, D. F., 64, 66, 133, 135, 142, 178, 181,
        206, 217, 251, 264
Hummert, M. L., 169, 170, 172, 182, 183
Hunn, B. P., 282, 287
Hunskaar, S., 59, 67
Hunt, W. C., 70, 89
Hunter, C. P., 70, 71, 72, 74, 75, 82, 85, 86, 90
Hurd, P. D., 9, 20
Hutchison, S. L., 39, 52
Hynes, D. M., 70, 89

I

Idler, E. L., 159, 163
Ingham, R., 69, 73, 90
Ingram, K. K., 35, 53, 109, 110, 111, 113, 114,
        115, 116, 117, 121, 122, 124, 125
Insua, J. T., 24, 28
Inui, T. S., 253, 264
Irvine, J., 39, 52

J

Jackson, D., 244, 246
Jacoby, L. L., 7, 20
James, S., 241, 246
Jamison, K. R., 72, 73, 91, 149, 150, 163
Janis, I. L., 35, 52
Janofsky, J., 110, 124
Jarrard, S. W., 271, 278, 279, 286, 290
Jay, G. M., 209, 219
Jaynes, L. S., 281, 286, 288
Jeffs, M., 72, 85, 90
Jemmott, J. B. I., 150, 162
Jennings, J. M., 6, 7, 19, 20, 133, 142, 169, 181,
        251, 253, 262, 264
Jensen, A. B., 70, 89
Jepson, C., 158, 164
Jessen, J. L., 134, 143
Jette, A. M., 203, 217
Johansson, B., 203, 219
Johnson, E. J., 34, 49, 52, 53
Johnson, M. M., 49, 52, 212, 217
Johnson, R. J., 109, 126, 159, 163, 201, 203,
        217, 219
Johnson, T. P., 159, 163
Johnston, W. A., 37, 53
Jones, T. R., 10, 15, 21, 146, 165, 185, 186, 187,
        197, 249, 250, 251, 260, 265
Joseph, G. M., 132, 142
Julian, M. W., 192, 196
Jurica, P. J., 141, 143

K

Kaesberg, P. R., 157, *163*
Kafry, D., 47, *54*
Kahle, L., 204, *217*
Kahneman, D., 34, 44, 46, 51, *52, 53, 54*
Kalish, J. R., 171, *181*
Kalsher, M. J., 281, *290, 296, 298, 302, 306, 308, 309*
Kamarck, T., 77, *89*
Kanani, R., 190, *196*
Kancel, M. J., 210, *217*
Kanouse, D. E., *298, 309*
Kaplan, R. M., 59, *67*
Kaplan, S. H., 151, *163*
Kaplan-DeNour, A., 72, *88*
Kapp, M. B., 109, 110, *124*
Kardaum, J. W. P. F., 99, *107*
Karnes, E. W., 278, *288*
Kart, C., 157, *163, 272, 288*
Kasimatis, M., 190, 194, 195, *196*
Katzman, R., 112, *125*
Kaufman, D. R., 130, 132, 133, 138, 139, *143*
Kausler, D. H., 133, *142*
Kazis, L., 56, 66, 170, 171, *181*
Kejriwal, S. K., 282, *289*
Kellenbenz, M., 102, *108*
Keller, M. L., 155, 157, *165*
Kelley, C. L., 10, *21*
Kemper, P., 203, *217*
Kemper, S., 8, 12, 20, 96, *107, 172, 173, 182, 244, 246, 279, 280, 288*
Kendrick, O. W., 203, *219*
Kendrick, R., 9, *20*
Kennealey, G. T., 57, 63, *66*
Kennedy-Moore, E., 190, *198*
Kessler, R. C., 192, 193, *198*
Ketcham, A. S., 73, *90*
Kethley, A. J., 271, 277, *289*
Kidder, D. P., 6, 14, 15, 18, *20, 21, 167, 169, 174, 176, 182, 187, 188, 189, 197*
Kim, H. M., 189, *196*
Kincaid, D., 14, 15, *21, 146, 155, 165, 176, 177, 179, 183, 189, 197, 205, 218, 259, 260, 265*
King, B., 169, 176, 178, 179, *182*
Kingsley, P. A., 271, 274, *287*
Kinne, D., 73, *90*
Kintsch, W., 132, 134, *142, 143, 250, 251, 252, 255, 265*
Kirscht, J. P., 36, *53*
Kitayama, S., 40, *53*
Klaaren, K. J., 47, *54*
Klare, G. R., 300, *309*
Klein, G. A., 37, 41, *53*
Klein, K. W., 306, *310*

Klein, L. E., 170, *181*
Kline, D., 237, *246*
Kline, D. W., 270, 272, *288*
Knäuper, X., 99, *108*
Knesevich, J., 112, *124*
Knight, C. C., 134, *143*
Kogan, N., 50, *54*
Kohake, J. R., 301, 302, *309*
Kosnik, W., 237, *246*
Kovar, M. G., 203, *218*
Kraetschmer, N., 39, *52*
Kramer, A. F., 135, *143*
Krampe, R. T., 128, *142*
Krantz, D. S., 56, *67*
Krenek, R. F., 268, 270, *289*
Kreps, G. I., 169, 170, *182*
Kroll, J., 59, *68*
Kromrey, J. D., 192, *196*
Kruse, W., 189, *196*
Kukull, W. A., 25, *28*
Kulik, J. A., 150, *163*
Kuller, L. H., 210, *217*
Kuman, V., 200, *216*
Kupper, L. L., 170, *182*
Kurman, R., 70, 71, 72, 74, 75, 82, 85, 86, *90*

L

Labouvie-Vief, G., 207, 208, 209, 215, *218*
LaFleche, G., 112, 120, *124*
LaFleur, S. J., 47, *54*
Lafronza, V. N., 6, *21*
Lagakos, S. W., 189, *196*
Lahar, C. J., 6, *22*
Lambert, L. D., 271, 281, *288*
Lampman, L., 72, 85, *90*
Lamson, N., 268, 270, 272, 283, 286, *289*
Lamy, P., 14, *20*
Langston, W., 256, *264*
Lapinska, E., 151, *162*
Lapp, D., 178, *183*
Larkin, J. H., 256, *264*
Larsen, R. J., 154, 160, *162, 190, 193, 194, 195, 196*
Larson, E. B., 25, *28*
Larson, E. J., 9, 10, *21, 22*
Larsson, U. S., 56, *67*
LaRue, C., 274, *288*
Lau, J., 24, *28*
Lau, R. R., 146, *163*
Lau, T., 24, *28*
Laughery, K. R., 268, 270, 274, 275, 277, 279, *284, 288, 290, 293, 294, 297, 299, 304, 306, 308, 309, 310*
Launier, R., 150, 152, *163*

Lautenschlager, G., 6, 7, 22, 64, 67, 189, 197
Laux, L. F., 281, 288
Lavin, B., 56, 67
Lavine, B., 60, 66
LaVoie, D., 6, 20
Lawson, E. J., 170, 181
Lawton, M. P., 199, 203, 218
Lazaro, C. G., 56, 67
Lazarus, R. S., 150, 152, 163
Lebowitz, R. L., 87, 91
Lee, J. W., 46, 54
Legaspi, A., 73, 90
Lehrer, R., 240, 247
Lehto, M. R., 270, 288
Leinster, S. J., 70, 73, 74, 88
Leirer, V. O., 134, 143, 174, 176, 177, 179, 182,
        223, 232, 249, 250, 253, 255, 256,
        257, 258, 259, 260, 262, 264, 265,
        271, 275, 276, 277, 286, 289, 301,
        303, 305, 309
Lemon, S. J., 153, 155, 163
Lenoir, G., 153, 155, 163
Leonard, S. D., 278, 288
Lerman, C., 153, 155, 163
Lerman, C. E., 56, 57, 66, 67
Lerner, N. D., 271, 281, 287
Leslie, W. T., 70, 71, 74, 91
Letenneur, L., 201, 216
Leventhal, E. A., 11, 14, 15, 16, 20, 21, 60, 61,
        67, 71, 85, 89, 147, 149, 150, 153,
        155, 157, 158, 159, 160, 161, 162,
        163, 164, 165, 197, 208, 212, 215,
        218
Leventhal, H., 11, 14, 15, 16, 20, 21, 60, 61, 67,
        71, 85, 89, 145, 149, 150, 152, 153,
        154, 155, 156, 157, 158, 159, 160,
        161, 162, 163, 164, 165, 186, 187,
        196, 197, 208, 212, 215, 218
Levkoff, S. E., 159, 164
Levy, B., 12, 20
Lewis, A., 241, 246
Lewis, S., 170, 171, 181
Ley, P., 65, 67, 236, 246
Lezak, M., 120, 124
Lichtenstein, E., 252, 264
Lichtenstein, S., 45, 53, 60, 68
Lichtman, R. R., 87, 91
Lidz, C., 113, 125
Lieberman, M. A., 72, 89
Light, L. L., 6, 7, 8, 20
Linton, M., 97, 107
Lipman, P. D., 241, 246
Lisle, D., 47, 54
Llewelyn, S., 236, 246
Llwewllyn-Thomas, H. A., 56, 68
Lo, B., 56, 60, 68
Lockery, S. A., 272, 288

Lockwood, G. A., 56, 68
Loewen, E. R., 177, 182, 259, 261, 264
Lorig, K., 146, 164
Love, R. R., 149, 164
Low, R., 244, 246
Luce, M. F., 34, 52
Luchins, A., 38, 53
Luchterhand, C., 149, 164
Lukaszewski, M. P., 172, 181
Lusky, R., 62, 63, 66
Lynch, H., 153, 155, 163
Lynch, J., 153, 155, 163

M

MacCrimmon, K. R., 50, 51, 53
MacDonald, E. T., 260, 264
MacDonald, J. B., 260, 264
Mackowiak, E. D., 176, 182
Maercker, A., 47, 52
Maggioni, A. P., 24, 28
Magurno, A. B., 274, 290, 298, 299, 301, 302,
        306, 309, 310
Mahler, D. A., 146, 150, 162
Mahler, H. I. M., 150, 163
Main, D., 153, 155, 163
Malec, J. F., 71, 91
Malmberg, B., 203, 219
Malpert, J., 174, 181
Mangels, J. A., 141, 143
Mann, L., 35, 52
Manton, K. G., 203, 218
Mäntyla, T., 253, 263
March, V., 12, 19, 56, 60, 66
Marcus, N., 244, 246
Margolis, G., 70, 73, 74, 89
Marks, R. G., 157, 162
Markus, H. R., 40, 53
Marshall, E., 84, 90
Marsiske, M., 209, 219, 271, 280, 288
Marson, D., 35, 53, 109, 110, 111, 113, 114,
        115, 116, 117, 118, 119, 120, 121,
        122, 124, 125
Martin, D. K., 201, 217
Martin, E. G., 304, 309
Martin, J. K., 72, 88
Martin, L., 94, 108
Martin, M., 14, 15, 16, 21, 188, 189, 197
Martin, R., 210, 217
Martz, B. L., 205, 214, 218
Marx, M. B., 159, 163
Maseri, A., 24, 28
Massie, M. J., 69, 73, 85, 90
Masullo, C., 120, 125
Matthews, D., 278, 288
Matthews, J., 60, 67
Mauri, F., 24, 28

May, F. E., 157, *162*
Mayer, D. L., 281, *288*
Mayhorn, C. B., 6, 10, 15, *21*, 167, 174, *182*, 185, 187, 188, 189, *197*, 249, 250, 251, *259*, *265*
Maylor, E. A., 176, *182*
Mazen, R., 155, *164*
McCarthy, R., 110, *124*
McCaul, K. D., 87, *90*
McClain, C. S., 59, *67*
McCorkle, R., 70, *90*
McCormick, E. J., 268, 272, 278, *289*
McCrae, R. R., 41, *53*
McDaniel, M. A., 6, 14, *19*, 176, *181*, 250, 260, *264*
McDonald-Miszczak, L., 169, 171, 176, 178, 179, *181*, *182*
McDowd, J., 228, *232*, 284, *288*
McEvoy, M. D., 70, *90*
McGhan, W. F., 179, *181*
McHugh, P., 65, 66, 114, *124*, 210, 213, *217*
McInturff, B., 110, 116, 118, 119, 120, 121, *125*
McKenna, N. A., 282, 283, 290, 306, *309*
McKibbon, K. A., 190, *196*
McPhee, S. J., 170, *181*
McQuellon, R. P., 70, 71, 74, *90*
McWilliams, M. E., 60, *66*
Mead, R. A., 179, *181*
Mechanic, D., 159, *165*
Meichenbaum, D., 151, *164*
Meisel, A., 113, *125*
Melton, L. J., 27, *28*
Menard, W. E., 250, 253, 255, 257, 262, *265*
Mengden, T., 190, *197*
Menon, G., 98, 99, 106, *107*
Mermelstein, R., 77, *89*
Mettits, E. D., 210, *218*
Meyer, B. J. F., 11, *20*, 37, 40, *53*, 60, 61, 62, 63, 64, 65, 67, 71, 74, 85, *90*, 134, *143*, 175, *182*, 207, 212, 214, *218*, 237, 239, 240, 246, *247*, 271, 280, 286, *288*, *299*, *309*
Meyer, D., 149, 153, 154, *164*
Miceli, G., 120, *125*
Michael, D., 241, *246*
Millar, K. U., 153, *164*
Millar, M. G., 153, *164*
Miller, D. C., 239, 240, *247*
Miller, J. M., 270, *288*
Miller, S. M., 57, *66*
Millner, L., 158, *164*
Misanchuk, E. R., 234, *246*
Mitchell, D. R. D., 134, *143*
Moffat, F. L., 73, 77, 89, *90*
Mohs, R., 112, 119, *126*, 210, *218*
Monsch, A., 112, *125*
Montamat, S. C., 25, *28*

Monty, R. A., 239, *247*
Moody, K. A., 167, 172, 174, 176, *183*
Moore, K. A., 171, *181*
Moore, W. P., 71, 74, *89*
Morrell, R., 6, 9, 10, 14, 15, 16, 18, *20*, *21*, 58, 67, 146, 155, *165*, 176, 177, 179, *183*, 188, 189, 191, *197*, 201, 205, 206, 214, 215, *218*, 241, 242, 243, 246, 256, 257, 258, 259, 260, *264*, *265*, 271, 274, 281, 284, 289, 301, *309*
Morris, J., 56, 67, 69, 73, *90*, 210, *218*
Morris, L., 170, *182*, 298, *309*
Morrow, D. G., 134, *143*, 174, 176, 177, 179, *182*, 223, *232*, 250, 253, 255, 256, 257, 258, 259, 260, 261, 262, 263, 264, 265, 271, 275, 276, 277, 286, 289, 301, 303, 305, *309*
Moskowitz, M. A., 56, *66*
Moss, M., 112, *125*
Mossman, D., 110, *124*
Mousavi, S. Y., 244, *246*
Moyer, A., 69, *90*
Müller, G., 96, *108*
Murdoch, B. E., 112, *125*
Murray, M. D., 205, 214, *218*
Musialowski, D. M., 170, *182*
Muss, H. B., 70, 71, 72, 74, 75, 82, 85, 86, *90*
Mutter, S. A., 44, 45, *53*
Myers, A. M., 202, *218*
Myers, R. E., 158, *164*
Myles-Worsley, M., 37, *53*

N

Narod, S., 153, 155, *163*
Nattinger, A. B., 70, *90*
Neale, J. M., 190, *198*
Neisser, U., 97, *107*
Nerenz, D., 154, 156, *164*
Nerlove, S. B., 149, *162*
Nesselroade, J. R., 190, 193, *198*
Newcomb, P. A., 69, 71, 72, 82, 85, 88, *90*
Nighswander, R., 176, *182*
Niles, P., 153, *164*
Nisbett, R., 147, *164*
Nissenbaum, H., 190, *197*
Noriega, V., 73, 77, 89, *90*
Norman, G. R., 132, *143*
Northouse, L. L., 72, 85, *90*
Northrop, L., 110, *124*
Nurss, J. R., 271, 278, 279, *289*
Nygren, M., 110, *124*

O

Obradovich, J. H., 231, *232*

O'Connor, T. W., Jr., 176, *182*
O'Hara, M., 72, *90*
Okun, M. A., 175, *183*, 253, 265, 271, 277, 289
Olshansky, S. J., 202, *217*
O'Muircheartaigh, C. A., 96, *107*
Orasanu, J., 41, *53*
Orbell, S., 17, *21*
Ory, M., 147, *165*, 170, *182*
Ostrum, J. R., 271, 277, 289
Otsubo, S. M., 281, *289*
Ouslander, J. G., 65, 68

P

Pagano, D., 24, *28*
Palmer, H. T., 10, *21*
Palmon, R., 134, *143*
Pariente, G. M., 176, 177, 179, *182*, 259, 260, 264
Parikh, N. S., 271, 278, 279, 289
Park, D. C., 6, 7, 8, 9, 10, 11, 13, 14, 15, 16, 18, 20, *21*, *22*, 58, 61, 64, *67*, 99, *108*, 109, 110, 121, *125*, 146, 155, *165*, 167, 169, 174, 176, 177, 179, *182*, *183*, 185, 186, 187, 188, 189, 191, 193, *197*, 201, 205, 206, 214, 215, 218, 241, 242, 243, 246, 249, 250, 251, 256, 257, 258, 259, 260, 261, 264, 265, 271, 281, 284, 289, 301, 309
Parker, R. M., 271, 278, 279, 289
Parmelee, P. A., 56, 66
Parrott, R., 151, *162*
Pasnau, R. O., 72, 73, *91*
Patel, V. L., 130, 132, 133, 134, 136, 137, 138, 139, *142*, *143*
Patrick-Miller, L., 160, *164*
Patsdaughter, C., 167, 172, 174, 176, *183*
Payne, J. W., 34, 36, 37, 49, *52*, *53*
Payne, S. A., 70, *90*
Pendleton, L., 56, 68
Pennebaker, J. W., 146, *165*
Pennington, N., 49, *53*
Pepper, S. C., 101, *107*
Perfetto, E. M., 272, 277, 287
Perkins, L. L., 157, *162*
Pesznecker, B. L., 167, 172, 174, 176, *183*
Pfau, M., 151, *162*
Phoenix, M., 260, *264*
Piasecki, M., 41, *54*, 207, *219*
Pierce, P. F., 56, 57, 59, 60, 61, 68
Pirkl, J., 237, 246, 286, 289
Pitts, J. S., 56, 68
Plein, J. B., 271, 277, 289
Pliske, R. M., 44, 45, *53*
Pogash, R., 41, *54*, 207, *219*

Pool, D., 110, *124*
Poole, A. D., 60, 68
Poon, L. W., 9, *21*, 58, *67*, 188, 191, *197*, 201, 205, 214, 215, 218, 242, 243, 246, 257, 258, 264, 271, 281, 284, 289, 301, *309*
Poses, R. M., 34, 35, *53*
Post, G. M., 41, *54*, 207, *219*
Poulton, E. C., 238, 240, *245*, 246
Pozo-Kaderman, C., 73, 77, 89, *90*
Pressley, M., 176, *181*
Price, A. A., 77, *89*
Price, P. C., 45, *53*
Prince, J. H., 238, *246*
Prohaska, T., 155, 157, 160, *163*, *165*
Pruchno, R., 110, *125*
Puglisi, J. T., 6, 7, *21*, *22*
Pulliam, C. C., 272, 277, 287
Purswell, J. L., 268, 270, 282, 289

Q

Qualls, C. D., 280, 288
Quinn, N. P., 190, *197*
Quinn, N. R., 149, *162*

R

Racicot, B. M., 281, 283, *289*, 290, 296, 298, 302, *308*
Rader, N., 65, 68
Raghubir, P., 98, 99, 106, *107*
Rampmaier, J., 189, *196*
Rapoport, S., 120, *124*
Rash, D. J., 244, *246*
Rashid, R., 306, *309*, *310*
Rasinski, K., 237, *246*
Ratajczak, H., 17, *20*
Ratcliff, G., 210, *217*
Ray, W. A., 27, *28*
Raymond, M. R., 192, *197*
Read, S. J., 206, 207, *217*
Redelmeier, D. A., 46, *52*
Reese, H. W., 206, *218*
Regier, D. A., 151, *162*
Reid, P. A., 87, *90*
Reifler, B. V., 25, *28*
Reilly, B. A., 47, *53*
Reinharz, S., 209, *218*
Reisberg, B., 200, *218*
Reitan, R., 120, *125*
Reitman, D., 24, *28*
Reynolds, P. M., 60, 68
Rice, G. E., 64, *67*, 134, *143*, 175, *183*, 239, 240, *246*, 247, 253, 265, 271, 277, 289
Rice, K., 173, *182*

Riley, D. M., 153, *162*
Ringseis, E. L., 301, 302, *309*
Rips, L. J., 97, 105, *107*
Robbins, J. A., 151, *161*
Roberts, D. M., 192, *197*
Robinson, D. S., 73, 77, 89, *90*
Robinson, J. D., 171, *181*
Robinson, J. N., 270, *287*
Robinson-Whelen, S., 251, 255, 259, *265*
Robitaille, C., 150, 152, 154, 161, *164, 165*
Rodeheaver, D., 206, *218*
Rogers, W. A., 6, *19*, 39, *53*, 228, *232*, 268, 270, 272, 280, 283, 286, 288, *289*
Rogers, W. H., 151, *163*
Roman, P. M., 72, *88*
Romney, A. K., 149, *162*
Romsaas, E. P., 71, 73, 74, 85, *91*
Ronis, D. L., 36, *53*
Rose, M., 110, *125*
Rosenberg, D. J., 231, *232*
Ross, E., 158, *164*
Ross, L., 147, *164*
Ross, M., 44, *52*
Ross-Degnan, D., 24, *28*
Roter, D. L., 151, *162*
Roth, L., 113, *125*
Rothert, M., 59, *68*
Rothstein, P. R., 297, 306, *309*
Rousseau, G. K., 268, 270, 272, 283, 286, *289*
Rovner, D., 59, *68*
Rowe, A. L., 306, *309*
Rowland, J. H., 69, 73, 85, *90*
Rowles, G. D., 209, *218*
Royle, G. T., 56, *67*, 73, *90*
Rubin, A., 70, 73, 74, *89*
Rudberg, M. A., 202, *217*
Rudd, P., 167, 169, *183*
Rulien, N., 179, *181*
Runnebaum, B., 189, *196*
Russell, F., 70, 71, 74, *90*
Russo, C., 11, *20*, 37, 40, *53*, 60, 61, 62, 63, 64, 65, *67*, 71, 74, 85, *90*, 175, *182*, 207, 212, 214, *218*
Russo, J. E., 45, *53*
Rusting, C. L., 141, *143*
Ryan, E. B., 171, 172, *183*

S

Sabo, D., 72, *90*
Sacks, H. S., 24, *28*
Saito, Y., 201, 202, *217*
Saljo, R., 56, *67*
Salmon, D., 110, 112, 119, *124, 125*
Salthouse, T. A., 6, 22, 37, 38, 42, *54*, 63, 64, *68*, 133, 134, 135, *143*, 169, 172, 183, 187, 188, 189, *197*, 214, *218*, 237, 245, 247, 251, 258, 265, 284, *289*
Salzman, C., 205, *218*
Samet, J. M., 70, *89*
Sanders, M. S., 268, 272, 278, *289*
Sanders, S. H., 191, *198*
Sandvik, E., 154, 160, *162*
Sanson-Fisher, R. W., 60, *68*
Santoro, E., 24, *28*
Sauvel, C., 201, *216*
Schaefer, E. F., 262, *264*
Schaefer, P., 11, 15, *20*, 60, 61, 67, 71, 85, *89*, 155, 157, *163, 164*, 208, 212, 215, *218*
Schaffner, W., 27, *28*
Schaie, K. W. S., 64, *68*, 110, 121, *124, 125*, 204, 206, 214, *218*, 237, 247, 252, *264*
Schain, W., 70, *91*
Schapiro, M., 120, *124*
Schegel, R. E., 282, *289*
Scheier, M. F., 77, 87, *91*
Schellhammer, P. S., 66
Scherer, K. R., 153, *164, 165*
Scheuring, B., 98, 101, 102, *108*
Schimmel, L. E., 59, *67*
Schmidt, H. G., 132, *143*
Schmitt, F., 109, *125*
Schmitt, N., 59, *68*
Schmitz, B., 194, *197*
Schneider, W., 36, *54*
Schoemaker, P. H., 45, *53*
Schooler, C., 241, *245*
Schooler, J., 47, *54*
Schreiber, C. A., 46, *52*
Schriver, K. A., 234, *247*
Schroeder, D. M., 87, *90*
Schulman, K., 153, 155, *163*
Schulz, R., 70, 77, *91*
Schumann, C. E., 239, *245*
Schwankovsky, L., 56, *68*
Schwartz, J. B., 160, *165*
Schwarz, N., 94, 95, 96, 97, 98, 99, 101, 102, 105, 106, *107, 108*
Scialfa, C. T., 270, 272, *288*
Scott, K. L., 274, 290, 298, 299, *310*
Scott, K. M., 240, *247*
Seaberg, E. C., 210, *217*
Segar, E. T., 25, *28*
Seidmon, E. J., 57, 63, *66*
Seiple, W., 229, *232*
Sekuler, R., 237, *246*
Shadden, B. B., 172, *183*
Shader, R. I., 27, *28*
Shaner, J. L., 169, 170, *182*

Shapiro, L., 27, 28
Shaw, A., 238, 247
Shaw, R. J., 7, 21, 177, 182, 259, 261, 264
Sheeran, P., 17, 21
Sheikh, J. I., 174, 176, 178, 182, 183, 249, 259, 260, 264, 265, 276, 289
Shevell, S. K., 97, 105, 107
Shiffrin, R. M., 36, 54
Shifren, K., 11, 18, 21, 22, 190, 192, 193, 194, 195, 197, 198
Shimamura, A. P., 141, 143
Shimp, L. A., 15, 22
Shinotsuka, H., 46, 54
Shoor, S., 146, 164
Shows, D. L., 34, 52
Siegrist, M., 244, 247
Silver, N. C., 271, 278, 286, 289, 294, 299, 310
Silveri, M. C., 120, 125
Simon, E. W., 64, 66, 206, 217
Simon, H. A., 57, 68, 130, 136, 137, 142, 143, 256, 264
Simons, M. A., 37, 53
Simpson, S. N., 271, 278, 279, 286, 290
Sinnott, J., 180, 183, 207, 208, 209, 215, 219
Sivak, M., 51, 54
Skovronek, E., 134, 143
Slade, P. A., 70, 73, 74, 88
Slovic, P., 47, 54, 60, 68
Smith, A. D., 6, 7, 21, 22, 64, 67, 97, 99, 108, 189, 197, 285, 289
Smith, C., 72, 90
Smith, C. A., 191, 198
Smith, C. R., 170, 181
Smith, D. G., 56, 57, 66, 67
Smith, D. H., 176, 183
Smith, D. M., 201, 217
Smith, J., 47, 52
Smith, M., 176, 182
Smith, S. R., 112, 125
Smith, T. W., 98, 108, 191, 198
Smith, V. L., 274, 288, 304, 308
Smyer, M., 56, 66, 110, 125
Snell, J., 46, 53
Snider, P. R., 69, 91
Snyder, C., 153, 155, 163
Sojourner, R. J., 298, 302, 303, 309, 310
Soler, J., 51, 54
Soloway, M. S., 57, 63, 66
Sovacool, M., 6, 21
Soviero, C., 170, 182
Spagnhol, J. M., 51, 54
Spilich, G. J., 134, 143
Spreen, O., 210, 213, 216
Spuhler, T., 190, 197
Staats, N., 110, 124
Stallones, L., 159, 163
Stanton, A. L., 69, 91

Staszewski, J. J., 132, 142
Staudinger, U. M., 47, 52
Steinwachs, D. M., 151, 162
Stewart, R. B., 157, 162
Stine, E. L., 6, 22
Stine-Morrow, E. A. L., 223, 232, 255, 257, 262, 264, 271, 275, 276, 277, 286, 289
Stoller, E. P., 147, 165
Stone, A. A., 190, 192, 193, 198
Stone, E. R., 47, 50, 54
Stone, M. D., 87, 89
Storandt, M., 112, 124, 251, 255, 259, 265
Strack, F., 94, 96, 98, 101, 108
Strauss, A., 156, 164
Strawbridge, J. A., 293, 309
Strayer, D. L., 135, 143
Street, R. L., Jr., 170, 183
Streufert, S., 41, 54, 207, 219
Strube, G., 97, 108
Strull, W. M., 56, 60, 68
Stuedemann, T., 18, 21
Stump, T. E., 201, 219
Sturr, J. F., 239, 240, 241, 247
Subar, A. F., 204, 217
Sudman, S., 94, 97, 104, 108
Sundarem, M., 120, 124
Sutherland, H. J., 56, 68
Sutton-Smith, K., 12, 19, 56, 60, 66
Svardsudd, K., 56, 67
Sweller, J., 244, 246
Szlyk, P. P., 229, 232

T

Talarcyzk, G., 59, 68
Talbot, A., 11, 20, 37, 40, 53, 60, 61, 62, 63, 64, 65, 67, 71, 74, 85, 90, 175, 182, 207, 212, 214, 218
Tanke, E. D., 176, 177, 179, 182, 223, 232, 249, 255, 257, 258, 262, 264, 265, 271, 275, 276, 277, 286, 289, 301, 305, 309
Tanner, M. A., 71, 73, 74, 85, 91
Taub, H. A., 239, 240, 241, 247
Taylor, C., 251, 259, 263
Taylor, J. L., 210, 219
Taylor, S. E., 72, 87, 91
Teimourian, B., 73, 91
Tennen, H., 194, 196
Tepper, A., 109, 125
Tesch-Römer, C., 128, 142
Tessler, R., 159, 165
Thal, L., 112, 125
Thomas, S. E., 203, 219
Thomason, M., 176, 182
Thompson, D. N., 239, 240, 247
Thompson, L., 134, 143

Thompson, S. C., 56, 68
Threlfall, S. M., 271, 275, 290
Till, J. E., 56, 68
Tognoni, G., 24, 28
Tonin, P., 153, 155, 163
Toone, B. K., 190, 197
Topol, E. J., 24, 28
Tourangeau, R., 98, 108
Tran, T., 160, 165
Trankle, U., 51, 54
Travis, C. B., 59, 68
Tritchler, D. L., 56, 68
Trock, B., 153, 155, 163
Troughton, E., 151, 165
Trump, D. L., 71, 73, 74, 85, 91
Tun, A., 7, 22, 237, 247, 253, 265
Turk, D. C., 151, 164
Tversky, A., 34, 44, 51, 53, 54
Tymchuk, A. J., 65, 68

U

Ung, E., 146, 164
Urrows, S., 194, 196
Usala, P. D., 190, 198

V

Valacich, J. S., 42, 54
van Belle, G., 210, 218
Vandeputte, D., 173, 182
Vanderplas, J. H., 238, 247
Vanderplas, J. M., 238, 247
van Dijk, T., 134, 143, 250, 251, 252, 255, 265
Varney, N. R., 210, 213, 216
Vaubel, K. P., 294, 306, 309
Venesy, B. A., 58, 63, 68
Vercruyssen, M., 228, 232
Vestal, R. A., 25, 28
Vetter, W., 190, 197
Veum, J., 70, 90
Viana, M., 229, 232
Vigilante, W. J., 271, 275, 289, 293, 301, 305, 309
Vogelzang, N. J., 57, 63, 66
Vogenberg, A., 176, 182
Volkman, N., 230, 232
von Eye, A., 64, 66, 206, 217
Vroman, G., 230, 232

W

Wagenaar, W. A., 97, 108
Wallace, L. M., 56, 68
Wallace, R. B., 25, 28

Wallach, M. A., 50, 54
Wallston, K. A., 191, 198
Walmsley, S. A., 240, 247
Walsh, D. A., 206, 207, 212, 217, 219
Wang, P., 110, 125
Ward, S. E., 146, 162
Ware, J. E., Jr., 151, 163
Watkins, K., 18, 21
Weber, E., 189, 196
Wechsler, D., 119, 125
Wedel, H., 56, 67
Wehrung, D. A., 50, 51, 53
Wei, W. W., 193, 194, 198
Weinberger, M., 205, 214, 218
Weir, T., 72, 89
Weissberger, F., 176, 182
Weisser, B., 190, 197
Wellisch, D. K., 72, 73, 91
Welsh, K., 112, 119, 126
Welsh, S., 204, 217
Wertheimer, M., 227, 232
Wesley, M., 70, 71, 72, 74, 75, 82, 85, 86, 90
West, R. L., 176, 183
Wetle, T., 159, 164
White, B., 191, 198
Wickens, C. D., 256, 257, 265
Wideman, M. V., 56, 67
Widmer, R. B., 151, 165
Wigton, R. S., 34, 35, 53
Wilholm, B. E., 14, 15, 19
Wilkes, W., 176, 182
Wilkins, A. J., 251, 260, 265
Williams, M. V., 271, 278, 279, 289
Williamson, G. M., 70, 77, 91
Willis, S. L., 64, 68, 109, 110, 121, 124, 126, 155, 165, 209, 210, 219, 252, 264, 271, 280, 288
Wilson, T. D., 47, 54
Wingfield, A., 6, 7, 22, 253, 265
Winslow, L., 237, 246
Wogalter, M. S., 256, 265, 268, 271, 274, 275, 277, 278, 279, 281, 282, 283, 284, 286, 287, 289, 290, 293, 294, 295, 296, 297, 298, 299, 301, 302, 303, 304, 305, 306, 308, 309, 310
Wolberg, W. H., 71, 73, 74, 85, 91
Wolf, T., 158, 164
Wolff, J. S., 256, 265, 282, 290, 301, 302, 309, 310
Wolfson, H. G., 56, 67
Wolinsky, F. D., 109, 126, 159, 163, 201, 203, 217, 219
Wood, C. T., 270, 287
Wood, J. V., 87, 91, 150, 165
Wood, P., 190, 193, 198
Woods, D. D., 231, 232
Woods, J. H., 247

Wright, B. D., 151, *161*
Wright, D. B., 96, *107*
Wright, P., 271, 275, *290*

Y

Yahnke, D., 70, *90*
Yates, J. F., 32, 33, 34, 35, 36, 38, 39, 40, 41, 45,
    46, 47, 48, 50, *52, 53, 54*
Yellen, S. B., 70, 71, 72, 74, 86, *90, 91*
Yen, J. K., 120, *124*
Yesavage, J. A., 178, *183,* 210, *219*
Young, C. J., 237, *246,* 280, 286, *288*
Young, S. L., 278, 281, *290,* 294, 298, 306, *309,*
    310

Z

Zachrisson, B., 238, 240, *247*
Zacks, R., 6, *20, 22,* 42, 43, *52*
Zarit, S. H., 203, *219*
Zautra, A. J., 191, *198*
Zedeck, S., 47, *54*
Zelinski, E. M., 134, *143*
Zimmerman, A., 145, *164*
Zimmerman, M. A., 151, *161*
Zozula, L., 139, *143*
Zsambok, C. E., 41, *53*
Zuckerman, M., 283, *290*
Zupkis, R. V., 12, *19,* 56, 60, 66
Zwahr, M., 6, 7, 9, 10, 11, *22,* 59, 62, 63, 64, 65,
    67, 68, 189, *197*

Subject Index

A

Age differences, *see also* Cognitive processes, age
    differences in
    behavior questionnaires, 93–94, 106
    and comprehension, 96
    and frequency scales, 99–100
    breast cancer treatment, 72, 74t, 76, 78t, 80t,
        83t, 85
        chemotherapy, 79, 82
        hormone therapy, 79, 84
        mastectomy, 71
        patient participation, 71
        radiation, 79, 84
    competency, 212–213, 215
    comprehension
        advanced directives, 9–10
        behavior questionnaires, 96
        pharmaceutical labels, 9
    decision making
        agents, 38–40
        conflict, 49–51
        modes, 37–40
        options, 41–42
        possibilities, 43
        realizations, 44–46
        values, 46–47
    medical experience, 8
    medication adherence
        and affective reactions, 154
        and automatic processing, 16–17
        and cognitive processes, 13–17
        and controlled processing, 13, 16

and environmental cues, 16, 17–18
and illness representation, 157
interventions for, 16–18
and lifestyle busyness, 15–16
model for, 15–16
and self-regulation, 155–157
    verbal ability, 7–8
    warning process
        and comprehension, 280, 281–282
        and familiarity, 275–276
        and risk perception, 279, 283
    working memory, 6
Alzheimer's Disease, *see* Consent capacity

B

Beliefs
    and medication instructions, 250–251
    and pharmaceutical labels, 303–305
Benzodiazepines, 27
Breast cancer treatment
    chemotherapy, 69, 70, 74t, 78t, 80t, 83t, 86,
        87
        and age, 79, 82
        and education, 71
        and insurance, 72, 81, 82
    and cognitive processes
        controlled, 11
        memory, 63
        prior knowledge, 61–62
        risk perception, 59
        verbal ability, 64

hormone therapy, 69, 70, 74t, 78t, 80t, 83t, 86
   and age, 79, 84
   and education, 71
   and insurance, 72
   and self-consciousness, 84
lumpectomy, 69, 70, 74t, 78t, 80t, 81, 83t, 86, 87–88
   and body image, 73, 79
   and education, 71
   and insurance, 72
   and self-consciousness, 82
mastectomy, 69, 70, 74t, 78t, 80t, 81, 83t, 86, 87–88
   and age, 71
   and body image, 73, 79
   and education, 71
   and insurance, 72
   and self-consciousness, 82
patient participation
   and age, 71
   benefits of, 56–57
   and education, 71
psychosocial variables
   age, 71, 72, 74t, 76, 78t, 79, 80t, 82, 83t, 84, 85
   body image, 73, 74t, 77, 79
   education, 71, 74t, 76, 78t, 80t, 85, 87
   income, 76, 78t, 80t, 83t, 85, 87
   insurance, 72, 74t, 76, 78t, 80t, 81, 82, 83t, 85
   life quality, 70, 71
   marital status, 72–73, 76, 78t, 80t, 85
   self-consciousness, 73, 74t, 77, 78t, 80t, 82, 83t, 87
   social support, 72–73, 74t, 78t, 80t, 86–87
   survival advantage, 70, 71
radiation, 69, 70, 74t, 78t, 80t, 82, 83t, 86, 88
   and age, 79, 84
   and education, 71
   and insurance, 72
and reconstruction, 69, 74t, 80t, 83t, 87–88
   and body image, 73
   and self-consciousness, 82, 87
research analyses
   bivariate, 75, 77–81
   multivariate, 75, 81–84
research limitations, 74–75, 84–85, 88
research methodology
   measures, 76–77
   participants, 75–76, 84

C

Chemotherapy, breast cancer and, 69, 70, 74t, 78t, 80t, 83t, 86, 87
and age, 79, 82
and education, 71

   and insurance, 72, 81, 82
Childbirth, 59
Chronic disease, 25–26
Clinical care, 26–27
Cognitive processes, *see also* Consent capacity; Medical expertise; Medication adherence
   and behavior questionnaires, 93, 94
   comprehension, 94, 95–96
   frequency estimates, 94, 96–97
   working memory, 94, 96–97, 106
   and breast cancer treatment
      controlled processes, 11
      memory, 63
      prior knowledge, 61–62
      risk perception, 59
      verbal ability, 64
   and home care equipment
      aging impact on, 229–231
      care determination, 226–227
      information processing, 225–230
      operation of, 227–228
      research agenda, 231
   and medication instructions
      adherence, 249–252
      age differences, 251–253
      communication, 250–252
      comprehension, 252–253
      discourse levels, 252
      patient beliefs, 250–251
      situation model, 252
Cognitive processes, age differences in, 3–5
   automatic processing, 5–8, 12–13, 18–19
      and aging stereotypes, 12
      and behavior, 7
      and knowledge structures, 7
      and medication adherence, 16–17
      and verbal ability, 7–8
      and working memory, 6–8
   comprehension
      and advanced directives, 9–10
      and pharmaceutical labels, 9
   controlled processing, 5–7, 11, 12, 18–19
      and information processing, 6
      and inhibitory function, 6
      and medication adherence, 13, 16
      and working memory, 6
   decision making, 10–13, 60, 64–66
   information processing, 8
   and medical experience, 8
   and medical intentions, 16–18
   medication adherence, 13–15
      and environmental cues, 16, 17–18
      interventions for, 16–18
      and lifestyle busyness, 15–16
      model for, 15–16
   and medication instructions, 251–253

Cognitive processes, decision making and
  age differences, 10–13, 60, 64–66
  cognitive abilities
    comprehension, 62, 63–64, 65
    memory, 62, 63–64, 65
    perceptual speed, 62, 63, 64
    reasoning, 62, 63, 64
    verbal, 63, 64
    working memory, 63, 64, 65
  competency, 58
  illness representation, 60–61
  information amount/type, 59–60
  and medical experience, 61
  medical treatment, 59
  medication adherence, 58
  patient participation, 55–57, 65
    informed consent, 56
  prior knowledge, 61–62, 65
  risk perception, 59, 65
  strategies for, 57–58
    alternative decomposition, 57
    first-difference rule, 57
    priori commitment, 57
    satisficing, 57
Communication
  of health information
    and chronic disease, 25–26
    and clinical care, 26–27
    and disabilities, 26
    and geriatric education, 24, 27
    informed consent, 23, 56, 109, 240–242
    and medical complexity, 23, 25–26
    and Medicare, 26, 27
    and medication effects, 25, 27
    and population heterogeneity, 24–25
    risks/benefits, 23, 24
    and system structure, 24, 26–27
  of medication instructions
    and adherence, 172–173, 249–252,
      261–263
    age differences, 251–252
  of patient decisions, 111–112, 113, 116,
    122
Competency, daily living, see also Consent ca-
    pacity
  age differences, 212–213, 215
  and education, 212–213
  instrumental activities of daily living (IADLs),
    199
    cognitive/physical, 200–202
    and health, 201, 203
    self-reported limitations, 201–203
  meal preparation, 199, 202
    food labels, 203–204
  medication behavior, 199
    comprehension, 205
    dosage interpretation, 205–206

physical activities of daily living (PADLs), 200
  problem solving
    declarative knowledge, 206–207
    personalized knowledge, 208–209, 215
    procedural knowledge, 207–208, 214
  qualitative analysis of, 209–216
    study description, 210
    task errors, 210–216
  task errors, 210–216
    incomplete processing, 211–214
    no attempt, 211–213
    prior experience, 211–213, 214–215
    random, 211–213
Comprehension
  age differences
    and advanced directives, 9–10
    and pharmaceutical labels, 9
  behavior questionnaires, 94, 95–96
  consent capacity, 111–112, 113, 115, 122
  decision making, 62, 63–64, 65
  estrogen replacement therapy, 64
  medication behavior, 205
  medication instructions, 252–253
  pharmaceutical labels, 9, 292f, 298–303
    application of, 300–303
  warning process
    age differences, 280, 281–282
    reading comprehension, 271t, 279–280
    symbol comprehension, 271t, 280–282
Consent capacity, see also Competency, daily liv-
    ing
  characteristics of, 109–111
  and comprehension, 111–112, 113, 115, 122
  and conceptualization, 110, 112, 113,
    115–116, 122
  criterion for
    by physician, 111, 116–121
    psychometric, 110, 113–116
  and decision communication, 111–112, 113,
    116, 122
  and executive function, 110, 112, 113,
    115–116, 120–121, 122
  and information processing, 111–113, 115,
    122
  and informed consent, 109
  model for
    cognitive neuropsychological, 111–113
    and neurocognitive change, 112–113
  neuropsychological tests for, 123
  research, 110, 113–121
    agenda, 121–122
    limitations, 121
    results, 115–116, 119–121
  and semantic memory, 110, 112, 113,
    115–116, 122
  and verbal recall, 110, 113, 115–116,
    119–121, 122

D

Daily living activities, *see* Competency, daily living
Decision making, *see also* Cognitive processes, decision making and
  age differences
    and conflict, 49–51
    and decision agents, 38–40
    and decision modes, 37–40
    and options, 41–42
    and possibilities, 43
    and realizations, 44–46
    and values, 46–47
  characteristics, 31–35
  and conflict, 48–51
    compensatory procedure, 48–49
    noncompensatory procedure, 48–49
    risk perception, 50–51
  deficiencies
    aims, 33
    competition, 33
    needs, 33
    outcomes, 33
    process cost, 33–34
  Einstellung effect, 38
  modes
    agency, 38–40
    analytic, 35–38
    automatic, 35–38
    rule-based, 35–38
  options, 41–42
  possibilities, 42–43
  realizations, 43–46
  research on, 32, 34–35, 36–37, 43, 44, 47, 50–51
  values, 32–33, 46–48
Disabilities, 26

E

Education
  and breast cancer treatment, 71, 74t, 76, 78t, 80t, 85, 87
  and competency, 212–213
  geriatric, 24, 27
Einstellung effect, 38
Equipment, home care
  and cognitive processes
    aging impact on, 229–231
    care determination, 226–227
    equipment operation, 227–228
    information processing, 225–230
    research agenda, 231
  home care overview, 223–225
Estrogen replacement therapy
  and comprehension, 64

  and controlled processing, 11
  and memory, 64
  and prior knowledge, 62
  and risk perception, 59
  and verbal ability, 64
Experience, medical
  and age differences, 8
  and decision making, 61

F

First-difference rule, 57

G

Gender, warning process and, 271t, 274
Geriatric Interaction Analysis (GIA), 170–171

H

Hormone therapy, breast cancer and, 69, 70, 74t, 78t, 80t, 83t, 86
  and age, 79, 84
  and education, 71
  and insurance, 72
  and self-consciousness, 84

I

Income, breast cancer and, 76, 78t, 80t, 83t, 85, 87
Informed consent, *see also* Consent capacity
  and cognitive processes, 56
  and communication, 23
  and consent capacity, 109
  form design, 240–242
Instrumental activities of daily living (IADLs), *see* Competency, daily living
Insurance coverage, breast cancer and, 74t, 76, 78t, 80t, 83t, 85
  chemotherapy, 72, 81, 82
  hormone therapy, 72
  lumpectomy, 72
  mastectomy, 72
  radiation, 72
Insurance policy design, 240

K

Knowledge
  and automatic processing, 7
  prior
    and breast cancer treatment, 61–62
    and decision making, 61–62, 65
    and estrogen replacement therapy, 62
  and problem solving

declarative knowledge, 206–207
personalized knowledge, 208–209, 215
procedural knowledge, 207–208, 214
and warning process, 277–278

L

Labels, food, 203–204
Labels, pharmaceutical, *see also* Medication instructions; Text design; Warning process
    attention capture, 292f, 293–297
        application of, 294–297
        contrast, 293
        habituation, 294
        location, 293
        pictorials, 294
        signals, 293–294
        size, 293
    attention maintenance, 292f, 297–298
        application of, 298
    and beliefs/attitudes, 292f, 303–305
        application of, 304–305
    and comprehension, 9, 292f, 298–303
        application of, 300–303
    improvement of, 307–308
    information processing model, 292–306
    instruction presentation, 251–252, 258
    and motivation, 292f, 305–306
        application of, 306
    purpose of, 291–292
    text design, 242
Lumpectomy, 69, 70, 74t, 78t, 80t, 81, 83t, 86, 87–88
    and body image, 73, 79
    and education, 71
    and insurance, 72
    and self-consciousness, 82

M

Marital status, breast cancer and, 72–73, 76, 78t, 80t, 85
Mastectomy, 69, 70, 74t, 78t, 80t, 81, 83t, 86, 87–88
    and age, 71
    and body image, 73, 79
    and education, 71
    and insurance, 72
    and self-consciousness, 82
Medical expertise
    and aging research, 133–135
        intentional tasks, 133
    and clinical information
        backward reasoning, 138–139, 141
        case recall, 135–137

diagnostic reasoning, 137–139
        forward reasoning, 138–139
    cognitive framework, 128–129, 132–133
        memory, 132–139, 140–141
    epistemological framework, 128–129
        diagnosis, 131, 132–133
        facets, 131, 132
        findings, 130–131, 132
        observations, 130, 131, 132
    levels of, 129, 132, 134–139, 140, 141
    models of
        compensatory, 128, 140
        strategy, 128, 140, 141
    and problem solving, 128–130, 132–133
    social/situational framework, 128–129
Medicare, 26, 27
Medication adherence
    affective reactions, 152–154
        age differences, 154
        fear, 153–154
    age differences
        and affective reactions, 154
        and automatic processing, 16–17
        and controlled processing, 13, 16
        and environmental cues, 16, 17–18
        and illness representation, 157
        interventions for, 16–18
        and lifestyle busyness, 15–16
        model for, 15–16
        and self-regulation, 155–157
    and decision making, 58
    illness control
        and caregivers, 151–152
        if-then-else rule, 150, 160
        and medical procedures, 150–151
    illness representation, 149–150, 157
        age differences, 157
    and instructions
        cognitive approach, 249–252
        communication of, 172–173, 249–252, 261–263
        interpretation of, 174–176
        simulated task, 258–261
    and memory
        instruction communication, 173, 251–252
        instruction interpretation, 175–176
        perceived adherence, 179–180
        prospective, 176–178, 180
    and memory strategies
        external, 177–178
        internal, 177–178
        metamemory, 178–180
    multidisciplinary approach, 145–147
    patient–physician relationship
        aging stereotypes, 169–171
        overaccommodative speech, 172–173

perceived adherence, 179–180
    processing model, 167–169
  processing model, 147–149
    patient–physician relationship, 167–169
    social-cognitive, 186–188
  self-regulation
    age differences, 155–157
    hypervigilance, 159–160
    and illness representation, 157
    risk management, 157–159
    and self-image, 154–155
Medication adherence research
  adherence influences, 186–188
    perceptual speed, 187
    prospective memory, 187
    working memory, 187–188
  agenda for, 161, 179–180
  cognition measures, 188–190
  methodology
    and disease type, 190–191
    and medication quantity, 191
  review of, 185–186
  statistical issues
    aggregate data, 193
    data stability, 192–193
    missing data, 191–192
    time-series analysis, 193–195
Medication effects, 25, 27
Medication instructions, *see also* Labels, pharma-
    ceutical; Text design; Warning pro-
    cess
  and adherence
    cognitive approach, 249–252
    and communication, 172–173, 249–252,
        261–263
    and interpretation, 174–176
    simulated task, 258–261
  cognitive approach
    and adherence, 249–252
    age differences, 251–253
    and communication, 250–252
    comprehension, 252–253
    discourse levels, 252
    and patient beliefs, 250–251
    situation model, 252
  communication of
    and adherence, 172–173, 249–252,
        261–263
    age differences, 251–252
  content of, 253–254
  design refinement, 253–258
  interpretation of
    and adherence, 174–176
  organization of, 254–256
    schemas for, 255
    signals, 255–256
  presentation of

oral, 257–258
    pharmaceutical labels, 251–252, 258
    time line icon, 254f, 256–257
Memory
  age differences, 6
  and behavior questionnaires, 94, 96–97, 106
  and breast cancer treatment, 63
  and consent capacity, 110, 112, 113, 115–116,
      122
  and decision making, 62, 63, 64, 65
  and estrogen replacement therapy, 64
  and medical expertise, 132–139, 140–141
  and medication adherence
    instruction communication, 173,
        251–252
    instruction interpretation, 175–176
    metamemory, 178–180
    perceived memory, 179–180
    prospective memory, 176–178, 180, 187
    strategies for, 177–180
  prospective
    and medication adherence, 176–178, 180,
        187
    and warning process, 285
  and warning process
    prospective memory, 285
    working memory, 279–280, 284–285

O

Overaccommodative speech, 172–173

P

Patient participation
  breast cancer treatment, 56–57
  informed consent
    and cognitive processes, 56
    and communication, 23
    and consent capacity, 109
Patient Self-Determination Act (1990), 9, 10
Perceptual speed
  decision making, 62, 63, 64
  medication adherence, 187
Population heterogeneity, 24–25
Prospective Memory for Medications Question-
    naire (PMMQ), 176–178

Q

Questionnaires, behavior frequency
  age differences, 93–94, 106
    and comprehension, 96
    and frequency scales, 99–100
  behavior judgments

comparative, 101–102, 106
noncomparative, 102
by physicians, 102–104
cognitive tasks for, 93, 94
    comprehension, 94, 95–96
    frequency estimates, 94, 96–97
    working memory, 94, 96–97, 106
scales for, 94, 95–96, 97–101
    and age differences, 99–100
    assessment of, 105–107
    and behavior judgments, 101–104, 106
    format recommendations, 100–101,
        106–107
    physical symptoms, 98
    and respondent bias, 94, 104–105

R

Radiation, breast cancer and, 69, 70, 74t, 78t,
        80t, 82, 83t, 86, 88
    and age, 79, 84
    and education, 71
    and insurance, 72
Reasoning, 62, 63, 64
Reconstruction surgery, breast cancer and, 69,
        74t, 80t, 83t, 87–88
    and body image, 73
    and self-consciousness, 82, 87
Rheumatoid arthritis, 61
Risk perception
    breast cancer treatment, 59
    childbirth, 59
    decision making, 50–51, 59, 65
    estrogen replacement therapy, 59
    warning process, 271t, 278–279, 282–283
        age differences, 279, 283

S

Satisficing strategies, 57
Signals
    medication instructions, 255–256
    pharmaceutical labels, 293–294
    text design, 238t, 239
    warning process
        caution, 278, 284, 293
        danger, 278, 284, 293
        warning, 268, 278, 284, 293
Social support, breast cancer and, 72–73, 74t,
        78t, 80t, 86–87
Speech Accommodation Theory, 172
Stereotypes, aging
    and cognitive processes, 12
    and patient–physician relationship,
        169–171

T

Text design, *see also* Labels, pharmaceutical;
        Medication instructions; Warning
        process
    and aging, 237–245
        advanced organizers, 238t, 239
        complex text, 240–244
        questions, 238t, 239
        signals, 238t, 239
        text structure, 238t, 239
        type size, 238
        underlining, 238t, 239
        unjustified text, 238
    cognitive overload theory, 244–245
    evaluation of, 234–235
    experience theory, 244
    informed consent forms, 240–242
    insurance policies, 240
    language of, 234
    layout of, 234, 235–236
    medication leaflets, 236
    pharmaceutical labels, 242
    prescription information, 242–243

V

Verbal ability
    age differences, 7–8
    and breast cancer treatment, 64
    and consent capacity, 110, 113, 115–116,
        119–121, 122
    and decision making, 63, 64
    and estrogen replacement therapy, 64

W

Warning process, *see also* Labels, pharmaceuti-
        cal; Medication instructions; Text
        design
    age differences
        and comprehension, 280, 281–282
        and familiarity, 275–276
        and risk perception, 279, 283
    and attention
        divided, 283–284
        selective, 284
    compliance costs/benefits, 271t, 282
    components of, 268, 269f
    and comprehension
        age differences, 280, 281–282
        reading, 271t, 279–280
        symbol, 271t, 280–282
    and familiarity, 271t, 274–278
        age differences, 275–276

general experience, 275
schemata, 275–277
technical knowledge, 277–278
and gender, 271t, 274
improvement of, 285–287
and memory
prospective, 285
working, 279–280, 284–285
overview, 270–272
person variables in, 268–270, 271t

and products, 267–268
risk perception, 271t, 278–279, 282–283
age differences, 279, 283
signal words
caution, 278, 284, 293
danger, 278, 284, 293
warning, 268, 278, 284, 293
social influence, 271t, 283
and vision, 271t, 272–274
warning variables in, 270